## ENVIRONMENTAL LAW AND ECONOMICS

In *Environmental Law and Economics*, Michael G. Faure and Roy A. Partain provide a detailed overview of the law-and-economics methodology developed and employed by environmental lawyers and policymakers. The authors demonstrate how this approach can transcend political divisions in the context of international environmental law, environmental criminal law, and the property rights approach to environmental law. Private law solutions and public regulatory approaches are also explored, including traditional command-and-control and market-based forms of regulation. The book not only shows how the law-and-economics framework can be used to protect the environment, but also to examine deeper questions involving environmental federalism and the effectiveness of environmental law in developing economies. In clear, digestible prose that does not require readers to possess a background in microeconomics or mathematics, the authors introduce the theory and practice of environmental law and economics that have been so critical in the creation of robust environmental policy.

MICHAEL G. FAURE is Professor of Comparative Law and Economics at Erasmus School of Law and Professor of International and Comparative Environmental Law at Maastricht University. He is also Academic Director of the Maastricht European Institute for Transnational Legal Research (METRO), the Ius Commune Research School, and the European Doctorate in Law and Economics (EDLE) programme. He is an attorney at the Antwerp Bar and publishes in the areas of environmental criminal law, tort and insurance, and economic analysis of accident law.

ROY A. PARTAIN is Chair and Professor of Commercial Law and Sustainability at the University of Aberdeen, as well as director of the PhD in Law programme and several LLM and LLB programs. His research explores the nexus between commercial law and sustainable development, including the liability issues arising from emergent and innovative technologies. He is a Member of the State Bar of Texas. He has advised and worked on research projects underwritten by ministries and research institutions in East Asia.

# Environmental Law and Economics

## THEORY AND PRACTICE

**Michael G. Faure**
Erasmus University School of Law and
Maastricht University Faculty of Law

**Roy A. Partain**
University of Aberdeen School of Law

CAMBRIDGE
UNIVERSITY PRESS

**CAMBRIDGE**
**UNIVERSITY PRESS**

University Printing House, Cambridge CB2 8BS, United Kingdom

One Liberty Plaza, 20th Floor, New York, NY 10006, USA

477 Williamstown Road, Port Melbourne, VIC 3207, Australia

314-321, 3rd Floor, Plot 3, Splendor Forum, Jasola District Centre, New Delhi - 110025, India

79 Anson Road, #06-04/06, Singapore 079906

Cambridge University Press is part of the University of Cambridge.

It furthers the University's mission by disseminating knowledge in the pursuit of education, learning and research at the highest international levels of excellence.

www.cambridge.org
Information on this title: www.cambridge.org/9781108429481
DOI: 10.1017/9781108554916



First published 2019

*A catalogue record for this publication is available from the British Library*

ISBN 978-1-108-42948-1 Hardback
ISBN 978-1-108-45429-2 Paperback

Contents

# Preface

This book has been in contemplation for a long time ...

It is our hope that this book can broaden the appeal of this methodological approach to environmental law. We believe that Law and Economics can be utilised to promote the very nature and purpose of environmental law, to protect, nurture, and defend the environment, however that in itself is defined.

We hope this book will provide accessible entry into the theory and theoretical models that have been developed for environmental law over the last several decades. Further, we hope that this book will evidence that policies designed with this method have been 'field tested' and found to be resilient and robust methods for protecting the environment.

We fully recognise that no school of legal methodology will likely be found to be 'complete' or acceptable to everyone, but we do hope to reveal with this book that environmental lawyers, researchers, and policymakers can readily utilise this Law and Economics perspective in composing their toolkit of effective legal rules and policies.

With that in mind, we hope you enjoy this book and use it to protect nature and her environment.

# Acknowledgements

This book and its many stages of drafting were carefully guarded, edited, and across-the-board improved by Mrs Marina Jodogne, for whose patience with its authors we are personally deeply grateful!

Special thanks are in order for Ms Agata Meysner, who singlehandedly deciphered many of our citations, corrected them, and created a much richer experience for our readers.

This book builds to some extent further on the volume *The Economic Analysis of Environmental Policy and Law: An Introduction*, which one of us co-authored with Göran Skogh in 2003. Meanwhile Göran sadly passed away and it is therefore to his memory that we want to dedicate this book.

# Abbreviations

| | |
|---|---|
| ADR | Alternative Dispute Resolution |
| ALARA | As Low As Reasonably Achievable |
| BAT | Best Available Technique (or Technology) |
| BATNEEC | Best Available Technique (or Technology) Not Entailing Excessive Costs |
| BPEO | Best Practical Environmental Option |
| BPM | Best Practicable Means |
| CAA | Clean Air Act |
| CAC | Command and Control |
| CAMPFIRE | Communal Areas Management Programme for Indigenous Resources |
| CAT | Catastrophe |
| CBNRM | Community-Based Natural Resource Management |
| CCS | Carbon Capture and Storage |
| CER | Corporate Environmental Responsibility |
| CERCLA | Comprehensive Environmental Response, Compensation, and Liability Act |
| CITES | Convention on International Trade in Endangered Species of Wild Fauna and Flora |
| CLC | Convention on Civil Liability for Oil Pollution Damage |
| $CO_2$ | Carbon dioxide |
| CSR | Corporate Social Responsibility |
| CWA | Clean Water Act |
| DEFRA | Department for Environment, Food and Rural Affairs (UK) |
| ECHR | European Court of Human Rights |
| EIA | Environmental Impact Assessment |
| EKC | Environmental Kuznets Curve |
| ELD | Environmental Liability Directive |

| | |
|---|---|
| EPA | Environmental Protection Agency (US) |
| ETS | Emission Trading Scheme |
| EU | European Union |
| EU ETS | European Union Emission Trading Scheme |
| GCCF | Gulf Coast Claims Facility |
| GDP | Gross Domestic Product |
| IEQS | Ivory Export Quota System |
| IPPC | Integrated Pollution Prevention and Control |
| IUCN | International Union for the Conservation of Nature |
| KWS | Kenya Wildlife Service |
| NAAQS | National Ambient Air Quality Standards |
| NGO | Non-Governmental Organisation |
| OPA | Oil Pollution Act |
| P&I Club | Protection & Indemnity Club |
| PCP | Private-Community Partnership |
| PWC | PricewaterhouseCoopers |
| $SO_2$ | Sulphur dioxide |
| TFEU | Treaty on the Functioning of the European Union |
| UK | United Kingdom |
| UN | United Nations |
| UNFCCC | United Nations Framework Convention on Climate Change |
| USA | United States of America |
| v. | versus |

# 1

# Introduction

## 1.1 WHY A BOOK ON ENVIRONMENTAL LAW AND ECONOMICS?

Sustainability and environmental law have never been more important. If there are new legal toolkits available for building a better, more sustainable world, there is a duty incumbent to explore and learn those new ideas, to transform our legal rules and institutions.

This book presents research drawn from literature on the economic analysis of environmental law.[1] Fundamentally, it presents a case that these methods share the established values and principles of environmental law,[2] yet they extend the set of legal policy options to address the needs of environmental protection and sustainable development.[3] Furthermore, it is shown that beyond the theoretical frameworks developed by environmental Law and Economics researchers, there now exists

[1] The terms 'economic analysis of environmental law' and 'environmental Law and Economics' are synonymous and interchangeable. The concept of 'economic analysis of environmental law' is distinguishable from the similarly named 'economic analysis of environmental policy', in that the former focuses on law and legal institutions whereas the latter focuses on economics and economic institutions; also, the latter tend to present a greater amount of mathematical content in their literature. Nevertheless, the two literatures are closely intertwined. Fischman and Barbasch-Riley limited their definition of environmental law to include research on legal issues of pollution, species or habitat conservation, land use, natural resource management, and climate change law (Fischman and Barbasch-Riley 2018, at 772).

[2] Driesen notes that environmental law still lacks a positive theory of environmental law; thus, it is quite likely that environmental law will continue to evolve much as Law and Economics is evolving (Driesen 2017, at 58).

[3] This argument of shared common legal principles was originally presented by Faure and Skogh (2003, at 19–39). The present book honours Professor Skogh's memory, as it extends and deepens the framework originally introduced by Faure and Skogh and additionally provides empirical case studies on the effectiveness of the models proposed in that earlier work. See De Sadeleer (2002, at 15–18) for the comparative reference to the principles of 'conventional' environmental law.

empirical data to evaluate the effectiveness of those models.[4] This book will demonstrate that the models of environmental Law and Economics have been proven effective in real-world settings.[5] Thus, there is a new legal toolset available to advance the goals of sustainability and environmental law.

Despite all the progress made in environmental law over the six decades since Rachel Carson's *Silent Spring*,[6] and then Earth Day 1970,[7] more is needed; the world needs to expand its environmental law perspective to include sustainability perspectives.[8] Daniel Esty's call for the inclusion of sustainability strategies in environmental law referred to a range of topics,[9] including the 'end of externalities',[10] a focus on 'choice' in lieu of mandates,[11] a systems approach that acknowledges trade-offs and interconnections of environmental protection efforts,[12] a priority on 'innovation', and the 'capacity to bring new technologies, information

4 Fischman and Barbash-Riley quote Diamond's definition for empirical research in their meta-study of empirical environmental law: 'the systematic organization of a series of observations with the method of data collection and analysis made available to the audience' (Fischman and Barbasch-Riley 2018, at 771).

5 While this might sound normative, and perhaps it is, so too is much of the existing literature of environmental law (Driesen 2017, at 59). He lists the normative goals of environmental law as (i) protecting public health and the environment, (ii) maximizing feasible reduction of pollution, and (iii) restraining disproportionately costly regulation. Id., at 83, 85, and 86. Given this formulation, we see much alignment between environmental law and environmental Law and Economics.

6 Carson 1962.

7 While presented primarily from the US perspective, the history of the subsequent decades was documented by Lazarus (2003). While it can be difficult to determine when environmental law first began as a school of research, Lazarus reports that the term 'environmental law' was first coined at the 1969 Conference on Law and the Environment, held at the Airlie House in Warrenton, Virginia. Id., at 47.

8 Esty (2017, at 3).

9 Id., at 5.

10 Externalities as an economic concept refer to those costs that remain excluded from the costs considered in an economic decision, such as within a firm's decision on maximizing revenue. In the context of environmental Law and Economics, it generally applies to the costs of environmental harms that are not responded to by those parties undertaking the activities causing those environmental harms. The topic is covered in detail in Section 2.3.

11 The technical term in the environmental Law and Economics literature is 'decentralisation', which refers to an alternative regulatory approach that avoids the use of a universal, central rule applied equally to all parties. Decentralised regulatory approaches provide responsive feedback to parties to enable them to find their own pathways to compliance with regulatory goals, thus enabling them to make the best use of their skills and resources in supporting the community's regulatory aspirations.

12 The technical terms in the environmental Law and Economics literature for 'trade-offs' include 'opportunity costs analysis' and 'cost–benefit analysis'. Opportunity costs analysis examines what must be given up to obtain a targeted goal or good. Cost–benefit analysis frames the same question from a more overtly financial perspective, to determine the ratio of what costs must be incurred to obtain how much benefit. The interconnectedness approach reflects well on the holographic model of information in the environmental Law and Economics method of analysis; this insight was noted by F. A. Hayek and is discussed in Section 2.4.1.

and learning to bear',[13] and an increased focus on proven results. As this book will evidence, these sustainability approaches are closely related to the ideas found in the literature of environmental Law and Economics. Indeed, many of those approaches were first developed in environmental Law and Economics research.

Thus, the need for a text such as *Environmental Law and Economics: Theory and Practice* is predicated on several observations.

First, environmental law and its sibling international environmental law have moved forward as critical and timely topics. Not only does the world face a global challenge from anthropogenic climate change, but the world is also facing novel environmental challenges from increasing levels of industrial pollution in developing economies, from advancing technologies such as carbon-fibre nano-technologies and genetic modification techniques, and from other large scale anthropogenic environmental events, such as the loss of the Aral Sea and the ongoing efforts to restore water flow to the lower Colorado River Basin. While the community of environmental lawyers has accomplished much in recent decades, new vital work continues to emerge, and the need for sound theoretical foundations for environmental law remains. The economic analysis of environmental law provides a theoretical core that enables novel responses to these emerging challenges.

Second, the literature of Law and Economics provides a solid theoretical foundation for environmental law, one that strongly supports the UN's 2030 Agenda for Sustainable Development and its seventeen Sustainable Development Goals. An extensive body of literature has emerged to support legal reasoning and jurisprudential decision making with tools based on models from environmental Law and Economics. Many of these tools have opened up new legal approaches for environmental regulators, such as EIAs, cost–benefit analysis, and hedonic measurement analysis. More importantly, the literature of Law and Economics enables models that inform on the flow and exchange of information and how to enable the production and distribution of that information on environmental policies to stakeholders and decision makers alike, facilitating environmental justice and equity.

Third, the models resulting from the economic analysis of environmental law enable ground-breaking pathways to opening interdisciplinary policy discussions on environmental issues. The issues raised in environmental problems are not merely legal problems but complex multifaceted challenges. The economic analysis of environmental law brings tools from both Law and Economics, but it is also informed by tools from political science, public choice theory, game theory, and

[13] The quote itself is from Esty (2017, at 5). The point on innovation and the avoidance of locked-in environmental standards reflects a substantial component of the body of literature in environmental Law and Economics. It will be addressed extensively in this book, but key lessons drawn from the economic analysis of law re-encourages the use of civil liability rules to support flexibility, the use of information revealing mechanisms (especially private regulatory mechanisms), and the use of smart regulatory mixes. See the discussions in Chapters 2, 7, and 9.

other schools of social science. By bringing these new tools to environmental legal analysis, policymakers and legal researchers can provide more robust answers.

Finally, the ability to work with theoretical models enables environmental lawyers and policymakers to more readily discover deeper symmetries and affinities in otherwise disparate environmental concerns, enabling solutions from one set of concerns to be mapped into new application for a second set of environmental concerns. This reflects the underlying paradigm of interconnectedness in sustainability.

In conclusion, the goal of this book is to enable environmental lawyers and policymakers to acquire familiarity and comfort with the literature of Law and Economics as applied to questions of environmental law. It covers a range of topics, beginning with explanations of the theory and its applications to environmental law, moving on to practical and historical applications of the same ideas. The book covers how this approach endeavours to minimise environmental harms and how this approach provides efficient compensation for those remaining harms. Discussions on democracy, federalism, and on the application of these tools in developing economies complete the book's coverage of environmental Law and Economics.

## 1.2 READERSHIP

This book is written both for academics and for students of social sciences interested in environmental policy. The book should be of interest especially for lawyers and economists.

Lawyers may find this book of interest to see how an economic analysis of environmental problems may lead to a better understanding of the rationales behind existing legal rules. In addition, economic analysis can be used as a useful tool to test current legislation. Economic analysis may not only lead to conclusions with respect to the efficiency of certain existing legal rules; it can also be used to test the effectiveness of legislative action. This means that economic analysis can show whether a certain set of legal rules can effectively lead to the result that the legislator claims the particular legal rule should have.

An economist might find some of the descriptions of economic notions, which are especially addressed towards the legal audience, too simplistic. However, some of the parts of this book may appeal to an economist, e.g. because the wide application possibilities of economic concepts to various social problems can, once more, be demonstrated.[14] In addition, it may well be new and interesting for environmental economists to read about e.g. the importance of liability rules and insurance in controlling environmental risks,[15] the similarities and differences

[14] On the expanding domain of economics, see Hirshleifer (1985).

[15] On the appeal of Law and Economics to both lawyers and economists, see Faure and Van den Bergh (1989b, at 21–22).

between safety regulation and taxes, and the economics of criminal sanctions for the protection of the environment.

The target audience for *Environmental Law and Economics: Theory and Practice* are thus environmental lawyers and policymakers who would like to deepen their toolkits by learning how to practically apply the principles of environmental Law and Economics to their arguments and proposals. It is hoped that this book will serve as both a handbook and a textbook for them; useful for practical litigators assembling and testing their arguments, for policymakers exploring their environmental options, and for lecturers and students exploring the intellectual frameworks enabling effective environmental policies.

Thus, *Environmental Law and Economics* is a book written for environmentalists who would like to benefit from several decades' worth of real-world environmental policy successes built from the theoretical models of environmental Law and Economics literature. The book provides both accessible introductions to the theoretical models and practical illustrations drawn from historical enactments.

It is hoped that this approach will enable lawyers and policymakers to build stronger environmental policies, based on a toolkit of environmental policy ideas that have been proven to be effective in a range of political and environmental settings.

## 1.3 METHODOLOGY

The economic analysis of law (also referred to as 'Law and Economics') methodology will be used. This method has known a rapid growth in the USA since the beginning of the 1970s and is also widely recognised in Europe now.[16] Significant is the foundation of a European Association for Law and Economics in 1984 in Lund, the existence of several academic reviews on this topic in Europe,[17] and the existence of several book series in many countries, including general handbooks on Law and Economics. Hence, we will not repeat general questions such as the usefulness of economic tools and more particularly the efficiency criterion to analyse legal rules, nor will we go into differences between economic methodology and legal theory. We can refer to a large body of literature on the topic.[18]

[16] In 1973, the first edition of Posner's seminal *Economic Analysis of Law* was published.

[17] More particularly the *International Review for Law and Economics* and the *European Journal of Law and Economics*.

[18] A reader interested in general books on Law and Economics can consult for example the latest edition from Posner (2014), Cooter and Ulen (2012), and Shavell (2004). An overview of literature per topic can also be found in the *New Palgrave Dictionary of Economics and the Law* (Newman 1998) and in the various editions of the *Encyclopedia of Law and Economics* (De Geest 2012).

The economic analysis we will use in this book belongs to what is sometimes referred to as 'new Law and Economics'.[19] The old economic analysis of law was still traditionally linked with taxation, regulation of markets, or competition law. Here lawyers used economists to help them to answer the questions lawyers had previously defined.

The new Law and Economics fits into the view that economics is a behavioural science that more generally analyses human behaviour, even if this is not strictly market oriented.[20] It reflects Hayek's perspective that markets are organs of information, enabling each participant the potential insight of the whole.

In addition to the economic analysis, also other social science theories will be used to explain the contents of legal rules, where appropriate. This is especially the case for theories related to public choice and rent seeking that attempt to explain legislation as a product of demand by powerful interest groups and supply by wealth maximising politicians.[21] Also in the environmental area it is highly useful to combine traditional Law and Economics with interest group theory.[22] This can provide useful insights if the positive analysis has shown that the legal system does not comply with the predictions of the model.

For many years now the traditional economic approach to law has been challenged by insights from cognitive psychology, showing that in many cases individuals are subject to a variety of heuristics and biases, limiting their ability to make rational choices. This domain of behavioural economics has also been translated to Law and Economics, creating the new domain of behavioural Law and Economics, where Cass Sunstein has played a prominent role.[23] These insights of behavioural Law and Economics are also quite important for the domain of environmental law and policy, for example pointing at the importance of specific differences between policy instruments as far as their ability is concerned to stimulate intrinsic motivation towards environmental protection.[24] These important insights will therefore also be incorporated in this book.

As far as the legal analysis is concerned, we will pay attention to principles of international environmental law and to European environmental legislation.[25]

[19] This concept has been introduced by Richard Posner and was used by Cento G. Veljanovski as title for a book, *The New Law-and-Economics: A Research Review*, to explain the difference between 'old' and 'new' Law and Economics (Veljanovski 1982).

[20] A classic book on this topic is by Becker (1976). Shavell wrote, 'As will become obvious to the reader, "economic" analysis of the law is not restricted to conventionally understood economic factors but also includes all manners of non-economic ones' (Shavell 2004, at xix).

[21] See Buchanan and Tullock (1962); see also Olson (1971).

[22] See inter alia Maloney and McCormick (1982).

[23] See Sunstein (2000); see also Sunstein (1997, 1999).

[24] See Frey (1992); see also Frey (1997).

[25] For general reference, see Birnie, Boyle, and Redgwell (2009); see Sands and Peel (2012); see also Jans and Vedder (2012).

In addition, examples from legislation and case law of some European Union Member States, the USA, and other legal systems will be provided as well.

The Law and Economics methodology will be combined with the comparative environmental legal analysis. This has a great advantage, since one will be confronted with the fact that solutions in various legal systems may inevitably differ. Law and Economics has the advantage that the solutions in the various legal systems can be looked at on a more principal level, without having the need to discuss the state of the law in a particular country in too much detail. When one addresses general problems such as the question what kind of legal instruments can be used to control a form of environmental risk, which could have manifested different solutions in various countries, we'll find that Law and Economics allows for a more general approach.

By starting from an analytical look at a specific problem that is provided by the economic analysis, we will then turn to the legal solutions in particular legal systems, when possibly also indicating whether an economic explanation for some of the established differences can be provided. Thus, we shall also try to apply the so-called comparative Law and Economics methodology, as has been advocated by Mattei and Siems.[26]

We previously indicated that the book is written both for lawyers and for economists and for all others interested in environmental law and policy. This inevitably has consequences for the depth both of the legal and of the economic analyses.

Solutions in the law will preferably be described in a global way, focusing on the essence of the legal solutions and eliminating legal details that have no importance for the value of the analysis itself and can only confuse the non-legal reader. For those interested in the details of the law, we shall provide references for further reading in footnotes. Not only do we try to present the law in such a way that economists can understand it. The same will be attempted as far as the economic analysis is concerned. Mathematical proof of certain statements will most often not be provided in this book and the economic analysis will be presented in a verbal way, easily understandable for lawyers. Once more, references in footnotes will help the interested reader to discover and explore further details.

We are not the first to compare legal approaches and economic approaches in environmental law. As Shi-Ling Hsu wrote of 'fair' pie-slicers and 'efficient' pie-bakers:

> Lawyers (including members of the legal academy) are educated and trained as pie-slicers, concerning themselves primarily with questions of fairness and justice, and frequently ignoring questions of efficiency. This is unfortunate because economics is a powerful complement to the law. Economists have also been myopic, still working mostly within a framework that routinely assumes that wealth transfers convert Potentially Pareto Superior policies into Pareto Superior policies, without

[26] Mattei (2000) and Siems (2014).

> laying much attention to whether, in fact, such transfers actually occur. Rather, the focus of most economic analysis is whether proposed policies maximize group utility or group wealth. This is the world of pie-baking.[27]

We hope that with this book we can add pie-baking skills to environmental lawyers and some pie-slicing skills to environmental economists, so that everyone can better coordinate in the kitchen of environmental policy development.

Finally, we should stress that in principle the book tries to provide a positive theory of environmental law. We do not attempt to use economics as the 'only value' for legal rule making. Ultimately, it is finally the legislator or the judge who will have to decide which solution will be chosen. Nevertheless, we shall focus on the policy implications of the analysis so that welfare implications of various legal instruments or solutions are revealed. In that respect, criteria beyond efficiency, such as equity, may play important roles in the analysis. Where possible, we shall also point at distributional consequences of various possible legal solutions.

Of course, this book cannot extensively deal with all problems of economic analysis, nor with all issues of environmental law. For instance, environmental taxes or pollution rights models are only briefly discussed; the same is the case for the law on nuisance.[28]

This book retains its focus to show that a Law and Economics approach can be a useful method in thinking about environmental law and policy. This is particularly the case if new legal systems are set up, such as is often the case in developing countries. Yet, the quality and effectiveness of environmental policy should not be determined solely through the use of economic methods, as we will demonstrate in the final chapter. As a kind of epilogue, that chapter summarises a number of issues discussed in this book, with special application to the situation of developing countries. One of the central issues will also be how an effective environmental law can be construed which respects the rule of law. These questions, of course, pass the boundaries of economics.

## 1.4 SYNOPSIS AND STRUCTURE

This book represents a coming of age in environmental law, one that benefits from theoretical models, a building base of enacted laws and case histories, and policies developed from the Law and Economics approach, and a building recognition of those successes in developing economies needing solutions for their own emerging environmental challenges.

In essence, this book uses the well-known Law and Economics methodology and applies it to problems of environmental law. It illustrates its theoretical models with examples drawn from real-world implementations. And this book presents these

[27] Hsu (2004, at 303–304).

[28] Aspects of nuisance law will only be discussed in relation to the first-use doctrine in Chapter 2.

materials with an international reader in mind, keeping the reading free from colloquial turns of phrase and excessive technical jargon.

The book will provide an introduction to the theory of environmental Law and Economics. The book will start by analysing environmental pollution in economic terms and then look at a variety of legal instruments and remedies that can be used to tackle environmental pollution. It will demonstrate the rational foundations of the theoretical models, show examples of where the models have become adopted into legal realities, and then provide empirical studies that affirm the validity of the environmental Law and Economics approach in solving environmental problems.

Then the book will turn to address the application of environmental Law and Economics. The strengths and limits of property rights, liability rules, and safety regulation will be reviewed, but attention will equally be paid to efficient standard setting. Next, the focus will be on environmental crime in an economic perspective and the compensation of environmental harm will be addressed in more detail, by focusing on insurance, but also alternative legal instruments to deal with environmental pollution. In each subject area, the book will provide examples from real-world acts of environmental legislation, drawn from a variety of countries, to illustrate the theoretical points made in the book; demonstrating that environmental Law and Economics has successfully transitioned from academic theory to practical enactments of environmental policy.

This book will cover environmental federalism, thus addressing the question how an optimal division of tasks between different layers of governance should take place within a federal system. Specific attention is also paid to principles of environmental law whereby the question is asked how these could be put into an economic framework.

Given the importance of environmental law and policy for developing countries, attention will be paid to the role of environmental law in developing countries. This will address the crucial question what type of specific challenges arise when implementing environmental policy in developing countries, but also the relationship between environmental protection and economic growth will be addressed.

Finally, we provide an essay on the overall theme of the book, to find a common thread of hopeful environmental law running through, as illuminated by economics. We hope that the epilogue will provide those readers who have made the journey through this text with us a final look back at the many arguments and ideas raised in the book.

# 2

# Environmental Harm and Efficiency

Environmental law provides laws, rules, and standards to protect a range of environmental conditions and settings from potential injury and harm. Environmental law begins with the recognition that legal rules and institutions could be responsive to these environmental injuries.

As environmental law has developed over time, the categories of included injuries have broadened. Early cases recognised injuries to private property, such as injured farmland or polluted riparian sources. More recently, environmental law has encompassed injuries that did not traditionally have standing, as recognised in the EU's Environmental Liability Directive. While environmental law has evolved to include a broader range of environmentally-related injuries, it remains focused on the prevention and precaution of those injuries, on the identification and characterisations of those injuries, on potential remediation and compensation for those injuries.

The economic analysis of environmental law enquires as to why there might be a need for environmental law; why might those injuries arise in the first place? One cause identified is the problem of missing information, known as 'externalities'. Externalities can occur when information necessary to make a full and complete decision is missing, or when information regarding costs imposed on third parties is not included by the actor. For example, a law could be adopted to ensure that a manufacturer receives the full set of costs of their production activities, including those costs passed on to other parties such as caused by pollution injuries. This topic is covered in Section 2.2.

Another issue identified by the economic analysis of environmental law is the application of Coase's Theorem to risky activities and environmental injuries, predicated on property rights.[1] Coase demonstrated that '[i]f transaction costs are

[1] It might be useful for readers to know that the phrase here of 'property rights' is different from the concerns raised by Lazarus, that traditional natural resource law was overly focused on the plenary authority aspect of real estate property rights, derived from *ad coelum* allodial rights (Lazarus 2003, at 50). The property rights discussed in the Coase-related sections address a far broader notion of property rights, including many notions traditionally referred to more simply as 'rights'.

zero and property rights over the relevant resources are well-defined, parties involved in an externality situation will bargain to an efficient and invariant resolution, regardless of to whom the property rights are initially assigned'.[2] This logically provides that when we do find unresolved negotiations, such as in environmental injuries, that transaction costs and the facility of negotiations are impaired; thus law might be able to provide new rules or standards to reduce those transaction costs and enable a more robust set of outcomes. Further, Coase recognised that the fundamental issue was the allocation of property rights, or as often stated, the misallocation of those rights. Thus, law could be an instrument to re-allocate rights to improve on the function of the market to enable private resolution of environmental risks and hazards. This topic is covered in Section 2.3.

A surprise might ensue for some readers, that while environmental Law and Economics is firmly located within the economic analysis of environmental law, this analysis is equally well founded on the recognition that markets do present various forms of market failure, even if granted the benefits of rationality,[3] and that instruments of law can improve the function of the market to better protect rights and lower the transactional costs of justice, enabling better jurisprudence. This approach extends to the economic analysis of environmental law, that markets surrounding environmental assets and activities present imperfect function and can be improved by legal instruments, resulting in improved appreciation and protection of those same assets. This topic is covered in Section 2.4.

In review, the economic analysis of environmental law builds on classical principles of environmental law, researches legal rules to restore a more complete awareness of impacts and costs of environmentally risky activities, seeks legal methods to enable improved discourse on environmental concerns leading to mutually beneficial outcomes, provides legal institutions to improve functionality of discovered market failures, and seeks to enhance our collective awareness of how we generate the norms and rules that underlay the legal processes and institutions of environmental legal advocacy.

## 2.1 PRINCIPLES OF ENVIRONMENTAL LAW, FROM AN ECONOMIC PERSPECTIVE

The economic analysis of environmental law begins with the same principles as all other analyses of environmental law;[4] namely that of the Polluter Pays Principle

[2] Medema (2014, at 66).

[3] The provision of individual rationality does not equate with the manifestation of functional rationality at a group or social level. See the above discussion on social choice theory. Separately, the notion of the fair bargain, as seminally modelled by Edgeworth, is now known to face substantial likelihood of failure, as demonstrated by Myerson and Satterthwaite (Myerson and Satterthwaite 1983, at 265–281).

[4] Chapter 5 of this book will explore seven fundamental principles of environmental law: (i) the principle of sustainable development, (ii) the principle of prevention at the source, (iii) the proximity principle, (iv) the precautionary principle, (v) the polluter pays principle,

(the Curative Model), the Principle of Prevention (the Preventive Model), and the Precautionary Principle (the Anticipatory Model).[5] But the approach taken to these principles is from a different perspective, the perspective of the actor making decisions on environmentally risky activities as analysed from models derived from microeconomic theory.

The economic analysis of environmental law examines how actors encounter these principles as an active process of applying rational decision-making tools to data and information related to the activities under examination. For example, how might a baker consider the impacts of their baking on the community surrounding their bakery? Would they only consider the data exchanges between them and their customers? What about the neighbour impacted by the smoke from the oven, or the villagers enjoying the smell of fresh bread?[6] Might the baker be aware of the yeasts present in the village for raising their breads, or might they consider how a local tanner's outflows have altered the water they use in their recipe?

Those examples can be shown to represent the key principles of environmental law. Might the baker consider how they might compensate those offended by the smoke of their oven, or how they might need compensation to filter water? Those are questions from the Curative Model, but economists might see those as questions of externalities, of crucial data missing from decision making on activities that impact others. Might the baker install a taller chimney; might the tanner use more bio-friendly chemicals in producing hides? Those ideas reflect the preventive model, but the economic analysis of tort law might see elements of precaution and decisions of how careful to be in a given risky activity.

Where the two modes of environmental legal research might be distinguished, and this is a necessary oversimplification, is that whereas classical environmental law primarily focused on the identification and protection of environmental victims, such as a wetlands or a protected species, economic analysis of environmental law has brought new focus on the potential environmental tortfeasors and how to impact their decision making to achieve similar results.

(vi) the principle of environmental human rights, and (vii) the EU's integration principle. But in advance of those discussions, this section presents an introductory connection from 'traditional' environmental law to its shared principles with the economic analysis of environmental law. See also Faure and Skogh (2003, at 5).

5 De Sadeleer (2002, at 15–18).

6 Lucretius is oft quoted '*Ut quod ali cibus est aliis fuat acre venenum*' (*De Rerum Natura*, Book IV, line 637, which translates as 'that which is nourishing food for one person might be a sour poison to another person'), and this is no less so than with many externalities. Anecdotally, one of the authors recalls the daily morning aroma of roasting coffee in downtown Houston, from the local Maxwell House factory. However, many people unaware of the coffee plant assumed that the smell was petrochemical in nature and would complain of the smell; those same people were likely to compliment on the same smell once they learned of its true origin. See 'Maxwell House, Good to Its Last Drop', *Houston History Magazine*, 17 March 2013; available at: https://houstonhistorymagazine.org/2013/03/maxwell-house-good-to-its-last-drop/

The classical principles of environmental law are the same principles that guide the economic analysis of environmental law. The means of discussion might appear different, or may gather different principles together in novel ways of analysis, but the underlying core principles remain the same.

## 2.2 POLLUTION AS AN EXTERNALITY

### 2.2.1 *External Effects for Firms and States*

The economic analysis of environmental law begins with actions, as it recognises the occurrence of 'risky activities', which place environmental settings in the path of potential harm. These risky activities are undertaken by actors;[7] the actors make choices, i.e. they make decisions, based on their awareness of the benefits and costs of their actions.[8]

The quality of the decision much depends on the quality and completeness of the data available to the decision maker.[9] Environmental Law and Economics recognises that better results will be obtained if the data presented to the actor is more complete and robust and attempts to determine what kind of legal rules or institutions might enable that improvement in available information and thus in decision making on environmental issues.

When actors are poorly informed as to the dangers and harms of their risky activities, they will not be able to make decisions that reflect the environmental norms and legal rules of their society.[10] Worse, if the actors are presented with better data on the benefits of the activity than the risks and harms, then they would likely overindulge in the risky activity.[11]

A key discovery results from this economic analysis of environmental law, that there are some activities which may be beneficial to a buyer and a seller, such as the production and consumption of pharmaceuticals, while simultaneously causing negative side effects for third parties. An economic activity that is volitional and

7 This is a key issue, as environmental consequences can also result from 'Acts of God'.

8 It is generally assumed that the actors are rational and that their choices are volitional in nature; even 'coercive' elements such as punitive legal rules are routinely modelled as foreseeable costs.

9 This is an analogue to the well-known adage from Computer Science of GIGO, 'garbage in, garbage out'; the original author is unknown. Similarly, Charles Babbage, the Victorian inventor of early computing devices, wrote: 'On two occasions I have been asked, "Pray, Mr. Babbage, if you put into the machine wrong figures, will the right answers come out?" . . . I am not able rightly to apprehend the kind of confusion of ideas that could provoke such a question' (Babbage 1864, at 67).

10 This statement assumes that a society or social group shares a common environmental perspective, of a shared *Grundnorm*; it is recognised by the authors that such is not always the case.

11 The inverse could also be true; if an actor is very aware of the dangers of a certain activity, but less aware of its potential benefits, then that actor would not undertake enough of that activity.

rational for two parties may have unnoticed impacts, and costs, for parties beyond the negotiated bargain; thus, the transaction actually includes more than the two original parties but the data from the extra parties remains external to the two parties' decision making and thus delicts can result.

Thus, while the manufacturer sells a product, and a buyer purchases the product, the market will expose a third party beyond this sales agreement to potential harm. For example, a drug manufacturer who receives profits from their sales but faces few of the costs induced by environmental injuries, e.g. damage caused to fish in stream impacted by chemical effluents, caused by their facilities, would likely produce too many products. Meanwhile, the fish are harmed and those individuals depending on those fish for food, sustenance, and a place of home are harmed without compensation or remediation.

This form of environmental pollution is described in environmental Law and Economics as being created by the existence of 'externalities'; of data missing from or ignored by the decision maker, as might happen when the market does not require the decision maker to pay those costs.[12] These side effects are indeed external to the industrial activity itself since the company committing the pollution is in principle not affected by the negative side effects it causes by its actions.

Environmental Law and Economics makes the argument that this form of pollution could be prevented by ensuring the decision makers include the externalised costs, to internalise them, by ensuring that they bear the costs of the injuries and damages they impose on those third parties. Environmental Law and Economics holds that if the costs, and any attending benefits, of the third party could be brought to bear on the original two actors, then the resulting new bargain would reflect the conditions obtained by a volitionally negotiated three-way bargain.

Precisely because pollution is an externality, the starting point of the economic analysis of environmental pollution is that a decision maker, such as the pharmaceutical company of our example, will not take into account the externality when it takes decisions on the production level and the investments in measures to avoid pollution, such as the instalment of a water treatment plant. Environmental pollution is considered by many scholars to be the classic example of an externality.[13]

Externalities do not only cause pollution problems for third party humans or communities; the impact could be transboundary or transnational in scope. From an economic perspective, the basic problem is that local industry, governed by local rules, exports environmental pollution to other legal jurisdictions downstream or downwind, leading to a de facto 'externalisation' of pollution problems.

[12] The etymology of the phrase externality is that the data, originally cost data, was not included in the decision making of the actor, and thus, was 'external' to the decision. The counterpart, of included data, is known as an internality; the act of including externalised data is to internalise the data.

[13] See generally Van den Bergh (1988, at 234).

Economists have often argued that the reasons for the transboundary character of environmental pollution problems are well known: local politicians will not have many incentives to act strongly against polluters who may be able to export large quantities of pollution outside the borders of the national territory. Thus the polluting activity could result in 'local' socio-economic benefits for the upstream nation (increased tax revenues and job security), whereas the costs of the negative effects are exported to the neighbouring downstream countries and the costs of those damages become externalised to the government of the upstream state governing their production and emission.[14] Because politicians need to be re-elected by the citizens within their particular state, their primary concern may not be with the transboundary effects of pollution caused by factories within their nation. Seen in this context, it is unsurprising that such an externalisation of pollution to other countries takes place.

### 2.2.2 *Internalising the Externality as Goal of Environmental Law*

The economic analysis of environmental law holds that if society can correctly assess the level of costs, to identify the full set of environmental impacts, then actors undertaking risky environmental activities should be able to set their behavioural standards to match society's environmental norms.

However, when environmental externalities exist, when actors are unable to discern the costs of environmental damages,[15] then those harms are likely to continue; for the market cannot function properly when data, especially cost data, is missing. By re-connecting that data to the actor, by making them aware of the costs they imposed on third parties, the decisions of the actor(s) will become responsive to those acts that create those environmental injuries and their damages.

This analysis indicates an economic goal of environmental law: environmental rules should (i) force the potential polluter to include in their decisions the damages caused by the pollution emitted by their activity choices by (ii) enabling the internalisation of related externalities back into their decision process.[16]

If those damages can be internalised into the potential polluter's decision process, then the polluter would be faced with new logical consequences. First option, they could decide to act as before, pollute, and pay the full damages. Second option, they could incur the costs of abatement technology. And the third option, they could choose to reduce their outputs to reduce their pollution levels and thus reduce the resultant damages. If society could set its standards clearly, then the potential polluter would be properly presented with the correct activity choices as the logical

[14] See Faure and Betlem (2008, at 129–191).

[15] This inability to discern damages accurately could be (i) due to inappropriate or insufficient awareness of environmental injuries, or (ii) due to failures of cost data to be communicated in the market.

[16] See Faure (1996, at 85–109).

choice; ergo, the pollution and its consequences will have become fully internalised by them prior to their actions.

In the absence of such a law, there would be no incentive for the polluting factory to take into account the pollution it is causing; in the absence of curative legal rules, the externality will not be internalised, and behaviours will not be changed. The potential polluter would not bear the damages of their pollution and they would continue to exclude it from their activity decisions.

The need for environmental rules to connect potential polluters to the consequences of their acts is clear from the economic analysis of environmental law. Thus, the scholar and policymaker of environmental law turn their focus to developing legal policies to solve the problem of externalities. Research has revealed a variety of legal instruments can lead to such internalisation results; a discussion of those instruments follows below, in Section 2.4, and then again in later chapters.

### 2.2.3 *EIAs and Internalising Externalities*

Externalities can also occur in transboundary and transnational contexts, not just within single jurisdictions. In the interstate context, legal instruments can be used to internalise transboundary externalities. International legal instruments are designed to prevent upstream states from 'exporting' their pollution problems to downstream states. To achieve these international results, one needs the body of international environmental law,[17] and also the use of national law, to fight transboundary pollution.[18]

An important class of instruments of internalising externalities are the various types of EIA. Generally speaking, an EIA is a process that leads to a formal statement concerning the set of potential impacts of a new project; it is 'an obligation to stop and consider environmental consequences before acting, a process that requires investigation and evaluation of the environmental impact of a proposed project or action before it goes forward'.[19] An EIA can inform decision makers on the environmental consequences of the particular activity.[20] Currently, 183 out of 197 (over 93 per cent) of the world's nations or jurisdictions, have embraced the concept of EIAs to some extent[21]; and given the present extent of the EIA rules and the use of them in international courts, the concept of the EIA has arguably evolved to that of 'general principle of law'.[22]

It is especially important that a variety of instruments have been developed which oblige potentially polluting states to organise an EIA in a transboundary context.

[17] See Sands and Peel (2012).
[18] See Van Dunné (1991, 1996).
[19] Yang (2018, at 4).
[20] Sands and Peel (2012, at 601).
[21] Yang (2018, at 2).
[22] Yang (2018, at 9 and 48).

The most important document in that respect is called the ESPOO Convention which was developed under the auspices of the United Nations Economic Commission for Europe (ECE). The ESPOO Convention obliges the state where a potentially polluting activity will take place, referred to as the 'party of origin', to ensure that, in accordance with the provisions of the convention, an EIA is undertaken for any listed activity 'that is likely to cause a significant adverse transboundary impact'.[23]

Similar instruments also exist at the regional level, for example within the EU, wherein specific directives relate to the assessment of the effects of certain public and private projects on the environment. Key amongst these EU directives is the Environmental Impact Assessment Directive.[24] Article 7 of this directive provided that where a Member State is aware that a project is likely to have significant effects on the environment in another Member State, the Member State in whose territory the project is intended to be carried out shall forward the information gathered for its own EIA efforts onto the other impacted Member State at the same time as it makes the EIA report available to its own nationals. In addition, this directive has been amended to bring it into line with the previously mentioned ESPOO Convention, as it is the convention for EIAs in transboundary contexts.[25] According to this amendment,[26] there shall be a consultation of the public and authorities in the neighbouring states, who can then communicate their opinion on the project to the authorities of the Member State on whose territory the project is located.

Practically speaking this means a 'party of origin' state would need to engage its impacted neighbours in a greater EIA process and enable the peoples of each country to provide feedback on the approval process for the new project. For example, if Belgium were to decide to locate a new nuclear power plant close to the Dutch and German border, then German and Dutch citizens would be granted a right of consultation and their opinion would need be communicated to the Belgian authorities deciding on the new plant.

In addition to this right of information and intervention in the administrative procedure one could also examine whether the location as such could be considered a violation of specific rules, such as the European EIA Directive (since the example takes place in Europe) or of the ESPOO Convention, or perhaps even of other principles of international environmental law.[27] A specific mention also deserved in this respect is the 1998 Aarhus Convention on access to information, public participation in decision making, and access to justice in environmental matters, which again provides possibilities for potential victims of a proposed activity

[23] Id., at 610–613.

[24] The original directive is Council Directive 85/337/EEC of 27 June 1985, but it has been many times amended.

[25] For more generally on EIA in the European context, see Jans and Vedder (2012, at 346–354).

[26] Directive 97/11, *Official Journal*, 7315.

[27] Sands and Peel (2012, at 601–623).

in a neighbouring state to obtain information and to have access to justice in order to acquire a potential remedy against the potentially polluting activity.[28] These examples show that many instruments have been developed, at the domestic as well as at the regional (for example European) and international level (such as the ESPOO and Aarhus Convention), all aiming at an internalisation of the externalities caused by environmental pollution.

To return to the earlier message on addressing transboundary externalities, those regional and international instruments can be considered as remedies countering the tendency of states to export their pollution problems, who would otherwise prefer to externalise the costs by addressing only the local impacts and not the transboundary impacts.

This introduction demonstrates how straightforward it can be to justify the need for environmental law, and international environmental law, on the foundations provided by environmental Law and Economics. Contrary to what might be expected by some readers, the economic analysis of environmental law recognises the failure of the market to prevent environmental injuries and it puts forward a theoretical framework based on the identification of environmental externalities as means to redress that market failure.

However, before turning to the question of which type of legal and policy instruments could generally be used to reach this internalisation of the externality, we should first discuss the work of Nobel Prize winner Ronald Coase, who has shown that legal rules may not under all circumstances be required to reach this internalisation of the externality.[29]

## 2.3 THE COASE THEOREM

### 2.3.1 *Reciprocal Nature of Harm*

Arthur Pigou is best known for formalising the ideas now known as externalities. By capturing these 'lost costs', market failures could be re-corrected to function properly. When the costs are environmental costs of pollution damages, the restoration of the market function enables the correct level of activity to provide for the socially desirable level of environmental engagement.

[28] Further on the Aarhus Convention, see Sands and Peel (2012, at 652–655) and for a discussion of access to justice at the European level, see Jans and Vedder (2012, at 228–237); see also Faure and Philipsen (2014).

[29] Technically, Ronald Coase won the economic equivalent to the Nobel Prize, which while often called the 'Nobel Prize in Economics' by the press, is actually the 'Swedish National Bank's Prize in Economic Sciences in Memory of Alfred Nobel'. Coase won the award in 1991 for 'his discovery and clarification of the significance of transaction costs and property rights for the institutional structure and functioning of the economy'; available at: www.nobelprize.org/nobel_prizes/economic-sciences/laureates/1991/

While one might re-connect those externalised costs in several different manners, traditionally, economists advocated the imposition of a tax on polluting activities in order to optimally internalise externalities such as environmental pollution. Since this idea builds on Pigou's work, this tax is usually referred to as a 'Pigouvian tax'.[30] By equalling the marginal tax rate to the marginal costs caused by the harmful activity, a potential polluter would face the correct costs of those environmental harms at the correct amount at every incremental decision point, preventing excessive production and polluting emissions. This makes sense if the polluter is the only one 'at fault' of the environmental injuries.

However, in his seminal article, 'The Problem of Social Cost', Ronald Coase opposed this idea; Coase stressed the reciprocal nature of harm.[31] In a theoretical twist on 'it takes two to tango', Coase observed that the pollution is not just caused by the fact that the factory is emitting harmful substances, but also by the presence of neighbours who are injured through the plant's emissions. Either party could yield ground and eliminate the conflict.[32]

Coase stressed that in these situations the actual point of conflict is a contrasting set of claims to the property right entitlements; that two parties seek to exercise rights that are somehow exclusive to each other. For example, a family has two children, a daughter and a son. The father may have given permission to the daughter to enjoy watching her favourite show on the TV. Meanwhile, the mother may have permitted their son to play a video game on the same TV. Both children arrive at the TV, with countervailing claims to rights of use, but just as clearly they cannot both have control over it at the same time. They will need to find some way to allocate the use of the commonly claimed right to the TV.

Similarly, Coase saw that the plant operator could claim a right to use the ambient air to emit and dissipate smoke, while a homeowner might claim an equally well founded right to enjoy the ambient air for breathing and refreshment. The problem is the underlying clash of claimed rights. The pollution problem could be solved unilaterally by either party yielding their claim to the other.

Lawyers traditionally see situations of environmental harm as rather one-sided affairs, wherein the factory operator limits the rights of the victims by emitting harmful substances. One could, however, equally argue that the victims limit the

30 Pigou (1951).

31 Coase (1960).

32 In examining property rights from a Coasean perspective, Lueck raises Arruñada's critiques, that Coase assumes a 'single-exchange' model of tort risk, that in a world of frequent sequential exchanges, that initial allocations may not be pre-determinative, that subsequent re-orderings may also lack determinative powers, but also acknowledges that Arruñada relied on an excessively narrow definition of transaction cost distinctly different from what is assumed in the models discussed in this book. See Lueck (2017, at 793–794).

right of the factory to perform its socially beneficial activities by their presence in the neighbourhood of the factory.[33]

One should therefore not automatically ask the question how the law should give incentives to force the factory to reduce emissions. First the question should be asked which of the several actors (factory or victims) should be limited in their property rights. The answer to this question will depend on which of the various actors could more efficiently take precautions to reduce or prevent the harm.

### 2.3.2 *Example of Conflicting Coasean Property Rights*

The Coasean results can be illustrated with a simple example. Assume the following facts:

- There is a neighbourhood with three individuals.
- In that neighbourhood is a factory emitting pollution.
- When exposed to pollution, each individual suffers $200 of damages.
- In the neighbourhood, only these three individuals can be damaged by pollution.[34]
- These three individuals have no means of preventing pollution nor the harm it causes them.

An ombudsman is called, reminded of the polluter pays principle, and is presented with several options:

- If nothing is done, the three neighbours will each continue to suffer for a total of $600 in damages.
- The factory could eliminate all the pollution by spending $300 to install a pollution removing filter.
- The three neighbours could be relocated to new housing, safely away from the pollution, for $400.

In this case, the ombudsman is likely to see that the factory could spend $600 to continue polluting as is, or it could spend $400 to relocate the neighbours away from the pollution, or, it could pay $300 to install the filter to eliminate the pollution from being emitted. The rational outcome would be for the plant to install the filter.

But what if the bill were to be faced by the residents, instead of the operator? That is, what if there was no pollution liability rule in place and the residents were left with merely 'self-curing' options? Well, they would still face the same three options: (i) they could do nothing and suffer $600 in damages, (ii) they could pay $400 for their own costs of relocation, or (iii), they could pay the operator $300 to install the

[33] The argument made herein is that when both parties present positive welfare value despite contrasting claims to exclusive property rights, then the Coase Theorem holds. No assertion is made that all plants are net positive welfare, nor that all victims are net damaged.

[34] Hence, in this example we disregard the fact that the emissions will also cause harm to the environment as such.

anti-pollution filter. Again, the logical outcome would be the same, that the filter would be installed, the only difference being who pays.

The theoretical question then arises of whether the optimal solution will always follow; in this case whether the filter will be installed.

Coase holds that if the transaction costs are zero an optimal allocation of resources will always take place, irrespective the contents of the governing legal rule. This is usually known as the Coase Theorem. To put it otherwise, Coase's Theorem holds that when the transaction costs are zero, the same invariant optimal outcome will result, no matter how the property rights were originally allocated.

This result, the symmetrical pathways to address the property rights problem, is considered quite revolutionary. It shows that when bargaining is possible between parties conflicting over pollution, then the optimal solution (in this case installation of the filter) will always follow, even if there is no liability for the pollution.[35] Even stronger: the result will also follow, irrespective of the legal rule, since parties may bargain around in efficient legal rules.[36]

Thus, the allure of Coase's Theorem; it does several important things for the economic analysis of environmental law. First, it provides theoretical foundations for understanding how the market would cure pollution if the market were fully functioning, albeit the question of who would bear the costs of the solution would differ. Second, the theorem enables us to detect market failure better, by noticing where that symmetrical result is not self-fulfilling. And finally, it enables to understand the importance of how to assign or re-allocate rights to enable the costs of cure most efficiently, by assigning them to the party which can cure at the least cost.[37]

### 2.3.3 *The Coase Theorem: A Few Constraints*

These powerful results of the Coase Theorem, however, merit a few cautionary comments.

First, a party must of course have resources available to pay for the filter if they are to actually pay for its installation. While industrial investors might be expected to be able to carry the costs to renovate their facilities, such is not always the case. Nor is it always feasible for the victims of environmental pollution to be able to bear the costs.[38] Thus, the optimal pathway may face a roadblock due to a simple lack of capital, or the high transaction costs of obtaining capital resources.

35 However, it is clear that the question of who will pay is affected by the initial allocation of rights and assets.

36 See Cooter and Ulen (2012, at 189).

37 This concept is well documented in common law but is oft called the 'least cost avoider' principle, after the usage of Guido Calabresi.

38 Christopher Stone is known for his question on standing for non-human participants in the environment; see Stone (2010). In this case, say for a tree suffering from pollution, the logic would hold the same as for a non-capitalized and legally incompetent person. See also footnote 40.

Second, the efficient outcome will not follow if one of the parties behaves strategically. For example, a party could file for strategic bankruptcy, or could raise the costs of negotiating by imposing novel difficulties of communication or of transactional sloth.

Third, it should be stressed that at first sight it is not clear which price the victims would have to pay to the factory for the installation of the filter if they faced a 'no liability rule' scenario. Depending upon its bargaining power, the factory could ask for more than the $300 in costs to cover the installation of the filter; arguendo, the negotiable range would be from the minimum of the $300 filter costs up a penny shy of the $400 in self-relocating costs.[39]

Fourth – and this is a crucial aspect – the Coase Theorem only deals with the efficiency effect of social problems, not with distributional aspects. Indeed, although the efficient results will hold in both cases (liability or no liability), there is a distributional difference: in the first case the factory pays for the filter; in the second case the victims pay for it. Hence, the contents of the legal rule will matter from the victims' perspective.[40]

This may be the reason why, from a policy perspective, the legislator sometimes intervenes to make the polluter liable even in situations where the conditions of the Coase Theorem are fulfilled. For the Coase Theorem demonstrates that the polluter pays principle is not the only pathway that could result in the same solution; additionally, it is not always the case that the polluter is the least cost avoider. Nevertheless, public policy often appears to prefer a social justice norm to require the implementation of the polluter pays principle.[41]

Fifth, the Coase Theorem is based on the zero transaction costs assumption. Although many Law and Economics scholars and environmental economists use the Coase Theorem as a starting point for discussing the role of environmental law and, more generally, the need for legal instruments to control environmental pollution,[42] a drawback is that the Coase Theorem only provides the symmetrical pathway results in a world of zero transaction costs. In some small cases of pollution, it might certainly be useful to apply the Coase Theorem as if the transaction costs were near zero.

[39] The theory of two-party negotiations was early addressed by Edgeworth and his early approach to game theory, best noted by his 'box' model; but the more recent Myerson-Satterthwaite Theorem has revealed the mathematical complexity and impossibility of a mutually beneficial bargain being achieved under four assumptions of fair conditions when the parties are both facing uncertainty of the utility (or value) of the negotiated goods to the counterparties of the trade. See Myerson and Satterthwaite (1983, at 265–281).

[40] Given the exploration of the standing of trees under the Coase Theorem, at footnote 38, here it is now obvious the importance of legal rules, from a distributional perspective, for those environmental participants with no or limited recourse to standing in civil liability cases.

[41] Indeed, many states and international agreements have implemented the polluter pays principle in their legislation and conventions. For details see Section 5.6.

[42] Baumol and Oates (1979); Frey (1992); Mishan (1971a); Oates (1983); and Schulze and D'Arge (1974).

However, in real life, the example of one factory emitting smoke that affects just three victims rarely exists. In most large-scale pollution cases the number of victims will be too large and transaction costs will be too prohibitive for the victims to act in a unified voice and strategy.[43]

One aspect of transaction costs is information. It was assumed that the victims and the polluter are fully informed about the damage and about the efficient preventive measures. In many cases that may not be a realistic assumption. In cases where transaction costs are indeed prohibitive the Coasean negotiations will not take place, and consequently some kind of intervention of the legal system is needed to effectuate the internalisation. But understanding the implications of the Coase Theorem will greatly enhance the policymaker's effort to design that curative legal rule.

Sixth, so far, we have assumed that the various rights are clearly defined and that negotiations take place on the basis of this allocation of rights. It was also assumed that the property of the neighbours could be valued objectively. However, in reality subjective valuations, for example determining the impact damages of a nuisance, could well exist and prevent effective negotiations.[44] These may hinder the attainment of an efficient solution through negotiations and can therefore also be considered as transaction costs on their own.

### 2.3.4 *Practical Value of the Coase Theorem*

Clearly, the most important implication of the Coase Theorem is that mutually beneficial agreements will be made when no transaction costs prevent parties from making such an agreement.[45] And countervailing, the immediate lack of such results gives evidence to the very impediments preventing that result.

Critics might argue that the zero transaction costs hypothesis of Coase's world will never be realised in the environmental context, so that one could question the usefulness of a discussion of the Coase Theorem for environmental law. But this misses the point, in many ways it is exactly the distance from that abstract result that informs the economic analysis of environmental law where the curative rule would be most useful, as to which re-allocation might make the greatest difference in addressing the environmental risks and harms.

First, we already stressed that there may be many pollution cases wherein the number of polluters and of their impacted neighbours are small enough in number and well acquainted enough with each other and the facts of the pollution to facilitate Coasean negotiations. In such a situation, reaching a Coasean bargain may be possible. For example, in some villages there may be small-scale pollution

43 On these drawbacks of the importance of the Coase Theorem for environmental problems, see Mishan (1971b); see also Kapp (1970).

44 See footnote 39 on the Myerson-Sattherwaite Theorem.

45 See Shavell (2004, at 84).

cases where polluters and victims do indeed know each other with the result that negotiations may enable a Coasean bargain to be reached.

Second, if transaction costs prevent efficient solutions through bargaining, one could examine what the nature of these problems is. If transactions do not occur, for instance because information on the nature of the harm or the potential preventive measures is lacking,[46] regulation could be targeted at increasing the information. If, for example, through mandatory disclosure of information transaction costs can be lowered, Coasean bargaining may again be possible.

Following that, the Coase Theorem demonstrates that prohibitive transaction costs should not necessarily lead to regulation determining the standard of safety; instead, the policymaker could also opt for a regulatory solution which facilitates bargaining. Such a solution is less interventionist; it is also more likely that efficient outcomes will occur through these efficient agreements instead of through mandatory regulation.[47]

Third, even starting from the assumption that an intervention of the legal system is unavoidable, the Coase Theorem still is useful since it may indicate an efficient solution to the legislator. Indeed, the legislator could ask what solutions parties would have agreed to if Coasean bargaining had been possible. This presumed result of Coasean bargaining could then be taken as the starting point for the legislative intervention. Thus, the legislative solution can 'mimic' the market.

Fourth, an important lesson of the Coase Theorem is that parties will, whenever possible (in low transaction cost settings, which allow for bargaining) contract around inefficient laws. And the observation of such behaviours could also be instructive in re-designing law to more efficiently address the environmental problem at hand.

### 2.3.5 *Transboundary Application of the Coase Theorem*

It was mentioned earlier that externalities do not only arise in a domestic setting between polluters and victims, but that states may equally have a tendency to externalise to other downstream states the harms and damages resulting from the pollution created in the upstream state. It could be argued that bargaining may also be possible through bilateral negotiations between states. Thus, a Coasean solution could be reached and there would be no need to use costly harmonisation measures.[48]

46 Asymmetry of information may indeed be one of the reasons why mutually beneficial agreements do not emerge. See Shavell (2004, at 89–91).

47 The only question one could ask is to what extent mandatory disclosure regulation is indeed effective in the sense of letting parties make better informed decisions. In the consumer areas there are some doubts whether the disclosure of information (for example forcing people to read before signing a contract) has indeed led to better decision making. See Faure and Luth (2011).

48 This argument was advanced by Cohen (1996).

In theory, for example, when only two states are involved, one upstream polluting state and one downstream victim state, bargaining should be possible, leading either the victim state paying the polluter state to install efficient pollution reduction mechanisms, or the polluting state taking those measures itself. However, in practice this type of efficient bargaining between states is rarely observed.

A variety of reasons may explain this.

One problem is that states are not necessarily the rational actors that are assumed to maximise their own utility, according to the Coase Theorem. States are represented by politicians who primarily seek re-election.[49] That may cause distortions as a result of which politicians may lack incentives to invest in solutions (for example investments in a water treatment plant) that would only provide benefits after their term in office.[50]

Another problem is that in some cases politicians may be insufficiently willing to represent the interests of a presumably smaller number of victims actually suffering the harm; as democratically elected members of government, their strategy to remain in place necessarily engages a calculus of plurality.[51] Examples can be drawn from coastal oil states, where the interests of coastal communities, e.g. fishing communities, are outweighed by the interests of much larger urban populations at a remove from the petroleum extraction activities.[52]

Moreover, as soon as the transboundary pollution passes across the boundaries of multiple states, and as the effluent presents chaotic flow and encounters other potential sources of pollution risks, complicated causation issues arise, and multiple parties must engage in complex negotiations. It becomes clear that in those events, bargaining is unlikely to generate efficient results due to the high transaction costs.

Again, those problems are evidence of Coase Theorem assumptions being dysfunctional and thus presenting an opportunity for environmental law to provide alternative transaction cost structures by changing the underlying allocations of rights, availability of information, and by improving the in-place legal institutions.[53]

[49] See Schäfer (2012). Also, the school of social choice theory expands the methods developed for the economic analysis of law to application in a political science context, with similar results.

[50] On similar problems with respect to the necessary investments in prevention of disasters, see Depoorter (2006).

[51] 'Public choice theory, which analyzes the political process using principles of economics, posits a very different vision of legislation.' Eskridge Jr. (1988, at 276). Public choice theory has this observation at the core of its methodology, in contrast to a microeconomics maxim and that a firm maximises profit, public choice theory observes that politicians maximise their time in elected office: 'Public choice theory argues that legislative behavior is driven by one central goal – the legislator's desire to be reelected.' (Id. at 288). Public choice theory is further explained in Section 9.3.

[52] This point could be made equally well with *Valdez, Alaska* v. *Los Angeles, California*, as with coastal communities in state with developing economies.

[53] Examples of such would include shifting the burden of proof, provision of scientific environmental data from collected EIAs, and the novel provision of transboundary tribunal or arbitral panels.

From the economic analysis of law, the transboundary character of externalities, as in environmental pollution, is one of the most clearly established reasons for shifting powers to a higher level of government.[54]

But even where Coasean negotiations were not facile to undertake, we notice that environmental agreements were reached which successfully reduced pollution levels.[55] Bargaining has also taken place via commissions that were instituted to manage transboundary waters. For the Rhine River,[56] and also the Meuse River,[57] one can notice that international commissions are called into life which should in principle facilitate cooperative solutions between parties. Early empirical evidence shows that, at least as far as the Rhine is concerned, environmental quality has substantially increased since the 1980s. Even though it is difficult to judge that these results are purely due to the intervention of these commissions, stakeholders hold that at least the engagement with the consensual approach, including the involvement of industry in the commissions, explains part of the success in gaining the increased willingness of industry to accept emission reductions.[58] Furthermore, this case does not concern intra-state negotiations, but rather negotiations held by the states in direct discussions with members of industry – enabled by a convention between the bordering states creating the necessary legal framework for such a voluntary agreement.

Hence, there are strong arguments from an economic perspective that shifting powers to a higher level of government is an efficient reaction to transboundary pollution. That explains why larger or federal government entities, such as the EU or the US government, tend to focus more closely on transboundary pollution problems.[59] Likewise, a central goal of international treaties at the core of international environmental law is this internalisation of transboundary environmental externalities. These results are all supported by the theoretical framework of environmental Law and Economics.

Stated point blank, evidence demonstrates that the development of novel legal institutions enabled groups previously unable to efficiently negotiate to reach Coasean outcomes, and thus to solve real environmental problems, matching the

[54] See Esty (1996, at 625); Oates and Schwab (1988). This is further explained in Chapter 13 dealing with environmental federalism.

[55] See for example the studies presented by the Environmental Law Network International (ELNI 1998). See also Innes and Sam (2008), who equally conclude that voluntary pollution reduction programmes can, provided they are carefully combined with regulatory and enforcement rewards for programme participation, be useful and effective tools to reduce pollution and save government costs.

[56] The Rhine flows through Switzerland, Austria, France, Germany, and the Netherlands.

[57] The Meuse flows through France, Belgium, and the Netherlands. Germany and Luxembourg join in its water basin.

[58] On the Meuse Commission, see Romano (2000, at 233–245); see also Peeters (2008).

[59] This will be discussed in further detail in Chapter 13, dealing with environmental federalism.

theoretical expectations drawn from models developed from the economic analysis of environmental law.

## 2.4 THE NEED FOR LEGAL AND POLICY INSTRUMENTS

### 2.4.1 *Determining Optimal Pollution Levels*

Friedrick Hayek taught that an important function of the price system is to transfer information.[60] According to Hayek, prices contain relevant, holographic information to be dispersed to the public at large; the economic analysis of environmental law extends that observation of the functions of that information system to application in environmental law.

The whole acts as one market, not because any of its members survey the whole field, but because their limited individual fields of vision sufficiently overlap so that through many intermediaries the relevant information is communicated to all. The mere fact that there is one price for any commodity – or rather that local prices are connected in a manner determined by the cost of transport, etc. – brings about the solution which (it is just conceptually possible) might have been arrived at by one single mind possessing all the information which is in fact dispersed amongst all the people involved in the process.[61]

We must look at the price system as such a mechanism for communicating information if we want to understand its real function – a function which, of course, it fulfils less perfectly as prices grow more rigid. (Even when quoted prices have become quite rigid, however, the forces which would operate through changes in price still operate to a considerable extent through changes in the other terms of the contract.) The most significant fact about this system is the economy of knowledge with which it operates, or how little the individual participants need to know in order to be able to take the right action.[62]

If the market mechanisms are not enabling information on environmental risks and harms to reach its proper audience(s), then law has a role to alter the market mechanisms to better ensure the creation, distribution, and utilisation of that environmental information.

The result of this chapter's analysis so far is that non-internalised externalities create market failures which can lead to environmental pollution. If acts of pollution

[60] Hayek won the 1974 Sveriges Riksbank Prize in Economic Sciences in Memory of Alfred Nobel, alongside Gunnar Myrdal, 'for their pioneering work in the theory of money and economic fluctuations and for their penetrating analysis of the interdependence of economic, social and institutional phenomena'; available at: www.nobelprize.org/nobel_prizes/economic-sciences/laureates/1974/hayek-facts.html

[61] Hayek (1945, at 519–530) (para. V. H.21), available at: www.econlib.org/library/Essays/hykKnw1.html; accessed 20 May 2017.

[62] Hayek (1945, at 526–527) (para. VI. H.22).

result in externalities that are not correctly reflected into the relative prices of products and services when presented to consumers, then demand will be too high (precisely because the price does not reflect the social costs caused by the pollution) and as a result, too much supply will be offered. By allowing the damage-costs information to be missing, excessive levels of pollution resulted.

The economic analysis of environmental law states that pollution predicated on missing information could be remedied by fixing the market's ability to correctly convey information. Because the transaction costs to enable access to the missing information were prohibitively high, an intervention of the law becomes necessary; environmental law in the domestic context, international environmental law in the transboundary context.

Of course, that leads to two additional questions. One question is what does the 'internalisation of the externality' precisely mean? Does it entail an obligation for potential polluters to reduce pollution to zero, in other words at all costs?

For reasons to be explored in Chapter 6, it turns out that the costs of reaching a level of 'zero pollution' would be prohibitively high,[63] as such a legal rule would amount to prohibiting any economic activity at all. Therefore, one important aspect of environmental Law and Economics consists in the search for 'optimal' levels of pollution, balancing the benefits of reduced pollution with the costs to human welfare to yet further reduce the levels of pollution.

A second question asks what legal tools or legal institutions might enable that 'internalisation of the externality'?[64] There are a range of options, including rules of civil liability, command and control public regulations, market-based instruments, suasive and voluntary instruments, and smart regulatory mixes. The key commonality across these tools are their ability to re-allocate rights, to correct market mechanisms to enhance the flow and availability of information, and their ability to internalise externalities that would otherwise enable the risks and harms of environmental pollution.

Finally, the economic analysis of environmental law enquires, if we are to begin identifying risky activities and environmental injuries, to be able to define environmental harms resulting from externalities, what standards or norms should we agree to as a group, community, or state in making those determinations? Economic

[63] It is also subjectively difficult to characterise the notion of 'zero pollution' as different researchers might prefer different baselines of comparison. Against what time or era should modern levels of activity be compared, to establish a notional 'zero pollution' level? Given mankind's impact on the earth goes back a very long way, and that even its experiences with agriculture and hunting have had environmental impacts for millennia, we will not suggest an approach in this book. We'll merely allow that the fundamental economic models reveal that no matter the baseline, its approach would become too costly to achieve in any realistic model of an economy.

[64] Other chapters of this book will deal with that question of instrument choice at greater length, see Chapters 7–13, but we present an introductory survey here in this section.

analysis of group decision processes, with regards to integrating social preferences,[65] and also to voting on social options,[66] have revealed that there are substantial challenges – what could be called 'social market' failures. Thus, the economic analysis of standard setting bears importance in studying environmental law; who should determine the standard and how might those standards be best determined? These issues are addressed in the various instruments later, in examining who the stakeholders are for each instrument.

### 2.4.2 *Rules of Civil Liability*

One of the oldest instruments of law, civil liability, has been found by the literature on the economic analysis of law to be one of the more robust tools in correcting the problems of internalising environmental externalities.[67] There are sophisticated models available, discussed at length in Chapter 8, that take into account the various rules of civil liability and of the multiple forms of tortfeasance;[68] this legal toolkit enables policymakers to create bespoke legal rules to address specific types of environmental externalities.

Under a regime of civil liability, courts can compel polluters to compensate victims by selection of specific rules. Choice of strict liability compels polluters to pay for damage done in all cases, without regard to efforts to avoid harm. Choice of the negligence rule compels polluters to pay if a certain level of care was not followed.

There is a major difference with civil liability rules from criminal rules and most forms of public regulation, that compliance with any particular standard of behaviour under a liability rule is not mandatory. Under civil liability systems, the polluter remains permitted to deviate as long as they are able to pay the price, i.e. to pay the adjudicated damages to the victim.[69] This flexibility of civil liability regimes provides logical incentives to avoid environmental risks without the need for policymakers

65 Arrow's Possibility Theorem, popularly known as his Impossibility Theorem, is the seminal model for examining the algorithmic complexities of establishing unified social preferences, such as in a hierarchical sense of norms or standards or in a social welfare function. See Arrow (1950, at 328–346). See also Arrow (2014).

66 While the algorithmic challenges facing voting systems date back at least to Condorcet, the theorem(s) of Gibbard and Satterthwaite established the impossibility of rational voting in a mirror to Arrow's findings on integrated preference ranking systems (Gibbard 1973, at 587–601; Satterthwaite 1975, at 187–217). For a beautiful demonstration of the symmetry of the two concepts, see Reny (2001, at 99–105).

67 See Shavell (2011).

68 In the first instance, for environmental injuries, one could select from a rule of negligence, a strict liability rule, a rule of trespass, or a rule of nuisance, amongst others. In the second instance, one might find injuries arising from unilateral or bilateral accidents, from singular or from multiple tortfeasors.

69 In that sense a liability rule can be considered as a price instrument, just like taxes and subsidies. See Wiener (1999, at 706–709).

and legislators to determine specific measures to reduce the effects or creation of environmental pollution.[70]

### 2.4.3 *Public Regulation: Command and Control*

Public regulation has by economists often been qualified as command and control (CAC) rules, consisting of an administrative system based on licences, permitting, and standard setting by administrative agencies.

The choice between liability rules and public regulation will be the subject of Chapter 9, but the economic analysis of environmental law finds that there are several key reasons to consider public regulations. Given the difficulty or impossibility of remediating certain types of environmental injuries, these theoretical recommendations from environmental Law and Economics in favour of regulatory standard setting is all the more important for environmental law.[71]

Public regulations may be more effective in setting standards in environmental contexts, because first, civil liability rules require an injury in fact before enabling the creation of a standard, and second, the necessary conditions for robustly functioning civil liability rules are often found to be lacking,[72] thus standards may fail to be set at all under certain circumstances.

A key problem of the CAC aspect of public regulations is that such regulations appear to suffer from 'stickiness', in that they lock-in technological assumptions at the time of drafting. The economic analysis of law shows that that the drafting of public regulations suffers from an array of transaction cost problem, which results in administrative reluctance to re-draft on a frequent basis. Thus, newer or better technologies or policies to avoid, prevent, cure, or remediate environmental harms could find themselves at odds with regulatory compliance; similarly, few incentives would be provided by public regulations to develop such improvements beyond the established regulatory requirements. Thus, environmentally beneficial innovations would lag and the environment would unnecessarily suffer higher levels of harm. Regulation will have to be enforced through public sanctions, often consisting of both civil penalties and criminal penalties. Sunset provisions have been recommended as means to dampen these problems.[73] Similarly, research supports the idea

[70] There are caveats such as the solvency of the polluter and an adequate assessment of damages by the judge. These caveats and related topics will be covered in Chapter 8.

[71] A CAC technology requirement in fact prescribes specific conduct of the operator. See Wiener (1999, at 706).

[72] In a nutshell, rules of civil liability are less likely to work as intended when parties face asymmetrical information on risks (creating strategic advantages), when parties face insolvency (reducing informational value of adjudicated damages), and when the threat of lawsuit is lacking or weak. The threat of lawsuits is weak when there is (i) a low probability of injury detection, (ii) a low probability of prosecution, or (iii) a low probability of enforced judgments.

[73] Ranchordás (2015, at 205).

of experimental regulations, enabling authorities a chance to test regulatory concepts before those ideas are used more broadly.[74]

However, CAC remains effective in many circumstances; and even its limited efficacy has been questioned meta-empirically, finding that CAC may have been more successful than many might have thought.[75]

An optimal design of public sanctions will be discussed in Chapters 6, 7, and 9, and environmental criminal law will be the subject of Chapter 10.

### 2.4.4 *Market-Based Instruments*

Command and control isn't the only way for public agencies to influence behaviour. A different approach, in fact already advocated as early as the 1920s by Pigou, is the use of financial instruments to internalise externalities. These economic instruments are often referred to as 'incentive-based', 'market-based', or 'economic' instruments.

The basic idea of those incentive mechanisms is to correct an externality by returning an appropriate fee or cost to the potential polluter. In that case, public regulation would not need to provide specific behavioural guidance, nor would bureaucrats need to audit the polluter's behaviour to those requirements. Instead, the restored information, the re-internalised externality, would provide sufficient information to guide the actor's behaviour.

The most commonly implemented are those Pigouvian taxes discussed earlier, but there are in fact a range of options, including positive payments such as subsidies for desired behaviours. For example, the polluter could be taxed according to the amount of pollution emitted; giving the polluter better incentives, tax-reducing incentives, for pollution reduction and more particularly for innovative investments in pollution reduction tools.[76]

On the other hand, if the polluters chose not to reduce pollution levels, then the state would have already collected capital resources from the polluter via the taxes, and as explored in Section 2.3, the state could then make its choice on how to respond to the pollution; it could (i) suffer damages and pay for remediation, or (ii) pay for costs of relocation, or (iii) pay the operator to install the anti-pollution technologies. Thus, the 'market-based' tax could enable the polluter pays principle to operate via the collection of the tax which could then be used by the state to act on the pollution.

This choice between market-based versus CAC instruments has been the subject of a lot of debate in the literature and will be discussed in further detail in Chapter 7.

[74] Id., at 206. She quotes Dan Farber as also being in favour of experimental regulatory design (id., at 220).

[75] Cole and Grossman (1999, at 889–891).

[76] Wiener (1999, at 714–726); Stewart (2007, at 151–152).

### 2.4.5 *Suasive Mechanisms*

Beyond CAC versions of public regulation and the market-based alternative of public regulation, a third option has emerged – that of the 'nudge', or the suasive mechanism. So-called suasive instruments, whereby the government does not necessarily impose specific duties on operators, but rather steers their behaviour in a particular direction. This could be achieved by use of 'defaults' in compliance efforts or by educational or informational publication campaigns.

In addition to (either mandatory or soft) government regulation there is also an increasing number of incentive-providing instruments which guide potential polluters to internalise externalities. Those suasive instruments can consist of government tools whereby pollution activity is not directly regulated per se, but it might be made mandatory that information on the polluter's environmental impacts be made available to the public. Another example of such a suasive instrument is where the government encourages private parties to offer environmental information.[77]

Information-based approaches can provide incentives for improved environmental performance through a variety of mechanisms.[78] In other cases voluntary environmental agreements are concluded between the government and operators.[79] These information-based approaches can in some cases be regarded as regulatory instruments if they are either required by law or the government provides inducements for their adoption.[80]

In perhaps an unusual reversal of the Pigouvian approach, in one case a mechanism was designed to reward parties that were 'negatively' impacted by the arrival and imposition of new wildlife preservation rules near Yellowstone National Park.[81] A private group, the Defenders of Wildlife, provided funds for those parties that assisted in the compliance efforts to support the Fish and Wildlife Service's efforts to reintroduce certain wolves into the park and its surroundings.[82] Ranchers were paid to offset the loss of sheep and cattle that occurred during that programme, to coordinate their interests with the goals of the Fish and Wildlife Service's programme.[83]

### 2.4.6 *Voluntary and Private Mechanisms*

In other cases, the government does not intervene at all and instruments are entirely developed by industry, for example via labelling and certification tools or via

77 Further on the development of those suasive instruments, and more particularly environmental information provision in international environmental law, see Sands and Peel (2012, at 624–664).

78 Stewart (2007, at 153).

79 For further details, see Glasbergen (1998).

80 Stewart (2007, at 152–154).

81 Lueck (1995, at 669).

82 Id.

83 Id.

mechanisms of corporate environmental responsibility (CER). To an important extent those instruments can also be considered as addressing the informational needs to facilitate Coasean negotiations.[84]

In some cases, operators will respond to a demand from for example particular consumer groups to deliver products or services of higher environmental quality, potentially also leading to higher prices. Eco-labels are one of the most widely employed tools by firms to communicate specific features of their products to consumers. The main purpose of eco-labels is to convey relevant environmental information about a product to the appropriate consumers through the product label.[85]

If signalling of higher environmental quality to specific consumer groups is possible, then product differentiation can take place and thus those consumer groups that have preferences for high environmental quality products and services could specifically be targeted by the industry. Corporate social responsibility (CSR) can thus be employed by operators as a means of product differentiation, and thus of economic gain.[86]

It should, however, be noticed that most agree that these private and voluntary strategies do provide an important additional tool next to formal government regulation, but not necessarily an alternative. Formal government regulation may still be necessary as the symbolic stick for the case when private regulatory instruments failed. Regulation remains important since certification and labelling schemes have in some cases been criticised as being mere 'green washing'.[87]

It should also be noted that increasingly one can notice an interaction between private and public regulation in environmental governance. For example, one of the conditions of compliance with public regulation may be the adherence to a private certification scheme. The polluter would be audited by a third party in order to receive a compliance-proving certificate; the polluter reveals information to obtain the certificate while the accreditor seeks to retain its reputation in evaluating compliance in order to retain its own licence to accredit certificates. This is an example of a private regulatory mechanism, wherein the public regulator creates an information revealing game between two non-governmental parties to ensure both informational and behavioural goals are achieved at low transaction costs to the public regulator.

### 2.4.7 *Smart Instrument Mixes*

What if no one legal instrument can fully address the circumstances of a particular environmental problem, then what? Gunningham and Grabosky established in the

84 See Lu and Faure (2016).
85 Martinez Gandara (2013, at 24).
86 Kitzmueller and Shimshack (2012, at 65).
87 See Martinez Gandara (2013).

seminal text, *Smart Regulation*,[88] that in fact all legal instruments have particular advantages, but also their own particular weaknesses; but they can be combined in bespoke arrangements.[89]

An important question in the 'choice of instrument' literature is therefore which type of policy instrument is indicated under which particular circumstances. The insight that no instrument alone can lead to optimal results also indicates that in most cases a combination of different instruments may be necessary to optimally internalise externalities. That leads to a growing literature on the search for smart mixes between different legal and policy instruments. The crucial question in that respect is how an optimal combination of a variety of legal and policy instruments can be designed to optimally internalise the externality caused by environmental pollution.

The remaining chapters in this book will try to indicate where those smart instrument mixes must be found and how bespoke solutions might best be tailored to the circumstances of the environmental risks and harms in consideration.

## 2.5 SUMMARY AND CONCLUSION

This chapter has presented the initial foundations of how environmental injuries are approached from the Law and Economics perspective.

We began with coverage of the fundamental principles of environmental law; how they can be reframed from a rational actor cum decision maker perspective. Once so reframed, the tools of Law and Economics can be brought to bear on policy questions within environmental law. Thus, it is paramount to recognise that the approach taken in this book is to build on the existing consensus in international environmental law and to provide it with new analytical tools to improve the design of legal rules and to enable prospective modelling of the effects of rules in pre-implementation stages of evaluation and deliberation.

We then discussed the Pigouvian idea of environmental injuries as economic externalities. The core idea of Pigou's model is that manufacturing costs that are excluded from the decision-making process will inherently not be reflected in the decision making of producers, and thus, manufacturing costs will be incorrectly perceived as lower than they actually are to the community-at-large, and that in turn will lead on to higher-than-optimal production levels. If those costs reflect injuries from pollution, then overproduction will co-produce 'surplus' environmental injuries, meaning those surplus injuries that are not already accounted by the costs of prevention activities or in repair and rehabilitation costs.

88 Gunningham and Grabosky (1998).

89 This choice of instruments is discussed in a detailed manner by Wiener (1999) and may also lead to hybrid regulatory approaches. See Stewart (2007, at 154).

Thus, a key objective, to ensure better decision making and to better prevent environmental injuries, is to find strategies to 'internalise' the cost externalities so that the marginal costs of the damages from the injuries can be included in the marginal analysis of the firm's production decisions. From another perspective, rational actors who are forced to bear the costs of the injuries resulting from their production activities will set optimal levels of production inclusive of minimising the costs of pollution injuries via reducing the incidence of those pollution injuries.[90]

We explored the complexity of environmental injuries that arise across non-singular jurisdictional zones of incidence. For example, State A may not be able to fully 'internalise' the costs arising from within State B, and thus, injuries arising in B might spread into A. The problem of internalising such transboundary Pigouvian cost externalities leads to questions of intra- and inter- state coordination and cooperation on environmental injuries. This question of coordination and cooperation leads to policy decisions on federalism and of international law to enable potential solutions to the transboundary concerns. And clearly, certain environmental injuries can only be rationally internalised if the appropriately broad and multi-jurisdictional legal frameworks are agreed to by the complete set of stakeholder jurisdictions. Such arrangements might not always be politically feasible or viable, but the Pigouvian model does enable policymakers to evaluate if workable solutions are available for adoption and to provide rational support for policy adoption.

We explored how Coase reformulated the basis of tort law, or of delict, by observing that injuries can be seen as resulting from oppositional claims to the same or similar bundles of rights; that the traditional tort law perspective of injurer and injuree might be missing important information useful for addressing tort law concepts. First amongst these concepts is the reciprocity of harm. Both a manufacturing plant and a village community might have claim to the ambient flowing air. The plant might claim the right to use that air to carry away emissions. The village might claim rights to access fresh air from the hills or mountains nearby. Depending on governmental permits or environmental protection rules, or maybe nuisance rules, the injury to access one's rights could be done either way in this example.

We discussed how policymakers might investigate conflicting Coasean property rights allocations. Key amongst those are the ability to negotiate and to re-allocate property rights in a market-based method. Another potential is for the state to re-allocate the rights when the ex ante allocation does not lead to an efficient pathway of negotiations.

90 In somewhat more detail, the actor would set the efficient level of production, and thus also the efficient level of pollution from their production activity, given the price structure of the market as reflective of the aggregate welfare function. Thus, the actor would set the pollution level at the level that best reflects society's revealed preference for pollution versus other goods and services.

That said, there were complexities in the Coasean framework. First, the actual costs of carrying out the re-allocation process, including the instrumental steps to avoid infringing on the rights of the other party, might exceed the budgetary provisions of one or both parties. Second, certain strategic behaviours could frustrate the efficacy of resolving the dispute, such as by increasing the transaction costs of the negotiating space. Coase's analysis primarily addressed efficiency in addressing social welfare and did not address issues of distributional issues such as parity or equity. In this regard, Coase's analysis is orthogonal to notions paradigmatically evaluated by Pareto and then by Kaldor and Hicks. Finally, the role of transaction costs in enabling or frustrating Coasean allocation processes cannot be sufficient underscored as both the core of the intellectual model and the root of its complexity in practice.

Also, the Coasean framework has conventionally been used for 'close-in-time' analyses. It is less clear how well the conceptual model holds up when the two groups at reciprocal risk operate in substantially different time frames, e.g. how the Coasean approach might address two groups separated by decades , as one might find in complex long-term industrial pollution such as governance of dumping sites of hazardous chemicals.

Despite the quick survey, earlier, of caveats surrounding Coasean analysis, its introduction of novel tools and insights does allow environmental policymakers and legislators to better foresee how to disentangle certain environmental conflicts and how to potentially redesign legal rules to more effectively enable prospective avoidance of environmental injuries and to also facilitate future efforts to resolve conflicting views on rights to better coordinate multiple actors and stakeholders in the environmental law space.

# 3

# Property Rights Approach to Environmental Law

One instrument which was not mentioned at the end of the last chapter, referring to the need for legal and policy instruments is property rights. There is also a good reason for that. As in fact the Coase Theorem already made clear, the allocation of clear property rights is a precondition for any type of environmental protection measure.

In his seminal article on the 'tragedy of the commons',[1] Hardin made clear that without the establishment of property rights a total destruction of the resource concerned could take place.[2]

Allocating property rights is, therefore, a basic condition to provide incentives to environmental protection (Section 3.1). In some cases an explicit allocation of property rights to environmental resources (such as wildlife) could provide a better protection to the resource than a CAC regulatory approach (Section 3.2). A specific case of conflicts between various property rights arises with temporary conflicts, i.e. when a polluting activity in fact only becomes polluting because the victims 'came to the nuisance'. In that case the question arises, how rights should be allocated in order to provide the correct incentives for pollution reduction to all parties involved (Section 3.3).

[1] Hardin (1968). That article and its arguments had been previously explored by the economist H. Scott Gordon, on a study on fishing access, in 1954. See Rose (2014, at 1258), citing to H. Scott Gordon, 'The Economic Theory of a Common-Property Resource: The Fishery', *Journal of Political Economics*, 1954, Vol. 62(2), 124.

[2] It is worth mentioning here that the economic model underlying Hardin's arguments has a symmetric model known in economics as the anti-commons model, wherein control over a right is open to many but the consumption of the right is limited to a few. A commonly given example is a permitting process where too many decision makers are involved. The risk of substantial welfare loss from open access commons and from anti-common processes has been demonstrated to be equal in value. See Buchanan and Yoon (2000), for a demonstration of the mathematical symmetry of the two models. See Bretsen and Hill (2009, at 727), for an introduction to this approach from a more legal perspective in the analysis of laws on water access.

TABLE 1 *Matrix of goods and services defined by excludability and rivalry*[3]

| | Subtractability or Rivalrous Character | | |
|---|---|---|---|
| | Rivalrous | Non-rivalrous | Anti-rivalrous |
| **Excludable** | Goods only one person can use at a time, but can control access to good. E.g. (i) private goods, (ii) a bite of food | Goods that we can all use at the same time without reducing others' enjoyment of same good, but can control access to good. E.g. (i) club goods, (ii) public museum, cinema | Goods that increase in value as more people use it, but can control access to good. E.g. a multi-player game |
| **Non-Excludable** | Goods only one person can use at a time, but no control over access to good – common pool resources. E.g. a fish in the high seas | Goods that we can all use at the same time without reducing others' enjoyment of same good, but no control over access to good. E.g. (i) public goods, (ii) math truths | Goods that increase in value as more people use it, but no control over access to good. E.g. cultural knowledge |

## 3.1 IMPORTANCE OF ESTABLISHING PROPERTY RIGHTS

### 3.1.1 *The 'Tragedy of the Commons'*

Two parameters that can broadly distinguish goods and services from one another are the degree of excludability and whether these goods and services are rivalrous, or subtractable, in consumption and production.[4] By using these criteria, goods can be classified in four categories, as shown in Table 1.

Common goods or common pool resources are generally typified by their costly and difficult exclusion of rivalry users. The rivalry manifests itself in the form that: resource subtracted by one user diminishes the resource available to the consumption of other actors. In other words, the resource is accessed in common by all but the goods generated are private. Common pool resources include Earth-system components, such as the atmosphere, marine and terrestrial ecosystems whose resources are regarded as depletable and renewable at the same time, as well as irrigation systems.[5]

[3] Faure and Skogh (2003, at 61).

[4] Ostrom et al., (1999, at 278–279).

[5] Private goods are mostly those being produced and traded in private markets, such as food, cars, clothing, and houses. Pure public goods are those that can be enjoyed free of charge by

From an economic perspective many environmental goods, such as the sea, the air and forests, especially tropical forests, can be classified as common pool resources, which are subject to high subtractability and low excludability.[6]

The problem with such an open access resource is that everyone could in theory take resources from the public provenance into private consumption or production; e.g. fish in the ocean or trees in a forest. As long as the marginal costs for accessing the resource remain below the resource's marginal benefit, such a non-excludable valuable resource will become subject to overharvesting (as in the case of public forests) or overhunting (as in the case of wildlife). It will therefore likely impair the continuous sustainability of such resources and lead to, for example, forest depletion,[7] or to extinction of the species.[8]

This phenomenon that open access (free-for-all) to resources will lead to the depletion of those resources has been described in a seminal paper by Hardin.[9] This 'tragedy of the commons',[10] resulting from the fact that no one is excluded from the use of the particular resource, leads to private ownership simply being established by the person who takes 'first access', known as the 'first mover'.[11] The first-mover advantage provides competing users with incentives to engage in a race whereby all try to harvest as much as possible and as quickly as possible from the resource in order to pre-empt claims or resource capture from others in the hunt.

The first-mover advantage has, for example, led to overexploitation of surf clams; to increase the catch, clam harvesters invested too much in equipment in order to be able to harvest clams rapidly.[12] Similarly, in oil extraction there has been a tendency to overcapitalise in order to pump more quickly since ownership rights are only

individuals at the same time without diminishing the utility, such as (tax-based) national defence, the law, court system, and (indirect private funding) search engines. Common goods and club goods are both impure public goods, which are not fully non-excludable and non-subtractable. Common goods might be non-excludable but can be congested, whereas club goods are the other way around. Club goods are not entirely subject to rivalrous consumption, i.e. only sometimes when there are too many users to a certain point, congestion becomes an issue, but users can be easily excluded, for instance, through paying fees or blocking clogged roads. Examples include cable TV, access to private parks, and swimming pools.

6 Cooter and Ulen (2012, at 146).

7 Id.

8 Faure and Skogh (2003, at 40).

9 Hardin (1968). 'Ruin is the destination toward which all men rush, each pursuing his own best interest in a society that believes in the freedom of the commons. Freedom in a commons brings ruin to all' (id., at 1244).

10 Here the term 'commons' actually refers to 'open access' (a free-for-all) regime, which is difficult to limit access, instead of a 'common property' regime. In the latter case, the size of the group is limited and behavioral rules exist to cure the tragedy of the commons.

11 Rose observes that many if not also most 'tragedy of the commons' events result not from a singular grab at open access common property, but rather from a sustained sequence of small acts, that to each individual their own act would appear small and of no consequence against the larger whole of the common property (Rose 2014, at 1263).

12 Litz (1994, at 335).

attached upon severance and extraction, not upon the discovery of the oil reserve itself.[13]

The above examples show that without rules regulating the use of those common resources (such as forests or oceans), exhaustion or extinction may be the result.[14]

The consequences are not limited to the immediate first use of the resource but may have substantial subsequent impacts on other benefits of the resources. In the case of forests, beyond timber and the forest as a resource itself, a forest also generates valuable ecosystem services, such as oxygen creation, watershed and soil protection, carbon sequestration, and biodiversity preservation, which can all be regarded as positive externalities or public goods.[15] These ecosystem services are equally threatened by the first-mover incentives embodied in unregulated forest resources.

These multi-vector impacts on public goods from the first-mover advantage underscore the importance of developing mechanisms that allow an exclusivity of control over such resources, i.e. vesting property rights.[16]

### 3.1.2 *Property Rights as a Remedy*

The importance of exclusive control (enforced via private property rights) is associated with a seminal article by Harold Demsetz,[17] who commented on the economy of hunting practised by North American Indians. The demand for meat and skins increased at the same time that hunting methods became more refined. As a consequence, the vast herds of buffalo that had roamed freely for centuries became nearly extinct. Beaver colonies in Canada, however, survived in spite of great demand and extensive hunting. Demsetz argued that the beaver colony survived because the Indian tribes in Canada divided the hunting territory amongst themselves. Thus, property rights were created, enabling the exhaustion of the resource to be avoided.

The 'property right' in beavers could be enforced because the domain of the beavers was relatively stationary. The Indians could enforce that 'outsiders' did not trap their animals.

However, the buffalo situation was different. The buffalo roamed over large areas, often beyond the zones of influence of any particular tribal group; furthermore, the

[13] Libecap and Wiggins (1994, at 87).

[14] Intriguingly, water markets have also been found to strongly resemble a 'tragedy of the anticommons'. See Bretsen and Hill (2009). They provide a list of three main factors in that analysis (id., at 782 and 783).

[15] Ostrom (1999, at 1).

[16] Possession is often a function of the technologies to observe rights and use and to enforce those exclusions to use; Rose has noted that technological innovations often reveal both new means of discerning extents of resources but also of already in process over-depletion of common property resources (Rose 2014, at 1264–1265).

[17] Demsetz (1967).

buffalo were hunted by different tribes and groups of settlers. Thus, exclusion was functionally impossible, and thus the hunting of the buffalo went functionally unregulated; it remained in every hunter's interest to have 'first possession', i.e. to capture and kill the buffalo first.[18]

Thus, Demsetz's theory holds that property rights will emerge, *sua sponte*, to internalise the externalities that follow from open access.

This change from open access to the creation of property rights will be more likely to occur when the costs of exclusion of non-owners are lower. When the resource is originally uncongested and the maintenance of the boundary for exclusion is expensive, open access can be relatively cheaper than private ownership.[19] However, as the resources approach depletion and as the costs of exclusion reduce, Demsetz's theory predicts that property rights will be created. This theory has found broad support in the literature; e.g. Smith found that the varying riparian and water rights laws in the USA, wherein several different sets of legal rules can be found, can be accounted for based on Demsetz's model, requiring only the factors of exclusion and modes of governance to be included.[20]

That perspective explains the incentives behind the invention of for example barbed wire, which lowered the costs of creating boundaries that could promote the privatisation of public lands.[21] Importantly, Demsetz not only claimed that the establishment of property rights would be efficient when the costs of exclusion fall below the gains enabled by exclusions, but he also made the stronger claim that this establishment would arise naturally, without coordination of interested parties, in a decentralised process.[22]

Similarly, Lueck found that the transaction costs of wildlife and land ownership, and the enforcement of those rights to exclusive use, could affect the modes of 'ownership' and the resulting forms of property rights institutions;[23] Lueck found ten modes of foreseeable property rights arrangements.[24] Further, Lueck was able to

[18] Lueck and Micelli (2007). The notion of first possession in US property law was grounded in the seminal New York case of *Pierson* v. *Post, Supreme Court of New York.* 3 Cai. R. 175, 2 Am. Dec. 264. 1805. (N.Y. Sup. 1805), wherein the court found that occupancy to a wild animal was required to render property rights in wildlife: 'The Pierson court found for plaintiff Pierson, that no interest in property can vest in an animal *ferae naturae* until it has been captured and brought in control, thus establishing the precedent of "the rule of capture" for US property law. However, it is an overstatement to suggest that actual physical control was required by Pierson; physical control was found necessary by Pierson when no other major indicia of occupancy was to be found, such as a mortally wounded or completely ensnared wild animal' (Partain 2012, at 253).

[19] Cooter and Ulen (2012, at 147).

[20] Smith (2008, at 475).

[21] Id.

[22] Demsetz (1967, at 353).

[23] Lueck (1995, at 638–640).

[24] Id., at 641. There are five systems wherein agriculture dominates: (i) landowners control wildlife, (ii) landowner leases out wildlife access in small units, (iii) wildlife remain unprotected, (iv) landowners contract for ownership of wildlife, and (v) government wildlife agency

evidence that this economic motive in the creation of property rights could account for the diversity of legal approaches taken across the common law community.[25]

Two more comments should be made concerning the importance of the allocation of property rights. One point is that the allocation of property rights is a necessary but not a sufficient condition for awarding an efficient mechanism to protect natural resources. After all, property owners may have sufficient incentives to protect their own resource (for example a forest) as a result of the allocation of property rights; but this provision of a property right would not necessarily also provide incentives to internalise negative external effects.

In the example of a tropical forest, a forest owner could still decide to use their forest exclusively as a palm tree plantation, providing the highest economic benefits to themselves, but potentially also creating losses for third parties, for example in the loss of biodiversity. Thus, while the provision of private property can enable a resource owner to be efficient with regards to internalised costs, it might not be responsive to externalised costs. As a consequence, legal and policy instruments still need to be combined with the allocation of property rights in addition to providing correct incentives for internalising externalities.

The second point is that an allocation of property rights does not necessarily imply an allocation of 'private' property rights. An alternative is the allocation of so-called common property rights. Common property rights allow the use of economies of scale in enforcing the exclusive rights to the asset. Rose examines a variety of studies on how social groups manage to coordinate the use of common property and to regulate the access to that property:[26]

> These community-based property arrangements have had some common characteristics. The first is that they limit access; not everyone can have access, but generally only the community of people contributing to maintenance. Second, transfer and movement in and out of the regime are not easy, so that group membership – and thus group know-how – is relatively stable. A third characteristic is related: the rules and conventions of the group are likely to be very complex, creating what scholars have called an anti-commons that actually protects the commons by preventing easy entrance and exit. A fourth characteristic is the reward system: aside from access to the commonly managed resource, other rewards and punishments are likely to be indirect, taking the form of prestige in the case of

controls game on private land. There are five systems wherein wildlife dominates: (i) wildlife owner controls farming, (ii) land used for wildlife and leased in parcels to farmers, (iii) agricultural uses of land ignored, (iv) small plots for wildlife are consolidated by contract for agriculture, and (v), government farming agency controls farming on private wildlife lands. All five of the 'agriculture-dominant' modes of property rights and the first three of the 'wildlife-dominant' modes of property rights were readily identified in historical practice by Lueck, but the last two modes of 'wildlife-dominant' modes of property rights were not recognised from historical records (id., at 641–642, see also Table 2).

[25] Id., at 650–651.

[26] Rose (2014, at 1258).

reward, and neighborhood disapproval and even shunning in the case of punishment.[27] (Underscoring added.)

An example is the agreement of common property rights between communities in Iceland, which prevented overgrazing of the animals in the common lands according to a specific formula.[28] Another example is Ellickson's work on ranchers in Shasta County in California.[29] In the literature, common property is viewed as an intermediate case between open access and private ownership.[30]

## 3.2 EXAMPLES OF PROPERTY RIGHTS APPROACHES TO WILDLIFE

In Cooter and Ulen's text book on Law and Economics, they wrote that the granting of property rights to previously openly accessible natural resources may have beneficial effects for the protection of that resource.[31]

This approach has been strongly advocated for natural resources and especially so for wildlife protection.[32] The theoretical basis for this property rights approach is that rational parties would be expected to steward their property so as to ensure the maximum benefit from their property, preventing both its wastage and its ruin, so that natural resources, such as wildlife, might be better protected as contrasted against the results of a CAC approach to protection.[33]

Of course, notionally, a state could have legal grounds to claim some notion of ownership in the wildlife within its borders.[34]

When the CAC approach is very difficult to enforce – for example, an absolute ban on trade in particular wildlife if demand for the product is so high that an illegal market will unavoidably emerge and that supply can also not be completely controlled inter alia because of corruption problems – then the property rights approach might be more effective.[35]

The theoretical literature for using a property rights approach to protect wildlife, and with a focus on elephants, can be found in the works of Demsetz and Hardin. The advice formulated by economists in these scenarios of growing herds is to

27 Id.

28 Eggertson (1992, at 423).

29 Rose (2014, at 1257).

30 Lueck and Micelli (2007, at 194).

31 Cooter and Ulen (2012, at 147).

32 Lueck (1989).

33 With the CAC approach we refer to the use of safety regulation, as discussed in Chapter 9, usually backed up with criminal law, discussed in Chapter 10. Further, the notions of CAC regulation can be distinguished from state efforts to financially support broader efforts at lower levels of subsidiarity in wildlife management. See Lueck (1995, at 634).

34 For example, the US Supreme Court historically once held in *Geer* v. *Connecticut* (1896), that that wildlife were owned by the states in trust for the benefit of the people of the state (Lueck 1995, at 633).

35 With respect to African elephants, inter alia McPherson and Nieswiadomy (2000).

impose a solution which incorporates local ownership in order to allow the local population to share in the profits resulting from wildlife utilisation.[36] The empirical support for their theoretical model comes from African countries such as Botswana, Namibia, South Africa, Zambia, and Zimbabwe; where property rights were established for the protection of elephants, the elephant populations increased in number.[37]

However, McPherson and Nieswiadomy stress that beyond the allocation of property rights, political (in)stability may equally be an important factor in the protection of wildlife. The economic logic is that those African leaders who have taken their position in power by force may be uncertain about their political longevity. Therefore, they may face high discount rates, inducing preferences for near-term gains and reducing the value of long-term gains, and thus they will pay less attention to future ivory production and the requisite protection of the elephants. Those instable leaders would face incentives to reap the benefits from ivory trade as quickly as possible.[38] Other literature equally showed that deforestation occurred more rapidly in countries facing political unrest.[39]

Heimert's elaborate study on the Law and Economics of the protection of elephants found that if no person owns the elephant, then 'rational actors each will seek to take the elephant before someone else does'.[40] Because the expected future value of the resource is zero, as it would be captured and removed by a first mover, there may be no incentive to invest in the future; thus, a strong bias towards resource depletion would be present.[41]

One solution may be to reduce demand. In practice, that seems unlikely as a complete elimination of ivory demand has never been accomplished: 'As long as there remains a demand for ivory, there will remain incentives for someone to kill elephants to supply the demand'.[42]

The alternative method of controlling supply would be to make that market for ivory an illegal market. This may undoubtedly lead to a cost increase, but as long as demand cannot be controlled, 'eliminating legal trade may be a fruitless attempt to eradicate trade in elephant tusks completely'.[43]

The only remaining solution according to this literature is the allocation of property rights – and empirical research seems to indicate that this approach has been relatively successful.[44]

36 Barbier et al. (1990, at 141–147).
37 McPherson and Nieswiadomy (2000, at 16).
38 McPherson and Nieswiadomy (2000, at 17).
39 Deacon (1994).
40 Heimert (1995, at 1490).
41 Id., at 1491.
42 Id., at 1492.
43 Id.
44 For a variety of examples see id., at 1493–1494.

### 3.2.1 Protection of Elephants

Heimert compared the approach in Kenya, based on an absolute protection of the elephants from poachers and a complete ban on all trade in elephants, with the approach taken in Southern African countries that share with the local people a portion of the proceeds earned from stewarded wildlife.[45]

The basic problem is that elephants are killed for two reasons: first, for their economic value (hides, tusks, and meat), second, because they are considered a danger and nuisance to the farmers and families – even without the demand for elephant products.[46] Their economic value alive for tourism is much lower than the value of their carcasses, as their hunters might consider the price of ivory plus the presumed avoidance of harms. Thus, there is a substantial opportunity cost of elephant preservation from the protection of elephants.[47] This means that elephant protection will only work if there is a guarantee that a part of the proceeds of elephant protection is also awarded to the local population.[48]

There are, as mentioned, two different possible approaches to elephant protection. The one that is followed in Zimbabwe and other Southern African countries is to allow limited killing of elephants in order to generate profits, inter alia from trophy hunting, but also (of course more debated) from the sale of ivory.[49] The proceeds of the elephants go to the local population and to anti-poaching control. The basic idea of this Zimbabwean model, referred to as CAMPFIRE,[50] is that this property-rights-based model provides incentives to local communities to protect the elephants, converting the elephant from an enemy into a protected source of revenue.[51] A quota of 1 per cent of the elephants can be hunted; the revenues from the sale of hunting permits ranges between $12,000 and $25,000. The proceeds go to the local community, to national wildlife protection, and to compensate damage to crops.[52]

The first advantage of this property right approach is that the owner knows that they may benefit from the elephant in the future and thus have an interest in conserving elephants in the present.[53] The second advantage from this idea is that by allocating property rights and allowing some trade, the wildlife can be better

45 Id., at 1473.
46 Id., at 1474.
47 Id., at 1480.
48 Id., at 1481.
49 Lueck addresses the question of when private owners of wildlife would be rationally expected to sell hunting licences; more licences would be expected to be sold as (i) the vastness of privately held range increased, (ii) as the density of the wildlife on that range increased, (iii) as the value of those herds increased in market value, and (iv) as the roam of the herds decreased (Lueck 1995, at 666).
50 CAMPFIRE is derived from Communal Areas Management Programme for Indigenous Resources.
51 Heimert (1995, at 1482–1483).
52 Id., at 1483–1484.
53 Id., at 1498.

protected, as creating a property right in the wildlife has reduced the incentive to kill elephants since poaching is now considered as stealing from the community.[54]

This can be contrasted with the regulatory approach that has been followed in Kenya, based on a total ban on hunting and on the sale of elephant products.[55] The primary problem in Kenya is that this complete ban on revenues from elephant culls leaves only the elephants' value as a tourist item.[56] The result is that poaching has continued and that there was no adequate protection of the animals. Furthermore, farmers whose crops were destroyed by elephants originally received compensation, but in 1989 that compensation programme was repealed as a result of lacking funds; human needs were also not included in the solution.[57]

Comparing the two programmes, Heimert finds that the elephant populations in Kenya under its 'protective strategy' were reduced substantially during the 1980s, whereas the elephant populations in Southern African countries increased substantially.[58] He therefore concludes, 'these results suggest that Zimbabwe's active management programme is the better method of preserving elephants'.[59]

### 3.2.2 *Effectiveness of CITES?*

A related issue is the effectiveness of the Convention on International Trade in Endangered Species of Wild Fauna and Flora (CITES).

CITES has three appendices in which species can be listed depending upon their degree of being endangered. Appendix I includes 'all species threatened with extinction which are or maybe effected by trade'; appendix II comprises animals that require regulation in their trade to avoid becoming endangered. Species listed on appendix I are protected by strict regulations that de facto eliminate any trade in those animal products.[60]

Originally, the African elephant was placed on appendix II in 1977, but elephant populations kept dropping. Next, in 1985, the Ivory Export Quota System (IEQS) was developed to provide each country with its own quota for the legal export of ivory. Since that quota system did not reach its goals either, in 1989 the African elephant was moved from appendix II to appendix I, leading to an effective ban on trade in ivory.[61] This ban was heavily debated by the Southern African countries that followed a property rights approach and their successful lobbying led to a relaxation

[54] Id., at 1495–1496. In a more collective sense of private motives for the same result, see Lueck (1995, at 663).
[55] Heimert (1995, at 1481).
[56] Id., at 1486.
[57] Id., at 1487.
[58] Id., at 1488.
[59] Id., at 1489.
[60] Id., at 1476.
[61] Id., at 1478–1479.

of the ban in 1997, allowing Zimbabwe, Namibia, and Botswana to sell a limited amount of ivory.[62]

The full ban on ivory trade was criticised in the literature since it would effectively reduce future profits and thus reduce the interest in conserving the elephants.[63] It was therefore held that 'international law, through CITES, has frustrated this goal by eliminating owners' incentives to protect elephants as their own property'.[64] Protective management (i.e. a ban) rather than active management (based on a property rights approach) hence 'coincides with an increase in the number of elephants killed by poachers'.[65]

The effectiveness of both regimes has also been tested empirically by McPherson and Nieswiadomy. They concluded based on regression analysis that 'elephant populations are more likely to thrive in countries that vest in their citizens some proprietary rights to the elephants'.[66]

However, they equally notice the importance of political stability as political instability is also partially responsible for declining elephant populations.[67] They therefore conclude that the impact of property right is quite compelling, but that at the same time establishing politically stable property rights in other African countries may not be an easy task. Thus, 'increasing political stability and representative government must accompany the establishment of property rights'.[68]

### 3.2.3 *Protecting Rhinoceros via Property Rights*

Similar logic provides support for a property rights-based approach to protecting rhinoceros. A complete trade ban was once imposed on black rhinoceros; nevertheless, a black market continued to flourish and poaching continued.[69]

The proceeds from rhinoceros-based activities could be substantial sources of income, e.g. a hunting licence could approach $100,000. These types of sums could provide substantial proceeds to finance more robust forms of protection and effectively reduce poaching. One rancher in Zimbabwe spends $22,500 each year to protect his seven rhinoceros. The costs for protecting those rhinoceros during those four years could be covered by allowing one rhinoceros to be killed. However, the ban on the sale of sustainable rhinoceros products substantially reduced the value of

62 McPherson and Nieswiadomy (2000, at 15).
63 Heimert (1995, at 1498): as a result of the ban, the elephant would become de facto an open access resource again.
64 Id., at 1505.
65 Id.
66 McPherson and Nieswiadomy (2000, at 23).
67 Id.
68 Id., at 24.
69 Heimert (1995, at 1502).

the herd to the rancher and 'failed to stop poaching or to halt the decline in the rhinoceros population'.[70]

An interesting study on private conservancies in Zimbabwe equally confirms that a complete ban on rhinoceros, as a result of a listing of the rhino on CITES appendix I in 1977, had no protective effect, and in fact, only brought rhinoceros closer to the edge of extinction.[71]

The rhinoceros population increased only when the responsibility for protection was shifted to private ranchers who 'were in a better position to protect the rhinoceros than anyone else in Zimbabwe. They also understood that the rhinoceros had to be an asset for those ranchers to protect them'.[72] As for the correct scale of investment in such ranches, that determination will depend on a range of factors, as discussed by Allen and Lueck.[73]

PricewaterhouseCoopers (PWC) reported that revenues from rhino protection could provide an 11 per cent return on capital; in contrast, revenues from cattle would provide only a 1 per cent to 3 per cent return on capital.[74] Rhino-based revenues could come from photo safaris and also from sustainable forms of hunting.[75] By granting the right to manage the wildlife to landowners, and by working with the local communities, protection was provided financial means to be effective.[76] Well defined property rights allowed the black rhinoceros to return from the brink of extinction.[77]

A similar story can be told on the protection of the white rhinoceros.[78] However, there too, poaching and criminal activities remained a big problem, driving up the costs of security. Those costs can be subsidised, as a positive externality is received by the public when rhinoceros survive, to support private land owners in their battle against fighting poaching through public-private partnerships.[79]

### 3.2.4 *Localised Management*

There is abundant literature focusing on the question how precisely the local populations should become more involved in the management of natural resources. Providing benefits to the local population, and thus incentives for protecting the targeted herds, is the general starting point, but there are various ways in which this

70 Id., at 1502–1503.
71 De Alessi (1999). Corruption was a major problem in failing to stop the poaching.
72 Id., at 5.
73 Allen and Lueck (1998, at 361), presenting eleven determinative issues in optimising capital investment and management approaches.
74 Id., at 6.
75 Id.
76 De Alessi (1999, at 11).
77 Id., at 13–14.
78 Pernetta (2014).
79 Id.

is brought into practice. Several detailed case studies focus on the specific way in which to involve local populations and how to allocate particular benefits to them.

The Community-Based Natural Resource Management (CBNRM) model, in which some property rights are allocated to the local population, either individually or in a group, was presented as an alternative to state controlled national parks. Under CBNRM programmes, local people financially benefit from wildlife protection; examples include receiving revenues from tourism and safari hunting as well as from the sales of wildlife-related products. CBNRM programmes might also generate jobs and revenues for community improvements such as infrastructure, schools, and roads.[80]

In particular cases, CBNRM has been criticised because no property-based benefits from wildlife protection accrued to the local community.[81] As a reaction to the criticism on community-based approaches, collaborative management techniques evolved, based on a partnership amongst various stakeholders.[82] In Kenya, management took place via the Kenya Wildlife Service (KWS), in which the state retained a substantial role in wildlife management, alongside of landowners and stakeholders.[83]

A problem with this model was that all wildlife remained owned by the KWS and not the local community. The management model did not change the economic interests of land owners who thus remained focused on removing wildlife from their land so they could continue their farming practices.[84] Moreover, herd in-breeding took place as a result of fencing-in the large animals. These observations confirm the criticism formulated earlier, that the Kenyan protection model does not provide sufficient incentives for protection as it did not allocate property rights in the wildlife to the local population.

A similar problem was found in a study on the gorilla conservation programme in Rwanda, where it was held that a crucial factor for success would be that local partners should equally benefit from a conservation project.[85] Equally crucial to stakeholder engagement, is that the local context is critical in the stewarding of expectations.[86]

The idea of shared ownership can be difficult to put into effective practice. A case study on Uganda concerning a 'private-community partnership' (PCP) showed that insufficient account was taken of political and contextual factors which undermined

80 McPherson and Nieswiadomy (2000, at 17–18).

81 Mburu and Birner (2007, at 379). A study on the implementation of collaborative wildlife management in Kenya established that there was insufficient devolvement of the control of wildlife resources to the local communities.

82 Id., at 380, e.g. the use of insured co-management.

83 Id.

84 Id., at 388. For a more formalised model on when farmers might better coordinate with wildlife planning, see Lueck (1995, at 614–642).

85 Rutagarama and Martin (2006, at 302).

86 Id.

the realisation of the common benefits,[87] warning that the complexity of the governance issues at stake in PCPs, and the different interests of several actors and stakeholders, could create a 'recipe for conflict' in the implementation of such a partnership.[88]

A co-management framework in which the local people only provide advice remains problematic as long as it lacks structural changes to provide them with meaningful authority and decision-making roles.[89] This was evidenced in a study on 'co-governance' of marine protection between the state Department of Conservation and an indigenous Maori group in New Zealand.[90] Indigenous rights need to be incorporated into the conservation framework, although the reconciliation of the fundamental customary rights (of the Maori) with public conservation goals remains difficult in practice.[91] Similar results were confirmed in a study by Mashale and others on the management of a nature reserve in South Africa, which failed as a result of unequal power relations, more particularly between the government and the local community.[92]

This is why the authors strongly argue in favour of partnerships based on community self-management rather than based on co-management.[93] This is in theoretical alignment with other institutional economic studies on agricultural contracts, which in general can be seen as efforts to coordinate the transaction costs of 'multiple margins for moral hazard and enforcement costs'.[94] This is ever more so where 'random forces affect production, so that inputs and outputs are costly to observe and, thus, subject to theft',[95] as in the stewarding of wildlife under the threat of poaching.

Although the previous authors consider co-management as a form of public-private partnerships,[96] other studies present public-private partnerships as an alternative to the CBNRM.[97] In an elaborate study for the International Union for the Conservation of Nature (IUCN), Borrini-Feyerabend discusses the various models of collaborative management of protected areas and provides many examples of involvement of NGOs and local grassroots groups in various projects.[98]

The important conclusion of this elaborate overview of different projects is that the specific institutional design of the management structure should be tailored to the locally specific needs.

87 Ahebwa, Van der Duim and Sandbrook (2012, at 306).
88 Id., at 316.
89 Id.
90 Dodson (2014).
91 Id., at 535.
92 Mashale, Moyo, and Mtapuri (2014).
93 Id., at 861.
94 Allen and Lueck (1995, at 450).
95 Id., at 448.
96 Mashale, Moyo, and Mtapuri (2014, at 860).
97 See inter alia Nshimbi and Vinya (2014).
98 Borrini-Feyerabend (1996).

### 3.2.5 *Conditions for Effective Management*

The previous literature review concerning the various state case studies related to the management of natural resources makes clear that the success of the particular management solution will be related to a few central elements such as:

(i) involvement of the local population;
(ii) award of direct benefits to the local population in a sustainable way;
(iii) tailoring the solution to the local needs, and
(iv) structuring the mechanism such that the local population has incentives for protection rather than for destruction of the particular natural resources.

As mentioned earlier, the theoretical and empirical literature make it clear that privatisation, i.e. awarding private property rights (in one form or another) may be an important condition to realise those goals.[99] Studies show that private land management of natural resources will lead to cost savings in achieving those goals.[100]

Sellenthin and Skogh proposed the allocation of property rights to the Scandinavian wolverine to solve the conflicts between the wolverines, that kill reindeer, and the Saami, the indigenous population of Northern Scandinavia to whom the reindeer belong.[101] Sellenthin and Skogh suggested that Saami villages could become the owners of the wolverines; as a result, reindeer breeding and wolverine protection would become joint operations. Sellenthin and Skogh provide conditions for property rights regime to be effective in protecting endangered species:

i. It must be possible to count the number of animals owned with sufficient precision.
ii. The animals need to be relatively stationary, vis-à-vis a migratory range.
iii. The major argument in favour of efficient property rights is decentralised information. Property rights should therefore be assigned to those stakeholders that have the necessary information, such as the Saami villagers.
iv. Conservation should in profitable activities. That can either be from private payments, such as for trophy hunting in the case of elephants and black rhinoceros, or the state could pay parties for conservation as a global public good.

[99] Lueck (1995, at 663), states that clearly defined rights in wildlife, and the existence of legal systems that will enable the trading of those rights, will act to increase the value of those herds and also increase the demand for legal measures that preserve that herd's sustainability.
[100] See e.g. the case of Florida's conservation land management by Holcombe (2009).
[101] Sellenthin and Skogh (2004).

v. Property rights need to be renegotiable. The initial assignment may not be fully adequate; as a result, negotiations have to enable inefficient allocation of the property rights.[102]

## 3.3 FIRST-USE DOCTRINE

We will now turn to a specific example of conflicting property rights, where various claims collide because of intertemporal differences.

### 3.3.1 *Economic Principles*

The first-use doctrine, also known as the 'coming to nuisance' defence, can be raised when an activity is begun in one state of circumstances, but then, other parties arrive to the location of the activity and make claims of the 'nuisance' of the pre-existing activity.[103]

For example, imagine a factory was located in a relatively sparsely populated area and is afterwards confronted with neighbours who 'came to the nuisance' and subsequently claimed compensation or even the relocation of the factory. If the harm to 'newcomers' can be prevented or reduced by preventive measures being taken by the pre-existing factory, and if the transaction costs are zero, then Coase teaches that the efficient preventive device will be installed irrespective of the legal rule.

On the other hand, if the transaction costs are prohibitive, then a liability rule could be employed to force the pre-existing firm to implement the preventive measures. If the conditions for liability are met, the existing firm will usually not be successful in claiming the coming to nuisance defence. This is because litigation of these issues usually deals with in an ex post perspective, when people have already moved to the neighbourhood of the factory and the question is simply asked from an ex post perspective whether additional investments in preventive measures could have reduced the harm. Liability law then drives an incentive to the firm to invest in efficient safety equipment, even though the victims 'came to the nuisance'.

The problem with this solution is that, looking at it from an ex ante perspective, it dispels incentives with potential victims not to settle in the neighbourhood of polluting activities.[104] However, it will generally, especially in densely populated areas, be difficult for citizens to choose their residence in such a way that they would never live in the neighbourhood of a factory. The factory on the other hand has the possibility of investing in preventive mechanisms to reduce harm for third parties,

[102] Id., at 245–246.

[103] This problem is widely discussed in Law and Economics literature, see e.g. Cooter and Ulen (2012, at 168–174); and specifically by Wittman (1980). See also Dewees (1992b, at 143); Epstein (1979, at 72–73); and Merrill (1985).

[104] See Wittman (1980, at 567–568).

such as relocating the factory. If the plant could identify the risk of encroachment and observe the liability rule, then the plant could also invest in the surrounding lands to prevent residential use of the lands at risk of exposure.

Many of these conflicting uses of property rights could be prevented if it could be established ex ante which area is best suited for a given activity.

Wittman argues that the goal of zoning is precisely to determine that best-suitedness; e.g. it is better to site a residential area in a beautiful hilly landscape with trees than to locate heavy industry there, taking into account limited heavy transport possibilities, the potential of heavy environmental degradation in this ecologically sensitive area, and other similar concerns. Ideally, zoning could lead to an ex ante fixing of a destination for certain areas.

Problems tend to arise ex post when there are no ex ante decisions clarifying the limited use of a certain area; in such cases, cost-effective measures may not exist to reduce harm to the citizens. In this respect one can think of airports that have taken all efficient noise abatement measures and nevertheless continue to exceed comfortable noise levels for its surrounding neighbours.

The question then arises how this conflicting use of the property rights has to be resolved in this ex post perspective.

One could examine whether the costs of nuisance have already been included in the price of a certain property, in which case the vendor would have built-in the capacity to pay compensation for the externality. Imagine if a new railway station were built and that the surrounding parcels of land were then sold for relatively low prices. The relatively low price paid by a prospective buyer can be considered as a compensation for future nuisance to be caused by the railway station. This will then exclude a subsequent claim by the property owner against the railway station. This is not only true for the original owner who purchased at a low price, but also for a subsequent purchaser who would become owner of the piece of land. Again, they should have been informed that the land is close to a railway station, which could be readily visible, and they could be informed that future nuisance to be caused by the railway station is already compensated for in the relatively low price they pay. On the contrary, if the price to be paid does not remain a 'low price', then the new price likely bears the information that the land around the railway station has accumulated benefits above and beyond the detriments, and thus no net nuisance exists for the average buyer.

Wittman therefore finds that the foreseeability of the nuisance is an important criterion. A neighbouring owner will have far more possibilities to claim compensation if the harmful activity (which was at first relatively innocent) expands in an unforeseeable way; for example, because the zoning designation of the area is changed. If the 'surprised owner' is compensated for the additional harms caused by that unexpected and unforeseeable expansion of the company this compensation is final. This means that they are compensated also for the fact that the price of their land will have decreased as a consequence of the expansion of the particular factory.

This entails that a potential new purchaser can purchase the land at a relatively low price, but that they cannot also claim compensation from the factory since it already paid compensation to the previous owner.

More difficult situations occur when the conflicting use of property rights cannot be resolved by paying monetary compensation for the resulting unreasonable nuisance. In some cases, the conflict of interest may be so serious that it can only be solved by the relocation of one of the two parties involved. This solution will typically be reached if the magnitude of the damage caused is much larger than the lowest relocation costs.

In a case where relocation is an efficient solution, Wittman states that it will need to be determined whose relocation costs are the highest in relation to the importance of the externality caused. For example, if the relocation costs of the existing factory were much lower than the relocation costs of a community adjacent to the factory, even if the neighbours had come to the nuisance, then the relocation of the factory would still be the efficient solution since that would be the overall cheapest solution from a welfare perspective.

Obviously, under this logic, the question of who came first will not play a role in answering the question of who would have to relocate, but it may still play a role in answering who would need to pay for the relocation costs. If the new neighbours came to the nuisance in a case of foreseeable harm, then one could claim that even though the factory will have to relocate (because of the lower relocation costs), the citizens who wrongfully came to the nuisance should be liable to pay some portion of the relocation costs of the factory. The latter and separate determination of who should pay, versus who should move, gives an important ex ante incentive to the citizens to choose wisely where to settle.

## 3.3.2 *Examples*

### 3.3.2.1 US Cases

We can now test these principles of Law and Economics doctrine by describing how case law has dealt with this 'coming to nuisance doctrine'. There are two US cases that are routinely discussed in the Law and Economics literature.

The first is *Boomer* v. *Atlantic Cement Companies Inc.*[105] Boomer and friends were the plaintiffs acting against a defendant cement company (Atlantic). The discussions in the Court specifically considered the question of what remedy (injunction or relocation) was most appropriate as a reaction to the nuisance caused by Atlantic to Boomer and friends. The majority opinion in the Boomer decision

[105] *Boomer* v. *Atlantic Cement Companies Inc.*, 26 *NY* 2d 219, 309 *NYS* 2d 312, 257 *NE* 2d 870 (Court of Appeals of New York 1970). Excerpts from this decision have also been given by Cooter and Ulen (2012, at 170–172) and Epstein, Gregory, and Kalven (1984, at 618–624).

argued that the plaintiffs should be awarded compensation for the infringement on their property rights. The argument against awarding an injunction (which would lead to closure of Atlantic Cement Company) was that company had invested $45 million in the company and that 300 persons were employed. This refers implicitly to the economic argument that the relocation of the company would probably cost more than the compensation due to the victims. The Court also held that so-called permanent damages should be awarded, which granted Atlantic Cement Company a permanent right to infringe on the neighbours' property rights, which can also be upheld against future owners of the adjacent properties.

In a dissenting opinion, Justice Jasen argued against the permanent damages, arguing that this would be the same as licensing a 'continuing wrong'.[106] Jasen argued that paying permanent damages would afterwards remove every incentive of the company to further reduce harm by investing in supplementary preventive measures. However, it appeared from the facts that there were no other supplementary preventive measures available that could have reduced the harm.

Another case that is often quoted is *Spur Industries* v. *Del E. Webb*.[107] This was a case in the 1950s in Maricopa County in Arizona, approximately fifteen miles west of Phoenix. The farmer Spur had an area suited for cattle and actually kept his cattle on that land. Webb, a project developer, bought 20,000 acres of agricultural land with the intention of developing a housing area that would be called Sun City. The first houses were built 2.5 miles north of Spur's cattle grounds, but in the end 500 houses were constructed and Sun City was expanding.

By 1967, Webb's project was only 500 feet from Spur's pastures. At that point, Webb found out that he was not able to sell the remaining land for residential housing because of the presence of Spur's agricultural activities. Webb therefore sued Spur for nuisance caused by smell and flies; Spur having at the time between 20,000 and 30,000 animals on his property.[108] The citizens of Sun City themselves did not file a suit against Spur; only the project developer Webb.

The Arizona Supreme Court decided that there was a so-called public nuisance because the farming activity by Spur seemed to harm a great number of citizens. In such cases an injunction to stop the harmful activities seemed more appropriate than just compensation, according to the Court. The Court held: 'Spur is required to move not because of any wrongdoing on the part of Spur, but because of a proper and legitimate regard of the Court for the rights and interests of the public'.

The Court then discussed the 'coming to nuisance doctrine'. Coming to nuisance would have constituted a valid defence if project developer Webb had been the only

106 It is the same as saying to the cement company, 'you may continue to do harm to your neighbours as long as you pay a fee for it'.

107 *Spur Industries Inc.* v. *Del E. Webb Development Company*, 494 p. 2d 701 (Arizona 1972).

108 An interesting detail is that the decision notes that a cow produces on average between 35 and 40 pounds of manure per day, so that 30,000 cows together produce more than 1 million pounds of manure per day, which may imaginably cause a smell and attract some flies.

victim. However, Spur's cattle apparently caused a nuisance to a great number of people (arguing from an ex post perspective). Spur on the other hand had not acted wrongfully since he could not have foreseen that in Maricopa County a practically new city would arise in the neighbourhood of his cattle. However, given the interests of the great number of citizens who were victimised, the Court decided that Spur had to relocate his cattle activities.

However, the project developer Webb is the cause for the duty to relocate that has been put on Spur. Webb indeed started activities in an agricultural area whereby it was perfectly foreseeable for him that future house owners could be harmed by the presence of the cattle.

Hence, the Court decided that Webb had to indemnify Spur for the relocation costs: 'having brought people to the nuisance to the foreseeable detriment of Spur, Webb must indemnify Spur for a reasonable amount of the cost of moving or shutting down'.

#### 3.3.2.2 European Examples

Problems of 'first use' unavoidably also arise in other legal systems. In countries which are traditionally highly populated such as Belgium and the Netherlands there is relatively little discussion on first use. This has a lot to do with the fact that alternative location possibilities are often lacking; and, it has been decided ex ante through zoning and planning laws which kind of activities should take place in which areas.

One can find some cases in which temporal priority seems to play a role. The Dutch Supreme Court had to deal with a case where Van Tol had first use and De Jong knowingly located himself close to the property of Van Tol. When De Jong sued Van Tol because he claimed to be harmed by over blowing seeds this claim was denied, taking into account that Van Tol had first-use rights and that the activities took place in an agricultural area.[109] Other examples in which an 'anteriority principle' is accepted in Dutch law are discussed in the literature.[110]

In Belgian law one can find some rare cases discussing the first-use doctrine. If a famous Belgian fries shop chooses its location next to a pig farm, the owner should not afterwards complain about the smell emitted from the pig farm.[111] On the other hand, Belgian law apparently also accepts that first use is not a defence against a duty to take additional preventive measures if these can reduce the harm.

[109] Hoge Raad (Dutch Supreme Court) 3 May 1991, *Rechtspraak van de Week*, 1991, at 120.

[110] See for instance Court of Appeals for The Hague, 28 December 1988, *BR*, 1989, 769 with case note by P. C. E. van Wijmen; see also the discussion of these cases by Van Acht (1993, at 225–226) and Faure (1994, at 164–167).

[111] Vredegerecht (Justice of the Peace) Beveren, 10 April 1990, *Tijdschrift voor Vrederechters*, 1990, at 347.

This duty to reduce the nuisance also exists if the victims came to the nuisance. The Court of Appeals of Ghent held in that respect that the newcomers may expect that the licensee of a factory will take the necessary measures to prevent the harm as much as possible.[112] If additional measures can therefore reduce the problem (e.g. of noise), the first use is no defence against the duty of taking these preventive measures.[113] If, however, additional reduction of harm through further preventive measures is not possible, newcomers cannot claim the closure of the factory.[114] From the facts it appeared that the harm caused in that particular case was relatively limited, compared to the probably much higher relocation costs of the company, which may have been a decisive factor in the decision.

Issues of temporal priority are also discussed in Norwegian environmental law. The fact that this is apparently a more important issue in Norway (compared with the Netherlands and Belgium) may have to do with the space that is available for alternative locations in Norway, which is largely lacking in Belgium and the Netherlands.

Endre Stavang discusses several Norwegian cases which are worth mentioning.[115] Temporal priority is explicitly discussed in cases on airport noise where plaintiffs came to the airport after it was built. In all cases the Norwegian Supreme Court denied compensation. In the first two cases the Supreme Court explicitly denied compensation on the ground that plaintiffs had chosen to come to the airport and thus were nearest to bear the risk of undesirable consequences of this locality choice. In the other two cases the Norwegian Supreme Court explicitly relies on the first-use doctrine, arguing that the airport was a first user.

Stavang discusses a couple of other cases as well. In one case, referred to as Hunton Bruk, a factory had come to the area in 1889, but started to produce a new product in 1957 with new technology. A lawsuit was started by four homeowners who came to the area after the factory had been constructed but before the new technology was installed. The factory argued that it was in the area first and that a new method of production was an expectable development of the activity. The Supreme Court, however, found the factory liable.

Temporal priority apparently plays an important role in French environmental liability law. French law distinguishes between liability based on public law (basically public authority liability) and liability based on private law. In both cases 'first use' plays a role.

112 Hof van Beroep (Court of Appeals) Ghent, 25 November 1968, *Rechtskundig Weekblad*, 1969–70, at 429.

113 Rechtbank van Eerste Aanleg (Tribunal of First Instance) Antwerp, 25 June 1981, *Pasicrisie Belge*, 1982, III, 66; Rechtbank van Eerste Aanleg (Tribunal of First Instance) Ghent, 12 March 1981, *Rechtskundig Weekblad*, 1982–1983, at 1327.

114 Antwerp, 17 February 1988, *Rechtskundig Weekblad*, 1988–1989, at 50.

115 Stavang's (1997) unpublished manuscript.

When a public work has been constructed before the victim 'came to the nuisance', under French law this constitutes a true immunity. Case law apparently holds that in that particular case no compensation is due to the victim or at least compensation can be considerably reduced.[116] The problem is, according to French legal doctrine, that such a temporal priority basically provides the public work a true 'right to pollute'.[117] The only limit to this right is that the public works that have been implanted earlier should not have led to greater nuisance. If the nuisance increased after the original installation, compensation will be awarded. An additional condition for compensation is that this aggravation of the nuisance was not foreseeable for the victim.

Similar rules apply in the context of civil environmental liability. Again, in 1976 the legislator more or less legalised existing nuisances and recognised a 'first-use doctrine'.[118] It is striking that this 'right to pollute', introduced in French law in 1976, was the result of lobbying by agricultural interest groups.[119] In the words of Prieur, this amendment was the result of the 'bad mood' of a few farmers resulting from abusive law suits filed by neighbours having their secondary residences in agricultural areas and subsequently complaining about noise created as a result of agricultural activities.[120] This immunity has been more or less reconfirmed in a legislative change of 1980, but is heavily criticised in the literature. It is held that as a result of this immunity, victims lose their access to justice against polluting activities.[121] Some even hold that this first-use doctrine protects polluters and may even constitute a violation of article 8 of the European Convention on Human Rights.[122]

### 3.3.3 *Economic Analysis*

If one applies the economic criteria advanced by Wittman and others to the cases discussed one could, as far as the US Boomer case is concerned, refer to Cooter and Ulen who argue that the attractive aspect of paying permanent damages is that the conflicting use of property rights is settled once and for all. As a consequence of the payments the externality is finally internalised.[123]

[116] See Prieur (2011, at 1074, No. 1277).

[117] Id.

[118] Id., at 1081, No. 1286.

[119] An article L421–9 was added to the Code de l'Urbanisme, holding 'Damage caused to the occupant of a building by nuisances resulting from agricultural, industrial or commercial activities do not give raise to a right to compensation when the construction permit related to the building that is exposed to the nuisances has been demanded after the existence of the activities that caused the nuisance and when these activities have been continued in the same circumstances'.

[120] See Prieur (1977, at 131).

[121] Prieur (2011, at 1083, No. 1288).

[122] Id., at 1084.

[123] Cooter and Ulen (2012, at 168–172).

Wittman, however, has considerable criticism on the Boomer case. He rightly argues that the first-use issue is not at all examined in the case, although it appears from the facts that the homeowners were in the area first whereas the harmful activity, in this case the cement factory, came later.[124] Wittman furthermore argues that the economic analysis the Court tries to engage in has many flaws. It does indeed argue that the employment of 300 people and the $45 million investments make the relocation costs for the cement factory higher than for the homeowners. This might be true in an ex post situation whereby the cement factory came to the residential area. This provides, however, a wrong signal for future companies who have to make a similar decision from an ex ante perspective. The Boomer decision seems to indicate that once a company has made considerable investments and the employees are there, the relocation is no longer necessary and a payoff with permanent damages will suffice.

Wittman correctly argues that the Court should have examined in an ex ante perspective whether the cement factory had a variety of possibilities of location and whether it chose its location in the residential area wisely. It is striking that in the assessment of the necessity to relocate, the Court only addresses the high relocation costs for the cement factory and does not even calculate the potential relocation costs for Boomer and the other homeowners (who even were there first).[125] Whether the Boomer case was correctly decided from an economic point of view is therefore hard to say since the Court did not involve all the relevant costs in deciding the case and did not at all discuss the issue that the homeowners were there first and the cement factory caused the nuisance by a potentially wrongful location decision.

This is different from the other US case *Spur* v. *Del Webb*. In that case the first-use issue is discussed by the Court. Looking at the decision from an economic point of view, one can say that it was totally unforeseeable for the cattle owner Spur that project developer Webb would come into that agricultural area. Nevertheless, the coming to nuisance defence that Spur invoked is rejected and he is forced to relocate since his relocation costs were lower than the relocation costs of the 500 homeowners. This makes sense from an economic point of view.

But since the project developer Webb was wrongful from an ex ante perspective by deciding to locate near an agricultural area with 30,000 cows, it is equally correct to decide that project developer Webb has to compensate Spur. Were this not the case, then this would give totally wrong incentives to future project developers. In that particular case an efficient solution is reached both from an ex ante as well as from an ex post perspective, since the activity with the lowest relocation costs has to relocate, while the prospective project developers will still have correct incentives ex ante by forcing Webb to pay for Spur's relocation.[126]

[124] Wittman (1980, at 558).
[125] Id., at 563.
[126] Id., at 566.

This type of solution is also referred to as a 'purchased injunction': the newcomer can 'purchase' an injunction, meaning that they can claim the closure of the activity that is causing the nuisance if they are prepared to compensate the relocation costs.[127]

The Dutch, Belgian, and Norwegian cases seem to comply with the economic rules of thumb sketched above. Coming to nuisance is accepted as a defence if the newcomer knowingly comes to the nuisance; if, in other words, the harm is foreseeable. This, however, does not eliminate the duty of the existing factory to invest in effective preventive measures, wherever possible. Foreseeability is apparently also a criterion in the Norwegian airport cases. The decision that plaintiffs who settled near the airport after it was built were denied compensation by the Norwegian Supreme Court can be understood: they had probably already been compensated because they could purchase their property at a lower price. Thus, this lower price already constituted an ex ante compensation for future noise caused by the airport.

This analysis only changes if the harm caused through the activities unforeseeably increases. This apparently happened in the Norwegian Hunton Bruk case. The activities had started in 1889 and only in 1957, after the homeowners came the area, was a new harm-causing technology implemented.

Even the heavily debated French provisions still seem to fit into the same economic analysis. Awarding a temporal priority at least has the advantage that it clearly signals to newcomers that they will not be entitled to compensation if the amount of the nuisances meanwhile has not been changed. The French statute in that sense provides incentives to potential victims (but rather also to project developers) to select the location of their projects carefully.

Unless this aggravation was foreseeable for the newcomer, the protection of the first user disappears from the moment that the nuisance increases. Again, this provision aims at providing incentives to newcomers to obtain adequate information not only on the current state of affairs, but also on potential foreseeable changes in the future.

The only problem with this type of legislation (or case law) is that the question is not asked to what extent the existing activity could, by using cost-effective preventive measures, still reduce the nuisance for the neighbours. Since these often constitute low transaction cost settings, the fact that the first user can often be the 'cheapest cost avoider' does not necessarily mean that the costs of those preventive measures will then also have to be paid by the first user. If optimal prevention by the first user is the optimal solution, an application of the Coase Theorem, also in this particular situation, shows that parties will bargain in order to implement the most efficient solution. This would even be the case if the newcomers were to pay the first user for the implementation of optimal preventive measures.

[127] See on this rule Calabresi and Melamed (1972, at 1115–1123); Ellickson (1973, at 738–748), as well as Epstein, Gregory, and Kalven (1984, at 628).

## 3.4 SUMMARY AND CONCLUSION

This chapter explored the idea of leveraging property rights to enable either better decision making by stakeholders, usually by changing the ex ante information and incentives, or by re-allocating rights as originally suggested by Coase.

We began with a discussion on Hardin's (in)famous 'tragedy of the commons', and explored it from the economic perspectives of rivalry (aka subtractability) and excludability.[128] We explored the impacts of observing the three states of rivalrous, non-rivalrous, and anti-rivalrous against both excludable and non-excludable, yielding six types of goods or services. Traditional property concepts, such as rules of first capture or first mover, could lead to inefficient use of resources.

We then discussed Demsetz's theory that property rights could emerge, *sua sponte*, to internalise the externalities that follow from open access; that property rights enable communities to re-balance the impacts of Pigou's externalities. We were cautious to remind readers that allocations of property, under Demsetz's theory, do not necessarily imply the establishment of private property rights. Again, the issues of rivalry and excludability came into view.

Cooter and Ulen advocated that if property rights could be granted for various natural resources, including wildlife, it would benefit the efforts to protect and conserve those resources. In particular, we focused on the ability of such property rights systems to protect and conserve more effectively than 'traditional' CAC approaches to protect wildlife and natural resources. A good deal of attention was given to the successes and failures of implementing the property rights approach in developing countries, especially for the protection of wildlife.

One approach is to consider the full range of 'services' from wildlife, including tourism incomes, sustainable harvests of meat, fur, or other aspects sought by consumers, and potentially hunting licences in accordance with the sustainable harvests; in part, this is to ensure that the local communities are aligned with the survival of the wildlife species under protection. We discussed CITES as to where it worked well and where it didn't, and we also examined how the CBNRM model can be used in supporting the survival of wildlife.

In some alignment with Demsetz's theory, Sellenthin and Skogh analysed the way in which the Saami could better coordinate the tensions of wolverine conservation and reindeer herding, by assigning property rights in a five-step manner.

We then departed from the discussions on wildlife and turned to the economic concept of 'first use' and how it illuminates the tort notion of 'coming to the nuisance'. We expanded on Coase's re-allocation of rights to better facilitate the transaction costs of settling disputes. That, in turn, enabled an exploration of how the decision of who should move to avoid a nuisance should be de-linked from who

[128] See the earlier discussion in Section 3.1.1, on rivalrous goods, exclusivity, and the tragedy of the commons.

should pay for that removal and relocation. We examined several scenarios of factories dealing with later arriving neighbours and how best to solve that conflict via this perspective of Coasean logic. Following Wittman, we discussed how zoning could be used to prevent conflicts; or, could at least be used to pre-assign the necessary rights to enable more efficient negotiations on how those spaces should be efficiently used. The chapter then explored several cases to reveal how the theory matched reality in the courtrooms and led to an analysis of the rule of 'purchased injunctions'.

Overall, the chapter provided both logic and examples from real life that the use of property rules and rights, even when not per se private property versions, could provide effective protection of wildlife and natural resources and could be considered an efficient complement to the CAC modes of behavioural regulation.

# 4

# Environmental Standard Setting

From the Latin, the etymology of 'to legislate' is to 'lay down', and from 'princeps', or 'that which comes first', comes principles. And in this chapter, we begin with the beginning of law, the settings of standards.

In the context of environmental law and regulations, standard setting takes on both normative and official meanings. Standards might be set as official policy statement and enactments, which we'll address in this chapter, or as legal principles or societal-judicial norms, as we'll later discuss in Chapters 5 and 8, respectively.

One of the most important tasks of environmental law consists of providing new incentives of guidance to the parties involved in risky environmental activities, to internalise the negative externalities related to the potential injuries or pollution. Chapter 2 indicated that this principal approach to internalising externalities leads to two subsequent questions, (i) through which instruments this internalisation can be achieved and (ii) how optimal pollution levels can be determined.[1]

This chapter will go further into this question of setting optimal levels of environmental risk to injuries, such as pollution. This process is sometimes referred to as 'environmental standard setting'. This chapter begins by explaining that the legal meaning and the economic meaning of standards may be substantially different (Section 4.1); next, we will distinguish the various environmental standards that have been developed and their meaning (Section 4.2). Lawyers have attempted to guide the process of standard setting by developing several principles of standard setting (Section 4.3), which can be analysed in economic terms as well (Section 4.4). Section 4.5 summarises and concludes.

1 See Section 2.4.1.

## 4.1 LEGAL VERSUS ECONOMIC MEANING OF STANDARDS

When economists generally use the word 'standard' they usually refer to what is called in legal terms a target standard or an environmental quality standard; referred to in the USA as an ambient quality standard.[2] This quality standard defines the optimal environmental quality for a certain environmental component. This can take different forms. The quality standard could broadly state how a particular habitat should be shaped in an optimal ecological way or it could simply refer to specific chemical parameters for an ecology. Economists have traditionally argued that the law should limit itself to setting these targets.[3]

When lawyers refer to standards, they usually refer to the regulatory measures, usually used and imposed by administrative agencies that prescribe for a factory causing the externality what measures to take to prevent harm. These measures can be imposed in general regulations such as statutory provisions but can also be found in the form of individual licences. In the environmental area they will often take the form of emission standards, prescribing the particular quality and quantity of the emissions into the environment. Non-compliance with such standards is usually enforced with administrative and/or criminal sanctions. Since in that particular case the actor is not free to choose the measures they wish to use, to reach an optimal environmental quality, this approach is by economists often referred to as the 'command and control' approach.[4]

In order to avoid confusion concerning the notion of standards we shall now distinguish between three types of standards:[5] (i) target or ambient quality standards, (ii) emission standards, and (iii) production or specification standards.

## 4.2 TYPES OF ENVIRONMENTAL STANDARDS

The balancing process between costs and benefits in order to set standards required by the economic model needs accurate information on the marginal costs of the various technical devices that could prevent harm, as well as information about the harm to the victims. Generally speaking there are three types of standards: quality or target standards, emission standards, and technology or production standards.[6]

In theory, information is needed on all polluters and victims. In cases where there are many polluters and victims there are obvious problems to obtain information

[2] Such as e.g. Baumol and Oates in their classic paper on the use of standards and prices for protection of the environment (Baumol and Oates 1971).

[3] Whereby economists, moreover, usually argue that the policy instruments to reach these targets should be incentive based, see e.g. Schultze (1977).

[4] For examples see Wiener (1999, at 706) and Stewart (2007, at 150).

[5] See also Richardson, Ogus, and Burrows (1982) and Ogus (1994a, at 150–173).

[6] Not everyone agrees to the terminology, for example, Coglianese and Nash refer to three standards as means standards, performance standards, and management standards (Coglianese and Nash 2017, at 42).

and to regulate all in detail. Practical simplifications are, therefore, crucial. A reduction of the problem is to abandon the search for optimal pollution and instead set politically realistic targets and try to reach them in a cost-efficient manner.

In practice, the regulation is usually formulated to achieve a general target, providing constraints or restrictions on the polluter's activities. Target or quality standards would leave it completely up to firms as to how to comply with the target set. With emission standards, there is less freedom of behavioural choice than with the quality standards. When emission standards are used the quality and quantities of the emissions are regulated. Still, emission standards leave much more freedom than the third category, specification or production standards, in which also the process or abatement technology would be described.

### 4.2.1 *Quality and Target Standards*

Environmental policy usually starts by defining the quality that a certain environmental component should have by setting a target or ambient quality standard. However, if there were only target standards this might lead to a problem. If the environmental harm is closely connected to the regulated activity, quality standard may suffice. In that case the administrative agency could, for example, determine the target for the quality of a certain creek. It would be the responsibility of the only factory emitting waste water into the creek to see that the target is achieved. However, in many cases the costs of determining the causal connection may be very high. This is particularly the case, for example, if not one but ten sources emit waste water on the particular creek. This example shows that whereas environmental policy can start from the ambient quality of an environmental component to be determined in target standards, it ought to take one step further as well by laying down emission standards that take into account how the quality standards can be reached.

Quality standards may therefore be addressed towards administrative agencies that are engaged in emission standard setting. They will have to take the quality standard into account when setting emission standards for individual sources. Hence, quality standards and emission standards can be closely related.

Quality standards are only of indirect importance for an industrial plant. The operator will usually not be the one responsible for complying with the target standards, but the targets will determine the emission standards laid down in their permit with which they have to comply. Quality standards as such can usually not be directly enforced upon polluters. The reason is that a specific pollution (for example of a river) will in many cases be the consequence of multiple emissions. Only in exceptional cases, for example when it is clear that one plant is the only one discharging waste water in a particular creek, could violation of the quality standard concerning the water in that creek be allocated towards that specific plant. But in many cases the presence of multiple sources and the resulting causal uncertainty will prevent that.

Thus, quality standards are usually addressed towards administrative agencies, which in turn will translate those quality standards into emission standards that can be directed at specific actors.[7]

Historically, quality standards prevailed in legislative Acts developed in the 1970s and 1980s, partially as a reaction to failing policies that had only been based on emission standards. This traditional CAC approach focusing on individual emissions of separate firms had the disadvantage that an agency would not envisage the effects of the overall pollution on the specific environmental component. Also, earlier non-market-based versions of emission standards gave few incentives for innovation in abatement technology to enable further reductions of environmental harm.

Policy therefore changed to increasingly make use of ambient quality standards, albeit these target (or ambient quality) standards are used in combination with emission standards. Beyond CAC-type regulation, target standards are increasingly availing themselves of alternative approaches, such as via market-based instruments (such as taxation or emission trading) in order to reach the overall emissions target.[8]

### 4.2.2 *Emission Standards*

The second type of standard which is often used in environmental policy are known as emission standards, also called emission limit values. In regulation theory, these are referred to as performance standards.[9]

The European Union's Integrated Pollution Prevention and Control Directive (IPPC) engages in the setting of emission standards. Emission limit values are defined in article 2(6) of the IPPC Directive as 'the mass, expressed in terms of certain specific parameters, concentration and/or level of an emission, which may not be exceeded during one or more periods of time'[10] These standards still leave some freedom to a potential polluter since the standards usually only determine the amount and quality of the chemical or hazardous substances that may be emitted into the environment.

Emission standards can be found in almost every legal system which has environmental legislation. Much environmental legislation originated by putting emission standards in general, non-environmentally oriented 'permits to operate', which

[7] See Driesen (2017, at 66), on effects-based standards implemented within the USA's Clean Air Act (CAA), the Clean Water Act (CWA), and the Resources Conservation and Recovery Act (RCRA).

[8] See further on the functioning of market-based instruments, Chapter 7.

[9] See Ogus (1994a, at 166–167): the performance standard requires certain conditions of quality to be met at the point of supply but leaves the supplier free to choose how to meet these conditions.

[10] Currently this is incorporated into the Industrial Emissions Directive 2010/75 (IE Directive). For details see Jans and Vedder (2012, at 365).

many factories were obliged to have from the mid-1800s. This permit was traditionally used as the instrument of the authorities to control the operation of a certain plant.

A next stage took place when various legal systems, usually in the 1960s and 1970s, started implementing sectoral legislation, protecting one specific component of the environment per enactment; e.g. surface water, ground water, air, or soil.[11] In some of these general Acts, specific emission standards for the emission of substances into these components were incorporated.[12] However, the system usually worked differently. The environmental Act would usually merely state administrative provisions, with the central goal of the legislation (protecting an aspect of the environment) and providing powers to administrative agencies to set emission standards in individual licences.

The USA has, from the Clinton administration to the Obama administration, demonstrated a strong preference for performance standards:

> President William Clinton, for example, urged his regulatory agencies to 'specify performance objectives, rather than specifying the behavior or manner of compliance that regulated entities must adopt'. President George W. Bush's regulatory team followed by advising agencies that performance standards are 'generally superior to engineering or design standards because performance standards give the regulated parties the flexibility to achieve regulatory objectives in the most cost-effective way'. President Barack Obama directed his administration to give preference to 'flexible [a]pproaches', including the use of 'performance objectives'.[13]

In some cases general emission standards were set industry wide at the national level in order to guide the standard-setting behaviour of local administrative agencies.[14] A deviation from these general standards then had to be motivated.

### 4.2.3 *Technology or Production Standards*

Technology specification or production standards go an important step further than emission standards, since they will regulate ex ante what kind of product technology

[11] Cole provides a history of that transition with respect to air quality laws in the USA (Cole 2012, at 23–31).

[12] See for the development of environmental law in the USA, Buzbee (2016).

[13] Coglianese and Nash 2017, at 39. Further, Coglianese and Nash list seven problems with performance standards: (i) 'teaching the test' problems in limiting innovation, (ii) increases in cost and complexity of the resulting regulations, (iii) sets limits on industrial imagination to achieve innovation, (iv) can become overly focused on one environmental goal to the detriment of other environmental goals, (v) no evidence that such standards reduce litigation over environmental policy, (vi) very dependent on existence of effective measurement and detection technologies to prevent methodological failure, (vii) appears to be fragile unless scientific causality certain (id., at 81–87).

[14] Coglianese and Nash note that one outstanding issue on discussing performance standards is that as of 2017 no major empirical work had been completed on the competitive efficacy of performance standards over traditional CAC regulation (id., at 40).

or abatement technology will have to be implemented by the licensee.[15] The advantage for the controlling administrative agency is that information costs in case of monitoring are extremely low: it can easily be detected whether the particular factory has installed the prescribed technology and whether the process is operating to intended specifications.

The disadvantages are, however, obvious from an economic point of view. Specification standards may become obsolete very rapidly; they also give no incentive for technological innovation since all the licensee has to do is to comply with the pre-prescribed specification. Specification standards may have important anti-competitive effects, in fact providing a monopoly to the producer of the prescribed technology if that technology is protected by IP rights.[16] The case for specification standards is generally rather weak, unless one could argue that the standard setter has better information than firms concerning the optimal protection technology or innovation activity. This is, however, rather unlikely.

### 4.2.4 *Optimal Standard-Setting and Cost–Benefit Analysis*

From the above it becomes clear that environmental policy at least needs quality standards to be set ex ante of any permitting or planning for risky environmental activities. Certainly, the technological risks to the environment, and the technological capacity to monitor and enforce the environmental standards, need to take careful consideration on the drafting of effective regulatory design.[17]

A policy of mere emission standards, not taking into account the environmental quality they should achieve, has proven ineffective. If emission standards are used, ideally first the optimal environmental quality is determined and afterwards emission standards for specific plants are fixed in such a manner that the aggregate pollution coming from the various emissions will not exceed the environmental quality standards set. The emission standards might take the form of regulatory standards of the CAC type (e.g. as licence conditions), but could also be implemented in other mechanisms, such as in emission taxes or in the form of a 'due care' standard in a liability case.

The question arises how cost–benefit analysis might interact with this standard-setting scheme.[18] First, cost–benefit analysis will first of all play a role when environmental targets are determined, as has been indicated above. At this second stage of defining emission standards, cost–benefit analysis could play a role. In an optimal

[15] See Driesen (2017, at 71) for discussion on the technology-based standards within the USA's CAA, CWA, and the RCRA.

[16] Ogus (1994a, at 167–168).

[17] Cole and Grossman (2018, at 909). See original article in *Wisconsin Law Review* (1999) at 887.

[18] More on this topic of cost–benefit analysis within the context of environmental law can be found in Sections 6.2 and 6.3.

world where the regulator sets emission standards in the public interest,[19] the administrative agency will take into account marginal costs of more stringent environmental standards and balance these against the marginal benefits in additional reduction of environmental harm.[20] This refined balancing process requires accurate information both on the expected environmental harm and on the marginal costs of the various technical devices that could prevent this harm. Further, the nuanced differences in two distinguishable sets of risks and technologies could require substantially different regulatory approaches.[21]

### 4.2.5 *Optimal Specificity*

Economists argue that in general, environmental standards should not be uniform across a jurisdiction or globe, but should be differentiated according to not only region, local needs, and branch of industry, but also preferences of the public.[22] Indeed, it is argued that in different regions citizens may have different preferences regarding the appropriate trade-off between environmental quality and industrial production.[23] An argument for differentiation can also be found in the economic literature with respect to optimal specificity; this approach has been advanced in the USA by Ehrlich and Posner,[24] and in the EU by Ogus.[25]

The theory of optimal specificity also has its impact on standard setting. From an economic point of view the environmental quality to be provided could differ according to differing preferences of citizens.[26] When externalities are local and prisoners' dilemmas are absent this would mean that target standards which reflect the local preferences of citizens could also be differentiated.

[19] Depending on whether either the parties in the market setting or an administrative agency can be assumed to have the best information this will lead to a choice for fixing emission standards via tort law (in which case they will correspond with a due level of care) or via regulation (in that case they will be incorporated as a condition of the administrative license). See more in Chapter 8 and Chapter 9.

[20] See further on the role of cost–benefit analysis in environmental standard setting, Sinden (2016, at 296–297), and see also Ogus (1994a, at 161–162).

[21] Cole and Grossman (2018, at 909). See original article in *Wisconsin Law Review* (1999) at 887.

[22] See on the local diversity and the impact on environmental standard setting, Wiener (1999, at 697–701).

[23] The risk that harm will be caused through, for example, hazardous waste may well vary depending upon factors such as population density or on specific hydrogeological conditions where the propensity to accumulate varies. Likewise, optimal specificity may play a role in designing proportionate rules for surface waters: the effect of particular emissions on lasting water quality will to a large extent also depend upon the particular local hydrogeological situation of that river; a pollutant may have a much greater impact in an area of small and still surface water versus the impact for a deep fast flowing river containing a large quantity of water.

[24] Ehrlich and Posner (1974).

[25] Ogus (1994a, at 168–170).

[26] Id., at 168.

The result of this reasoning would be that environmental quality within a federal system could vary according to the individual preferences of the citizens. This economic argument therefore in principle leads to an environmental federalism where the environmental quality between Member States could differ as long as there are no transboundary effects.[27] Politically, however, this idea of differing environmental quality between entities within one federal system is sometimes difficult to accept or coordinate. One could make a political case for harmonised quality standards, arguing that a federal system could guarantee a basic environmental quality for all of it citizens. The legal instruments to reach this goal would, then, be the setting of quality standards to which the environmental components, such as groundwater, should in principle correspond everywhere in the jurisdiction.

Therefore, as a result of different local circumstances the emission limit values to reach a similar environmental quality may well vary.[28] In principle, the differentiation of emission standards should be carried through as long as the advantages of further differentiation outweigh the administrative and information costs that are incurred with a highly detailed standard-setting process. The costs of meeting a certain level of environmental protection may well vary according to location-specific circumstances.[29] This inevitably leads to the conclusion that where the environmental quality target to be reached is uniform, the emission limit values have to vary according to the location-specific circumstances and will therefore be differentiated.

## 4.3 COST–BENEFIT ANALYSIS AND GUIDELINES OF STANDARD SETTING

### 4.3.1 *What Are These Guidelines?*

The question arises how the economic notion of cost–benefit analysis, discussed earlier in this chapter, can be related to the specific legal standards just presented.[30]

Depending on the legal instrument chosen to reach the desired environmental quality, this weighing of marginal costs versus marginal benefits will either take place by the administrative agency during the standard-setting process or by the judge presiding a tort case when a due care rule must be established or examined.

Legal scholarship has also asked how a guideline for environmental standard setting could be given.[31] This question seemed important first to give the judge some indication of what the balancing of interest means in practical environmental cases they have to decide. Second, guidelines can steer the standard-setting behaviour of

[27] See Chapter 13 on Environmental Federalism. See also Faure (1998a, at 173).

[28] See Ogus (1994b, at 30–32).

[29] Kolstad (1987) and Faure and Lefevere (1995a).

[30] See further on the legal formation of differentiated standards also Ogus (1994b, at 31–32).

[31] See further Ogus (1994a, at 165–171).

administrative agencies when no clear instructions from the legislator were explicitly delivered. Third, the general principles in the guidelines could aid the operator of a plant when no fixed environmental standards are ready, to inform them what kind of process or abatement technology should be chosen. This line of research brought about an interest in formulating general principles of standard setting. To be clear, these principles are rather guidelines to constrain the behaviour of administrative agencies or to guide the judiciary; they should not be confused with general principles of environmental law, which will be further discussed in the next chapter.

Coming from a UK tradition where environmental policy traditionally relied more on general principles than on fixed emission standards, there is now also an increased discussion of the usefulness of general principles of standard setting on the continent.

The following principles or guidelines can now be found in the literature and some of them also in legal documents:

- BPM: Best Practical Means
- ALARA: As Low As Reasonably Achievable
- BPEO: Best Practical Environmental Option
- BAT: Best Available Technique (or technology)
- BATNEEC: Best Available Technique (or technology) Not Entailing Excessive Costs.[32]

In the next subsections, we will provide a quick review of a couple of these principle frameworks.

#### 4.3.1.1 BPM in the United Kingdom

The general principles of standard setting were first developed within the Common Law legal systems, especially in the United Kingdom where its policymakers have relied on the BPM concept for a century. This concept formed the basis for the limitation of the emissions for all environmental components; it first gained a legal basis in the different versions of the Alkali Act 1906.[33] Scholars report that the BPM principle implicitly formed the basis for the formulation of standards and enforcements in all environmental fields.[34]

The BPM concept as such has never been explicitly defined, but in the CAA 1956 the concept was defined as 'reasonably practicable ... having regard amongst

[32] For a discussion of the legal meaning of some of these principles see Faure and Ruegg (1995, at 39–60) and Ogus (1994a, at 207).

[33] In section 7 of the Alkali Act 1906, plant operators were required to use the BPM with respect to certain registered industrial processes in order to prevent the emission of noxious or offensive gases or to render those gases which are discharged harmless and inoffensive. For a more recent formulation, see the Health and Safety at Work Act 1974.

[34] See e.g. Ball and Bell (1991, at 212).

other things to local conditions and circumstances, to the financial implications and to the current state of technical knowledge'.

For each section of industry, so-called BPM notes existed as guidelines for agencies to help them specify the BPM for any particular plant. Specifying BPM was thus left in practice to the discretionary powers of the agencies, and by implication, to the individual officers of the relevant ministries. Moreover, there was a distinct problem with keeping these BPM notes up to date.[35]

Besides a range of source-directed measures, BPM notes also contained emission standards, in the form of so-called presumptive limits, non-statutory standards formulated by the chief inspector. These standards provided a basis for negotiation between industry and the ministry officials. If these presumptive standards were being met (for instance, emission limits), then it was presumed that any legislation was being complied with and that the BPM were being used. When a firm failed to operate a process within these standards, in principle this indicated a prima facie breach of the BPM standard and so was taken as presumptive evidence that the BPM had not been applied. The breach of such a standard, however, did not mean by definition that they were not applied. BPM notes and presumptive limits, therefore, had no binding legal force.[36]

The British experience with BPM shows very clearly the problems one may experience when using vague, elastic notions. On the other hand, it is possible to use the flexibility of these notions in a positive way, to be stringent and lenient exactly where appropriate according to, for instance, local conditions, and to be able to react relatively smoothly to changed circumstances.[37] This was exactly the philosophy behind the BPM concept,[38] and this philosophy can be found behind the concept of BATNEEC too.

#### 4.3.1.2 ALARA in the Netherlands

The Dutch legislator did not seem inclined to define or explain vague notions of law, such as BPM, in statutes. These notions were only to be found in advisory notes and only in the matter of water pollution and its prevention.[39]

35 See inter alia Frankel (1974, at 14).

36 See inter alia Wood (1989, at 100) and Hughes (1992, at 321).

37 See Ball and Bell (1991, at 78).

38 Practicability, flexibility, and discretion could be considered to be the keywords within this philosophy (Lomas 1990, at 62).

39 BPM was considered as one of the foundations of environmental policy in general. See Drupsteen (1991, at 21). In advisory reports the authority responsible for the granting of licences in the Water Act (the Minister of Transport and Communications) was given guidance on how to translate the BPM into licence conditions (the so-called CUWVO-reports, which are reports from the Coordinating Commission concerning the execution of the Water Act).

Only the ALARA principle had been granted a place in a statute;[40] it can be found in Dutch legislation concerning radiation, based on a European directive.[41] In a statutory instrument to the Dutch Nuclear Power Statute (the Besluit Stralenbescherming Kernenergiewet), the principle has been implicitly defined. Section 21 of this regulation states that anyone working with radioactive substances has a duty to stop and prevent irradiation and contamination as far as this is reasonably achievable, to limit the consequences of contamination as far as this is reasonably achievable, and in cases in which irradiation and contamination cannot be avoided, to take precautions to limit both as far as is reasonably achievable. This provision thus creates a duty of care for persons who work with radioactive substances. The provision, however, does not create a statutory duty for administrative agencies to take this principle into account when deciding about the granting of licences and the content of licence conditions. In case law it has been determined, however, that agencies must show in their decisions that this ALARA principle has been taken into account.[42]

In January 1993 the ALARA principle was also laid down in the Dutch Environmental Act, the Wet Milieubeheer.[43] The formulation of the principle in this Act is slightly different than as presented within the Nuclear Power Statute. In section 8.11 of the statute the principle is defined as a direct duty of care for the agencies concerned to make sure that 'as far as negative consequences for the environment cannot be prevented by subjecting licences to conditions, licences must be subjected to conditions which offer the largest protection possible against these consequences, unless this request would be unreasonable'.

In order to evaluate the applicable state of the art which is required to comply with the ALARA principle, reference is made to BTM and BPM. According to the comments given by the environmental minister during the parliamentary debate preceding the Environmental Act,[44] it was his intention to keep the level of pollution in the different environmental media as low as possible by using the BTM.

The BPM are to be considered as a minimum, to be used only if the BTM standard is considered 'unreasonable'.[45] The ALARA principle, as formulated in the

[40] This ALARA Principle can more generally be found in nuclear legislation. For details see Lierman and Veuchelen (2005).

[41] See *Official Journal* of 15-7-1980 EC/1980/836.

[42] See the president of the Administrative Court (Vz.AG RvS), 17 March 1989, *Tijdschrift voor Milieu en Recht*, nr. 88, and more recently a case by the Administrative Court of 27-3-1991, *Administratiefrechtelijke Beslissingen* 1991, nr. 537.

[43] The Wet Milieubeheer is a comprehensive environmental Act, replacing all (or at least most of the) existing environmental Acts, which all are about only one environmental medium or deal with only one sort of pollution.

[44] Parliamentary Documents of the Dutch Chamber of Representatives, 1990–91, 21 087, nr. 13, 33–34.

[45] The term 'unless ... unreasonable' implies, according to the mentioned explanatory note, that the agency concerned must clarify why in this particular case conditions which offer less protection must suffice. See the Parliamentary Documents of the Dutch Chamber of

Wet Milieubeheer, clearly does not include a duty of care for (industrial) polluters to stop or prevent pollution when involved in certain activities. The ALARA principle, thus, seems to have a relatively limited function.

#### 4.3.1.3 BATNEEC in the IPPC Directive

This BATNEEC notion also plays a crucial role in the directive of 24 September 1996 concerning integrated pollution prevention and control, the so-called IPPC Directive.[46]

What constitutes BAT has been defined in the IPPC Directive and that has remained unchanged in the later directives. According to article 2(11) of the IPPC Directive 'best available technique' shall mean, 'the most effective and advanced stage in the development of activities and their methods of operation which indicates the practical suitability of particular techniques for providing in principle the basis for emission limit values designed to prevent and, where that is not practicable, generally to reduce emissions and the impact on the environment as a whole'.

> Reference to some sort of a cost–benefit test is now made in the definition of 'available techniques': 'available techniques shall mean those developments on a scale which allows implementation in the relevant industrial sector, and their economically and technically viable conditions, taking into consideration the costs and advantages, whether or not the techniques are used or produced inside the member state in question, as long as they are reasonably acceptable to the operator'.[47]

Here one can find a clear reference to the fact that costs and benefits should be taken into account where the availability of the technique has to be considered.

Article 13 of the (2010) IE Directive states that an exchange of information concerning best available techniques shall take place between the Member States, industries concerned, and environmental NGOs. This information exchange will then lead to the drafting of documents on what precisely constitutes the BAT in a particular sector of industry.[48]

## 4.4 STANDARD-SETTING GUIDELINES AND ECONOMIC ANALYSIS

Although one can therefore find a reference to the economic cost–benefit test in the notion of BAT, the precise contents of this concept is still rather vague.

Representatives, 1990–91, 21 087, nrs. 13, 34. The minister admits that the costs are an important factor here, whereby, however, in principle the branch of industry concerned should be the point of reference, not the individual plant.

46 As mentioned earlier, this 1996 directive was replaced in 2008 by Directive 2008/1. Later changes took place in Directive 2010/75 on industrial emissions (IE Directive).

47 Article 2(12)(b) of the IPPC Directive and Directive 2008/1/EC.

48 For details see Jans and Vedder (2012, at 365).

The question arises what this notion of BAT and other general principles of standard setting, discussed above, mean from an economic point of view.

To be clear: prescribing BAT does not mean that the use of certain pollution control technologies should be directly mandated,[49] given the fact that such specification standards would be largely inefficient. The idea is rather that the knowledge on the BAT would be translated into an emission standard. There are various ways in which this could work.

First, it cannot be denied that although one can recognise a reference to the economic cost–benefit test in the BPM and BATNEEC notions, the precise contents of these legal concepts remains rather vague. In the application of these general principles an economic evaluation method could be used. The BATNEEC notion specifically gives room for an explicit application of the marginal cost / marginal benefit test when deciding what the 'excessive costs' are. Since BATNEEC refers to 'excessive costs' the well-known marginal costs / marginal benefit test which was applied to determine the level of optimal care in tort law can now explicitly be used in the environmental standard-setting process. There is still room to make this legal notion more concrete. As we mentioned above, within the framework of the IE Directive this concretisation now takes place on the basis of an exchange of information between Member States, industries concerned, and environmental NGOs.

Second, one could state that some of these guidelines apparently coincide with the economic evaluation method of environmental standards as developed in the positive economic analysis of law. The British experience with the BPM standard shows that apparently similar questions are asked as in the economic model. For instance, in defining the term 'practicable', the question of when costs are excessive will have to be answered. Although the reference to economic notions still seems rather vague in this BPM concept, it becomes more explicit in the BATNEEC principle. Indeed, the notion of 'not entailing excessive costs' seems to refer to the more refined incremental Learned Hand standard,[50] which takes into account marginal costs and marginal benefits.

A first tentative conclusion could, therefore, be that the legal system seems to apply the economically relevant notions in using general principles of environmental law such as BPM and BATNEEC. The conclusion that the economic principles of standard setting are followed in BATNEEC is of course only warranted if indeed both marginal benefits in reduction of damage are considered as well as costs. If the

[49] Salzman (2013, at 374).

[50] This Hand formula is based on a US case decided by Judge Learned Hand (*United States v. Carroll Towing*) where Judge Hand stated that 'Liability depends upon whether B is less than L multiplied by P), (B<P.L)', whereby P stands for the probability of injury, L for injury and B for the burden of precaution. Later this formula was refined in the literature by mentioning that rather than comparing absolute costs and benefits, marginal costs should be weighed against marginal benefits. This is therefore referred to as an incremental Learned Hand standard. See inter alia Landes and Posner (1981b, at 885).

practice of environmental standard setting only took into account whether the absolute costs are reasonable and disregarded the benefits, this would not be compatible with the economic cost–benefit test. It will, therefore, depend upon the actual practice of standard setting whether we can draw the positive conclusion that these general principles fit into the economic test or not.

Several problems still remain to be solved. For instance, the question arises whether a BATNEEC standard should be set for an entire branch of industry or merely for one individual firm. In addition, the standard might be set at a different (higher) level if the initial assumption of risk neutrality is relaxed. Risk aversion of potential victims might lead to a higher standard, which means that the marginal costs will not be considered quickly as 'excessive'. But, although there are of course many questions that still need to be examined with respect to the application of this BATNEEC notion, economic analysis provides the appropriate tools for an evaluation of these 'excessive costs' of BATNEEC. If lawyers will use the available economic tools for such an evaluation, the use of BATNEEC can lead to more efficient environmental standards than would be the case if the term 'excessive' were to be analysed with other vague legal notions, such as equity.

Third, these general guidelines of standard setting can be of major importance if the conditions of a permit are outdated or simply silent with respect to a certain kind of pollution. The weaknesses of the standard-setting process through administrative agencies are well known: the administrative authorities cannot regulate all possible emissions in a singular permit; the technology may change; or the conditions in the permit can simply be too weak because the agency might be 'captured'.[51] Some of these problems may be cured by using these general guidelines. These guidelines could be binding upon the operator of a plant as a kind of residual duty in case the conditions of the permit are silent. One could also go one step further and consider these principles also as binding upon the administrative authorities that set the conditions of the environmental permit. Eventually, one could even consider the possibility of a review of permit conditions that violate, for instance, the BPM standard. In sum, these guidelines might play a role in rationalising the standard-setting process.

Fourth, these guidelines of standard setting could guide either the judge in a tort case when fixing the standard of due care under negligence, or the administrative authority when fixing the conditions of a licence.

Finally, it should be recalled that ideally the various notions mentioned in this chapter are coordinated in a smart manner: environmental policy should start from a definition of the desired environmental quality. Next, the BATs should be determined and those should be translated into emission limit values. That is also how for example in Europe the 2010/75 Directive on Industrial Emissions is conceived.

[51] The problems related to capturing and the influence of private interest on environmental regulation will be discussed in detail in Section 9.2.

The directive forces administrative agencies to set emission limit values (emission standards). Article 15(3) of the IE Directive requires that emission limit values are set on the basis of BAT. However, article 15(4) of the IE Directive allows for less stringent emission limit values when the imposition of BAT would lead to disproportionally higher costs compared with the environmental benefits due to the geographical location or the local environmental conditions of the installation concerned. This provision therefore explicitly enables an extra cost–benefit analysis.[52] However, article 18 of the IE Directive equally provides that stricter emission limit values than those based on BAT may be set when this is required to meet environmental quality standards.

## 4.5 SUMMARY AND CONCLUSION

This chapter on standard setting began by exploring the differences between legal and economic notions of standards and what standard setting means in both research disciplines. We then further clarified the legal concept for environmental law, wherein we set out three forms of standards to be set: (i) target or ambient quality standards, (ii) emission standards, and (iii) production or specification standards.

Target standards are the preferred type of standard when a decentralised approach across a jurisdiction is feasible, because it enables a variety of methods to achieve the environmental goals; each party can select their own mode of achieving those goals.

Emission standards set specific amounts of chemical or energy emissions for each potential emitter. Emission standards are also known as performance standards, because they provide administrative guidance on how each emitter should perform with regards to quantity or quality of emissions. Emission standards, however, do not per se determine the particular technology to be used by the emitter.

Perhaps the least decentralised approach to standard setting is to use production standards, also known as specification standards, which provide specific guidance on the precise technology to be used by the emitter to address their emissions.

We then discussed optimal standard setting, considering issues of how precise to be in setting standards and of how to consider the metrics of evaluating the relative optimality of those standards; including a discussion on the use of cost–benefit analysis as a common tool in optimal standard setting. We also reviewed cultural relativity, that different cultural communities might place various environmental goals in different priorities; e.g. one community might be more concerned about marine environments while others might take more issue with air pollution. We found that there are solid reasons for community policy preferences to vary and that a follow of that is a variety of preferred environmental standards. This multijurisdictional awareness for differences in preferred standards can be more easily

[52] See also Jans and Vedder (2012, at 366).

coordinated when no transboundary effects are present from a given harm, but could cause coordination problems when those transboundary concerns are more substantial.

We then discussed a variety of guidelines for establishing environmental standards, including (i) BPM: Best Practical Means, (ii) ALARA: As Low As Reasonably Achievable, (iii) BPEO: Best Practical Environmental Option, (iv) BAT: Best Available Technique (or technology), and (v) BATNEEC: Best Available Technique (or technology) Not Entailing Excessive Costs.

After reviewing several of these guidelines from examples of historical implementation, we reviewed their fitness from a theoretical perspective. We found that these guidelines were less motivated from a theoretical optimality but rather by a sophisticated sense of Simon's notion of satisficing, to make informed efforts to approach an answer sufficiently close to reduce the overall transaction costs of the determination process. Many of the concepts imbedded in the guidelines, such as 'best' or 'reasonably' are inherently contextual judgments and would reflect knowledge afforded to the decision maker, which might be unevenly available across time and communities, leading to diverse results.

In conclusion, standard setting is clearly at the heart of environmental law – to set environmental goals, predicated on community preferences, to better achieve desired levels of environmental welfare or services. But the task of standard setting is as complex as the set of environmental challenges facing a community as it is complicated by the particular goals desired in diverse communities. Standard setting is then also a question of 'environmental federalism'; the guidelines for setting standards for local injuries and global injuries might differ substantially.

# 5

# Principles of Environmental Law and Environmental Economics

## 5.1 INTRODUCTION

In this chapter, we explore how the analytical tools from the Law and Economics literature provide insights into the role and functions of the norms known as 'principles of environmental law'. While many lawyers may assume that the notion of a legal principle, especially that of environmental legal principle, would be low in economic content or context, we provide here a contrarian view; that the principles of environmental law do have an economic context and, in many cases, that economic insight is key to understanding the proper role and function of those principles.

De Sadeleer's seminal *Environmental Principles* provides a case-by-case analysis of how various key principles of environmental law co-emerged with various economic trade rules within the EU.[1] For environmental rules provide for very different modes of production and industry, and thus have tremendous effects on competition, trade, and free markets. As such, the environmental principles have been often included within founding documents of the EU, such as those located in article 11 and in article 191(2) of the Treaty on the Functioning of the European Union (TFEU):

> Article 11– Environmental protection requirements must be integrated into the definition and implementation of the Union's policies and activities, in particular with a view to promoting sustainable development.
>
> Article 191(2) – Union policy on the environment shall aim at a high level of protection taking into account the diversity of situations in the various regions of the Union. It shall be based on the precautionary principle and on the principles that preventive action should be taken, that environmental damage should as a priority be rectified at source and that the polluter should pay. (Underscoring added.)

[1] De Sadeleer (2002).

Within the EU, the connections between closer economic integration and environmental policies are built into the founding documents and are broadly seen as mutually conducive to the success of the EU and to the benefit of welfare across the EU's Member States.

It is understood that such is not the position of environmental law in the USA, where one is more likely to encounter a Samuelsonian 'guns vs butter' debate on economic growth and environmental protections. Instead of that perspective, this chapter attempts to demonstrate to the reader that there is broad theoretical support from the Law and Economics literature for many established principles of environmental law, and that to some extent, many of those principles are in fact derived from that Law and Economics literature. These themes will be additionally expanded and enhanced when re-encountered in later chapters as well.

In quick summary, this chapter provides the reader with the understanding that the Law and Economics literature both supports and coordinates with the established set of environmental law principles.

In legal doctrine concerning environmental law and policy increasingly attention is paid to the importance of the general principles of environmental law, such as the principle of sustainable development, the polluter pays principle, and the precautionary principle. Originally these principles were formulated as non-binding legal doctrines, but increasingly they can also be found in documents with legal binding force, such as in the EU's charter documents or in specific environmental enactments.

As far as constitutions are concerned, we can point at the fact that increasingly modern constitutions in western European countries are trending to explicitly provide for a right to a clean environment.[2] As far as treaties are concerned we can for instance point at the principles contained in the Rio Declaration of 1992.[3] Thus we now have decades of explicit incorporation of these principles into official enactments of law.

With the incorporation of these principles into constitutions and treaties, a debate began concerning the status and legal significance of these principles. Originally serving as general policy guidelines, guiding the behaviour of states in making environmental policy decisions, but over the past decades, legal scholars and courts began to hold that these principles are more than merely guidelines and do have some legal binding effects.

Before starting this overview, we should point out that the principles of environmental law, discussed here, should not be confounded with the guidelines for standard setting from the discussion in Chapter 4, such as BAT, ALARA, and

[2] These environmental rights in constitution will be further discussed below in Section 5.7.

[3] For an overview of these principles see Jans and Vedder (2012, at 41) and Sands and Peel (2012, at 187–237).

BPM. Those principles of standard setting are legal principles which guide the standard-setting behaviour of administrative agencies.

We shall now discuss the sources, the contents, and possible economic interpretation of a few principles. We start with the crucial notion of sustainable development (Section 5.2) and then discuss in turn the prevention at source (Section 5.3), the proximity (Section 5.4), the precautionary (Section 5.5), and the polluter pays principle (Section 5.6). Then we briefly discuss the relationship between environmental law and human rights (Section 5.7) as well as the integration principle (Section 5.8). Section 5.9 summarises and concludes.

## 5.2 SUSTAINABLE DEVELOPMENT

### 5.2.1 *Sources*

The principle of sustainable development can be found in a number of legal documents, spreading back through history.[4] The term 'sustainable development' was chosen in 1987 in a report of the World Commission on Environment and Development, which published its report 'Our Common Future', usually referred to as the Brundtland Report after the name of the commission's chairperson, Ms G. Harlem Brundtland (Norway). The Brundtland Report defines sustainable development as 'development that meets the needs of the present without compromising the ability of future generations to meet their own needs'. This refers, according to legal doctrine, at least to the need to preserve natural resources for the benefit of future generations and to the aim of exploiting natural resources in a manner which is 'sustainable'.

The notion of sustainable development can, as we already mentioned, also been found in the 1972 Stockholm Declaration and the Rio Declaration, which states in principle 4 that the 'right to development must be fulfilled so as to equitably meet the developmental and environmental needs of present and future generations'.[5]

Two decades earlier, in the USA's National Environmental Protection Act of 1969, the US Congress set out a federal statute that reads similarly to principle 4 of the Rio Declaration:

[4] For an accessible guide to the history of both the concepts of sustainable development, and of the etymological pathways of the various terms that have been used in multiple languages for this concept, see Grober (2012). He finds that the modern concept of sustainable development can be sourced to the vocabulary that emerged in Europe to address forestry management, to ensure stable timbering over multiple generations, with a particular reference to 1804, in Georg Ludwig Hartig's early forestry textbook, as perhaps the first modern use of *nachhaltigkeit* or 'sustainability', with this sentence in translation: 'no long-term forest can be imagined or expected, if the yield of timber is not calculated with regard to sustainability'; see Grober (2012, at 117).

[5] See further on the principle of sustainable development, Sands and Peel (2012, at 206–217).

> Sec. 101(a) [Enrolled as 42 USC § 4331]. The Congress, recognizing the profound impact of man's activity on the interrelations of all components of the natural environment, particularly the profound influences of population growth, high-density urbanization, industrial expansion, resource exploitation, and new and expanding technological advances and <u>recognizing further the critical importance of restoring and maintaining environmental quality to the overall welfare and development of man</u>, declares that it is the continuing policy of the Federal Government, in cooperation with State and local governments, and other concerned public and private organizations, to use all practicable means and measures, including financial and technical assistance, in a manner calculated to foster and promote the general welfare, <u>to create and maintain conditions under which man and nature can exist in productive harmony, and fulfill the social, economic, and other requirements of present and future generations of Americans</u>. (Underscoring added.)

Thus, the basic concept of sustainability is increasingly found in domestic legislation and in international conventions, with similar notions and norms across those instances.[6]

### 5.2.2 *Legal and Economic Interpretation*

An important aspect of the notion of sustainable development is the commitment to integrate environmental considerations into economic and other developments. This aspect of the notion of sustainable development is probably the most important from a legal point of view.[7] It is this notion of integration that lays at the basis of important instruments such as environmental impact assessments and explains the necessity to take the needs of present and future generations into account.[8]

This notion of sustainability also corresponds to notions of environmental Law and Economics we have discussed above. The idea of sustainability requires a development, taking into account consequences for all generations, ours as well as future generations. In that sense this sustainability notion corrects a strict economic reasoning which would argue that there is little reason to invest today to protect future generations, since only the net present value has to be taken into account.

However, this notion of sustainability can be directly connected to Pigou's economics of externalities, with negative externalities occurring in future timeframes in contrast to the economic activities occurring in the present time frame. Thus, sustainability is another metaphor for ensuring that all of the consequences of one's economic activities are fully reconciled and included in the decision making;

6 For further sources of the principle of sustainable development, see Barral (2018).

7 On the integration of environmental and economic development, see Pallemaerts (1995, at 60–77) and Sands and Peel (2012, at 215–217). The integration will be discussed separately in this chapter. See Section 5.8.

8 See Sands and Peel (2012, at 209).

the policy problem then becomes one of how best to model those future risks and costs into current decision making so that only those activities which are genuinely welfare improving over the very long run are undertaken. Or, put another way, how to best ensure that pathways that appear rewarding in the short run but reduce welfare in the long run are not begun. For the policymaker, there is a question of how to include both those risks and costs of environmental injuries and to also ensure that the positive externalities of a preserved ecological and environmental services are somehow integrated with decision making.

Interestingly enough this notion of 'sustainable development' is also used to promote the production of 'sustainable products' and to argue in favour of the recycling of products, which corresponds with economic reasoning.

### 5.2.3 *Valuing Future Generations*

The question how to value the rights of future generations has a lot of impact for the implementation of sustainability. The key question is how to rationally compare the quantity and quality of eco-bundles both for today's societies and for all subsequent generations to ensure that each generation receives no less of an eco-inheritance than previous generations. Key to this problem is that we lack information on future technologies, on future cultural preferences, and on a variety of issues that could affect how to plan for that goal of sustainable eco-inheritances.

Where there is debate in the Law and Economics literature is not on whether to pursue sustainability, which is commonly agreed to, but rather on how best to rationally provide models to support policymakers in their efforts to create useful and efficient legal rules to achieve the goals of sustainability under this problem of missing and costly information about future needs and preferences.

In Chapter 6, we will point at Law and Economics literature to examine modelling methods and their difficulties to evaluate environmental harm from an economics perspective, including attention to the interests of future generations. The central question in sustainable planning is to discover how some kind of intergenerational equity can be taken into account in environmental valuation.[9]

Howarth and Norgaard showed that the valuation of environmental services and the way in which society cares for future generations are somehow interdependent. They claim that the valuation of non-market goods and social objectives are intertwined.[10] However, the question arises in what way environmental policy should actually take into account interests of future generations. This is particularly important in the context of Chapter 6, where we shall point at the importance of cost–benefit analysis for environmental policy.

9 Krutilla and Fisher (1985).

10 Howarth and Norgaard (1992, at 473–477).

The next question that arises is how to decide whether benefits to future generations should give rise to costly preventive measures today. Revesz demonstrated a distinction should be made between harm caused as a result of environmental injuries with a low latency period versus actions with long latencies, which may affect distant future generations. Would discounting to reflect the passage of time between the exposure and the harm be appropriate in these cases?

Revesz argues that discounting is appropriate when engaging with present generations. However, he equally argues that upward adjustments of the value of life need to be undertaken to account for the dread and involuntary nature of environmental carcinogens as well as for the higher income level of victims. By not performing these adjustments the regulatory process risks undervaluing human life.

In contrast, Revesz holds that in case of harms to future generations, discounting is ethically unjustified. He holds that it would simply be a means of privileging the interests of the current generation.[11]

## 5.3 PREVENTION AT SOURCE

### 5.3.1 *Sources*

The preventive principle requires action to be taken at an early stage and, if possible, before damage has actually occurred. This preventive approach can be found for instance in the 1972 Stockholm Declaration and in principle 11 of the 1992 Rio Declaration which requires states to enact 'effective and environmental legislation'.[12]

The norms underlying the prevention principle lay within the traditional norms of tort and delict law, that all members of a community have a recognised right to a 'status quo' of zero non-volition injuries. In this vein the rights to be free of trespass or nuisance can be found connected to the prevention principle.[13]

### 5.3.2 *Legal and Economic Interpretation*

The preventive principle means that actions should be taken before pollution, damage, or environmental impairment has occurred.[14] Generally this preventive principle in international environmental law requires an activity which may cause damage to the environment to be prohibited or controlled to protect the environment at an early stage. The basic idea is that it should be avoided that the damage is only repaired after it has occurred.

[11] See Revesz (1999).
[12] See Sands and Peel (2012, at 200–203).
[13] For a further analysis of the prevention principle, see Duvic-Paoli (2018).
[14] See further for a detailed and systematic analysis of the prevention principle, De Sadeleer (2002, at 61–90).

The idea that all polluting or damaging activities are subject to licensing and therefore prohibited unless allowed by administrative authorities can be considered as an expression of the preventive action principle. A related principle is that of rectifying damage at source. This refers to the fact that environmental impairment should be avoided as close as possible to its source in order to avoid expansion of pollution. The principle of preventive action can also be found in international environmental law.[15] It seeks to minimise environmental damage as an objective itself.

The prevention principle also corresponds with the economic criteria for safety regulation which will be discussed in Chapter 9. The whole idea of ex ante regulations is indeed that in some cases ex ante measures have to be imposed, since ex post liability might not have a sufficient deterrent effect. As detailed in that chapter, ex post liability is only functional with a substantiated injury-in-fact and given the oft irreversible character of environmental injuries, ergo it is functionally to provide compensation and not restoration. Given awareness of a basic liability rule with established liability consequences, potential tortfeasors will be aware of the eventual costs of any created injuries and would rationally avoid those costs.[16] Another problem is the repeatable nature of the injury; is it a sufficiently frequent activity that an established rule is useful for many actors, such as 'routine' chemical leaks from plants, or is the accident and resultant liability rule so unique as to be rarely re-invoked, such as might result from super-scale events or guarded technologies?

Once more one can state that the prevention principle, arguing that prevention is better than cure, of course complies with basic notions of environmental economics. The costs of taking preventive action, meaning investments in abatement technology are usually much lower than curing the environmental damage after it occurred.

## 5.4 PROXIMITY PRINCIPLE

A principle which in fact constitutes an application of the source principle in cases of waste is the proximity principle.[17] Article 191(2) TFEU provides that environmental damage should as a priority be rectified at source.[18] In the European context for a long time it has been unclear whether the basic freedoms necessary to establish the common market, such as the free movement of goods, also apply to waste. The question arose how this notion should be interpreted with respect to problems of

15 Duvic-Paoli (2018, 162–163); Sands and Peel (2012, 200–203).

16 Given competitive conditions, the tortfeasor will continue its activities so long as its marginal costs are smaller than its marginal revenues, so the setting of those marginal costs by the court will be crucial to correctly setting effective environmental standards.

17 See on the relationship between the source principle and the proximity principle, Krämer (2018), and see generally on the proximity principle, Reese (2018).

18 See Jans and Vedder (2012, at 48–49).

trade with waste. This fits into a more general discussion in European environmental law on the question whether individual Member States may restrict the free movement of goods for reasons of environmental protection. An elaborate case law has been developed with respect to this trade-off between the free movement of goods and environmental protection.

### 5.4.1 *Free Trade versus Environmental Protection*

According to the provisions of article 34 and following of the TFEU, 'quantitative restrictions on imports and all measures having equivalent effect' are prohibited between Member States. A Member State cannot blindly restrict or prohibit the import of a certain (polluting) product. First it should be examined whether such a prohibition or restriction is in accordance with article 34. As genuine quantitative restrictions between Member States no longer exist the interpretation of the notion 'measures having equivalent effect' is the most relevant part of the provision.

In the Dassonville case,[19] the European Court of Justice decided that 'all trading rules enacted by Member States which are capable of hindering, directly or indirectly, actually or potentially, intra-community trade are to be considered as measures having an effect equivalent to quantitative restrictions'. Every potential import hindrance, with or without distinction to domestic or imported products, falls in principle under this prohibition.[20] In this respect one can for instance think of a general national prohibition to use a certain polluting compound (such as asbestos) or introducing a maximum admissible concentration of a certain compound in products. In both cases these national rules can potentially have the same effect as formal restrictions on imports if for instance all national products already comply with the standard, but imported products have to be adapted to this standard. As this could potentially raise the costs of import it would hinder trade; therefore, they also fall under the prohibition of article 34. This broad prohibition of import restrictions as interpreted in the Dassonville case would mean that the goal of the realisation of the common internal market is considered that important that also products that are harmful to the environment can cross the national borders of the Member States without any limitation.

### 5.4.2 *Exceptions to Article 34: Trade-Restricting Measures*

There is however an important exception that can be found in article 36 TFEU. This exception allows Member States to restrict intracommunity trade if the measures taken are justified 'on grounds of ... the protection of health and life of

[19] ECJ 11 July 1974, *Procureur du Roi* v. *Dassonville*, Case 8/74, ECR [1974], at 837.

[20] The ECJ has recently importantly limited the scope of Dassonville. See ECJ 24 November 1993, *Keck and Mithouard*, Joined Cases C-267/91 and C-268/91, ECR [1993], at I–6097.

humans, animals or plants'.[21] These measures 'shall not, however, constitute a means of arbitrary discrimination or a disguised restriction on trade between Member States'. The grounds on which Member States can restrict intracommunity trade on the basis of article 36 have been interpreted in a series of decisions of the European Court of Justice. The measures taken have to be necessary and proportionate to the goal to be reached.[22] The example of a prohibition of asbestos, as being a substance dangerous to the health and life of humans, animals, and plants, could well be justified by the exceptions mentioned in article 30. On the other hand, the Court also decided that a general import prohibition on non-dangerous wastes cannot be justified under article 30.[23]

Another important exception to article 34 was, however, created by the European Court of Justice in the Cassis de Dijon case.[24] The Court held that a national trade-restricting measure can be justified if, firstly, it applies in a non-discriminatory way to both national and imported products, secondly, if the goal of this measure is a mandatory requirement (such as public health in the Cassis de Dijon case) and, thirdly, if the impact of the measure is proportionate to the interest that needs to be protected by it.

This idea was extended to the field of the environment in the Danish bottles case,[25] where the European Court decided that the environment can be qualified as a mandatory requirement. The Court held that environmental protection is an interest that can justify a national environmental policy with trade-restricting effects, such as in casu a mandatory system of returnable containers for beer and soft drinks. Since this Danish bottle case, it is accepted that environmental protection can be one of the 'mandatory requirements' which can restrict the applicability of the free trade principle of article 34.

This exception of the Cassis de Dijon/Danish bottles case is in fact broader than the one offered by article 36. For the applicability of article 36 it is necessary that human, animal, or vegetal life or health is at stake, whereas this is not required under the rule of reason of the Cassis de Dijon/Danish bottle case.

However, an important condition for the applicability of the rule of reason of the mentioned cases is that the national measures taken apply to national and important products in a non-discriminatory way. But even this non-discrimination principle has been alleviated importantly in the already mentioned Walloon waste case. The Court held in that case that the principle of preventive action at source, which

[21] See further on these exceptions and the relevant case law, Jans and Vedder (2012, at 261–280).

[22] ECJ 20 May 1976, *De Peijper*, Case 104/75, ECR [1976], at 613.

[23] ECJ 9 July 1992, *Commission* v. *Belgium*, Walloon waste, Case C-2/90, ECR [1992], at I–4431. See further Jans and Vedder (2012, at 261–268).

[24] ECJ 20 February 1979, *Rewe-Zentral AG* v. *Bundesmonopolverwaltung für Branntwein* (Cassis de Dijon), Case 120/78, ECR [1979], at 649.

[25] ECJ 20 September 1988, *Commission* v. *Denmark* (Danish bottles), Case 302/86, ECR [1988], at 4607.

implies that all regions or local authorities are entitled to adopt measures to limit transport of waste and to ensure that their disposal takes place as close as possible to their place of production, can justify an import restriction that only applies to foreign waste. The Court held that there was no violation of the non-discrimination principle although the prohibition in the Walloon regulation only applied to foreign waste.

This principle of preventive action at source, which was introduced as a general principle of environmental policy in the Single European Act, is apparently considered to have priority over the freedom of trade and non-discrimination principles.

### 5.4.3 *Trade of Waste between Efficiency and Ethics*

To some extent these problems have been set aside as a result of the Basel Convention,[26] which now regulates the transboundary movement of waste. How can these issues of the trade-off between free trade and environmental protection be addressed from an economic point of view?

At first sight there is a lot to say in favour of free movement of waste from an economic point of view for the simple reason that there might be economies of scale advantages if trade is allowed. It is for instance very well possible that the French are able to incinerate waste at lower costs than the Dutch or the Belgians, so that a trade of waste from Belgium or the Netherlands to France would be welfare increasing.

Some countries might still be able to use certain rest-products for secondary goals, so that recovery of the waste in another Member State is possible. Trade of waste for reasons of recovery is always welfare-enhancing. This is also principally allowed under the Basel Convention, since it does not apply on waste transports if the waste is re-used or recycled.[27]

However, there is always the danger when waste is shifting borders that a loss of control takes place. This lack of monitoring by administrative agencies might increase the probability that the waste escapes any control and is therefore discharged in an illegal manner. To prevent this one could principally argue that trade of waste may be welfare-enhancing, provided that there is an effective control on transboundary shipment of waste.

The possible protection of a domestic industry has been shown in a case of the European Court of Justice when the relationship between competition and the proximity principle had to be decided. National regulations may force the local industry to bring all industrial waste to one, perhaps monopolised, waste treatment plant or incinerator, and prohibit all export of waste on the basis of the proximity principle. In those cases, the question arises whether the national Member States

[26] See further on the Basel Convention, Sands and Peel (2012, 568–571) and Jans and Vedder (2012, 492–499).

[27] For details on the Basel Convention, see Voinov-Kohler (2017).

have the right to force their national industry to an expensive waste treatment on the basis of the proximity principle, or whether the export ban should be considered illegal.

The European Court of Justice decided against an 'abuse' of the proximity principle to justify an export ban on waste. Such a general export ban (by in casu the Netherlands) was held to violate European Law.[28]

Thus, one could argue that a proximity principle might create inefficiencies if phrased in a strict meaning that the waste should in principle be treated at the source. The logic of the proximity principle does indeed restrict welfare-enhancing trades with waste. However, there are with respect to the trade with waste apparently limits to the economic reasoning. It might well, for instance, be efficient to ship waste to the Sahara Desert and store it there at relatively low costs where the potential environmental harm is very low. These kinds of trades are not only prohibited by international conventions but might also be problematic from an ethical point of view. There is apparently a strong ethical appeal of the proximity principle, being the idea that a community should basically treat its waste problem itself and not export it to its neighbours. Looking to the Calabresian maxim from the Law and Economics literature to search for the 'least cost avoider', the principle might be supported if the creators of the waste are uniquely and better informed on the contents of the waste and of its potential remedial processing, storage, and disposal.

Nevertheless, the proximity principle also has its limits. Perhaps the local creator of the waste is not well informed or is limited by local regulations on waste process, and thus, cannot cure the waste at a competitive cost? Might that create problems of economic fairness?

## 5.5 PRECAUTIONARY PRINCIPLE

### 5.5.1 *Sources and Contents*

The precautionary principle can inter alia be found in article 191(2) TFEU, wherein it is simply stated that Union policy on the environment 'shall be based on the precautionary principle'.[29] European law itself contains no definition of this precautionary principle.

The precautionary principle dictates that if there is a strong suspicion that a certain activity may have environmentally harmful consequences, it is better to act before it is too late. In that sense the precautionary principle goes a step further than the prevention principle, since the precautionary principle would dictate that action

[28] European Court of Justice, 25 June 1998 Case C 203/96, *Chemische afvalstoffen Dusseldorp B.V.*

[29] Jans and Vedder (2012, at 41).

has to be taken precautionary, that one should not wait until scientific evidence incontrovertibly shows a causal connection between a certain activity and possible environmental damage. This principle therefore is important in all those cases where there is presumption, but no clear and convincing scientific evidence yet of certain undesirable environmental effects. Even in the absence of absolute proof the precautionary principle dictates that tentative and indicative scientific data might be sufficient ground on which to take measures to protect the environment.[30]

This precautionary principle can also be found in international environmental law.[31] Within the context of international environmental law it would mean that internal legal action has to be taken to address highly threatening environmental issues such as ozone depletion and climate change, even if full scientific certainty of climate change, for example, were not yet available.[32] And in this sense perhaps lays its potential power, to legally require action under international law for events not yet fully formed and thus creating a powerful policy tool; it effectively shifts the 'burden of proof' for hesitance on matters of international environmental law to those who hesitate to undertake novel policies. This could have both positive and negative consequences.

The precautionary principle finds its legal basis inter alia in principle 15 of the Rio Declaration, which provides that 'where there are threats of serious or irreversible damage, lack of full scientific certainty shall not be used as a reason for postponing cost-effective measures to prevent environmental degradation'.[33]

The precautionary principle has now been adapted in several international environmental treaties. One example is the 1992 Baltic Sea Convention which states that preventive measures are to be taken 'when there is reason to assume "that harm might be caused" even when there is no conclusive evidence of a causal relationship between inputs and there alleged effects'.

Another example constitutes article 3(3) of the well-known UN Framework Convention on Climate Change (UNFCCC) of 9 May 1992, which states:

> The Parties should take precautionary measures to anticipate, prevent or minimise the causes of climate change and mitigate its adverse effects. Where there are threats of serious or irreversible damage, lack of full scientific certainty shall not be used as a reason for postponing such measures, taking into account that policies and measures to deal with climate change should be cost-effective so as to ensure global benefits at the lowest possible cost.

Here one can note that the economic notion of cost–benefit analysis is linked with the (legal) precautionary principle.[34]

30 Id., at 43–47.

31 For a detailed discussion see De Sadeleer (2002, at 91–225) and De Sadeleer (2016).

32 See for instance Sands and Peel (2012, at 217 and ff.)

33 Id., at 218.

34 For a precise interpretation of the precautionary principle in the UNFCCC, see De Sadeleer (2016, at 24–29).

Both the legal interpretation and the economic meaning of this precautionary principle are highly debated.[35]

### 5.5.2 *Economic Interpretation*

The precautionary principle is also debated from an economic point of view. Economists may have no problem with the principle that preventive action should be taken (prevention is better than cure), but might have more worries with a principle forcing policymakers in governance and in industry to invest resources in precautionary measures when there is scientific uncertainty on the need to take these measures.

A potential criticism is that in this way the principle will lead to overregulation and limit human activity to too great an extent. Or, given the assumed uncertainty of the causal connection between various activities and any particular environmental harm, it is foreseeable that sometimes the presumed curative action could be ineffective or worsening and cause material misdirection of policies, counterproductively resulting in more harm and not less.

Some have argued that forcing citizens to invest in costly preventive measures when there is no evidence that this may lead to a reduction of environmental harm would bring about a waste of scarce resources.[36] Ogus has also argued that a strict application of the precautionary principle would lead to inefficiency.[37] Ogus gives the example of the display screen equipment directive 1990,[38] which governs the use of display screens throughout the industry and commerce. It requires employers inter alia to meet standards relating to e.g. the design of the screen, desk, and chair, and environmental factors. Ogus argues that while health problems which may potentially arise from the use of display screens have been the subject of concern and debate, there is no hard evidence indicating serious effects. To realise benefits which are thus highly speculative, the directive imposes substantial costs.[39]

In such a strict application the precautionary principle could indeed lead to inefficiencies. A new approach to the precautionary principle would be to shift the burden of proof and require the person who wishes to carry out the activity to prove that it will not cause harm to the environment.[40] But in this interpretation potential polluters are required to incur substantial costs when conclusive proof of a lack of a causal link cannot be provided. This shows that the precautionary principle essentially deals with the question how regulatory standards should be set when

35 For a summary of the literature see Haritz (2011).

36 This point has been made in the various works of Viscusi. See for instance Viscusi (1983, at 793; 1989, at 65–107).

37 See Ogus (1995, at 325–338).

38 Directive 90/270, *Official Journal*, 1990, l 156/14.

39 Ogus (1995, at 330).

40 See Sands and Peel (2012, at 222).

there is uncertainty concerning potentially harmful effects. The precautionary principle indicates that under uncertainty regulatory action may have to be taken where the scientific evidence suggests that lack of action may result in serious or irreversible harm to the environment.

### 5.5.3 *The Use of the Precautionary Principle*

Doctrinally the legal and economic approaches strongly diverge.[41] It has already been noted that lawyers enthusiastically support the precautionary principle, while economists warn that it may be too costly and that it would stifle economic activity and innovation.

Ultimately, the computational complexity of the precautionary principle complicates its use as a decision-making support tool – when does one know enough about the risks to invoke the precautionary principle? One is reminded of Rumsfeld's quote on uncertainty in policy formation:

> Reports that say that something hasn't happened are always interesting to me, because as we know, there are known knowns; there are things we know we know. We also know there are known unknowns; that is to say we know there are some things we do not know. But there are also unknown unknowns – the ones we don't know we don't know. And if one looks throughout the history of our country and other free countries, it is the latter category that tend to be the difficult ones.[42] (Underscoring added.)

It is noticeable at the policy level that policymakers on the one hand embrace the precautionary principle and on the other hand warn that a too far-reaching interpretation of the precautionary principle would simply become too costly.

This is clear from the European approach to the precautionary principle. This emerges from a review of the European Commission's approach to the precautionary principle.[43] On 2 February 2000 the European Commission published a communication on the precautionary principle. The purposes of this communication are, first, to establish guidelines for applying the principle and, second, to avoid unwarranted recourse to the precautionary principle as a disguised form of protectionism. The Commission accepts that recourse to the precautionary principle acknowledges that scientific evaluation does not allow the risk to be determined with sufficient certainty. This is referred to as risk assessment. The implementation of an approach based on the precautionary principle should accordingly start with a

[41] For an excellent summary of the literature, see Wiener (2018).

[42] 'DoD News Briefing – Secretary Rumsfeld and Gen. Myers; Presenter: Secretary of Defense Donald H. Rumsfeld' (12 February 2002, 11:30 AM EDT); available at: http://archive.defense.gov/Transcripts/Transcript.aspx?TranscriptID=2636

[43] Communication from the Commission on the precautionary principle [COM(2000) 1 final of 2 February 2000].

scientific evaluation which identifies the degree of scientific uncertainty. The precautionary principle continues to play a role at the second stage: namely that of risk management. Based on the scientific evaluation about the level of uncertainty, decision makers then have to accept the political responsibility to determine the 'acceptable' level of risk for society. How this is done is important, yet it is not something readily addressed in most formulations of the principle.

When measures are necessary to give effect to the precautionary principle, the Commission indicates that these measures should similarly be based on an examination of the potential benefits and costs of action or lack of action. The Commission stresses that this is not merely an economic cost–benefit analysis; instead policymakers should take a much broader perspective and include non-economic considerations, such as the efficacy of possible options and their acceptability to the public. Resulting measures taken to give effect to the precautionary principle should be reviewed periodically in the light of scientific progress and amended as necessary.

The approach of the European Commission indicates that some of the fears of economists about a too rigid interpretation of the precautionary principle seem to have been incorporated in this communication. An important point is that, when the precautionary principle is applied, the Commission explicitly states that account should be taken of the potential benefits and costs of action and of a lack of action. In other words, precisely as economists had proposed, both cost–benefit analysis and opportunity costs analysis should constitute integral parts of the procedural life of the precautionary principle.

Some in the USA have expressed concern of how to implement the precautionary approach in terms of introducing the necessary evidence into court proceedings; the particular concern is the historical Frye and Daubert tests for scientific evidence and whether the precautionary principle might fall askew of the evidentiary conventions.[44]

## 5.6 POLLUTER PAYS PRINCIPLE

### 5.6.1 *Sources*

Probably one of the most well-known principles of environmental law is the polluter pays principle. This principle is incorporated both in European and international environmental law.[45] Article 191(2) TFEU states that Union policy shall be based on the principle 'that the polluter should pay'.

Legal scholars point at the fact that as soon as one starts to interpret the polluter pays principle as a legal principle, difficulties accumulate, such as the questions of who is a polluter, what is pollution, what should be paid for; the need for clarity on

44 Smith and Steenburg (2015, at 76–79).
45 See Schwartz (2018).

who is responsible for an environmental tort is not always as simple as one might hope, as Coase made quite clear.[46]

The polluter pays principle can also be found in international environmental law.[47] For instance principle 16 of the Rio Declaration provides that: 'National authorities should endeavour to promote the internalization of environmental costs and the use of economic instruments, taking into account the approach that the polluter should, in principle, bear the costs of pollution, with due regard to the public interest and without distorting international trade and investment'.

### 5.6.2 *Economic Interpretation*

The simple way in which it is formulated in environmental policy 'that the polluter should pay' is from an economic perspective ambiguous to say the least.[48] Nevertheless, it has been often remarked that the polluter pays principle is perhaps one of the easiest principles to coordinate with economic models: 'Conceptualizing the polluter pays principle as an eminently economic principle as in line both with its origin (OECD, 1975) and with some of its most representative definitions that explicitly endorse the criterion of cost internalization, such as the above-mentioned principle 16 of the Rio Declaration.'[49]

The question of course arises what the polluter pays principle means from a legal point of view.[50] Jans and Vedder argue that the whole standard setting in environmental law forces potential polluters to make various investments to comply with the statutory standards. Thus, the standard-setting process within environmental law helps to ensure that the polluter bears the costs of pollution; straddling the goals of both efficiency and equity.[51] The community must ensure that by laying down standards and environmental charges that the persons who are responsible for pollution in fact bear the costs.[52]

One could argue that the fact that polluters have to pay for environmental harm equals the duty to internalise externalities. This is one of the starting points of environmental economics. It was on the basis of this polluter pays principle that Arthur Pigou advocated the use of environmental taxes as the main instrument to internalise externalities.[53]

One of the problems with the Pigouvian approach is that the only solution thereby envisaged to environmental problems is the fact that the polluter should

46 Coase (1960). See the discussion on the Coase Theorem in Section 2.3.

47 See Sands and Peel (2012, at 228–233).

48 The polluter pays principle is included in many legal instruments inter alia of the OECD and the EU. For a detailed description see Sands and Peel (2012, at 228–233).

49 Woerdman, Arcuri, and Clò (2008b, at 573).

50 For a detailed legal analysis, see De Sadeleer (2002, at 21–60).

51 Woerdman, Arcuri, and Clò (2008b, at 574).

52 For details see Jans and Vedder (2012, at 49–51).

53 See Pigou (1951).

be exposed to the social costs created by the polluting activity. It has been the major achievement of Ronald Coase to demonstrate that, by addressing externalities as a one-sided problem – namely the factory causing harm to the victims – this is a too one-sided approach. One could as easily argue that it is the presence of the neighbours – the potential victims – which in fact limits the rights of the operator of the factory. Harm from this perspective is not one-sided but reciprocal and symmetrical.

According to the Coase Theorem, the problem is rather the conflicting uses of overlapping property rights. The optimal solution is not necessarily that 'the polluter should pay'. As the Coase Theorem illustrated, a victim pays model – in the sense that victims pay for preventive measures – could equally lead to the optimal solution. Accordingly, one problem with a one-sided presentation of the polluter pays principle is that it neglects the insights from the Coase Theorem. To achieve optimal pollution abatement, it is not necessary that the polluter pays either the prevention costs or the damage costs; indeed, Calabresi has suggested a 'least cost avoider' principle for tort law in general, with clear applications here that when victims might be the least cost avoider then they might bear a duty to prevent the environmental injury.

There is a second problem with a one-sided presentation of the polluter pays principle. If it is transposed to environmental liability, the polluter pays principle would be interpreted as a duty imposed on polluters to pay not only the costs of prevention but also for any environmental damage that might occur. This would be the functional equivalent of a strict liability rule.

Although there are strong arguments in favour of a strict liability rule,[54] particularly when ultra-hazardous activities cause the pollution, in some cases a negligence rule could equally lead to an optimal internalisation of the externality. A negligence rule requires polluters to pay for the costs of prevention. Since the polluters will be considered to have complied with the due care requirement, they will not have to pay compensation for the victim's damage, but remember, taking due care does not assure that no injuries will result. The negligence rule merely sets the costs of prevention and damages into two piles, with the tortfeasor being told to pay for prevention and the victim being warned that they will pay for damages if the tortfeasor pays for prevention. Thus, the negligence rule illustrates that polluters can be given optimal incentives to prevent injuries by paying the costs of 'due care' activities, all-the-while not being required to pay for the costs of those injuries that do in fact occur despite taking 'efficient due care'.

These examples show that the polluter pays principle is more ambiguous than might first appear. If a broad interpretation is applied and the polluter pays principle is considered only as the obligation of the injurer to internalise externalities, then the polluter pays principle is in line with economic analysis. However, internalising

[54] As we will argue in Section 8.2.

the externality does not necessarily imply that polluters should in addition compensate victims for the environmental harm caused. Thus, pay but not pay.

## 5.7 ENVIRONMENTAL LAW AND HUMAN RIGHTS

We should also mention that an interesting debate has been taking place concerning the role of environmental protection versus other human rights.[55] Human rights approaches to environmental protection have become increasingly popular in legal doctrine.[56] This is closely related to the question whether the right to a clean environment should be considered as a human right.[57]

Increasingly, international environmental law recognises such rights. For instance, in the 1972 Stockholm Declaration it was declared that man's natural and man-made environment 'are essential to his well-being and to the enjoyment of basic human rights – even the right to life itself'. Nevertheless, it is less clear when an environmental degradation will have to be considered a breach of the individual human rights.[58]

### 5.7.1 *Environmental Rights in Constitutions*

In many national constitutions, the right to a clean environment is formulated as a basic human right.

For instance, in 1994, an article 20a was added into the German constitution (Grundgezetz), which made environmental protection a state principle. Article 20a of the German constitution emphasises a principle of precaution and an environmental duty to all state levels to effect the goal of environmental protection. It does, however, not grant an actionable right to the citizen. Thus, according to German legal doctrine, article 20a does not provide a 'fundamental environmental right'.[59]

Other constitutions also guarantee the protection of the environment. The Greek constitution of 1986 guarantees in article 24 the protection of the environment, formulated as a duty of the state.[60] Further, article 21 of the Dutch constitution provides for a legal basis for environmental protection. It was introduced in the constitutional revision of 1983 and states that the duty of the government is aimed at the habitable status of the land and the protection and improvement of the

[55] Hsu presented a similar argument in suggesting that the concept of 'fairness' in environmental law has three main elements; (i) an equalizing distribution of burden and benefits, (ii) the avoidance of retroactive regulation, and (iii) elements drawn from retributive justice (Hsu 2004, 313–319).

[56] See Boyle and Anderson (1996).

[57] See on the relationship between environmental principles and the right to a quality environment, Boer (2018).

[58] See Sands and Peel (2012, at 777–780).

[59] Rody (1996) and Seerden and Heldeweg (1996, at 157).

[60] Sioutis (1996, at 193).

environment. But similar to Germany, this legal doctrine holds that the article states an obligation on the government without actually serving as a legal basis for claims by civilians against the state.[61]

### 5.7.2 *ECHR Case Law*

These developments in modern constitutions are in line with pleas in environmental legal doctrine to introduce environmental human rights in the law.[62] The formulation of 'environmental protection rights' in constitutions or conventions usually refer to a duty of the authorities to protect the citizens against environmental degradation. It is, however, usually argued as well that these so-called economic and social rights do not confer individually actionable subjective rights to citizens.

There are, however, a number of highly interesting cases where citizens have used the traditional human rights, notably the right as laid down in the European Convention on Human Rights of 1950 to argue that some cases of environmental pollution might constitute a violation of these traditional human rights by the government. Several articles of the convention have been used in that respect.

This is for instance the case for article 1 of the first protocol to the European Court of Human Rights (ECHR), which protects private property. The ECHR recognised in the case *Fredin* v. *Sweden* that 'in today's society the protection of the environment is an increasingly important consideration' and tested whether the interference with a private property right to achieve environmental objectives was proportionate or disproportionate in the context of article 1 of the first protocol. It held that this interference was not inappropriate, meaning that environmental protection measures can in fact override private property rights.

The question has also risen whether severe cases of environmental pollution might be considered as a breach of article 8 of the ECHR, which provides that, inter alia, 'everyone has the right to respect for his private and family life, his home . . . and there shall be no interference by a public authority with the exercise of the right except such as is in accordance with the law and is necessary in a democratic society in the interests of the economic well-being of the country'. Citizens living in the neighbourhood of Heathrow Airport alleged that in a breach of article 8, excessive noise forced them to endure unreasonable disturbance caused by air traffic, whose flying was in accordance with UK governmental regulation. The court rejected the argument, arguing that it was to strike a fair balance between the competing interests of the individual and the community as a whole. The court apparently judged that this fair balance had not been upset, inter alia given significant measures to abate noise pollution that had been taken by the government, in

[61] See Seerden and Heldeweg (1996, at 274).
[62] See in this respect for instance Verschuuren (1993; 1995, at 421–445).

alignment with international standards. Moreover, some nearby residents had been compensated for disturbances resulting from aircraft noise.[63]

Compare the case of *Lopez Ostra* v. *Spain* (1994), where the ECHR held that there was indeed a violation of article 8 of the European convention because of the pollution caused by a waste treatment plant. The expertise showed an unacceptable emission of toxic fumes and damage to the health of the people living in the immediate vicinity of a waste treatment plant. Physicians testified that they found the health of Mrs. Lopez Ostra's daughter had been seriously damaged and that they had recommended her to move away. The court held that there was a violation of article 8, as the town had allowed the plant to be built on its land and the state of Spain had subsidised the plants' construction. The court considered in this case that the state did not succeed in striking a fair balance between the interests of the town's economic well-being – that of having a waste treatment plant – and the applicant's effective enjoyment of her right to respect for her home and her private and family life.

EU legal doctrine holds that this case can have important implications, especially for countries in Europe with less developed legislation and rules to prevent environmental problems caused by outdated and ill-equipped factories. That case shows that serious environmental issues can lead to standing under article 8. This case also shows that there is apparently less of a distinction between traditional human rights, where it was accepted that they were actionable, and social rights where it was generally held that they were not. Thus, this case could be read as enabling a fusion between human rights and social rights.[64]

### 5.7.3 *Economic Interpretation*

There is no specific Law and Economics literature addressing how one can view the emergence of environmental rights in constitutions. There are, however, concepts in other areas of Law and Economics literature which might apply to the developments of those rights which can be viewed.

First, one approach is to view the expression of environmental protection in the constitution as mostly of a symbolic nature. Important fundamental rights are protected in the constitution. The mere fact that the constitution maker considers environmental protection of such importance that it becomes of constitutional value provides an important signal to the population. In that sense, arguing that it has symbolic value does not at all mean that it would be unimportant, quite to the contrary.

In Law and Economics scholarship it is stressed that incorporating particular norms in legislation can have a strong so-called expressive value.[65] Although this

[63] Compare in this respect the discussion on the first-use doctrine in Section 3. 3.
[64] For a detailed analysis of this case see Heringa (1995, at 196–204).
[65] See Cooter (1998) and Jacob (1980).

expressive function of the law is often stressed in relation to the criminal law, it can have its value for constitutional rules as well. In that respect, incorporating environmental protection into the constitution could thus have an important expressive function, pointing at the importance of environmental values and putting them on an equal footing with other values protected in the constitution.

Second, another function of such a constitutional protection could simply be gap-filling: more particularly in legal systems where the legislator or executive would fail to put an effective environmental legal framework in place (which may sometimes be the case in developing countries), granting environmental values constitutional status may be important at the level of adjudication. That would therefore imply that the environmental protection incorporated in the constitution could also lead to an increased environmental protection via the judiciary. This is of course clear in the case law of the ECHR, which used a broad interpretation of article 8 to grant protection against gross violations of environmental rights. To the extent that environmental norms in constitutions therefore become actionable, they can be considered as fulfilling an important gap-filling function, providing an extra tool to internalise externalities where the first-best instruments (standard setting via administrative agencies) would fail.

## 5.8 INTEGRATION

### 5.8.1 *Integration of Laws: Codification*

The notion of integration has many different meanings in environmental policy.[66] Sometimes the notion integration is used to refer to a harmonisation or coordination of legislation or procedures. This type of integration usually refers to the bringing together of various environmental Acts into one document. One can note an evolution in environmental law whereby originally all the several components of the environment (air, water, soil) were protected separately in various pieces of legislation, such as in the CWA (1972), and the CAA (1963, 1970) as enacted by the USA.

In the 1980s many legal systems decided to bring together all these various Acts into one 'integrated' piece of environmental legislation. One example is the Environmental Management Act in the Netherlands; another one is the Flemish decree on environmental policy, which also aims at codifying the whole body of environmental law. Usually the goal of this type of codification or harmonisation of legislation is to harmonise the procedural steps for environmental permits, even if different permits for the various environmental components may still exist.

Therefore, one could notice that the development of various environmental statutes to protect various components of the environment was in fact a first step.

[66] For an overview see Faure (2000, at 174–182).

The next step, taking place now, is to move from this so-called sectoral to integrated legislation. This type of 'integration' does not necessarily say very much on the contents of law, but has more to do with the fact that all environmental law can then be found in one legal document, a Code or a general Act on environmental policy, depending upon the legal system.[67]

From an economic point of view, one could, however, argue that this 'integration' already has the major advantage that it is much easier for the citizens to receive information on the contents of legislation when they just have to consult one legal document. Information costs are reduced through codification. Administrative costs might for the same reason be lower as well and if information on the contents of environmental legislation is improved through codification this might also lead to better compliance.

### 5.8.2 *External Integration*

There is a second notion of integration, which is usually referred to as external integration.[68] This can be found in article 11 TFEU. This provides that the environmental protection requirements must be integrated into the definition and implementation of other community policies, in particular with a view to promoting sustainable development across the whole of the EU.

The goal of this notion of external integration is that environmental protection should not only be of concern for environmental decision makers but should be an important consideration when other non-environmental policies are shaped and implemented. As far as the European community is concerned, this integration principle as laid down in article 11 TFEU therefore aims at a total 'greening' of other community policies.[69] Jans and Vedder consider this as 'one of the most important principles of EC law', but at the same time they rightly mention that still a lot of questions arise with respect to the precise meaning of this integration principle.[70] At least this leads to a general obligation on the European community institutions to reach an integrated and balanced assessment of all the relevant environmental aspects when adopting other policy measures.[71]

This notion of integration of environmental concerns into other policy areas is also know in international environmental law. Sands and Peel consider the commitment to integrate environmental considerations into economic and other

[67] For instance, in Sweden an environmental code was introduced. See also for Germany, Kloepfer (1996, at 87–100). See, on one of the first examples, the Danish Environmental Protection Act 1991, Pagh (1996, at 143–153).

[68] For a detailed discussion of the notion of external integration, see Grimeaud (2000, at 207–218).

[69] See Krämer (1995, at 82).

[70] Jans and Vedder (2012, at 22).

[71] Examples of where this can play a role are discussed with references to case law, by Jans (1995, at 17–23).

development as an element of 'sustainable development'.[72] Sands and Peel rightly point at the fact that this integration principle has an important legal consequence, being that environmental information has to be collected, e.g. through the conduct of environmental impact assessments when economic policy or economic projects are developed.

At the international level this integration issue is in close proximity to the 'right to development' discussion, initiated by developing countries. Therefore, developing countries have often been careful, by introducing specific language into treaties to safeguard their future development possibilities, limiting the extent to which international environmental regulation might limit such development.[73]

### 5.8.3 *IPPC*

There is a third meaning of the notion of integration, which can inter alia be found in the well-known Directive on Integrated Pollution Prevention and Control of 24 September 1996 (IPPC Directive).[74] This notion of integration,[75] as introduced in the IPPC Directive, is related to the prevention of emissions into air, water, or soil, wherever this is practicable.[76] Integration in that specific meaning refers to an integration of decision making, because of the interchangeability of externalities.[77] The idea is that integration is necessary to take into account the total pollution costs to prevent the shifting of emissions by firms. Therefore, the basic idea is that in an integrated decision making where the effects on all environmental components are taken into account at once emission limit values can be set efficiently.[78]

### 5.8.4 *Economic Interpretation*

What can be said about this notion of integration from an economic point of view? The concept of integrated pollution control itself fits in the economic idea that the legal instruments should be shaped in such a way that the externalities caused by the environmental pollution are internalised as much as possible.

A classic problem with a non-integrated pollution control system is that it does not take into account the possible interchangeability of emissions. In practice, rules are very fragmented and sectorally administered, thus once environmental regulation is

72 See Sands and Peel (2012, at 215–217).

73 For further details see id., at 215–217.

74 *Official Journal*, L 257/26 of 10 October 1996.

75 It was this notion of integration that we briefly discussed in Chapter 4.

76 For more on the IPPC Directive, see Chapter 4.

77 See further on the legal interpretation of this principle of integration, see Montini (2018).

78 The way that this is achieved in the IPPC Directive is mentioned in article 7. This provides that the Member States should guarantee the coordination of the procedures for the grant of a permit 'to guarantee an effective integrated approach' where more than one competent authority is involved.

established in one sector, one can often see a shifting of the environmental problems to other less controlled or regulated sectors. Strict controls on emissions into water, for example, have frequently led to installing water purification equipment which in its turn produced sewage sludge which was again dumped on land. Instead of internalising the costs of environmental pollution, these attempts at rule-making merely shifted the problem of water pollution into soil pollution, thus also shifting the cost externalisation from one party to another, without sufficiently internalising the cost data into holistic decision making to prevent a misallocation of activities and resources. Internalising the externalities however refers to all possible forms of emissions from a certain entity, therefore integrating these different concerns in the decision-making process.

Preventing the shifting of emissions has indeed been advanced as one of the central goals of the IPPC Directive. The original proposal explicitly mentioned under the specific objectives of operation that the directive aims at preventing pollution emissions from larger installations 'so that pollution problems are solved rather than transferred from one part of the environment to another'.[79] The considerations preceding the directive mention that 'separate approaches to controlling emissions into the air, the water or the land alone may encourage the shifting of pollution across environmental media rather than protecting the environment as a whole'.

The advantage of an integrated approach therefore is that the externalities of all possible environmental injuries, whether air-based, water-based, or soil-based, can be integrated into one decision-making procedure as a result of which emission limit values are set in such a way that the industry has proper incentives to match environmental policies and no incentives to shift its emissions from one compartment of the environment to the other.

Whether the end-result of this procedure will also be efficient, will first largely depend upon the procedure and the involved authorities and their ability and willingness to take into account the various possible emissions and set standards in such a way that a shifting is indeed prevented.

A second condition is that not only limit values for the various types of emissions are set in a balanced manner, but that also enforceability of standards can be guaranteed. Article 14 of the directive stipulates that the Member States shall take the necessary measures to ensure that the conditions of the permit are complied with by the operator. An integrated pollution control system will only be successful if not only the standard-setting process is integrated, but also the enforcement system. Since the enforcement and implementation of the directive is left to the Member States, the true value of the integration will depend on their approach.

An integrated approach towards the pollution problem is desirable not only because of the risk of transfer of emissions, but also to enable an efficient calculation

[79] COM (93) 423 final, at 25.

of the costs and benefits. Indeed, if one agrees that the $mc = mb$ test should play a role when emission limit values are set, it is desirable that a standard-setting authority should take simultaneously into account all injuries in order to be able to decide what the optimal standard to reach the target quality should be.

The concept of an integration of pollution control systems can also be defended by referring to the reduction of administrative costs this will probably bring. A separate licensing procedure for every possible emission from a large plant leads to high costs, both for the industry and for the bureaucracies involved. One can therefore expect that industry would welcome an integrated approach. This has the advantage that industry only has to address itself to one counter instead of having to apply for three or more licences before it can start up its activities. The original proposal of the directive also aimed at a streamlined decision-making process: in principle, decisions with respect to a permit had be taken within six months.[80] This deadline was unfortunately dropped in the final text of the directive.

In general, there can hardly be any criticism on the concept of integrated pollution control itself. Also, the notion, which is stressed many times in the explanatory memorandum, that the aim of integrated pollution control is to prevent emissions and to minimise emissions to the environment as a whole, fits into the economic approach.[81] There it has also been stressed that legal instruments should be used to induce a potential polluter to prevent emissions in the first place.[82]

## 5.9 SUMMARY AND CONCLUSION

We began this chapter on environmental principles with a discussion on sustainable development. We discussed the origins of the phrase in legal contexts from both the EU and the USA. The core concept, to pursue a path of increased human welfare while also enabling all future generations an equal or better set of environmental conditions, can readily find context in economic theory. For example, if future generations are considered within a Pareto optimality context, then only those activities that are agreeable to all generations would be Pareto improvements. Similarly, if all of the potential Pigouvian externalities were to become identifiable, both the positive and negative externalities, then growth could proceed on a path of sustainable development, as the impacts on future generations from those externalities would be integrated.

However, one of the challenges we discussed was the complexity of integrating the values and preferences for future generations who remain unable to directly

[80] This was at least the case in article 7(2) of the September 1993 version of the proposed directive; but, the phrase was unfortunately deleted in the June 1995 common position.

[81] The explanatory memorandum stated with respect to the proposal: 'It is founded upon a preventive approach to pollution control', in COM (93) 423 final, p. 14.

[82] In this respect we can also refer to the discussion concerning the preventive principle in Section 5.3.

voice those concerns to present-time policymakers. Even if those voices were heard, there are questions of how the concept of an interest rate and of discounted cash flow might affect policy decisions.

We next turned to the preventive principle. Ideally, the preventive principle means that actions should be taken before pollution, damage, or environmental impairment has occurred. The goal is to prevent pollution at the source of the pollution, to prevent injuries by acting as local to the tortfeasor locus of activity as possible.

If injury does result, then the proximity principle states that the pollution or injury should be addressed as close as possible to the source of the emission or injury. We explored this principle from a discussion on waste and whether waste should be required to be treated and processed at source or if treatment could be allowed at a location further removed from the source but that provided a more efficient method of handling that waste. Economic theory generally was found to prefer an efficient location so long as Pigouvian concerns are adequately addressed. We then reviewed EU case law which has examined the concept of waste as an industry that could avail itself of economic protections afforded all industries in the EU, particularly from free trade and freedom of movement principles that facilitate a common economy.

We then discussed the precautionary principle, which requires that if there is a strong suspicion that a certain activity may have environmentally harmful consequences, that one should act before the anticipated injury would occur. The precautionary principle guides that one should not wait until scientific evidence incontrovertibly shows a causal connection between a risky activity and its possibly resultant environmental damage. Perhaps the key concern from the Law and Economics literature is the difficulty for decision makers to evaluate the risk of needing to take action based on incomplete information; this causes both problems of determining when sufficient concerns have risen to precipitate action taking, and thus of when some sense of fault might arise, and also of inefficient use of resources in attempting to achieve the goals of the precautionary principle. The transaction costs of implementing the precautionary principle are thus complex and potentially inefficient. And inefficient efforts, it might bear repeating, mean that inefficiency on achieving one's environmental goal would result in fewer resources being available to achieve other equally important environmental goals. As we reported above, the EU Commission has indicated that precautionary measures should be based on an examination of the potential benefits and costs of action or lack of action – that policymakers should take a much broader perspective and include both economic and non-economic considerations. Thus, the implementation of the precautionary principle, from a Law and Economics perspective, in consideration of the complex transaction costs and of the complexities of the potential externalities, must be taken with more consideration than the preventive principle, which in most cases would be expected to be injury and cost reducing.

The polluter pays principle would appear to be as strongly based on Pigou's theory of externalities as on legal notions of justice, that tortfeasors should render damages for the injuries that they caused. Yet, the Law and Economics literature, from Coase forward, has found that such a framework might not be as rigorously valid as might at first appear. Coase's observation that either side of an injury could efficiently avoid that result and Calabresi's maxim to search for the 'least cost avoider' have made implementation of the polluter pays principle both less obvious and less compelling. Another concern raised was that the polluter pay principle in effect is a call for strict liability, which can be shown to be less effective than a rule of negligence for certain environmental scenarios. Thus again, while the Law and Economics literature supports aspects of the polluter pays principle, it also finds the principle more complex and non-linear than might have been hoped for by policymakers.

Human rights, particularly rights of humans to certain standards of environmental services or qualities, have grown in popularity and have found home in many constitutions and legal conventions. As the ECHR has said, 'in today's society the protection of the environment is an increasingly important consideration'. In essence, the allocation of human cum environmental rights is at its core an act of Coasean re-allocation, to provide one group with ex ante rights to reduce the transaction costs to achieve an efficient outcome for all parties.

Perhaps hidden within the concept of integration is the economic concept of reducing transactions cost. Integration enables various externalities, impacting diverse aspects of ecological and environmental wellness, to be brought together in a unified solution and strives to prevent individualised rules from interfering in each other's environmental goals. Integration, both forms of it, presents a legal form of preventive principle, in that if legal rules can be coordinated to prevent an environmental injury, then they should be so coordinated.

Overall, the Law and Economics literature has been in broad alignment with many of the key principles of general environmental law; however, economic analyses of those principles add useful complexity to the implementation of those principles.

# 6

# Pricing Environmental Harm

## 6.1 INTRODUCTION

From the discussion in Chapter 2, it follows that in a setting of prohibitive transaction costs and in the absence of a legal rule, there will not be an internalisation of the externalised costs of pollution. Some kind of policy instrument is necessary to effectuate this process of cost internalisation.

Before addressing the variety of legal instruments that can be used to control environmental pollution, the first question to be answered is what this internalisation means in practice. To what level should the potentially polluting company take into account the pollution? In other words: what kind of measures should be taken to avoid environmental injuries and should all injuries be avoided at all costs?

A related question is how a 'price' can be put on environmental pollution. Indeed, if one wishes to measure the benefits of investments in costly precautionary measures then one must have a counterbalancing idea of the measurement of environmental damages.

In this chapter, we will first sketch some basic principles of cost–benefit analysis, as applied to environmental policy (Section 6.2). This will also include a discussion of economic methods to assess environmental damage. It will equally be examined in what way these principles of cost–benefit analysis can also be found in environmental law.

Then we will examine how cost–benefit analysis is applied in environmental policy (Section 6.3) and address economic methods to evaluate environmental damage (Section 6.4). Section 6.5 summarises and concludes.[1]

[1] See the various meanings of these standards in Section 4.1.

## 6.2 IMPORTANCE OF COST–BENEFIT ANALYSIS FOR ENVIRONMENTAL POLICY: GENERAL

### 6.2.1 *Importance for Environmental Policy*

This question, how the optimal level of pollution should be determined, has been addressed from different angles by economists. Hereunder, we explore the historical pathway of how the method of cost–benefit analysis became a central tool of environmental economic analysis.[2] Cost–benefit analysis can be defined simply: '[m]odern regulatory cost–benefit analysis is a systemized method of comparing the expected advantages and disadvantages of proposed policies'.[3] But how did this method come to focus so centrally in environmental law?

The historical starting point is usually the work of Pigou, who advocated that cost externalities caused by a damaging activity could be corrected by a public authority imposing a tax against that activity, by setting that tax rate equal to the marginal social damage caused by each instance of the damaging activity.[4]

In this Pigouvian tradition, Baumol and Oates proposed the use of standards and prices for environmental protection.[5] They proposed a predetermined set of standards for environmental quality and advise the imposition of unit taxes to achieve these standards. This pricing and standards technique enables policymakers an effective method to implement a Pigouvian tax.[6] This Baumol–Oates approach has, since the 1970s, been the starting point for environmental economic analysis.

This approach, however, provides only a partial answer. As we shall show in the remainder of this book, taxing is just one of the possible instruments which can be used to reach the desired environmental quality.

The question remains: how could the 'optimal environmental quality' be determined, taking into account a possible conflict with values other than environmental quality. At a more practical level, the question arises how a choice could be made; e.g. between different abatement techniques that can be used to reach this optimal environmental quality?

2 We recognise that not all readers will be able to agree that the environment and its protection can be modelled in via cost–benefit analysis, but we do hope to illuminate the strengths, weaknesses, and best approaches to handling requirements for, or presentations of, cost–benefit analyses. We take note of the many modes of jurisprudential resistance to the concept of including cost–benefit analysis within broader environmental law; see Hsu (2014), inter alia, for recent coverage of the diversity of voices in that regard.

3 Rowell (2014, at 1218).

4 See further on environmental taxation in Section 7.3.

5 Baumol and Oates (1971, at 42–54).

6 There are two basic steps. First a standard of environmental quality will have to be determined. This refers to the use of ambient quality standards which determine the quality to be achieved of a certain environmental component; see Section 4.2.1. Second, the optimal tax to reach this environmental quality will have to be determined.

These questions are traditionally answered in environmental economics using cost–benefit analysis. Cost–benefit analysis is often used in environmental policy to balance an aspect of environmental quality against other policy interests in order to determine the optimal environmental quality of a certain environmental component. Or cost–benefit analysis might be used after the optimal quality standard has been set and the choice will have to be made between a variety of different processes or abatement techniques which can be used to reach this environmental quality.

Cost–benefit analysis has a long tradition in environmental economics and its models and literature brought their insights to Law and Economics researchers. We can therefore refer to the general literature applying cost–benefit analysis in environmental policy and provide a brief summary of the main principles of cost–benefit analysis, mainly for those who might be unaware of this literature.[7]

Oates pointed out that a cost–benefit study involves four essential steps:[8]

- The first is simply an enumeration or listing of the various forms of benefit and costs inherent in the examined activity.[9]
- The second step is to assign actual monetary values to the various forms of benefits and costs.
- The third step involves the selection of a rate of discount for the evaluation of benefits and costs that are expected to accrue in future years.
- Finally, the present discounted sum of the entire expected future stream of benefits and costs will be calculated.

If that sum is positive, then the analysis suggests undertaking that activity will increase welfare, and a negative sum suggests a decrease in welfare if undertaken:

> [I]f society is to make the most of its scarce resources, it should compare what it receives from pollution control and environmental protection activities with what it gives up by taking resources from other users. It should measure the values of what it gains (the benefits) and what it loses (the costs) in terms of the preferences of those who experience these gains and losses.[10]

7 See Mishan (1974) generally on cost–benefit analysis, Ackerman et al. (1974) on environmental economics, and Oates (1976, at 864–891) for the review of this book; see also Abelson (1979), Cocker and Richards (1992), Field (1994), and Tolley, Graves, and Blonquist (1981). As for the complicated cost–benefit analysis issues arising in climate change analysis, inter alia, see Cole (2008) for a survey of those issues emerging in studies of multi-generational cost–benefit analyses.

8 Oates (1976).

9 Hsu points out that many scholars who resist the application of cost–benefit analysis will have trouble with the presentation of scientific certainty as needed for the implementation of cost–benefit analysis, and he refers to the development of a postmodernist model of science, building on Kuhn's paradigmatic model of science, as the root of that discontent with cost–benefit analysis reliance on scientific models of environmental impairment (Hsu 2014, at 67).

10 See Freeman (1997, at 187–207).

In addition to the attention of environmental economists for cost–benefit analysis we should also point out that in public finance since the 1950s, public policies have been advocated to control externalities on a 'marginal costs equal marginal benefits' basis.[11]

Practically speaking, this weighing of marginal costs and benefits will mean that the marginal costs of further pollution abatement will be compared with the benefits from a further reduction in environmental damage. If a choice has to be made between various environmental techniques (either production processes or abatement techniques) which are all available at different costs and which can all lead to different levels of reduction of damage, first environmental engineering will have to be applied to provide information on these various production technologies and abatement techniques. If the marginal costs of environmental harm reduction efforts were to be available, and if the reductions in environmental harm could be measured, then all of these different techniques could be compared by their ratios of marginal benefits and marginal costs, and thus the most efficient environmental technique could be selected from those options.[12]

Investing in expensive cleaning technology that would not additionally reduce environmental damage would be inefficient since scarce resources would be wasted. A balancing process weighing marginal costs and marginal benefits can be used both to determine an optimal environmental quality, but also to make a choice concerning the optimal way to reduce environmental harm.[13]

### 6.2.2 *Limits of Cost–Benefit Analysis*

This brief sketch of the importance of cost–benefit analysis for environmental policy cannot provide for an in-depth discussion of economic theory on this particular point. It seems important to remember that generally economists agree that environmental policy should be based on some weighing of costs and benefits.

It is, by the same token, also important to stress that although these principles may be accepted, there is also considerable critique on the use of cost–benefit analysis with respect to environmental problems. One weakness is that a cost–benefit test does not indicate to whom the benefits accrue and who bears the costs.[14] In other

[11] See for this literature on policy analysis e.g. Friedmann (1984), Stokey and Zeckhauser (1978), and for an overview see Rose-Ackerman (1992b, at 14–19).

[12] In the legal system, uncertainty concerning possible hazardous environmental consequences of certain industrial activities are also taken into account in the so-called precautionary principle. See in that respect the discussion in Section 5.5.

[13] The fact that one production process (e.g. a form of clean production technology) or a specific abatement technique (e.g. a certain water treatment plant) would be considered as optimal according to the marginal cost = marginal benefit test does not automatically mean that the law should prescribe this process to be followed by every firm on the market. Later we will discuss how this balancing process will be translated into a legal standard.

[14] Oates (1976, at 56).

words, it does not take into account distributional matters.[15] That said, policymakers can bolt-on requirements for distributional analysis as part of the cost–benefit model; such was encouraged in the USA by Executive Order 13,563.[16]

This raises several questions. How can the benefits of environmental policy be calculated? One question is whether the benefits will be addressed merely from an anthropocentric perspective, merely focusing on a reduction of risk to human health or from an egocentric perspective. Another question is how benefits should be measured if it concerns a reduction of a possible threat to an entire ecosystem. The question arises whether the traditional 'willingness to pay' test, which relies on market criteria, suffices to value environmental damage.

Of course, it is not possible within the scope of this brief presentation to discuss all the complexities of environmental cost–benefit analysis in detail. At this stage, however, a few additional comments should be made.

Our first comment is on the impact of risk averse parties on cost–benefit analysis methods. From the moment that risk aversion is introduced, it might well be worth spending additionally on pollution abatement to remove the disutility of risk aversion from individuals that are exposed to risk. The optimal amount of pollution abatement measures might, therefore, be higher in case of risk aversion. This explains to some extent why certain industries are required to invest in safety techniques to levels at which at first sight no additional gain in reduction of damage could be achieved. This is the case for safety investments required from petrochemical industries, but especially from the nuclear sector, the nuclear risk being very sensitive in the public opinion.

However, in many cases, such as with nuclear risk, it might be very difficult to make an accurate estimate of the probability of the loss and to foresee the expected magnitude of the damage. This uncertainty explains the high levels of safety investments that are required and which might well be worth the additional benefit in further reduction of the risk.

This brings us to our second comment, being that in many cases an accurate cost–benefit analysis is of course not possible. This is especially the case if new techniques or substances are introduced. This is not an argument, however, against the cost–benefit analysis for novel concerns, nor for banning those products from the market until better informed cost–benefit analysis can occur. For some potentially hazardous products a registration procedure will be used and for potentially hazardous technologies a licensing scheme will be applied. Although the information might be poor, the licensing/registration boards can set standards given the best

[15] Or as Rowell put it, 'cost benefit analysis is notoriously poor at managing distributional issues' (Rowell 2014, at 1219).

[16] 'Where appropriate and permitted by law, each agency may consider (and discuss qualitatively) values that are difficult or impossible to quantify, including equity, human dignity, fairness, and distributive impacts' (id., at 1229, with citation to Exec. Order No. 13,563 sec. 1(c), 3 C.F.R. 215, 216 (2012)).

available information on the potential risk, such as it appeared, e.g. through pre-testing.

There are other structural cases that make the application of cost–benefit analysis more complicated, mostly focused around the mathematical treatments of long time periods.

Rowell drew attention to the problems of applying cost–benefit analysis in 'intertemporal relationships', as they violate Coase's observation of reciprocal risk; this is due to them not functioning within the same time frame, potentially at a great temporal remove from each other, so that the actions of the first party cannot be negotiated with the second party:[17]

> Resources, information, harm, and risk can only be transferred from the present to the future. The future cannot do the reciprocal: the future can pay no money to the present; can convey no information; can collect no damages; can impose no risk.
>
> Consider in this light the classic economic insight by Ronald Coase that risks and externalities are reciprocal. Coase's insight does not apply intertemporally: risks and externalities are not reciprocal across time because time is unidirectional. The present can impose risks on the future, but the future cannot impose reciprocal risks on the present.[18] (Underscoring added.)

And for added clarity:

> [T]he future is completely dependent—physically, financially, emotionally, and literally—on the present. The future can make no credible threats, can bring no carrots to the bargaining table, can in fact only with difficulty, and through a proxy, express interests or preferences.[19]

This clearly causes problems for the usage of cost–benefit analysis when well-known events occur in the face of environmental law, such as the impact of an ancient chemical plant on future residents or the impacts of historical green gas emissions on future residents facing the results of anthropogenic climate change. The future cannot negotiate with the present or past, and the modelling of time in cost–benefit analyses of these types of intertemporal events requires strong assumptions on how to model intertemporal equity effectively for the needs of policy deliberation.

Another time-based problem is the issue of uncertainty about the timing of the injury, as many risks can lay dormant for very long time periods without specifically foreseeable moments of injury. For example, as discussed above, nuclear waste may lay in storage for millennia before an injury occurs, so should the model reflect a thousand years, one hundred thousand years, or a million years? The examination by the Environmental Protection Agency (EPA) of the Yucca Mountain nuclear storage site assumed a reference of ten thousand years, whereas the National

[17] Rowell (2014, at 1217).
[18] Id., at 1225.
[19] Id., at 1227.

Academy of Science recommended modelling up to one million years; clearly these alternatives, being two magnitudes of time different, could result in substantially different cost–benefit analysis results.[20]

Huber provides some remedies; first, he observes that common law's evolution towards fee simple reduces the problem of temporal spillovers.[21] On the other hand, if the value of the land is reduced to below zero, as certain forms of environmental degradation can achieve, then internalisation of the temporal damages can only be remedied if the present owner cum environmental-waster undertakes the effort to restore and remediate; abandonment would force the externality onto future holders of title.[22] While that abandonment of land is difficult to achieve in real property law, corporate insolvency performs a symmetrical task, enabling the creation of temporal externalities.[23] He explores, not to conclusion, the potential to leverage bonding to better ensure that corporations do not create such temporal spillovers.[24]

As a result of the scholarship on these temporal matters, Revesz, Livermore, and Rowell have recommended that cost–benefit analysis be reserved for those conditions wherein the parties are sufficiently co-temporary to enable Coase-type negotiations of risk.[25]

## 6.3 COST–BENEFIT ANALYSIS IN ENVIRONMENTAL LAW AND POLICY

One of the central questions when addressing the instruments to control environmental policy is whether these chosen instruments can give incentives to adopt an environmental policy (at government and at the individual firm level) that corresponds as much as possible with these principles of weighing marginal costs versus marginal benefits.[26]

Cost–benefit analysis plays a role in legal practice in the sense that most legal cultures continue to retain rules admitting the existence of some level of pollution, that those legal cultures have not required environmental pollution to be brought to a zero-level of emissions no matter what that might cost; thus, judges are left

20 Id., at 1232–1233.
21 Huber (2017, at 45).
22 Id., at 47.
23 Id., at 47–48. He refers to Superfund-type sites as instances of these corporate created temporal externalities, wherein many of the responsible firms are simply long non-existent or presently insolvent.
24 Id., at 55.
25 Rowell (2014, at 1235), citing to Revesz and Livermore (2008).
26 Hsu writes that some discomfort for some environmental lawyers with cost–benefit analyses and other encroachments into environmental law from economics may potentially arise from motives of self-preservation, that such economic toolkits might reduce the role of lawyers in environmentalism generally ( Hsu 2014, at 31–32).

addressing this balancing question, examining the costs and injuries of pollution against the benefits of the activities giving rise to that pollution.[27]

### 6.3.1 *Cost–Benefit Analysis at the European Level*

Cost–benefit analysis has become a popular and broadly used tool for policy analysis across many policy issues and at many levels of governance; this is especially true for environmental policy. Sunstein has paid considerable attention to the influence of cost–benefit analysis in the US 'regulatory state'.[28] As far as Europe is concerned, Ogus has argued that policymakers generally, but also with respect to environmental policy, should take into account cost–benefit analysis in policy design.[29]

The importance of cost–benefit analysis for environmental law and policy is stressed at a variety of instances and with respect to different levels of government. As far as the European level is concerned, we should more specifically point at article 191, al. 3 (formerly article 174, al. 3) of the TFEU,[30] which provides that:

> in preparing its policy on the environment, the Union shall take account of:
> - available scientific and technical data;
> - environmental conditions in the various regions of the Community;
> - the potential benefits and costs of action or lack of action;
> - the economic and social development of the Union as a whole, and the balanced development of its regions.

Here the Commission is explicitly given the duty to take into account potential benefits and costs of action in preparing European environmental policy.

Ogus addressed a variety of European directives aiming for minimum harmonised standards for 'essential requirements'. He investigated the Use of Work Equipment Directive 1989,[31] the Display Screen Equipment Directive 1990,[32] and the Fresh Meat Directive 1991,[33] and although these are only slightly related to environmental policy, his analysis also has importance for European environmental policy. He argues that in the drafting of these directives scientific evidence was only used to identify the hazards, but that in no case a serious effort at risk assessment was made estimating the likelihood of the hazards occurring. In addition he argues that arguments relating to the cost implications for implementing these directives carried

27 Epstein notes that the case history of the liability rule for nuisance, a foundational element of environment law in common law, inherently evidences that 'the nuisance law has always tolerated low-level background interferences under a live and let live principle, which recognizes the simple fact that moving to a pollution free environment is too costly' (Epstein 2016, at 146).

28 Sunstein and Pildes (1995, at 3–129).

29 Ogus (1995, at 325–338).

30 Consolidated version published in the *Official Journal* C326/1 of 26 October 2012.

31 Directive 89/655, *Official Journal*, 1989 L393/13.

32 Directive 90/270, *Official Journal*, 1990 L156/14.

33 Directive 91/497, *Official Journal*, 1991 L268/69.

little weight in working groups of the Council of Ministers.[34] He argues that these examples are symptomatic of a general quality problem relating to European regulation which is, according to him, to a large extent caused by the fact that the institutional structure of the EU enables special interest groups to exert a significantly greater influence on law making than others.[35]

Ogus proposes to improve the quality of European regulation by introducing a mandatory economic appraisal of all legislative proposals at the European level. Taking the example of US regulatory agencies which had to submit comprehensive cost–benefit analysis of legislative proposals, Ogus proposes to amend the existing *Fiche d'impact*, in which the European Commission currently signals whether a proposal may have a significant impact on business, to include a more thorough US-style cost–benefit analysis. According to Ogus the Commission should, prior to forwarding legislative proposals, address the question, inter alia, of whether there is an acceptable cost–benefit relation for public action and indicate the expected impact on employment, competitiveness, costs, and innovation.[36] This increased and explicit significance of cost–benefit analysis at the European level would be a powerful device to counteract the strategic behaviour of special interest groups.[37]

This shows that although there is explicit mention of the need for cost–benefit analysis in some European documents, such as article 191, al. 3 of the TFEU, Ogus powerfully demonstrates that there was still much left to be desired and a lot of room for an increasing use of cost–benefit analysis, which might lead to a general increase of the quality of European regulation, including at the environmental level.

### 6.3.2 *Economic Analysis of Soil Clean-Up*

One of the most debated issues in environmental law nowadays is probably the area of soil clean-up.[38] An interesting question related to the use of cost–benefit analysis is on what kind of criteria the decision to clean up a polluted soil should be based.

In most European countries the decision to clean up (with the subsequent question of liability to pay for clean-up costs) is made by administrative authorities. In some countries, such as the Netherlands, these clean-up sites were already identified in the late-1970s, and extensive cleaning operations have already taken place or are still in the course of execution. In other countries, such as Belgium,

34 Ogus (1995, at 331).

35 The influence of industrial lobby will be further discussed in Chapter 9 which deals with regulation.

36 This proposal is equally supported by the Molitor Report, giving the views of a group of independent experts appointed by the Commission (Report of the Group of Independent Experts on Legislative and Administrative Simplification, 1995).

37 Ogus (1995, at 338).

38 This brings about an interesting set of legal questions, some of which will also be discussed in this book, e.g. the question of negligence or strict liability (Section 8.2), retroactive liability (Section 8.7) and causal uncertainty (Section 11.6).

polluted sites have only been discovered more recently and important decisions concerning clean-up still have to be made.

From an economic point of view, one can understand that it would be important to base a clean-up decision on the already mentioned balancing of marginal costs and marginal benefits. The various costs of different modes of a clean-up operation will in most cases be known. The benefits on the other hand associated with these different clean-up techniques are not always that easily assessed. One difficulty in the calculation of the benefits is whether the destination of the soil can be taken into account when fixing criteria for clean-up. Indeed, the question whether a site should be cleaned up and to what level may well depend upon the future destination of that site. If for instance the future destination is the construction of a factory and health risks are totally excluded, one may not insist on a highly costly clean-up of that particular polluted soil. A total clean-up might well be inefficient, given this future destination.

If, on the other hand, that particular site were to be re-used for vegetable growing in the near future, the potential health damage caused by industrial chemicals might well outweigh the marginal costs of a clean-up action.[39] Therefore, from an economic point of view it seems to make sense to take into account the future destination of a particular soil when deciding upon a possible clean-up.

In that respect it would be interesting to examine on what kind of criteria the administrative authorities base their decision to clean up. Could an administrative authority decide that a particular polluted site can only be used for certain industrial goals in the future and not for vegetable growing anymore? A related question is whether an administrative authority could require a total clean-up of any given patch of land merely for ecological reasons, notwithstanding the future destination of the particular soil.

The reason why it seems efficient to take into account the future destination is that there is a relationship between the possible magnitude of the harm and the level of efficient care discussed above. The higher the potential damage, the more care will be required. Precisely this magnitude of the damage may well depend upon the future use of the soil. Therefore, it seems useful to weigh the costs of clean-up on the one hand against the benefits in reducing possible harm on the other hand, the latter also depending upon the future destination of a site.

Interestingly enough, this idea now seems to be accepted as well in legislation concerning soil clean-up. For instance, in the Netherlands the classic 'multifunctional criterion' is now relaxed, and also in Flanders a new Soil Clean-Up Decree provides for a ground of excuse for the owner of a polluted soil who is in good faith, i.e. who was not aware of the fact that the particular soil was polluted.[40]

39 An economist would of course also argue that an obvious alternative would be not to use that particular site for vegetable growing in the future any more.

40 According to article 31 §2 of the Soil Clean-Up Decree of 22 February 1995, there is no duty to clean up in case of historic pollution if the user of the soil was in good faith (Deketelaere 1995, at 135–142).

## 6.4 ECONOMIC METHODS TO EVALUATE ENVIRONMENTAL DAMAGE

An important question relating to the 'pricing' of environmental pollution is how environmental damage should be assessed. This is of importance also for cost–benefit analysis, since the perceived benefits of protective measures will also depend upon the assessment of environmental damage.

This brings us to an important topic related to the pricing of environmental pollution. The valuation of environmental damage is important for the just mentioned cost–benefit analysis, but also when the compensation due in a tort case has to be established. Economists have established a variety of techniques for valuing environmental damage.

One method is the so-called hedonic price technique: 'Hedonic damages are intended to compensate victims for the loss of enjoyment of life's pleasures.'[41] This can be done after the injury, or by using certain survey techniques, before the injury. This is based on the analysis of market data from transactions in private goods and services which are related to the characteristics of the public good under consideration. In other words, in the hedonic price technique the value of changes to the natural environment are analysed by the perceived economic changes these changes have caused in affiliated markets of goods impacted by the environmental event. There are basically three models of 'willingness to pay' within this technique: (i) the consumer's willingness to buy safety or environmental protection, (ii) the willingness to assume additional risk for a certain pre-payment, and (iii) cost–benefit analysis as required under regulations for governmental purposes.[42]

A modeller might assume that housing values would reflect the variation in the quality of surrounding environmental goods. House prices can be a function of natural surroundings such as the presence of parks and forests. On that basis an evaluation of environmental improvement could be undertaken based on an estimation of the house price function. This approach has, for example, been applied by Hoch and Drake,[43] Harrison and Rubinfeld,[44] and Nelson,[45] and for a critical analysis see Maler.[46]

An alternative method is to ask individuals to state their willingness to pay for environmental improvement directly, using a survey questionnaire. This is referred to as contingent valuation and is based on a hypothetical allocation procedure for the particular public good. This more direct approach is based on, for example,

41 Smith and Steenburg (2015, at 70).
42 Id., at 73–74.
43 Hoch and Drake (1974, at 268–295).
44 Harrison and Rubinfeld (1978, at 81–102).
45 Nelson (1978).
46 Maler (1977, at 355–369).

Davis,[47] Bradford,[48] and Bohm,[49] and for a comparison of both methods of analysis see Pommerehne.[50] There is a lot of discussion of contingent valuation in the USA since it is being used under some environmental laws.[51]

Another option is the use of travel cost studies to estimate environmental benefits. Travel cost studies have been used to measure the benefits of recreational options.[52]

Given the debates over how to analyse environmental problems with uncertain scientific frameworks, or those that last over many generations, there have been calls for cost–benefit analysis models to be published with greater transparency, especially with regards to sensitivity analyses that reflect how the model forecast changes with alternate assumptions as input.[53] This might also be important when analysts have trouble concurring on correct temporal elasticities or uncertain estimates of economic growth, which all feed into the time value discounting of many cost–benefit analysis models.[54] Also, when extremely hazardous results are possible but with unreliable or uncertain probability curves, then perhaps 'safe minimum standards' could be modelled alongside more traditional implementations of cost–benefit analysis to better provide analysis of these odd fat-tail models.[55]

## 6.5 SUMMARY AND CONCLUSION

While Goethe may have taken umbrage at pricing the world and its majestic environments, the literature of Law and Economics encourages us to recognise that this can be both a useful operation and a revealing operation.[56] And to price an aspect of environmental services need not mean a direct 'price to acquire rights to injure' perspective, but rather can reflect the damages imposed on the community from the event of the injury, of the opportunity costs of the events around the environmental injury. Further, there can be a calculation of the costs necessary to completely avoid the events enabling the injury; at what cost can the commercial activity be undertaken in a manner that enables an environment to remain clear of injury.

47 Davis (1963, at 239–249).
48 Bradford (1970, at 775–791).
49 Bohm (1971, at 55–66).
50 Pommerehne (1988, at 363–400).
51 See Hausman (1993) for a critical analysis.
52 Krutilla (1967, at 777–786).
53 Cole (2008, at 70 and 81).
54 Id., at 79.
55 Id.
56 We note the more technical arguments against viewing Nature through the lens of economics, such as those raised by Heinzerling, that 'Even when the methods are applied in good faith by neutral or environmentally inclined investigators, we will see that the results tilt strongly toward endorsement of business as usual, and rejection of health and environmental protection' (Hsu 2014, at 45, quoting from Ackerman and Heinzerling [2000, at 36]).

The Baumol–Oates approach, to determine a set of environmental quality standards to facilitate the imposition of marginal cost-correcting unit taxes, enables a functional start at implementing a Pigouvian tax system. But no environmental system is simple enough to fit on a menu, so the function of an approach will necessarily be limited to an incomplete set of externalities.

Under most forms of cost–benefit analysis, the use of marginal costs for environmental losses requires an understanding of the marginal benefits of the activity that caused those injuries, if they are to be aligned for optimal community welfare. However, those costs and benefits may accrue to many diverse stakeholders, present and future, and it may be quite difficult to complete the set of information required to fully implement marginal analysis.

We found that indeed the concepts of placing metrics, particularly economic metrics, on environmental losses is fraught with difficulties. Nevertheless, the very exercise of contemplating through the potential losses and benefits we find likely to be beneficial in the design of environmental standards and regulations. In some sense, this can be seen as another aspect of the precautionary principle, to consider taking action even when the data is not fully established of the causal risk. Examination of the potential pricing of environmental impacts both heightens identification of risks and may also serve to evaluate which paths of actions are most in alignment with the established environmental standards and policy goals.

In practical terms, both the EU and the USA have enacted rules requiring various forms of impact assessments, usually inclusive of the economic measurements discussed above. And econometricians have responded by developing tools, such as hedonic measurements and contingent valuation systems.

In some manner, rational efforts will remain necessary to identify environmental risks, to draft effective standards and rules in response, and to enable meaningful compliance and enforcement that result in those environmental goals being achieved. To make use of mathematical notions, to make use of data, to be able to compare the various alternative pathways for their comparative impacts on communities and ecologies, is but the same. Yet, it is also as sure that due to complexity and the transactional costs of accessing the necessary information, these efforts will remain, for the most part, incomplete. Nevertheless, the literature strongly supports making these efforts; experience from practical implementation has found them to be of benefit, both in the ex ante design of rules and in the ex post review of the rules.

Thus, a case is made that reasonable efforts to determine the prices and costs of environmental impacts can yield useful information that can be instrumental in the design and operation of environmental standards and rules, especially if those models of cost–benefit analysis can be published with high standards of transparency.[57]

[57] Cole (2008, at 80).

# 7

# Market-Based Instruments

## 7.1 INTRODUCTION

For several decades, environmental laws have expanded beyond a CAC-type of regulation to include more diverse regulatory approaches. Economists increasingly pointed at several disadvantages of imposing pollution standards via government regulation.[1] Thus, they have in recent years worked with Pigou's message of the 1920s that taxation could be used to internalise externalities.[2] Already in Chapter 2, we indicated the importance of market-based instruments.[3]

Since the 1960s, Dales pointed out that social welfare could be increased by trading in pollution rights.[4] The literature calls these economic or market-based instruments. Such instruments are advanced for a number of years by policy analysts as a reaction to CAC regulation. Using market-forces and information strategies instead of relying on state enforcement of public regulation sounds modern and flexible; no surprise then that the Law & Economics literature has found itself a popular toolset for politicians looking to solve environmental challenges in times of fiscal austerity.[5]

However, terminology can be misleading.

One could argue that all legal and policy instruments can be considered as 'economic' as long as they give appropriate incentives to polluters for an efficient reduction of the externality caused by the pollution. Also, liability rules are 'economic' in the sense that liability gives incentives to polluters to prevent environmental harm. Nevertheless, liability rules are traditionally not included in 'economic' instruments. With this concept one usually refers to instruments

1 Freeman and Kolstad (2007) and Sterner (1999).
2 This topic was introduced in Section 2.3.
3 See Section 2.4.4.
4 Woerdman, Arcuri, and Clò (2008b, 567), citing to Dales (1968).
5 See Stewart (2007, at 151–152).

whereby only the environmental targets are defined, but whereby it is largely left to the polluters to find the optimal instruments to reach the particular targets. Thus, integral parts of economic instruments are incentive driven-ness and flexibility.

Section 7.2 first summarises the limits of CAC mechanisms. Next, the essential role of environmental information in markets is stressed, no matter which type of instruments is employed (Section 7.3). Then we will discuss the principles behind environmental permit trading (Section 7.4), payments for ecosystem services (Section 7.5), and environmental taxation (Section 7.6). Economic instruments have different 'elasticities' and distributional effects on environmental welfare, which we will address in Section 7.7. Section 7.8 summarises and concludes.

## 7.2 ROLE OF ENVIRONMENTAL INFORMATION IN THE MARKETS

We began with a focus on information itself and of its role in the marketplace.

Fundamentally, both legal theory and economics theory assume that the actors involved are decision makers. In law, a decision maker might become culpable or liable for both their manner of decision making and the results of their decisions. In economics, the decision maker is viewed as an optimiser, managing their resources to achieve their preferred goals; with efficiency as a meta-goal to enable the achievement of many goals as possible given their constrained budget of resources. But for each vision of decision makers, information is a critical ingredient. For lawyers, to act contrary to what you know might be prudent, based on the available information, could lead to recklessness; knowledge with regards to criminal acts could lead to issues of scienter and imply differing levels of criminality. For economic actors, missing information could lead to either inefficient or inaccurate decisions, resulting in wasted resources and missed opportunities and goals.

Actors in environmental settings cannot safely undertake their activities unless they have a sufficiently complete set of information from environmental sciences, on local ecologies, of the potential reactions and consequences of the activity to be undertaken, and a comprehensive set of stakeholders both present and future. Shy of those sufficiency conditions, decisions on how to best undertake that activity without causation of injuries is likely to be at best wasting of the actor's resources and worst result in complicated sets of injuries, as their decision-making process will be flawed.

The most difficult information to obtain, for environmental law issues, is the information related to the ex post consequences of the environmental impact and of the complete collection of resultant injuries. The tortfeasor may be aware of some of the impacts caused by their behaviours, but both incomplete monitoring and potentially incomplete scientific understanding of the event could lead to many injuries being unknown to the tortfeasor and thus not included their decision-making process about the activity. Similarly, victims may have incomplete or no knowledge about the original activity and derivatively might not be tracking potential impact from that event; thus, victims are quite likely to possess poor information about the risks they are facing and thus would not be able to include those sets of information in their own decision-making processes, which might otherwise include preventing that activity or taking their safety precautions.

As we will detail more in Chapter 8, the role of information, particularly missing or inaccurate information, can materially frustrate the design of legal rules to motivate proper behaviours from tortfeasors or to provide guidance to victims. Indeed, legal rules themselves generate information. Rules of civil liability transform the costs of damages, as rendered from a causal finding of tortious injury, into ex ante information of expected, 'foreseeable', costs of causing accidents. Legal rules found in public regulations also create standards of expected behaviour and ex ante determined consequences for violations of those standards. Again, from both the economics perspective and from the legal perspective, these types of information generated from legal rules are to be included in decision making.

Thus, the role of information, from the various sciences, from ecological setting-in-place of the activity under consideration, to data gleaned from legal rules, all of these forms of environmental information are critical to creating the optimal decision-making opportunities to evaluate the consequences, both beneficial and adverse, from actually undertaking that activity.

The importance of environmental information as a prerequisite for effective decision making cannot be overstated, especially in light of so-called market-based instruments that greatly depend upon the reasonableness of decision makers in the market to carefully balance a multitude of issues and costs to enable the market to perform its role and thus to enable additional tools to protect the environment.

## 7.3 REGULATION BY COMMAND AND CONTROL

Before looking at environmental taxes and emission trading, this section summarises the criticisms on the CAC approach.

First, traditional CAC systems focused on permits and licensing have been criticised since the 1970s for controlling specific emissions while disregarding the holistic effect of the emissions on environmental quality, which was deteriorating.[6] A result of that misguided micro-focus on a subset of environmental impacts was that, notwithstanding severe emission controls, total environmental quality was seriously reduced.

We already mentioned that one of the features of market-based instruments is that they rather define targets to be reached instead of the methods how to reach those particular targets. It is in that sense no surprise that in the US context emission trading developed within the context of the CAA. The CAA had indeed defined particular target standards, which

6 See also Section 4.2.

were referred to as National Ambient Air Quality Standards (NAAQS).[7] Within market-based instruments, the focus is therefore on target or environmental quality standards, rather than on controlling emissions. This criticism does not invalidate per se a CAC approach, since this instrument could also be used within a system that would largely focus on target standards. However, there are several other criticisms that can be formulated.[8]

Second, use of CAC requires optimal standards and optimal enforcement measures entailing high information and enforcement costs.[9] If enforcement is suboptimal, then profits can be earned by increasing the risky activities or by reducing efforts of prevention and precaution, enabling more pollution.[10] Enforcement and information costs can be reduced by relying on industry information.[11]

Third, compliance with regulatory standards (e.g. of a permit) does not provide continuous incentives to reduce pollution or to invest in environmentally friendly technology.[12]

Fourth, the CAC cannot ensure equalisation of marginal pollution costs among different polluters and thus the government winds up distorting the market and pricing winners and losers. Because administrative agencies face prohibitively high information and regulatory costs, they will not normally be able to determine the efficient emission for each polluter and may demand comparable reductions by polluters. This creates inefficiencies and reduces social welfare losses if the possibilities for pollution abatement differ.[13] Polluters that possess an ability to abate the pollution above the set regulatory standard would not have any incentives to do so, financial or otherwise.

Fifth, polluters bear the costs of complying with regulatory standards but may not be required to pay for residual damages associated with the pollution created while in compliance with the standard.

This list of concerns shows that there are considerable disadvantages in the traditional CAC approach: regulatory standards are often too general, inflexible, and poorly differentiated.

7 Hahn and Hester (1989).
8 Faure and Ubachs (2003).
9 Ranchordás (2015, at 203), especially with regards to the knowledge asymmetry facing regulators of innovative technologies and services.
10 See Tietenberg (2000).
11 However, the private interest theory of regulation suggests that industry can benefit from distorting information. On which more in Section 9.3. See also Grossman, Clearley, and Cole (2006, at 9), with reference to relying on data created and collected by the insurance industry.
12 Ranchordás (2015, at 202).
13 Rosen (1999).

In support of more frequent horizontal modes of enforcement within the EU, Van Zeben offered many reasons why traditional modes of CAC might be less robust than optimally sought:

> In cases of extremely detailed and overly prescriptive standards, dynamic efficiency may suffer and reduce incentives for technical innovation or other cost-effective responses. This may lead to a situation where the regulated parties do only that which is absolutely necessary to comply with the set standards. Because of the high level of expertise needed to set these standards, the system is also sensitive to the problem of regulatory capture, where regulators (and thus regulation) are manipulated through information dissymmetry to pursue the regulated enterprises' interests rather than the public interest. Moreover, C&C regulation based on technological conformity can be very burdensome for private parties to implement, which can lead to over-enforcement; stringent enforcement of legislation may then lead to a general decrease in innovation and production. Paradoxically, enforcement may often be difficult and costly, which, depending on the prioritization of time and funds, can lead to under-regulation. In contrast, the lack of incentives due to lack of dynamic efficiency will increase the risk of non-compliance. Additional challenges include the increasing complexity of regulatory networks and the growing need to differentiate and prioritize between certain violators, all of which make maintaining the level of enforcement needed to deter environmental pollution difficult.[sic][14]

Steinzor found four key reasons that CAC public regulations failed to ensure environmental policies were attained: (i) fiscal budget cuts to limit the capacity of the regulatory authority, (ii) political attacks in Congress and elsewhere have demoralised public servants working on environmental regulation and enforcement, (iii) statutes and regulations have stagnated without necessary updates to current challenges, and (iv) a congelation of the rule-making process at the administrative level has prevented new rules from being developed.[15]

An optimal environmental policy needs adaptable instruments which on the one hand provide more flexibility (taking into account the individual possibilities of optimal pollution abatement of each polluter) and on the other hand provide optimal incentives towards environmental technological innovation (and not merely compliance with a regulatory standard).[16]

After having addressed the disadvantages of the traditional CAC approach, we thus better understand why environmental policy analysts are increasingly interested in the so-called economic instruments. An impressive amount of literature has dealt

[14] Van Zeben (2010, at 246–247).

[15] Steinzor (2016, at 213). Her policy review was in line with determining if additional criminal law sanctions should be brought to bear against environmental malfeasants, but the analysis equally holds as to why regulation wasn't effective in the base case.

[16] Some studies have found that CAC can be as effective as market-based mechanisms when the abatement costs of those pollutants are comparatively low and when monitoring costs, for both CAC or market-based mechanisms, are high. See Cole and Grossman (2018, at 937).

with the various aspects of comparing the traditional CAC approach via regulation with more incentive-based mechanisms, referred to as economic or market-based instruments.

Yet, one lesson from this literature review is that it is complicated to compare general public regulation with market-based instruments because the superiority of one toolset or another is very much dependent upon the specific context, type of environmental injury, institutional design, or legal culture within which the set is applied.

Research shows that a traditional regulatory approach can lead to significant reductions, for example of waste water emissions, and encourage the implementation of less polluting production techniques in the long run.[17] As long as CAC approaches are designed with at least one eye on cost-saving, incentive-based systems are not necessarily superior to CAC.[18]

Therefore, one has to be careful with too sharply distinguishing the two approaches to public regulation. After all, CAC approaches also include a wide variety of measures, some of which are quite crude, but others also producing results as efficient as economic incentives.[19]

A few examples of empirically examined success stories of market-based instruments, at least as far as reducing emissions is concerned will be provided based on empirical literature. That does, however, not necessarily imply that similar results could not have been reached with a regulatory approach.[20]

## 7.4 ENVIRONMENTAL PERMIT TRADING

### 7.4.1 *Basic Principles*

If a state chooses to limit the overall amount of emission for a given month or year, it could do this in one of two ways. First, it determines emission limits per actor and issues permits to the specific actor. However, fine-tuned regulation, such as traditional permit schemes, asks for an expensive and burdensome bureaucratic work. This could be overcome by the increasingly popular marketable permits as introduced by Dales,[21] such as the National Sulfur Dioxide Trading Program and Regional $NO_x$ Trading Programs.[22] Thus, the second approach is to determine a national emissions target, to render an initial allotment of emission permits, but to also allow a 'secondary' market for private actors to re-sort the initial allocations to

[17] See for example Stephan (1988, at 401–422).

[18] See Oates, Portney, and McGartland (1989, at 1233–1244).

[19] See Oates (1985) and Oates (1990, at 289–296).

[20] For an overview of the literature, see Ackerman and Stewart (1988, at 171–199); Stewart (1988, at 153–169; 2000, at 171–244). See the contributions in Freeman and Kolstad (2007).

[21] Dales 1968.

[22] See Barde (1995, at 218–220); Freestone and Frenkil (2009); Nash and Revesz (2001); Oates (1990, at 290–293); Stavang (2005).

better match their needs without challenging the set 'net emissions' goal of the authority.

Marketable emission permits are issued to polluters up to the amount predetermined by policymakers. The market price and willingness to pay determines which actors will pollute. Many different distribution schemes are possible. Permits can for example be auctioned or distributed for free.[23] Cole described this process, as implemented within the 1990 amendments to the Clean Air Act, as creating rights to 'own' parcels of air that can thereafter be polluted by the holder of those rights; he draws an analogy to rights to own land for the purposes of creating a landfill.[24]

Marketable emission permits have several key advantages: first, the regulator determines directly the quantity of emissions; second, contrary to the tax system they adapt to inflation; third, marketable permits may gain more acceptances because regulators are already familiar with permits. Marketable emission permits enable carbon reductions to occur at the lowest marginal costs and have been modelled as being welfare efficient.[25]

Marketable permits also have a number of disadvantages: first, initially permits are usually allocated via grandfathering (thus free of charge) according to past emissions records. It can be assumed that initial rights to use the environment are assigned to the polluters; second, there are concerns that pollution will be transferred to another region; third, volatility of permit prices causes uncertainty about future price developments and results in suboptimal investment in energy supply, particularly renewables; fourth, marketable permits are criticised because a polluter's profits can increase while pollution levels remain the same. Taxes by contrast will not only improve the level of pollution but also raise revenue for the government.

### 7.4.2 *Design Issues*

Despite its theoretical appeal to economists, emissions permit trading encounters problems regarding its legal and institutional design that are underestimated by economists.[26] For that reason substantial concerns are raised by lawyers concerning emission permit trading.[27]

From an economic perspective auctioning is the preferred allocation method; that all emissions in a period are equally regulated by permit without regard to source or operator. In practice, however, free allocation rewarding (old) polluters (grandfathering) and hindering new entries is often employed in practice. Worse, Turner, Pearce, and Bateman argue that marketable permits can be used to create

[23] For a comparison, see Weishaar (2007a).
[24] Cole (2011, at 29).
[25] Woerdman, Arcuri, and Clò (2008b, at 568).
[26] Woerdman (2004).
[27] See e.g. Winter (2009).

entry barriers if incumbents start hoarding them.[28] The relationship between interest group lobbies and the emission trading system is discussed by Svendsen.[29] Early actors as well as cleaner companies might need to buy rights from firms that have polluted more and can thereby be disadvantaged. Another substantive objection is that grandfathering runs counter to the basic meaning of the polluter pays principle.[30] Yet, alternative allocation criteria need to legally also respect the legitimate expectations of firms based on traditional permits. Indeed, research has suggested that in such cases, that grandfathering might not distort the results for future trading and thus ought not be a barrier to an efficient trading mechanism.[31]

Thus revocation, even partial revocations, of traditional permits must correspond to legal criteria, such as ensuring reasonable transition periods. Additional financial instruments could be considered to mitigate the undesirable effects of grandfathering; the setting of a maximum price on the tradable rights could be analysed.[32]

### 7.4.3 *The EU Emissions Trading Scheme*

Europe chose emission trading as the instrument to implement the Kyoto Protocol and address the challenges posed by climate change. It is therefore interesting to briefly address the European Union's Emission Trading Scheme (EU ETS).[33] The EU ETS entered into force on 1 January 2005 and covered the main sources that emit $CO_2$,[34] encompassing some 12,000 installations representing close to half of Europe's emissions of $CO_2$. As of 2012 it also began to cover aviation activities (Directive 2008/101/EC). The EU ETS is the biggest domestic emissions trading system established thus far. The first trading period ended in 2007 and the second trading period ran till the end of 2012. After the revision of the EU ETS Directive (Directive 2003/87/EC was amended by Directive 2009/29/EC only three years after the system's introduction) in the third trading period (2013–2020), auctioning is being phased in while grandfathering gradually declines. Specific provisions for industries facing international competition are provided for. Furthermore, the trading system's scope is enlarged, incorporating additional greenhouse gases and sectors.[35]

Although many different legal design issues and institutional questions have been addressed in the development of the EU ETS, it is interesting to review some issues associated with allocation and enforcement. The economic literature has stressed

28 Turner, Pearce, and Bateman (1994, at 184).
29 Svendsen (1998, at 133–144).
30 Nash (2000); Peeters (2003).
31 Woerdman, Arcuri, and Clò (2008b, at 577 and 579).
32 Victor (2001, at 102 ff).
33 For details see Peeters (2016).
34 See Dornau (2005).
35 Massai (2009).

the superiority of auctioning as allocation mechanism since it prevents over-representation of industry's emissions projections.[36] The European Commission, however, limited auctioning to 5 per cent in the first and 10 per cent in the second trading phase. In the third trading phase auctioning is increasingly gaining importance.

This large volume of free allocations (grandfathering) has given rise to a number of interesting legal and economic questions. For example, it has been examined if free allocation constitutes a form of state aid. Although the European Commission considers that free allocation is state aid, the academic literature is much more divided on the issue.[37] The reason why free allocation rather than auctioning was chosen is that a free allocation serves the interest of incumbents and thus could help to make the ETS system more acceptable for industry.

The EU ETS Directive 2003/87/EC lays down specific provisions relating to monitoring and enforcement. Member States are expected to impose a 100 Euro penalty per allowance (see article 16 of Directive 2003/87/EC as amended) that is not surrendered to cover emissions. Operators remain obliged to surrender allowances for illegal emissions. A 'market-based' instrument such as emissions trading needs adequate information on the actual emissions and enforcement measures that are taken against violators, so as to mitigate any incentive for free riding and to ensure the system's environmental effectiveness.[38] In addition, a 'naming and shaming' provision has been introduced, meaning that Member States shall ensure publication of the names of operators who are in breach of requirements to surrender sufficient allowances (article 16(2) of the directive).[39]

### 7.4.4 *Efficacy of Emission Trading Systems*

Emissions trading enables owners of pollution permits to trade with each other, buying and selling those rights to match emission and capital budget needs of each firm.[40] We discuss below the comparable performance of emission trading versus the policy efficacy of environmental taxation.

#### 7.4.4.1 The 'Living Legend' of the US SO2 Trading Programme

Whereas environmental taxes and charges on emissions were popular in Europe, emission trading methods were employed early in the USA.[41] Thus, since the 1980s

36 Baldwin (2008).
37 De Sepius (2007) and Weishaar (2007b).
38 Baldwin (2008); Peeters (2006a); and Peeters (2006b).
39 Meanwhile, the directive has been adapted. For more recent evolutions, see Peeters (2016).
40 See Section 7.1.
41 Conniff 2009. For a recent overview of the North-American greenhouse gas emission trading systems, see Endres (2011, at 114–120) and Hodas and De Armey (2016).

there has been abundant US research showing the effectiveness of trading in pollution rights. An early example might include research by Wallace Oates from 1986 concerning the well-known US emission trading system for air pollutants.[42] He reported that such trading made real headway in certain regions and that the system was successful.[43] Also Hahn and Hester claim that the trading programmes concerning the CAA have led to considerable cost savings, albeit that the cost savings may have been less than anticipated.[44] A problem is that trading may in some cases have increased emissions, more particularly where the pollution rights that were sold were previously not being fully utilised by the owner. Nevertheless, the $SO_2$ cap and trade programme has maintained its label as a 'living legend' of market effectiveness. To note, the total annual health benefits associated with the $SO_2$ emission reductions under the programme were estimated to be more than $50 million per year in 2010.[45] Keohane estimated the annual cost savings resulting from the trading programme to be $150 million.[46]

The enthusiasm concerning the trading system in the US Clean Air Act not only comes from its environmental effectiveness, but also from its cost-saving aspects, at least when referring to compliance costs for industry.[47] Ellerman also showed that the administrative costs for running the emission trading system under the CAA are significantly less compared with a traditional regulatory system.[48] Other US studies examining the trading programmes under the Clean Air Act provide a roughly similar picture.[49]

### 7.4.4.2 Effectiveness of the EU Emissions Trading Scheme

Too many studies to be mentioned here have addressed the effectiveness of the EU ETS.[50] The case of the EU ETS is an interesting one simply to show the difficulties in interpreting the results of empirical research. Europe chose with Directive 2003/87 of 13 October 2003 to give emissions rights basically for free to existing industry as a result of so-called grandfathering.[51] Again, the private interest theory of regulation can explain why emission trading with grandfathering was chosen instead of an

42 Oates (1986, at 261–265).

43 Id. See also Oates and McGartland (1985, at 222).

44 Hahn and Hester (1989, at 151).

45 See Burtraw and Palmer (2004, at 47); see also Ellerman (2007, at 50, showing that the $SO_2$ emissions trading programme caused significant reductions in emissions).

46 Keohane (2007, at 224).

47 Burtraw and Palmer (2004, at 59) (noting the 'perceived success of the $SO_2$ program in reducing compliance costs' has boosted a number of similar legislative proposals).

48 Ellerman et al. (2000, at 294–296); Ellerman (2004, at 92); and Endres (2011, at 270–282).

49 See for example Nash and Revesz (2002, at 333, 335, discussing the design of emissions trading programs more generally) and Tietenberg and Johnston (2004, at 29–30).

50 See for example the contributions in Douma, Massai, and Montini (2007).

51 Directive 2003/87, establishing a scheme for greenhouse gas emission allowance trading within the Community and Amending Council Directive 96/61/EC 2002, *Official Journal* L275, 32, 36 International Emissions Trading Association, High Level Group on the Emissions Trading

environmental tax.[52] This should not come as a surprise, since grandfathering of course serves the interests of industry better than costly taxation measures.[53]

Also not surprising, at least at first sight, is that grandfathering, in other words giving away allowances free of any charge, may lead to over-allocation of emission rights.[54] As a result of this over-allocation in early 2007, the price of allowances dramatically dropped below €1.00.[55]

This low price for allowances provides evidence of over-allocation by the European Member States.[56] However, it is more difficult to answer the question whether this necessarily makes the whole EU ETS ineffective in providing incentives for emissions reductions.

At first sight one may be tempted to argue that this is the case: why would any company invest in emission abatement equipment if a tonne of $CO_2$ emission rights could be purchased at a price of lower than €1.00? Marginal costs of pollution abatement are undoubtedly higher. However, Kuik and Oosterhuis convincingly argue that the over-allocation could be partly the result of investments in technological and other innovations which precisely caused the emissions reductions.[57] They showed that the EU ETS led to an additional abatement of between 50 and 200 million tonnes and equally showed that this emission trading scheme played a key role in long-term decisions of companies to develop innovative technologies, with more particularly a strong impact on the steel industry.[58] The fact that the price of a tonne of $CO_2$ dropped below €1.00 (at the beginning of 2007) does not necessarily mean that this ETS had no incentive effect on innovation and would thus be ineffective. Quite the reverse may be true as well, being that the demand for emissions simply dropped since the introduction of the EU ETS precisely had the desired effect of reducing those emissions.[59]

These observations are of course not meant to argue that there is no room for improvement of the EU ETS; the institutional design could certainly be improved and that has to a large extent also occurred with the promulgation of the second ETS Directive.[60] However, one has apparently to be very careful in correctly

Scheme, 2006, available at: http://ec.europa.eu/enterprise/policies/sustainable-business/files/environment/hlg/docs/contribution_ieta_en.pdf

52 See Section 9.3.

53 See Ellerman (2005, at 90) and Sterner and Hammar (2005, at 31).

54 See e.g. Baldwin (2008).

55 See Communication on climate change, 'Building a low-carbon economy – The UK's contribution to tackling climate change', at 149, 150, fig. 4.2, 2008, available at: www.theccc.org.uk/pdf/TSO-ClimateChange.pdf

56 See for example Woerdman, Clò, and Arcuri (2008a, at 143–144).

57 Kuik and Oosterhuis (2008, at 212–214, 221).

58 Id., at 217, 220.

59 Id., at 217.

60 See generally Directive 2009/29 amending Directive 2003/87/EC so as to improve and extend the greenhouse gas emission allowance trading scheme of the Community, 2009 *Official Journal* L140/63 (EC).

interpreting results of empirical research: the price of one tonne of $CO_2$ falling below €1.00 does not necessarily mean that the EU ETS is ineffective; one has to interpret this in the correct context.

Still, notwithstanding these relatively enthusiastic evaluations one has to remain cautious. One problem is that by merely analysing whether there has been any effect on firm behaviour as far as reducing emissions is concerned, one does not take into account whether additional and further going reductions could equally have been achieved with other instruments (such as taxation). The conclusion that the EU ETS is effective (in the sense of having some effect) does therefore not imply that it is optimal. Indeed, Baldwin argued that the transaction costs of trading systems can be high, referring to the EU ETS as 'an administrative nightmare'.[61] Without taking into account the relative costs of EU ETS one can therefore not argue that the system would be cost effective as well. The mere fact that the EU ETS may have been effective in providing incentives for technological change leading to emission reductions does therefore not mean that there is no room for improvement, thus increasing the effectiveness. It therefore bears mentioning that the use of emissions or energy taxes in sectors covered by the EU ETS has received some scholarly attention. Authors do appear to be rather cautious about the desirability of such complementary approaches, particularly if they represent unilateral action by Member States.[62] Further improvements in the legal and institutional design of the emissions trading system may well reduce its costs and thus increase its effectiveness.[63]

## 7.5 PAYMENTS FOR ECOSYSTEM SERVICES (PES)

Payments for Ecosystem Services (PES) are a relatively new entrant into the field of market-based policy tools.[64]

> In economic terms, PES seeks to internalize the positive externalities (that is, the third-party benefits) generated by natural systems, creating incentives for landholder behaviour that ensure service provision. In some circumstances, PES can create additional revenue streams for conservation and has been described as 'making trees worth more standing than cut down'.[65] (Underscoring added.)

PES's economic function builds on the notion of hedonic pricing but in a more active sense – in ecosystem services, parties preferring preservation of species or

[61] Baldwin (2008, at 193–215).

[62] Böhringer, Koschel, and Moslener (2008) and Eichner and Pethig (2009).

[63] For the recent evolutions concerning the EU ETS, see Peeters (2016).

[64] While it remains unclear as to the first instance of ecosystem services, it can be documented that in 1995, there were only three references found to exist in the research literature. Salzman et al. (2018, at 136).

[65] Id.

habitats, or other environmental 'services', pay other parties to engage in protective acts or to avoid damaging acts – it is, thus, an active sense of economic engagement, to transform environmental policy and goals into some form of market-based transaction, into a volitional, utility optimising, contract for environmental policy and goals.

> The idea of more fully assessing how our impacts on nature (both degrading and restoring) are affecting human wellbeing is compelling. Considering ecosystem services can help assess trade-offs and consequences of impacts (e.g. by considering whether an increase in or change in location of timber harvest may have downstream effects on the water supply and health of local communities). This level of consideration can also help provide a more complete understanding of the benefits of an action. For example, a community may protect a local wetland to provide flood protection, but in doing so that community also is providing groundwater recharge, water filtration, and habitat for important species.[66] (Underscoring added.)

In Salzman et al.'s recent survey on PES systems, it was found that over 550 PES programmes are currently in existence, that their present funding level is estimated at over US$36 billion, and a search of research literature published in 2016 found over 1,900 PES journal references.[67]

The key, of course, to this marvellous innovation is the financing of the payments. Their survey found three major categories of financing in the existing PES systems: (i) user or consumer financing,[68] (ii) governmental financing, and (iii) compliance PES, which would include payments required under other regulatory structures – the EU's carbon credit trading schemes are given as an example.[69]

To date, the largest application of PES systems has been in the preservation and protection of watersheds, with 387 PES programmes identified, predominantly in China and South America.[70] Next, 120 PES systems were found in support of biodiversity and habitat programmes,[71] and, 48 PES systems were found engaged with protection of forests and policies engaged with land use carbon sinks.[72]

Most of these programmes present challenges in judging their effectiveness; as programmes may not have achieved useful baseline data sets before commencing, or ongoing data collection efforts may be incomplete.[73] Study has found that the creation and implementation of PES systems within common law jurisdictions

66 Sharon et al. (2018, at 9).
67 Salzman et al. (2018, at 136).
68 Users or consumers could include individuals, corporate actors, non-governmental agencies, and public actors. Id.
69 Id.
70 Id., at 136–137.
71 Id., at 138.
72 Id.
73 Id., at 140.

appears to have been more successful, especially when litigation played a founding or critical role, if the new PES vector of attention was drawn to already well recognised environmental rights instead of efforts aimed at attempting to establish new environmental legal recognitions.[74] But it is worth noting that a global survey found many, if not also most, of the existing PES systems functioning in civil law jurisdictions,[75] where it might be easier to add new elements of codification or acts of ministerial agency to establish novel environmental concepts into a PES system.

## 7.6 ENVIRONMENTAL TAXATION

The idea of a tax for environmental pollution was first developed by Arthur C. Pigou.[76] This concept states that pollution can be reduced to socially desirable levels by increasing a firm″s marginal private costs by means of a tax to reflect the marginal costs of society. Since polluters' production costs are increased by the Pigouvian tax to reflect costs of society, firms should maximise profits by reducing activity levels to the social optimum.[77]

Environmental taxes have a certain appeal; they invoke the polluter pays principle by internalising the Pigouvian externalities of pollution, they would appear to provide incentives to reduce pollution and to encourage innovation at those sites with the most efficient cost structures to achieve that improvement, meaning that more capital is available for a broader set of goals, including other environmental goals.[78] It has been suggested that the transaction costs of achieving environmental goals by taxation instead of by CAC policies might be easier to bear on society.[79]

### 7.6.1 *Basic Principles and Advantages*

Environmental taxes have a few potential advantages, especially when compared to CAC regulation:

First, a pollution tax entails less total abatement costs than the emissions standard does. However, total compliance costs for firms may be higher with environmental taxes since polluters will not only have to abate emissions but are also liable to pay the tax for non-abated emissions; but this is part of a Pigouvian tax's purpose to reduce production by raising costs of production with the inclusion of the formerly excluded externalised costs.

[74] Sharon et al. (2018, at 14–17).
[75] See Salzman et al. (2018).
[76] See earlier in Sections 2.3 and 6.2.
[77] Groosman (2000). See also Turner, Pearce and Bateman (1994).
[78] Hsu (2008, at 32 and 33).
[79] Id., at 32.

Second, pollution taxes levied on inputs via existing authorities have a lower risk of evasion than fixed emission standards that are controlled via irregular on-site inspections. Emissions used as tax base require sufficient control and monitoring to limit the risk of evasion. Nevertheless, such control and monitoring are likely not cheaper nor less demanding than the control and monitoring under regulatory standards, thus no particular gains will be found there.

Third, pollution taxes provide continuous incentives for abatement to reduce the tax burden and abatement costs.

Fourth, taxes induce investment in research and development.

Finally, taxes may induce substitution of inputs that reduce other environmental harmful substances.[80]

### 7.6.2 *Critical Issues*

The effectiveness of a system of environmental taxation depends on a number of critical issues.

First, failure to set an appropriate tax rate that enables the equalling of marginal benefits and of the marginal costs of pollution would undermine the effectiveness of the tax to achieve a full internalisation of external costs. The Pigouvian tax is a simple incentive-based mechanism capable of inducing behavioural changes. To set an optimal tax rate, governments require optimal information; the obtaining of that information would face substantial transaction costs and would likely fail to be completely gathered.[81]

Second, the effectiveness of taxes also depends heavily on demand and supply functions. Only if the functions are flat (elastic) will a price increase lead to a significant change in the consumption or supply patterns and render the tax effective. The presence of inelastic price demand, on the other hand, will result in little to no behavioural change.

Third, Environmental taxes require that emissions are monitored as closely as possible to ensure its effectiveness even if that is difficult and if the monitored pollution contains multiple substances. To avoid such a difficulty, 'proxy variables' are sometimes employed, although their use is not theoretically consistent with the model of Pigouvian tax.

Fourth, taxes have regressive effects on some income categories – although it is debated exactly which categories and to what extent – thus,

[80] Faure and Weishaar (2012, at 408).

[81] See for an elaborate criticism, Fullerton, Leicester, and Smith (2010).

distributional aspects must be considered appropriately to ensure an equitable result for the community.

Fifth, some authors have alternatively raised complaints that environmental taxes normalise thinking about pollution as an economic problem instead of as a 'moral' problem against the sanctity of the Earth.[82] These scholars would rather see criminal law brought to bear on emitters, forbidding them from an 'illegal' trade in purchasing 'pollutable clean air'.[83]

It also bears mentioning that other approaches towards environmental taxes could be developed that do not have anything in common with Pigouvian taxes. Albrecht proposes a pragmatic classification of sustainable products, [84] which benefit from low VAT levels to green-up the tax system.[85] Also, others have opined that tax-based mechanisms retain many characteristics of CAC regulatory approaches,[86] so perhaps it can be viewed as an intermediate step between the two approaches.

### 7.6.3 *Some Success Stories*

There is a long tradition now with using the so-called Pigouvian taxes to provide incentives for emission reduction.[87] Those interested in a historical survey can have a look at literature providing detailed overviews,[88] or can be referred to the global conferences on environmental taxation which are held on an annual basis as a result of which impressive volumes are produced, equally providing evidence of successes obtained with environmental taxation.[89]

Just to mention a few success stories:

- In the Netherlands water pollution by fourteen industries responsible for 90 per cent of total water pollution decreased by 50 per cent between 1969 and 1975 and by another 20 per cent by 1980.[90] Half of this reduction was, so the evidence shows, due to an effluent charge.[91]

82 Hsu (2008, 37).

83 Id., at 34 and 37.

84 Albrecht (2006).

85 See Kosonen and Nicodème (2009) for a comparison.

86 Hsu (2008, at 41).

87 Although it has been noted that the use of environmental taxes has been more pronounced in Europe than in the USA, see Hsu (2008, at 29).

88 See for example the contributions in Harrington, Morgenstern, and Sterner (2004).

89 The Global Conference on Environmental Taxation has completed nineteen annual conferences at the time of the drafting of this book; the nineteenth conference having been held on 26–28 September 2018.

90 See Dewees, Duff, and Trebilcock (1996).

91 Id., at 326–327.

- A similar success story comes from Germany where various scholars provided evidence that a system of charges on waste water led to a considerable reduction of emissions.[92]

Interestingly, most of these European legal systems had (and still have) a combination of effluent charges with emission standards.[93]

Still the evidence shows that these significant investments in water treatment plants were not due (only) to the threat of administrative and/or criminal sanctions in case of violation of emission standards, but to the taxation.[94] Comparative research by Bongaerts and Kraemer comparing the water pollution charges in France, the Netherlands and Germany came to the same conclusion that effluent charges provide a strong incentive to invest in water pollution abatement equipment.[95] The authors argue that the effect is especially strong in Germany where the charges are reduced by 50 per cent for emitters who meet the emission standard.[96]

Also, a study by Morley on environmental taxation in EU Member States and Norway confirms a significant negative relationship between taxes and pollution.[97] That study confirms that the current use of environmental taxes to reduce the EU's levels of pollution appears to be effective.[98] This is not surprising, because given an incidence of environmental taxation, companies will see costs investment in pollution-reducing technological innovation as potentially offset by the eventual reduction in taxation; thus environmental taxes can be seen as spurring innovation in pollution reduction.[99]

### 7.6.4 *The Influence of Private Interest*

One should, however, not immediately become overly enthusiastic, since there is equally evidence that special interest groups can also be as active when it comes to designing a taxation system as they were in affecting the development of public regulation. It is for example remarkable that pollution permits are introduced on a large scale in the USA, but that taxation systems were traditionally more popular in Europe than in the USA.[100]

Buchanan, together with Tullock, has argued that this should not come as a surprise, since firms will prefer emission standards or emission trading (especially

92 See Brown Jr. and Johnson (1984, at 929, 933–937, 943–945); see also Frey (1972, at 149, 151).
93 Laskowska and Scrimgeour (2002).
94 See Brown Jr. and Johnson (1984, at 929). See also Frey (1992, at 149–151).
95 See e.g. Bongaerts and Kraemer (1987, at 12, 15).
96 Bongaert and Kraemer (1987, at 12–19). They also argue that it is therefore difficult to disentangle the separate effects of charges and emission standards.
97 Morely (2010).
98 Id., at 15.
99 Hsu (2008, at 30).
100 See Buchanan and Tullock (1975, at 139–147).

when emission rights are grandfathered) to taxes,[101] because such standards with grandfathering have the advantage that they can serve as barrier to entry to new firms, thus raising the profits of existing firms.[102] Taxes on the other hand do not preclude entry by new firms and represent an additional cost to the existing firms on the market.[103] In fact, environmental taxes avoid the perverse incentives that can sometimes preserve installed polluting capital infrastructure, when other forms of governance might be more readily open to grandfathering, such as technology choice standards.[104]

It should not come as a surprise that interest groups representing industry will oppose taxation and that as a result charges are rarely introduced 'in the textbook form'.[105] Governments often use these fees as a revenue generating device for public services rather than as an instrument of environmental policy, as predicted by economic theory.[106] As a result, there is also a lot of evidence of inefficient environmental taxation and not surprisingly the likelihood of these inefficiencies increase the larger the power of the interest group involved. A few examples can illustrate this.

Belgian research showed that, whereas a general tax to internalise externalities created by the power generating sector could create important welfare gains, the Belgian regulation is structured in such a way that 'independent power producers escape most of the air pollution regulation' imposing the tax.[107]

In the Netherlands a regulatory digressive energy tax was introduced in 1996.[108] As a result the larger the energy use was, the lower the tax would be.[109] This tax therefore only gives incentives to increase the use of energy rather than decreasing it. The main concern of the policymaker was to increase competitiveness of Dutch industry rather than serving any ecological goal.[110]

Similar problems arose in China. O'Connor reports on pollution charges on air emissions, waste water discharges, noise, solid waste, and radioactive wastes introduced in China at the end of the last century.[111] Charge rates were set slightly above average operating costs of pollution control facilities in order to provide incentives for compliance.[112] However, in practice they were not indexed to inflation, as a result of which their real value eroded over time, resulting of course in 'weak incentive(s)

[101] Id., at 142–146.
[102] See Hahn (1989c, at 107).
[103] Id.
[104] Hsu (2008, at 31).
[105] Hahn (1989c, at 107–108).
[106] Id., at 107.
[107] See Bigano, Proost, and Van Rompuy (2000, at 149).
[108] Ministry of Housing (2004, at 1, 2).
[109] Faure and Ubachs (2002, at 301–329).
[110] Id., at 323–324. See also Faure and Ubachs (2005, at 521–532).
[111] O'Connor (1998, at 96).
[112] Id.

for further pollution reduction'.[113] Efforts to raise the charge met, not surprisingly, 'strong opposition from industry'. Considerations of political acceptability may limit the possibilities to introduce efficient taxation systems.[114]

Similar problems arise concerning the introduction of market-based instruments and more particularly pollution charges in developing countries.[115] Some have advocated that, more particularly for developing countries, market-based instruments such as taxation would be well suited. These would, at least on paper, be perfect instruments since they could be implemented at lower costs than CAC regulation.[116]

However, others have argued that implementing market-based instruments is only possible in a context where a decent institutional and administrative structure is available.[117] These conditions will often not be met in the case of developing countries.

The empirical evidence largely seems to confirm this point: in those countries where at least some institutional structure is available, e.g. to set and collect environmental taxes in the public interest, then environmental taxes may work effectively.[118] If these institutional conditions are not met it may become very hard to implement pollution charges.[119] There is evidence that institutional inertia in the economic and political system led to a debacle of pollution charges in Russia.[120]

However, in cases where a successful collection is possible and where environmental charges are combined with other instruments, including traditional standards, they can lead to an overall improvement of environmental compliance, provided of course there is an effective enforcement. This was shown in a study by Kathuria with respect to three successful cases of reducing water pollution: Malaysia, Poland, and Columbia.[121] Kathuria argued that it was the combination of charges with other instruments that led to the overall improvement in environmental compliance.[122] A similar result was also found in a study of environmental policy instruments in eight developing countries by Jordan and others.[123] They showed that even though many countries moved to the introduction of market-based instruments, regulation still remained the dominant instrument for pollution

[113] Id., at 96–97.

[114] Id., at 108.

[115] For an overview of experiences with introducing pollution charges in transition economies, mostly in Central and Eastern Europe, see Bluffstone and Larson (1997).

[116] Blackman (2009, at 101), quoting Panayotou (1995, at 19).

[117] See e.g. Bell and Russell (2002, at 64–66).

[118] Id., at 69–70.

[119] Id., at 70.

[120] See e.g. Söderholm (1999, on file with the author). See generally Kozeltsev and Markandya (1997, at 128, explaining the period of Russian regulation, including the difficulties in implementing economic incentives).

[121] See Kathuria (2006, at 423).

[122] Id.

[123] Jordan et al. (2003, at 1–24).

control.[124] Also Blackman showed in a study concerning Columbia's discharge fee programme that the reason why pollution loads dropped significantly after the programme was introduced was not so much because of incentives provided by the discharge fees, but rather as a result of incentives created through the programme 'for regulatory authorities to improve permitting, monitoring and enforcement'.[125] Above it was mentioned that although earlier research on environmental taxation in China was rather sceptical of its effectiveness, especially due to political pressure not to increase the tax rate,[126] later research seems to indicate that China's discharge fee programmes have had a positive influence on pollution levels.[127]

In closing, it is useful to remember that environmental taxation can be phrased as a Coasean allocation of rights: 'environmental taxes confer an entitlement upon society at large to be free of pollution (an entitlement that can be purchased by the polluter)'.[128]

Thus, environmental taxes will likely operate best wherein the legal institutions are capable of defending those rights of the public, of identifying those 'purchasers' of 'pollutable clean air', and having recourse to effective and efficient tax collection institutions.

## 7.7 ELASTICITIES AND DISTRIBUTIONAL EFFECTS ON ENVIRONMENTAL WELFARE

Environmental policies, especially effective policies, change the strategic behaviour of certain parties, but the consequence of those changes can have serious distributional effects, often on other smaller or weaker parties.

When an economist discusses the behavioural impacts of policies on a certain party, they will often use the economic idea of elasticity. Elasticity reflects exactly what it sounds like, how flexible a party is with response to policy effected changes, say in price, cost, or quantity. By understanding the elasticity of economic policies, such as implemented to enable the goals of environmental law, we can model how various impacted parties would be expected to modify their behaviour due to the change in policy.

First, a quick review of a couple standard definitions:

> Price elasticity of demand is defined as the percentage change in the quantity of good demanded that results from a 1 percent change in price.[129]

[124] Id., at 20.
[125] Blackman (2009, at 117).
[126] See O'Connor (1998, at 96–97, noting the influence of industry pressure).
[127] See more particularly, Wong and Wheeler (2005, at 184, no. 15).
[128] Hsu (2008, at 34).
[129] While the price elasticity of demand is one of the most common forms of elasticity, there are in fact many types of elasticity studied by economists. An informal definition can be stated as a measure of sensitivity; how much percent will a second factor be impacted by a 1 per cent

> The demand for a good is said to be elastic with respect to price if its price elasticity is less than −1 . . . The demand for a good is inelastic with respect to price if its price elasticity is equal to −1.[130]

We have two resulting concepts, 'elastic' and 'inelastic' responses. When something is very elastic, small changes in price will greatly change the quantity demanded.[131] When something is inelastic, great changes in price will result in little to no change in quantity demanded.[132]

Elasticity reveals that not all parties respond identically to a common policy. Thus, it is not as simple that a tax on a product or activity will reduce that activity; it might or might not, depending on the measure of elasticity for that party. If a tax is applied to an elastic good, a party will want less of that good; if the good is inelastic, then the tax will not alter their demand in any substantial way. In the elastic case, they reduce their consumption of the taxed item; but in the inelastic case, they'll continue to purchase the same amount of the taxed item as before but that will result in a smaller budget for their other purchases.[133]

And of course, that change in price could be from Pigouvian tax, an eco-tax, or from any additional imposition of costs or fee, as it need not be a tax.[134]

When we expand our scope of view from a single party to a collection of parties, for example the set of companies engaged in a polluting act, it could well be that each company's elasticity to the policy tools is unique, some displaying elastic responses and others displaying inelastic responses.

This diversity of elasticities across the regulated parties could cause a singular environmental policy to have multiple and different results on the various regulated parties.[135] For example, when smaller plants are less elastic than larger plants in responding to regulatory requirements to reduce polluting emissions, the small may find themselves unable to adjust to the new regulations as cost-effectively as the larger plants, and thus may be pushed out of the market.[136] This could be contrary to regulatory intent, as regulators may have assumed an equal but proportionate impact

change in a first factor? Thus, the price elasticity of demand asks, how sensitive is demand to a change in price?

[130] Frank (2010, at 111–112). Frank's *Microeconomics and Behavior* is a standard textbook for microeconomics. The definitions presented here are for a general audience.

[131] Id., at 114.

[132] Id.

[133] See Sandmo (2003, at 7): 'A green tax reform may improve efficiency, but it does so at the cost of redistributing income from the poor to the rich. This is particularly important in the case of energy taxes. Expenditure on energy, particularly for heating and cooking, weighs more heavily in low-income budgets, so that higher energy prices redistribute income in disfavour of the poor'.

[134] Of course, the cost, fee, or tax need not be based on a market-based instrument, the same economic logic and result will hold for costs, fees, or taxes imposed by traditional CAC-type regulations too.

[135] Moloney and McCormick (1982, at 105).

[136] Pashigian (1984, at 4–5).

across all plants, but the difference in elasticity could yield competitive advantages to some polluters while disproportionately impacting other polluters; policymakers will want to be sure of the relevant elasticities facing the agents to be regulated prior to launching new policy measures to better assure the desired policy outcomes.[137]

The complexities that this might entail for environmental policy planners was set out by Konar and Cohen:

> Increased pressure due to new information about environmental hazards may be focused either on an entire industry or within specific firms in an industry. In some cases, consumers may look at alternative product lines that are less polluting or otherwise change their aggregate consumption habits to reduce the demand for an entire product category. In this case, the negative impact following environmental disclosures is industry-wide.
>
> Corresponding to this effect, however, might be a positive impact on other industries whose products now look relatively more favorable. The extent to which this new information is likely to affect industry-wide valuation will depend on the availability of close substitutes, the price elasticity of demand for that product, and other "elasticity" factors related to the demand for green products. Similarly, new information on environmental hazards may have firm-specific effects as some firms within an industry now look more or less favorable than others in that same industry. Even if aggregate demand for a product line is not affected or even positively affected by this new disclosure, differential emission rates across firms may create new winners and losers in that industry.[138] (Underscoring added.)

Policymakers that seek to tax activities that could give rise to environmental injuries must carefully understand the relative elasticities of demand to ensure that the tax will actually fall on the correct party and thus create the correct incentives; as Ogus pointed out:

> However, the alleged winner-loser dichotomy must be explored with greater care: if costs are incurred by losers under an interventionist law, who ultimately bears them? The answer is not simply shareholders of the firms subject to the regime, but also their employees and consumers of their products or services (the exact distribution of the burden will vary from case to case according to the degree of price elasticity in the relevant capital, labour and product markets).[139] (Underscoring added.)

Fullerton found that this area remains empirically lacking in detail, but what data does exist evidences the importance of the concept for policymakers:

[137] Beyond theoretical models, empirical support exists to affirm that environmental taxation affects the elasticity of demand for 'abatement goods and services'. See inter alia Sinclair-Desgagné (2008, at 21).

[138] Konar and Cohen (1997, at 113).

[139] Ogus (1999b, at 413).

> Few have studied labor adjustment costs, especially from climate policy. In one exception, Deschênes (2010) looks at the effect of energy costs on labor demand. He finds a negative cross-price elasticity. Since the cap and trade bill that passed the U.S. House of Representatives in 2009 would raise electricity prices by about 4%, his preferred estimate suggests that U.S. employment would fall by 460,000 (about 0.6%). That estimate captures the effects on industries that react to their own higher electricity costs by reducing employment.[140] (Underscoring added.)

The effects of elasticity and inelasticity mean that a policy maker might create an environmental policy aimed at corporate-owned plants that emit pollution, but the underlying customers' or employees' relatively inelastic demand vis-à-vis the elastic of the plant owner may enable the actual burden of those costs to be shifted away from the owner to the customer or employees; this is called policy 'pass-through'. Not only would this shift the burden of costs to unintended parties, but it would also send a signal to parties who are not the direct decision maker who is the corporate owner of the plant. Thus, the policy effectiveness would be materially reduced in such a case.

A quick example from environmental law; building on Palmer and Riera concerns on taxes against energy products and the impacts on distributional equity: 'All environmental policy related measures lead to redistribution but, in the case of environmental taxes (and other economic means of generating income), the impact on family income gives special cause for concern as, on many occasions, the environmental tax is levied on the usage of assets that are a prime necessity, such as water resources or energy.'[141]

When a party's demand for crude oil is elastic with regards to changes in price, an increase in price would result in less demand for that oil. On the other hand, when a party is inelastic in demand for crude oil, then higher prices will not dent their demand for oil but will instead reduce their budget for other commodities or services; this could result in net welfare reduction while also not affecting oil consumption behaviour.[142]

And on water, Olmstead and Stavins found that the lower income households were more affected by environmental policies, due to their greater inelasticities of demand:

> What does economic theory tell us about the equity implications of water pricing as a conservation tool? If water demand management occurs solely through price increases, low-income households will contribute a greater fraction of a city's aggregate water savings than high-income households, in part because price elasticity declines with the fraction of household income spent on a particular good. The empirical evidence supports this conclusion. Agthe and Billings [1987] found that

[140] Fullerton (2011, at 8).

[141] Palmer and Riera (2003, at 672).

[142] Frank (2010, at 119).

> low-income households exhibited a larger demand response to price increases in Tucson, Arizona. Renwick and Archibald [1998] found that low-income households in southern California communities were more price responsive than high-income households. Mansur and Olmstead [2007] found that raising prices to reduce consumption would cause a greater consumption reduction for low-income than for high-income households.[143] (Underscoring added.)

This can have complex impacts on environmental regulatory design, constraining where public regulatory measures might be effective tools of behavioural change.[144] A corporate refiner may be able to pass the costs of the tax on crude oil through to the end consumer, who may demonstrate highly inelastic demand for that crude oil, having no alternative choice to fuel their work vehicle or their family car, at least in the short term.

Other distributional problems can occur from the imposition of taxes or permit costs; those are the downstream 'knock on' consequences of the changes in market activity that occur due to the effective change in behaviour of the targeted party. Reduced economic activities, such as reduced visits to a tourist location due to incidence of an eco-tax, will reduce need for beds, hotel staff, and affiliated services such as restaurants.[145]

This understanding of the effects of relative elasticities also implies that efforts to ensure the application of Pigouvian taxes and efforts to deliver on the polluter pays principle could be frustrated in such scenarios, that the ultimate costs or forbearances may lay at some remove from the party making the polluting decision.

## 7.8 SUMMARY AND CONCLUSION

In this chapter, we reviewed the concept of 'market-based' instruments from both legal and economic perspectives.

We began with a focus on information itself and of its role in the marketplace. Fundamentally, both legal theory and economics theory assume that the actors involved are decision makers. In law, a decision maker might become culpable or

[143] Olmstead and Stavins (2009, at 5).

[144] Moloney and McCormick found that when elasticity effects were taken into account, that regulatory efforts to create economic incentives to motivate behavioral changes would be effective when three conditions were met: 'First, the restricted input level must have been cost minimizing at some output before the restriction. In other words, there must be an output level where the firm would voluntarily choose to emit the same level of pollution as that mandated by the law. Second, the restricted input cannot be inferior – pollution must increase with output. Finally, the input restriction must drive a wedge between the pre- and post- regulation average-cost curves that are increasing in size. Average cost subject to the regulation must be more inelastic than average cost where there is no restriction on technology or inputs' (Moloney and McCormick 1982, at 104–105, underscoring added).

[145] Palmer and Riera (2003, at 672); they note the effect but also suggest that the effects might not be as large as feared for the specific eco-tax in their case study, the eco-taxes for the Balearic islands east of Spain.

liable for both their manner of decision making and the results of their decisions. In economics, the decision maker is viewed as an optimiser, managing their resources to achieve their preferred goals; with efficiency as a meta-goal to enable the achievement of many goals as possible given their constrained budget of resources. But for each vision of decision makers, information is a critical ingredient. For actors undertaking risky activities with potential for ecological injuries, missing information could lead to either inefficient or inaccurate decisions, resulting in wasted resources for the actor and missed environmental opportunities and goals for the community at large.

Actors in environmental settings cannot safely undertake their activities unless they have a sufficiently complete set of information from environmental sciences, on local ecologies, of the potential reactions and consequences of the activity to be undertaken, and a comprehensive set of stakeholders both present and future. Shy of those sufficiency conditions, decisions on how to best undertake that activity without causation of injuries is likely to be at best wasting of the actor's resources and worst result in complicated sets of injuries, as their decision-making process will be flawed. The Law and Economics literature details how information can be generated from legal rules drawn from both private and public spheres; indeed, much of the literature is concerned with designing legal rules to become more effective in creating useful information to improve both private and public decision making.

We examined the market-based tool known as marketable emission permits or as tradable permits. This approach begins with setting of target standards for jurisdiction wide emission goals. Then, each emitter receives an allotment of emission permits that determine on a quantity basis how much they can emit, usually on an annual basis. These permits are essentially emission standards, sometimes including aspects of technological specifications that might normally fit within production standards. But the innovative part is allowing firms to sell those permits across to each other.

Whereas public regulations tend to provide poor incentives for enhancing beyond their encoded norms of performance, the ability to sell permits does provide incentives if holders of permits can find greener solutions at prices attractive enough to sell off their permits. Perhaps the installation costs of the greener technology can be covered by the revenue from selling the permits, or perhaps the factory needs to upgrade for other reasons but includes additional green technologies as a means to create revenue from sales of the permits. Further, there is potential to link jurisdictions so that markets could extend across multiple zones; such is recognised in the UNFCCC's clean development mechanism, which enables developed economies to reap carbon credit offsets for investing in carbon-reducing operations in developing economies – enabling both countries to benefit in the process.

There will be problems if certain emitters are unreasonably grandfathered or if the conditions of resale are too limiting; nevertheless, the concept of tradable permits enables new opportunities for governing and reducing emissions.

The economic theory to support environmental taxation goes back a long way, but many researchers would cite to Pigou as the seminal innovator. Simply put, taxes increase the costs of an activity and thus make it less attractive to undertake, especially if an activity is motivated by commercial reasons. Pigou advocated for placing taxes on activities that led to negative externalities; that by carefully adding tax costs to the activity so that the marginal costs could become accurate, fully reflective of the externalities, then marginal analysis could become effective for the firm and the community at large. Again, Coase's analysis of transaction costs complicates this concept, particularly with the question of against whom should the taxes be levied.

A discussion on price and demand elasticities revealed the complicated nature of market responses to changing costs. When an actor is inelastic in demand to a certain good, say crude oil, then higher prices will not dent their demand for the product, but will instead reduce their budget for other commodities or services. On the other hand, when that demand is elastic, an increase in price would result in less demand for that product. If a tax is levied against a form of pollution, but the commercial actor has no functional alternative in the market, and is thus facing an inelastic demand for that activity, then the tax will not reduce the activity that creates the hazard; instead, the price will either be absorbed by the consumer if they are also inelastic in demand or by the producer if the consumer is elastic in demand. Thus, taxing activities that could give rise to environmental injuries must carefully understand the relative elasticities of demand to ensure that the tax will actually fall on the correct party and thus create the correct incentives.

In conclusion, we found that market-based instruments worked best alongside more traditional forms of public regulation, that market-based instruments are not robustly implemented as a stand-alone alternative to traditional forms of public regulation. As an early prelude to the discussion in Section 9.5, when properly harmonised, market-based instruments can reinforce and support the effectiveness of public regulations, and vice versa.

# 8

# Liability Rules

After having discussed how cost–benefit analysis can be used to define how environmental pollution can be internalised, we will now turn to a few legal instruments to see what problems arise when they are applied to environmental pollution. The first instrument which we address in a more detailed way is the use of liability rules.

First the economic principles of accident law will be discussed (Section 8.1); then these principles will be applied to environmental harm (Section 8.2). Some problems merit specific attention, such as causation (Section 8.3) and the question whether environmental liability should be limited (Section 8.4) or channelled to a particular operator (Section 8.5) and how one should address joint and several liability from an economic perspective (Section 8.6). Finally, we will examine whether new liability rules should apply retrospectively to environmental problems which were caused in a distant past (Section 8.7). In addition, we review some of the empirical literature with respect to the effects of liability rules (Section 8.8). Section 8.9 summarises and concludes.

## 8.1 ECONOMIC PRINCIPLES OF ACCIDENT LAW: INTRODUCTION

### 8.1.1 *The Goal of Tort Law*

The economic analysis of law in general and of accident law more specifically starts from the belief that a legal rule for liability and of responsibility for damages will give incentives to potential parties in an accident setting to alter their behaviour.[1]

Critically speaking, economists tend to place more emphasis on the deterrent function of tort law, with a principle derived from their models that it is more

[1] See Shavell (2004, at 176–206). Epstein, in demonstrating that the economic freedoms of the marketplace ('freedom of contract'), where not at odds with civil liability for environmental injuries, provides a historical survey of courts supporting environmental litigation claims during the heights of American industrial era between 1850 and 1900 (Epstein 2016, at 145).

economically robust to remain uninjured than to seek compensation and restitution;[2] not unlike the quote from Ben Franklin: 'an ounce of prevention is worth a pound of cure'.[3] But especially the delicate nature of ecological communities and the complexity if not impossibility of complete restoration to prior pre-injured conditions, this perspective to focus on deterrence well serves the goals of environmental law, generally.

Lawyers tend to attach more value to justice and compensation goals of accident law, to identify a wrong doer, punish them, and to provide compensation to the victim. While this might provide emotional justice for the human victims, it is less clear what sense of justice emerges for the rest of the environmental and ecological injured; would a frog know that justice was rendered in its honour? The costs of social justice borne by the tortfeasor and the costs of the damages paid to the victim, or to the restoration fund in trust, would provide ex post costs that could be reasonably foreseen by potential environmental tortfeasors and those costs integrated ex ante in decision making to reduce the overall risk of injury. Thus, this approach too has its merits from the Law and Economics approach.

This 'victim protection' argument is also discussed in the Law and Economics literature.[4] When it is discussed, however, it is often stressed that the best path to protect victims is to avoid victimisation in the first place. Of course, no one will argue that prevention of accidents is not a way of victim protection as well. This difference in accents between both approaches is also characterised as an ex ante versus an ex post vision. Whereas lawyers tend to be more interested in the accident problem ex post, where there is a victim that needs to be compensated, economists look at the accident problem in an ex ante perspective by asking the question how an ex post finding of liability will influence ex ante the incentives of potential parties in an accident setting for care taking.

Of course, the economist is looking at accumulative welfare, and models reflect, especially considering the complexities of ex post cures, that ex ante avoidance is in general a more robust strategy. The legal perspective appears to be framed by the nature of legal work itself: that rarely do clients appear prior to becoming injured, rarely does a client gain standing before incurring an injury, and rarely will a judge offer an injunction to prevent such dangerous activities. Thus, the law has evolved primarily in that context and it is therefore understandable that lawyers have a habit

[2] It was first developed by Guido Calabresi (Calabresi 1970).

[3] Benjamin Franklin, *Pennsylvania Gazette*, 4 February 1735. The full quote was indeed in reference to safety considerations, it focused on the prevention of home-based fires: 'In the first Place, as an Ounce of Prevention is worth a Pound of Cure, I would advise 'em to take care how they suffer living Coals in a full Shovel, to be carried out of one Room into another, or up or down Stairs, unless in a Warming pan shut; for Scraps of Fire may fall into Chinks and make no Appearance until Midnight; when your Stairs being in Flames, you may be forced, (as I once was) to leap out of your Windows, and hazard your Necks to avoid being oven-roasted.'

[4] Schwartz showed that rules of tort law may serve both the aims of deterrence and corrective justice (Schwartz 1997, at 1801–1834).

of being overly focused on those parties already injured, versus a focus on overall prevention, as the economists since Brown, Calabresi, and Shavell have called for.

In *The Costs of Accidents*, Guido Calabresi makes a distinction between primary, secondary, and tertiary accident costs.[5] Primary accident costs are the costs of accident avoidance and the damage that finally occurs, secondary costs refer to the equitable loss-spreading, and tertiary costs are the costs of administering the legal system. Tort law should give incentives to a reduction of total social costs of accidents. Thus, Calabresi's central goal of tort law was given: it should give incentive for a minimisation of all accident costs, across (i) the tortfeasors costs to avoid, (ii) the victim's cost of damages and injuries, and (iii) the costs of society to support legal institutions to coordinate and protects the relevant legal rights.

This is a deep movement in the legal paradigm from a focus on justice for the injured victim to a broader sense of the costs that injuries charge against society at large, that torts hurt more than just the 'victim' of the tort. This notion of Calabresi has been taken up later by economists that have formalised this issue.[6]

Let us address the first goal of tort law being the minimisation of primary accident costs: the costs of accident avoidance and the expected damage. Indeed, from a social point of view accidents do not only cause costs from the moment an accident occurs and a harm is suffered; potential parties in an accident setting, both injurers and victims, make investments in care to avoid the occurrence of an accident. Sometimes costs of care taking are very clear and visible. We can refer for instance to the investments made by firms to reduce environmental pollution by investing in water-cleaning equipment or the investment to install safety controls to avoid product defects. But also, the mere fact that in a traffic accident case both injurers and victims are limited in their freedom of movement, for instance because they have to drive or work carefully, is considered as a cost by economists. A difference is further made between so-called unilateral accidents, in which only the care taken by one of the parties (the injurer) can influence the accident risk, and bilateral accidents, in which the behaviour of both parties can influence the accident risk. In a bilateral accident situation, the goal of accident law should therefore be to give incentives to minimise the total costs of care taking by the potential injurer and the potential victim and the expected damage that will occur in case of an accident.[7]

Economists use cost–benefit analysis to determine what level of care would lead to such a minimisation of the social costs of an accident. Not surprisingly this can be found where the marginal costs of care taking equal the marginal benefits in accident reduction.[8] Indeed, since care taking has its own costs as well, a legal rule should not give incentives to avoid every possible accident that could occur, but only

5 Calabresi 1970.

6 Here we refer more particularly to Brown (1973, at 323–349); Diamond (1974, at 107–164); Landes and Posner (1981b, at 851–924); Shavell (1980a, at 1–25).

7 This distinction has been made by Shavell (1987, at 7).

8 Id.

those accidents that could be avoided by investments in care, of which the marginal costs are lower than or equal to the marginal benefits in accident reduction.

It might well be that extremely high care could additionally contribute to a reduction of the accident risk, but the marginal costs of care taking in that case might well be much higher than the additional benefit from accident reduction. Investments in care would in that case be inefficient and scarce resources would be misapplied.[9]

A substantial assumption herein is the idea of opportunity costs; that resources expended to reduce one risk will not be available to mitigate risks elsewhere, so we should seek a strategic set of policy choices to mitigate the greatest sum amount of costs from the risks across many activities. Thus, a need to be efficient with resources for each individual activity to ensure that society gains the greatest improvement in overall reductions of the costs from all risky activities across that society.

These levels of care, where marginal costs of care taking equal marginal benefits in accident reduction, are referred to in the literature as optimal or efficient care levels.[10] Liability law should therefore give an incentive to potential parties in the accident setting to adopt this optimal care level.

Before going into the detail of the analysis, it is good to repeat that the economic model assumes that a potential tortfeasor (in environmental terms a polluter) can take measures to prevent the pollution. This is referred to as costs of accident avoidance or prevention costs. In some of the economic literature these avoidance costs are also referred to as costs of precaution. For environmental lawyers that may be slightly confusing, given the difference between prevention and precaution highlighted above.[11] It is important just to recall that from the economic perspective, prevention costs are simply investments that can be made that positively affect the probability of an accident (environmental injuries) occurring.

We will begin with a discussion on the theory for optimal liability rules in unilateral accidents, before moving on to consider optimal liability rules for bilateral accidents.

### 8.1.2 *The Unilateral Case*

Starting from a clean slate, let us consider what outcomes would be expected if there were no liability rules for resultant injuries. If there were no liability at all, then the tortfeasor would have no obvious incentive for precaution or exercising 'due care'; therefore, in a no-liability situation the cost externality from the environmental

[9] This finding only holds in a risk neutral setting. In case of risk aversion higher investments in care might well be efficient since a reduction of accident risk will in that case also remove the disutility of risk from a risk averse person.

[10] See Landes and Posner (1981b, at 870) and Polinsky (1983).

[11] See Sections 5.3 and 5.5.

injuries will not be internalised, too many risks will be taken, and an inefficient outcome will follow, leading to too many injuries and associated costs.[12]

Our immediate analysis, below, focuses on how liability rules impact the precautionary and preventive strategies of potential tortfeasors. However, as Shavell modelled, this is not the only area of behaviour impacted by these rules. Shavell observed that the court took observation of one type of data –that which indicated fault or aspects of intensity, such as evidence of recklessness. This set he called precautionary efforts. But he also observed a second set of data, oft ignored by courts. In an example, imagine a bicycle rider who likes to juggle fire batons as they ride. In the case of an accident, courts are likely to enquire whether the cyclist exercised any due care at the time of the accident, did they take efforts to avoid injury, and similar questions on precaution. However, the court would not have foundations to enquire about their other bicycling excursions, how often they rode, how long they rode on average, or if other days' rides had gone well. Shavell called this set of issues 'activity level' issues, and activity levels also operate to determine the risk of an activity, but for various legal reasons, these activity level questions rarely come up in court. We'll address those issues later in Section 8.1.4.

#### 8.1.2.1 Negligence

Looking at a unilateral accident situation one can state that two legal rules, a rule of negligence and a rule of strict liability, would give the injurer incentives for taking optimal care.

If a negligence rule is adopted the injurer will take optimal care, provided the due care required in the legal system is equal to the optimal care as defined in the model.[13] This can be easily understood. If the judicial system sets the due care standard correctly the injurer can avoid liability by taking due care. Thus, they will have to spend care to avoid the accident, but if they do so they can avoid paying the expected damage. The injurer could take more care than the legal system requires them to do under a negligence rule, but they will have no liability-based incentive to do so since they can already escape liability by following the due care standard.

The injurer could also spend less on care than the legal system requires them to. In that case they will have lower costs of care taking, but they will have to pay damages in case an accident occurs. Since the optimal care standard was defined as exactly that level of care where the marginal costs of care equal the marginal benefits in accident reduction, taking less than the due care standard will not be interesting for the individual injurer since it will increase their total expected costs.

[12] We assume of course that there are prohibitive transaction costs which prevent efficient bargaining between the tortfeasor and the victim. Otherwise the Coase Theorem (see Section 2.3) could apply.

[13] Shavell (1980a, at 8) and Calabresi (1975a, at 658).

Thus, a negligence rule will lead to an efficient level of precaution for each risky environmental act, as long as the legal system defines the due care as equal to the optimal care of the model.

### 8.1.2.2 Strict Liability

A strict liability rule will also lead to the optimum.

The reason is quite simple. A strict liability rule basically says that the injurer has to compensate in any case, no matter what care they took. It is sometimes argued that this will lead the injurer to take excessive precautions or to take no care at all since they are liable anyway. Neither of these statements seems true.

By making the injurer strictly liable, the social decision is in fact shifted to the injurer. In the case of a unilateral accident, it simply means that they have to bear all the social costs of accidents, being their own costs of care taking and the expected damage.[14] Therefore, they will take exactly the same decision, being to minimise their total expected accident costs. We discussed in the model that this can be reached at the optimal care level. Therefore, the injurer will take optimal care for each risky act since this is the way to minimise their total expected costs. Spending more on care would increase their costs of care taking inefficiently and spending less on care would increase the expected damage inefficiently.

### 8.1.2.3 Differences

This leads to the conclusion that in a unilateral accident setting both a negligence and a strict liability rule will lead to a minimisation of the social costs of accidents. There remain differences between both rules as far as the secondary and tertiary costs are concerned.

Do victims receive compensation? Under a negligence rule in principle no cases of liability could be found, since a rational injurer would always follow the due care standard required in the legal system and would thus never have to compensate their victim. Under a strict liability rule, however, victims would always receive compensation, as some accidents would still occur, given whatever rational levels of precaution and activity were chosen by the rational injurer.

Does risk aversion play a role? If the assumption of risk neutrality is relaxed and if only one of the two parties were risk averse, for instance the victim, the choice between negligence and strict liability could result in a preference for one of these rules, depending upon which party is risk averse.

Do the administrative and information costs of both rules differ from each other? The strict liability rule seems to have the disadvantage that a legal case will follow with every accident since the injurer is always bound to compensate. Court costs can

[14] Polinsky (1983, at 39) and Shavell (1980a, at 11).

therefore be expected to be high. However, the negligence rule seems to have high information costs for the judge since they will have to determine in a particular case what the marginal costs and marginal benefits of care taking were.[15]

### 8.1.3 *The Bilateral Case*

Analysis can be extended to include those situations wherein the victim also is able to make a decision that will impact on how the risky activity plays out. What if the victim could take their own strategy ex ante to affect the ex post results of the risky activity, how might we provide incentives to both parties to better guide them to a robust result?

Until now we assumed that the optimal care level for the victim would be zero. The question arises which liability rule is optimal if one also wishes to give incentives to the victim to follow an optimal care level. Thus, the question, which liability rule can provide incentives simultaneously to both the injurer and the victim for efficient care taking.

Strict liability will, for the above given reasons, still give incentives to the injurer to take efficient care. The victim, however, will realise that they receive full compensation. A simple strict liability rule would therefore be suboptimal since it will not provide the victim with an incentive for efficient care.[16]

Victims can be given incentives for optimal care taking if the strict liability rule is combined with a so-called contributory negligence defence. This rule means, in its hardest form, that the victim will not receive any compensation from the injurer if they did not follow the due care the law requires from a victim. A strict liability rule combined with such a contributory negligence defence will provide optimal incentives to both the injurer and the victim. The victim will take optimal care to avoid that they will have to bear their own loss. The injurer, knowing that the victim will take optimal care will still have an incentive to take optimal care under the strict liability rule to minimise their expected accident costs.[17]

A negligence rule will provide the victim with an incentive for optimal care taking. The reason is that injurers will, under negligence, always take due care to avoid liability. Under a negligence rule a victim therefore carries in principle their own loss and therefore has optimal incentives to minimise their expected accident costs.[18]

A third possibility is the combination of negligence with a contributory negligence defence. The difference with a simple negligence rule would be that with a defence of contributory negligence, the injurer would not have to compensate a

[15] Brown (1973, at 343); Calabresi (1975a, at 666, n22) and Shavell (1987, at 9).
[16] See Shavell (1987, at 11).
[17] Id., at 12–13.
[18] Id., at 14.

victim that behaves contributorily negligent, even in cases where the injurer did not follow the due care level and therefore was also negligent themselves. Such a rule will in principle also provide optimal incentives for both injurers and victims.

There is, however, debate in the literature on the use of adding a contributory negligence defence to the simple negligence rule. Some authors claim that this is useless since the simple negligence rule will also provide the victim with an incentive to take care.[19] However others, including Posner, claim that it is certainly useful to add a contributory negligence defence to the negligence rule, to provide the victim with some incentives to self-protect.[20]

Summarising we should note that when also the behaviour of the victim can influence the accident risk, a liability rule should be chosen to account for this bilateral accident situation: the victim should be given an incentive for care taking as well. This result can be achieved both with a strict liability rule combined with contributory negligence and through a negligence rule.

### 8.1.4 *The Activity Level*

A further refinement to take into account is the fact that other factors than care can influence the accident risk. In the literature attention has especially been paid in this respect to the influence of those activities not routinely taken into account in judicial settings; the literature refers to this concept as 'activity level'.[21]

In simple words, this means that the chance to be involved in an accident will not only be influenced by the 'care' which is taken when exercising the activity, but also by other behavioural acts, such as the number of times one engages in the activity. And these differences in categories exist because of the way courts tend to examine the evidence for a particular accident, to examine the details of that one unique act in isolation.

Taking the simple example of traffic accidents, one can argue that the chance that one will be involved in a traffic accident not only depends upon the care taken by the driver (and victim), but also upon the number of kilometres driven in a certain time period. The more one drives, the larger the statistical probability that one will be involved in an accident. But the court will likely focus on a narrower set of details, such as speed at moment of accident and care rendered in the moments immediately surrounding the accident event. Years of experience, frequency of

[19] Id., at 15; Veljanovski (1981, at 133).

[20] See Posner (1986, at 252–253) and for mathematical proof, Landes and Posner (1981b, at 881–883); in the same direction goes Chelius (1976, at 297). It would take us too far to discuss this difference at great length in this book. It is, moreover, less important in the environmental context, since we will subsequently claim that there is a strong case for strict liability in environmental cases.

[21] See Adams (1989); Diamond (1974, at 107–164); and Shavell (1980a, at 1–25).

travel, and other such considerations are often not examined in tort cases, despite the obvious role that data might have in foreseeability and risk planning.

Hence, it has been stressed that a liability rule should not only aim at providing incentives for optimal care taking but should also provide incentives for adopting an optimal activity level.[22] Thus, the recognition of the concept of 'activity level' should play an important role in the choice of legal rules between strict liability and negligence.

If once more, we first assume that accidents are unilateral and only the injurer's activity can influence the accident risk, one can argue that negligence will not be optimal. Negligence indeed only provides incentives to the injurer to take optimal care, but not to adopt an optimal activity level.[23] The reason is that when the judge determines the due care level required in the legal system, they cannot incorporate the activity level exercised by the injurer. In other words, the judge will not be able to determine what an optimal activity level is, and thus would not hold an injurer liable because of negligence since they engaged too often in a certain activity.

Only a strict liability rule will provide the injurer with an incentive to adopt an optimal activity level. The reason is that adopting an optimal activity level is just another way for the injurer to minimise their total expected accidents costs. Since strict liability means that the injurer will have to compensate the total accident costs, they know ex ante that they will have to bear their own costs of care and the expected damage. Therefore, they will weigh not only their costs of care, but also the number of times they engage in the activity against the resulting expected loss. From this it follows that in case of a unilateral accident only strict liability will provide incentives to the injurer to adopt an optimal activity level.[24] At the policy level this means that strict liability seems more attractive in situations where the victim cannot influence the accident risk, neither through taking care, nor by adopting an optimal activity level.

This picture, however, changes if one moves once more to the bilateral accident situation. The problem is that in that particular case the victim will, under strict liability with a contributory negligence defence, not have an incentive to adopt an optimal activity level. The activity level of the victim will indeed not be taken into account when judging whether the victim was contributory negligent or not. Only under negligence will the victim have an incentive not only to take optimal care, but also to adopt an optimal activity level since under negligence a victim will be fully exposed to their loss.[25]

The conclusion is therefore that in a bilateral accident situation one should examine which activity is mostly influencing the accident risk. Strict liability is

[22] Id., at 22.
[23] Id., at 2.
[24] See also Shavell (1987, at 24–25).
[25] Id., at 29.

more effective in situations where one wishes to provide incentives for activity changes to injurers, whereas negligence seems more appropriate in situations where the activity of the victim is the most important factor influencing the accident risk. One example could be where a pharmaceutical company produces an important anti-cancer medication at some risk to the environment, and policymakers have determined to place the costs of those risks on that company instead of the local community, then they should use a rule of strict liability to incentivise the company to create less risk by reducing overall production. If the policymakers preferred to shift the costs of those risks to the local community, a rule of negligence would leave the community at risk of cost-bearing every time an accident occurred while the company was exercising due care; thus the community would receive an incentive to avoid being in the vicinity of the risk or to reduce their activities that increase their risk exposure to the pharmaceutical plant's risky activities.[26]

## 8.2 NEGLIGENCE VERSUS STRICT LIABILITY TO CONTROL ENVIRONMENTAL HARM

### 8.2.1 *Economic Criteria*

One possible liability rule which will give the polluter an incentive to spend on care to reach the optimal standard is the negligence rule. Assuming that under a negligence rule the potential polluter will only have to pay compensation if they spend less on care than the legal system wants them to (due care), the firm will have an incentive to spend on care, since it is a way to avoid liability which will maximise their utility. Provided that the legal system defines the due care level as the optimal standard, a negligence rule will therefore give the polluter incentives to follow the optimal standard. Also, a strict liability rule will lead to optimal incentives for care taking for the polluter, since taking efficient care will minimise the expected accident costs which the potential polluter has to bear under a strict liability system.[27] Therefore, the literature generally accepts that both a negligence rule and a strict liability rule will provide a potential polluter with incentives to take the efficient care level. However, this is only valid in a unilateral accident setting, i.e. an accident whereby only the injurer can influence the accident risk. If victims were also given incentives for accident reduction, a contributory negligence defence should be added to the strict liability rule. Under negligence, victims will always have an incentive to take efficient care as well since they will in principle not be compensated by the injurer who, under a negligence rule, will take efficient care to avoid liability.

[26] In considering who might be the more robust recipient of the risk exposure to the costs of the accidents, the policymakers will be facing a question of robust Coasean allocation of rights, from Section 2.3

[27] Polinsky (1983, at 39); Shavell (1980a, at 11); and Shavell (1987, at 8).

However, as we just discussed, the accident risk is not only influenced by the level of care, but also by the number of times that the parties are involved in the risky activity, i.e. the activity level. An optimal liability rule should also give the parties in a potential accident setting incentives to adopt an optimal activity level. A negligence rule will not give optimal incentives to the injurer to adopt an optimal activity level since the activity level is not incorporated in the due care standard which the court applies.[28] Under a negligence rule, the injurer only has an incentive to take efficient care (to escape liability) but not to adopt an efficient activity level. Under a strict liability rule, on the contrary, an injurer has an incentive to adopt an efficient activity level since this is also a way to minimise the total expected accident costs which they have to bear. In a unilateral accident model, strict liability is the efficient liability rule since it leads both to efficient care and to an optimal activity level.

The reason that is often advanced in legal literature in favour of strict environmental liability is that strict liability will help the victim in obtaining compensation since they are released from the heavy burden of proving fault under the negligence rule. However, from a deterrence point of view victim compensation is not as such a goal of accident law. The duty of the injurer to compensate their victim is only an instrument to reach deterrence efficiency. Moreover, the victim compensation argument to introduce strict liability for environmental pollution is not that convincing in all cases. Indeed, many legal systems qualify every violation of a statutory or regulatory norm as a civil fault.[29] Most industries are subjected to extensive safety regulation. Hence, in these systems the victim only has to prove the violation of one of these regulations to establish a fault. If, in addition, the victim can prove a causal relationship with the loss suffered, they will be able to claim compensation. In many accident cases this burden of proof will therefore not be as heavy as has been argued.

It is, therefore, at least questionable whether a strict liability rule substantially improves the situation of the victim in comparison with an already existing broadly interpreted civil fault regime.

It should also not be overlooked that under the general fault regime of tort law, no limitations apply, and the victim is entitled to full compensation. In many of the environmental cases where strict liability was first introduced, more particularly in the international conventions concerning nuclear accidents and oil pollution, financial caps and other limitations on the victim's rights were introduced. The alleged compensating benefit of the strict liability is therefore doubtful.

Although the classic victim compensation argument may as such not justify the introduction of strict liability for environmental pollution, there are however economic reasons based on deterrence efficiency for introducing a strict liability rule.

[28] See Adams (1989); Diamond (1974, at 107–164); and Shavell (1980a, at 1–25).

[29] See generally on the interaction between regulation and tort law, the contributions in Van Boom, Lukas, and Kissling (2007).

Environmental pollution can in some cases be considered as a unilateral accident. This is more particularly the case when environmental damage is the result of an ultra-hazardous activity such as a nuclear accident. In this case we noted that the advantage of the strict liability rule is that it will give the injurer an incentive both to adopt an optimal activity level and to take efficient care. Since the victim cannot influence the accident risk, strict liability seems to be the first-best solution to give the potential polluter optimal incentives for accident reduction.[30]

In sum, if we apply the criteria of Shavell, determining the choice between negligence and strict liability to the environmental case, there seem to be strong arguments in favour of an introduction of strict liability. In many cases environmental pollution will be truly unilateral in the sense that only the injurer's activity can influence the accident risk, which constitutes a strong case for strict liability.[31] In other cases the victim will certainly be able to exercise an influence on the risk as well. One can more specifically think about situations where the victim has the possibility to mitigate damages after the accident occurred. However, in those cases it is not the victim's activity level, but their level of care which influences the accident risk. This can be controlled by adding a contributory or comparative negligence defence to the strict liability rule.

### 8.2.2 *A Few Refinements*

#### 8.2.2.1 Information Differences

Many scholars argued that there is indeed a strong case in favour of strict liability in case of environmental harm; this will give the potential injurer optimal incentives for accident reduction, and hence for optimal internalisation.[32]

There is, however, another important aspect of the difference between negligence and strict liability which should be mentioned. This concerns the fact that the application of negligence requires high information costs from the judge, who will have to set the due care standard. The information necessary to weigh costs and benefits and fix the optimal care may not be readily available for the judge.

Strict liability shifts all costs to the injurer, who will then have to define the optimal care level. If one therefore assumes that, as may be the case with environmental harm, the information on optimal precaution is better available with industry than with the judges, this constitutes an argument for strict liability.

30 See Faure (1995a, at 21–43).

31 In some cases it will be the victim's activity that caused the harm, e.g. if the victim knowingly came to the nuisance. This may then lead to a denial of a claim on compensation. See in that respect the discussion on the coming to the nuisance doctrine, in Section 3.3.

32 See e.g. with respect to environmental liability Endres and Staiger (1996, at 79–93) and Monti (1994).

Note that in some cases there may be an information advantage with the regulator. This is, as we will discuss below, an argument in favour of regulation, but not necessarily against strict liability. This information advantage may therefore constitute an additional argument in favour of strict liability for environmental harm.

This, however, assumes that the court has accurate information on the amount of the damage. If courts err in assessing damages, strict liability will lead to under-deterrence and thus negligence would have been more robust.[33]

#### 8.2.2.2 Insolvency: Strict Liability versus Negligence

There are other reasons why the seeming advantage of strict liability should be taken with salt. Until now, it was assumed that the injurer has sufficient money at stake to pay compensation to the victim. If, however, the amount of the damage exceeds the injurer's wealth, a problem of under-deterrence will arise. Under strict liability the injurer will consider the accident as one which is equal to their total wealth and will therefore only take the care necessary to avoid an accident with a magnitude equal to their total wealth. If that wealth is lower than the magnitude of an accident, they will take less than the optimal care and therefore a problem of under-deterrence arises under strict liability.

Insolvency is less of a problem under negligence since under that rule the injurer will still have an incentive to take the care required by the legal system, as long as the costs of taking care are less than their individual wealth. Taking due care remains indeed a way for the injurer to avoid having to pay compensation to the victim. If there is thus a potential accident setting whereby the magnitude of the loss is higher than the injurer's wealth (which can often be the case in environmental liability), this constitutes an argument in favour of negligence rather than strict liability.

#### 8.2.2.3 Positive Externalities

There is another issue which has been mentioned in the literature which reduces the arguments in favour of strict liability. Gilead rightly pointed out that many activities create not only harmful externalities but also positive externalities, which may be a reason to be somewhat cautious with strict liability.[34] This is a consequence of the fact that strict liability incorporates activity level changes, whereas a negligence rule does not. It is not always obvious that increases in activity levels are socially undesirable.[35] Think about the manufacture of drugs. Most of this activity creates huge social benefits. One should therefore be careful with the argument that

[33] If, in other words, courts can more easily observe the socially desirable level of precaution than the exact amount of external harm, a negligence rule should be favoured. This point has been made by Cooter (1984, 1343–1523).

[34] See Gilead (1997, at 589).

[35] Gilles (1992, at 319).

strict liability is needed to internalise risk and control activity levels if the externalised benefits of an increased activity were neglected.

Finally, there is one other nuance which has to be added. Until now, we assumed a strict liability rule whereby the injurer is 'merely' held to compensate the damage they caused to their victim, not less but also not more. Problems may arise if strict liability is combined with other features which may expand the burden of liability on enterprises. One could think of a removal of the burden of proving causation,[36] joint and several liability, and high (punitive) damages for (non-pecuniary) losses. These are formally different issues than the simple choice between negligence and strict liability. However, according to Trebilcock,[37] it was especially because of these other features that the strict liability regimes in the USA were experienced as 'crushing'. The final judgment on the efficiency of strict liability may also depend upon these other issues, such as causation and the magnitude of the damages awarded.

### 8.2.3 *Strict Liability in Environmental Law*

#### 8.2.3.1 International Level

If one confronts the reasoning from the economic literature in favour of strict liability with developments in conventions, statutes, and case law, it is certainly fair to state that there is a strong tendency towards strict liability for the environmental risk.

At the international level we can inter alia refer to the international conventions concerning nuclear accidents and oil pollution. Although these conventions show various inefficiencies, such as the introduction of financial caps, they did introduce strict liability for activities which are typically unilateral and which therefore seems to correspond with the economic doctrine. In addition, we can point to the interesting Convention of Lugano on Civil Liability for Damage Resulting from Activities Dangerous to the Environment (1993).[38] In this convention the signatory parties agreed to a strict liability for environmental damage; however, this convention never entered into force.

There is one international, or at least regional, instrument which can also be mentioned, being the European Union Directive 2004/35/EC on Environmental Liability with Regard to The Prevention and Remediation of Environmental Damage.[39] This Environmental Liability Directive (ELD) of 21 April 2004 has as a key objective to prevent environmental harm through the incentives generated by

36 See Faure and Hartlief (1998, at 681–706).

37 Trebilcock 1987, at 929–1002.

38 For comments on this convention see e.g. Bauw (1993); De Boer (1993, at 225); Spier and Sterk (1992, at 591); and Sterk (1994).

39 *Official Journal* L143/56.

potential liability, based on the idea that if operators are exposed to financial liabilities for damage, they will be induced to adopt measures and develop practices to minimise the risk of environmental damage.[40] The basic liability rules of the ELD are the following: for operators that undertake an activity which is covered by the EU legislation listed in Annex III of the ELD, strict liability applies for damage to EU protected natural habitats and species, damage to waters covered by the Framework Directive, and soil pollution, if the damage exceeds the applicable thresholds. If the damage to the environment is the result of a non-listed occupational activity, fault-based liability applies and only the damage to EU protected natural habitats and species is recoverable under the ELD. This regime covers activities that are not deemed dangerous to the environment.[41]

This distinction made in the ELD between the two liability rules of negligence and strict liability is very much in line with the lessons from the economic analysis. The activities listed in Annex III can often be considered as hazardous and thus as unilateral activities. In those situations, it is important to control the polluter's activity through a strict liability rule. Even if hazardous activities are bilateral in nature, there remains a case for a strict liability rule, since the hazardous activity will have a far more important influence on the risk than the victim's activity.

The same is not the case for the non-hazardous activities (non-listed in Annex III), where a fault rule applies.

However, it was mentioned earlier that strict liability entails a larger risk of insolvency creating under-deterrence than a fault-based rule. For that reason, it is important to add a mandatory solvency guarantee to a strict liability regime. It is in that respect that the ELD shows a major weakness. Mandatory insurance was rejected by the EU legislature. The ELD only requires in article 14(1) that Member States would take measures to encourage the development of financial security instruments and markets by the appropriate economic and financial operators, including financial mechanisms in case of insolvency, with the aim of enabling operators to use financial guarantees to cover their responsibility under the ELD.[42] There is a major weakness of the liability regime in the ELD as it has been stressed in the literature that introducing a strict liability regime without the accompanying mandatory solvency guarantees may lead to a serious problem of under-deterrence.[43]

#### 8.2.3.2 Strict Environmental Liability in Statutes

It may be clear that with the implementation of the ELD many European Member States had to implement the strict liability, at least related to the (rather limited)

[40] See Goldsmith and Bergkamp (2013, at 3).
[41] See Brans (2013, at 42–43).
[42] For details see Bergkamp, Herbatchek, and Jayanti (2013, at 118–138).
[43] See Faure and Grimeaud (2003, at 192–193).

scope of the ELD. However, many EU Member States already had introduced strict environmental liability in statutes. Strict liability could for example be found in the German Water Pollution Act of 1957,[44] and in the subsequent Umwelthaftungsgesetz of 1990;[45] another example constitutes the Danish Act on Strict Liability for Environmental Damage.[46] Given the limited scope of the ELD, some specific statutes in Member States also expand the scope of strict liability for environmental damage beyond the scope of the ELD regime.[47]

Of course, many examples of strict liability for environmental damage can also be found outside of the EU. For example, Switzerland has a special strict liability which was introduced in the federal Act on the protection of the environment.[48] Other legislation focuses specifically on particular aspects of the environment such as water pollution.[49]

The federal statutes on environmental law within the USA have also brought strict liability rules to bear on environmental injuries. Perhaps the best-known instances of strict liability in environmental contexts is that of Comprehensive Environmental Response, Compensation, and Liability Act (CERCLA): [50]

> [A]ny person who accepts or accepted any hazardous substances for transport to disposal or treatment facilities, incineration vessels or sites selected by such person, from which there is a release, or a threatened release which causes the incurrence of response costs, of a hazardous substance, shall be liable for . . .

Another well-known example is the Oil Pollution Act of 1990 (OPA),[51] which provides strict liability for:

> Notwithstanding any other provision or rule of law, and subject to the provisions of this Act, each responsible party for a vessel or a facility from which oil is discharged, or which poses the substantial threat of a discharge of oil, into or upon the navigable waters or adjoining shorelines or the exclusive economic zone is liable for the

44 Brüggemeier (1991, at 85–91).

45 Id., at 91–92; Simon (1996, at 13); and Wagner (1991a, at 175). A translation of the German Environmental Liability Act can be found in Markesinis (2002, at 871).

46 For a comment see Pagh (1995, at 15). According to Betlem, liability under this Act is already excluded if the conditions of a licence are followed (Betlem 1995, at 302); this would indeed seriously limit the scope of liability.

47 See on the scope of the ELD regime, Bergkamp and Van Bergeijk (2013).

48 For details see Widmer (2002).

49 For a comparative overview see Koch and Koziol (2002, at 405–407).

50 See 42 U.S. Code § 9607(a)(4): 'CERCLA is often described as imposing strict liability. In many respects this description is justified. To prove liability the plaintiff need not show fault on the part of the defendant, and proof of the defendant's care or lack of fault is often not a defense. One can even incur liability without knowing that one was handling hazardous wastes."' George W. Dent, 'Limited Liability in Environmental Law', 1991, Faculty Publications. Paper 334, at 153.

51 33 U.S. Code § 2702(a).

removal costs and damages specified in subsection (b) that result from such incident.

It is clear from these two examples that they follow the idea of an accumulated or stewarded hazard that escapes control of the operator, and thus closely follow the spirit of Rylands.

#### 8.2.3.3 Strict Environmental Liability in Case Law

Finally, we can point at tendencies in case law to shift from negligence towards strict liability. In many areas this shift took place without the formal introduction of a strict liability rule, but instead simply by broadening the fault concept. This evolution could also be seen in the area of environmental damage. Especially as far as the liability for soil clean-up costs is concerned, the foreseeability requirement has often been relaxed, which also substantially lowers the burden of proving negligence.[52] Tendencies towards expanding the scope of liability for environmental harm via case law could be found in many jurisdictions. One can point to the famous *British Rylands* v. *Fletcher* case, where a strict liability rule for damage caused by bursting reservoirs was instituted.[53] This nineteenth-century doctrine is now widely applied to many cases of environmental harm; albeit it has evolved in several pathways, each with their own variations.[54] Another example can be found in German case law, where a reversal of the burden of proof was accepted in a 1985 environmental case.[55]

It's worth mentioning that strict liability can be found in a variety of corners in common-law-based environmental law, as nuisance and trespass are often effective avenues for establishing standing for environmental lawsuits. As Shapo wrote, 'Trespass is the strictest of strict liability torts.'[56]

## 8.3 CAUSATION

Another issue of particular importance in environmental liability is causation. In environmental liability the problem will often arise of uncertainty concerning the causal link between an event (e.g. an emission) and a certain outcome (e.g. health damage). The question then arises how the law should deal with causal uncertainty if scientific evidence were to report that there is a 40 per cent probability that a cancer was caused by the wrongful act, but a 60 per cent probability that the cancer came from another source (the so-called background risk).

[52] See Faure and Hartlief (1996a, at 235) and following for a sketch of these evolutions.
[53] See Zweigert and Kötz (1998, at 708) and Mullis and Oliphant (2011, at 195–200); see also the Cambridge water case, discussed in the next section.
[54] See discussion at Faure and Partain (2017); at Section 3.4.1.
[55] Discussed by Markesinis (2002, at 880–881).
[56] Shapo (1997, at 541).

### 8.3.1 *Importance of Causation*

Already early Law and Economics papers have stressed the importance of causation in tort law.[57] Shavell explains why it is important to limit the liability of the injurer to those cases in which they really caused the accident.[58] If the requirement of causation did not have this limiting effect, this would mean that potential injurers would withdraw from many activities which are as such socially beneficial.

In the absence of a causation requirement it would mean that a manufacturer, for example, could also be held liable for damage which has not been caused by their activities and which the manufacturer could therefore not influence or reduce. Such a liability not respecting the requirement of causation would be considered as 'crushing', according to Shavell.[59]

It is of course, equally a case of injustice from a more legal perspective, to be punished for what one has not done wrongly.

### 8.3.2 *Causal Uncertainty and 'Probability of Causation'*

Landes and Posner provide an example of this category.[60] Imagine a community where the ambient environmental conditions lead to 100 new cases of cancer every year. (One can imagine either a giant city or a small village, for the purposes here the maths works the same way.) Suppose that a nuclear power plant, newly built in the community's locale, wrongfully emits a certain amount of ionising radiation into the environment, of which it is clear that exposure to this radiation will increase the rate of new cancers from 100 to 111. Economic theory holds that the nuclear power plant should only be liable for the 11 additional cancer cases, because only these cancer cases could have been prevented through the power plant.

In other words, the power plant should not be liable for the so-called background risk, the 100 cases that would occur anyway; it should only be liable and responsible for the excess risk it brings, so only the 11 additional cases.

This corresponds with the argument of Rizzo and Arnold that the causation should be equal to the objective marginal product of an activity, being the amount in which the activity has contributed to an increase in the accident risk.[61]

The practical problem is, however, that it is not possible to identify which of the 11 persons would not have received cancer had there been no radiation from the nuclear power plant. Hence, the causal uncertainty in this particular case is that

57 We can e.g. refer to Calabresi (1975b, at 69); see also Epstein (1973, at 151–204); Landes and Posner (1983, at 109–134); Landes and Posner (1987, at 228–255); and Shavell (1980b, at 463–516).

58 Shavell 1985a, at 587–609.

59 See Shavell (1987, at 108).

60 See Landes and Posner (1983, at 123–124; 1987, at 242).

61 Rizzo and Arnold (1980, at 1399, 1410–1414; 1986, at 219–226).

there are 111 victims whereby in 11 cases the harm (the cancer) was the consequence of the tort (the emission). For each individual, taken separately, the probability that their disease was caused by the specific radiation was not even 10 per cent. If one would now allow each of the 111 victims to claim full compensation from the nuclear power plant this would not only be inefficient, but also largely unreasonable. Landes and Posner claim that, taking administrative costs aside, the efficient solution would be that each victim should have the possibility of claiming 10 per cent of their damage from the power plant.[62]

In the literature it is generally argued that there should only be liability to the extent that the activity contributed to the accident risk, meaning that on the basis of statistical evidence the liability should be constructed in such a way that the polluter will never be held liable for the background risk (which they did not cause), but only for the excess risk.[63] First a so-called probability of causation will have to be determined.

This probability of causation formula originates from radio-biology and nuclear medicine, where it has always been important to determine what the probability is that a certain cancer has been caused by a certain exposure to radiation. The American National Council on Radiation Protection and Measurements announced in a statement of 30 September 1992 that this probability of causation method is accepted to determine whether a certain disease has been caused by a particular radiation.[64] On the basis of this method the American National Institute of Health made tables to determine what, given certain circumstances and exposure to certain doses, the 'probability of causation' will be.[65] These tables show that, although there is a lot of controversy, it is scientifically not impossible to provide guidance on the probability of causation.[66]

### 8.3.3 *Threshold Liability versus Causal Apportionment*

The interesting question now is how the law should react when this probability of causation is known. From a Law and Economics perspective the question arises what kind of a legal rule can lead to a limitation of the liability to the excess risk and exclude liability for the background risk.

Traditionally there was a choice between two legal rules – one with a binary 'all or nothing' character, the other with a sliding scale approach.

62 Landes and Posner (1983, at 124).

63 See Gold (1986, at 376–402); Kaye (1982); and Rosenberg (1984, at 851–929).

64 National Council on Radiation, Protection and Measurements Statement No. 7, 30 September 1992; see also Bond (1981, at 108–111).

65 Report on the National Institute of Health at Hock Working Group to develop radio-epidemiological tables, NIH Publication No. 85, 2748, Washington, 1985; see also Ketchum (1985, at 967–972).

66 See Estep (1960, at 259–304) and Mettler and Moseley (1985).

One possibility is to award 100 per cent compensation to the victim once a certain threshold is passed, e.g. a 50 per cent liability. This is usually referred to as a threshold liability. This rule, which was applied in the USA for a long time, is considered to be inefficient and unjust. It is inefficient since it may lead to under-deterrence if e.g. the probability is always just below the threshold (e.g. for 10 per cent) that the cancer was caused by the emission. If the threshold is just passed (e.g. 60 per cent probability) there will be full compensation, which may be unjust. In that case the threshold liability rule forces a firm to compensate (at least partially) for damage which it can never have caused from a statistical point of view.

The alternative is to translate the probability of causation by awarding the victim a proportion of their damage. When the chance, as was the case in our initial example, is 40 per cent that the harm was caused by the tort, the victim will be awarded 40 per cent of their loss. The advantage of this solution from an efficiency point of view is that the injurer is precisely exposed to the excess risk which they cause.

In addition, this proportional liability rule may also be preferable from the victim's point of view. Indeed, in many cases the victim would have received nothing under a threshold rule, if the 50 per cent threshold had not been passed. The threshold rule is indeed an 'all or nothing' approach; in those cases, the victim would at least have received 40 per cent compensation under a proportionate liability rule. Economic analysis generally holds that only the proportional liability rule will give optimal incentives for accident prevention.[67] It is important to mention that in some modern policy proposals with respect to causation, this proportional liability rule has been introduced. It is for example the case in the 'Principles of European Tort Law', which have adopted proportional liability for example when multiple victims suffered harm, but it remains uncertain whether a particular victim's damage has been caused by the activity, while it is likely that it did not cause the damage of all victims. In that case, article 3:103 of the 'Principles of European Tort Law' holds that the activity is regarded as a cause of the damage, suffered by all victims in proportion to the likelihood that it may have caused the damage of a particular victim.[68] Also, in the domestic law of various countries a proportional liability rule is now introduced.

## 8.4 FINANCIAL CAPS

An important feature of environmental liability, especially in the liability regime of many international conventions, is a limitation of the compensation.[69] The question

67 See Faure (1993); Makdisi (1989, at 1063); Landes and Posner (1984, at 417–434); and Robinson (1985, at 779–798).

68 Article 3:103(2) of the 'Principles of European Tort Law' (European Group on Tort Law, 2005, at 47).

69 We more particularly refer to the conventions on nuclear liability and on liability for marine oil pollution, mentioned earlier.

arises how one should consider these financial limits on the amount of liability to be paid by the injurer from an economic point of view. These limitations, also referred to as 'caps' are often advanced as an argument 'to keep the risk insurable'.

### 8.4.1 *Economic Analysis of Caps*

#### 8.4.1.1 When Costs Are Not Fully Internalised

Earlier we advocated that there are good reasons to favour a strict liability rule for environmental damage, the main reason being that only strict liability would lead to a full internalisation of the environmental risk. Only with full strict liability would the potential injurer have an incentive to adopt an optimal activity level. This full internalisation is only possible if the injurer is effectively exposed to the full costs of the activity they engage in, and derivatively held to provide full compensation to any victim.

A disadvantage of a system of financial caps is that this will seriously impair the victim's rights to full compensation. But if the cap is indeed set at a much lower amount than the expected damage, this would not only violate the victim's right on compensation, but the above-mentioned full internalisation of the externality would not take place either. From an economic point of view a limitation of compensation therefore poses a serious problem since there will be no internalisation of the risky activity.

If one believes that the exposure to liability has a deterrent effect, a limitation of the amount of compensation due to victims poses another problem. There is direct linear relationship between the magnitude of the accident risk and the amount spent on care by the potential polluter. If the liability therefore is limited to a certain amount, the potential injurer will consider the accident as one with a magnitude of the limited amount. The amount of care spent by the potential injurer will be lower and a problem of under-deterrence arises.[70] The amount of optimal care, reflected in the optimal standard, being the care necessary to reduce the total accident costs efficiently, will be higher than the amount the potential injurer will spend to avoid an accident equal to the statutory limited amount.

In fact, if a certain industry is protected by a statutory limitation of compensation, this also constitutes an indirect subsidisation of that particular industry. That subsidisation is very clear in the case of nuclear accidents, where international conventions (and domestic statutes) limit the amount of the subsidy to an amount which is substantially lower than the estimated costs of a nuclear accident. The financial limit on the liability of the nuclear power plant operator has therefore in the literature been qualified as a subsidy.[71]

70 Landes and Posner (1984, at 417).

71 See inter alia Dubin and Rothwell (1990); Faure and Fiore (2009); and Heyes and Liston-Heyes (1998).

#### 8.4.1.2 A Remedy to Uninsurability?

One could question whether statutory caps on liability are adequate answers to uninsurability. When discussing environmental liability insurance, we will show that competitive insurance markets have worked out all kinds of devices to cope with large risk as well. Reinsurance, co-insurance, or pooling of risks are well-known phenomena that allow insurers to provide large amounts of insurance coverage. Hence, the high magnitude of the risk itself does not make environmental liability uninsurable per se.

More principally, one can also question whether, even in cases where there is a limited availability of insurance coverage (which is already hard to judge for the legislator, if possible at all), this should lead to a limitation of the liability of the injurer. If it appears indeed that the possibilities of obtaining liability insurance coverage are limited to a certain amount, there is no reason to limit the liability itself to that same amount, which could reduce incentives to manage risks efficiently and thus potentially increase the risk of an accident and of insurance costs.

A clear alternative would be to introduce a duty to insure up to the available amount of insurance coverage, but to keep the liability of the injurer unlimited. In several EU Member States, inter alia in Germany, an unlimited liability has been imposed upon operators of nuclear power plants, but at the same time the duty to seek financial security has been limited to a specific amount, for example €2.5 billion in Germany.[72] This will on the one hand have the advantage that the duty to insure is limited to realistic amounts, whereas on the other hand, the incentives for care taking by the injurer remain at least partially in existence because the injurer is still exposed to risk in case the magnitude of the harm is higher than the insured amount. In sum, from an economic point of view there are very few convincing reasons to limit the amount of compensation due to the victim. If insurability problems exist, they can be solved by limiting the duty to insure.

### 8.4.2 *Legal Analysis of Caps*

Reality is, however, often very different. For instance, in the area of nuclear liability some countries have seriously limited the liability of the licensee of a nuclear power plant. In Belgium the limitations were so low that the victim's right to compensation was reduced to less than 1 per cent of the average costs of an accident.[73]

The reason that these caps are often introduced can be found in interest group theories.[74] In the 1950s the nuclear industry feared that the future of nuclear power could be endangered by unlimited liability. In the preparatory documents preceding

72 For details see Faure (2016a, at 129–130).

73 For estimates see Faure (1995a, at 29–31).

74 Interest group theory and public choice will be further discussed in Chapter 9.

the Paris Convention on Nuclear Liability it can clearly be read that the goal of the regulation of nuclear liability was not so much the protection of victims, but the protection of the nuclear industry itself.[75] There is qualitative evidence of the influence of the nuclear industry both in drafting the international conventions and especially in the national implementing of legislation.[76] Both insurers and the nuclear industry lobbied in a joint profit maximising strategy, for the limitation of liability.

One should, however, note that objections against statutory caps on liability are also raised in legal literature. Legal authors of course argue that a limitation would be contrary to the principle of full compensation of victims;[77] also the economic argument is advanced that a limitation – specifically in case of professional liability – would lead to a reduction of the quality of the services.[78] Finally it is also argued that granting a limitation to a specific group of professionals would violate the equality principle, since there are no specific reasons to protect one group by financial caps whereas others would still be exposed to full liability.[79]

### 8.4.3 *Contractual Limitations*

Although there are, in sum, very few arguments in favour of a statutory limitation of the liability, this does not mean that there may be no reasons for a contractual limitation in insurance policies. In many insurance policies these limitations already exist, since an insurer will hardly ever provide unlimited coverage for the liability risk.[80] A contractual limitation could take two forms. First, an insurer could consider lowering the amount of liability coverage generally. Such a general undiscriminated reduction might, however, be difficult to sell to the intermediaries. It might be more appropriate to focus on the specific components of the damage where an increase may be expected. Depending upon the legal system, this may for example be the case for the amounts awarded for pain and suffering. If an insurer expects substantial increases in these amounts in a particular legal system, a contractual limitation of the insured amounts for pain and suffering may be appropriate.

## 8.5 LIABILITY CHANNELLING

There is one more feature of the environmental liability regime as it has been worked out in international conventions on oil pollution and for nuclear accidents which deserves a review. This is the so-called liability channelling, which per se

75 For an interesting analysis in that respect, see Vanden Borre (2007, at 262–266).
76 Faure (1995a, at 33–35).
77 See Hartlief and Tjittes (1990a; 1994).
78 See Wessels (1995a, at 235; 1995b, at 54).
79 See Faure and Hartlief (1995, at 313).
80 Insurance will be discussed in further detail in Chapter 11.

directs all of the potential liability from an accident to a single party, even if multiple participants are readily identifiable. It means that a victim of a nuclear accident could only sue the licensee or operator of that nuclear power plant and could not sue a third party, even if the loss was actually caused by the third party.

### 8.5.1 *Examples*

Under channelling, the liability is attached to one party who becomes fully liable for the damage.[81] Channelling is often exclusive. Channelling statutes indicate which (of many possible) parties can be held liable for the loss.[82] The result is that the victim can only sue the 'channelled' injurer and not another party who might have contributed to the loss.

As already indicated earlier, channelling of liability can be found in international conventions with respect to nuclear liability and marine pollution.[83] For example, under the Paris Convention on Nuclear Liability, liability is channelled to operators.[84] According to the convention, only the operator and no one else is liable for the damage caused by a nuclear accident.[85] The 'operator' is defined as 'the person designated or recognised by the competent public authority as the operator of that installation'.[86] The Paris Convention is the only legal basis for a claim against the nuclear operator in case of an incident.[87] Additionally, according to the Convention on the Liability of Operators of Nuclear Ships of Brussels,[88] 'except as otherwise provided in this Convention no person other than the operator shall be liable for such nuclear damage'.[89]

The 1969 International Convention on Civil Liability for Oil Pollution Damage (CLC) created a channelling of liability for oil pollution damage to the tanker owner.[90] The tanker owner is defined as 'the person or persons registered as the owner of the ship or, in the absence of registration, the person or persons owning

81 Wang (2011, at 82–83) for a discussion of channelling in the nuclear industry and in cases of oil pollution.
82 Id., at 82 ('It means that only the statutory channelled party shall be exclusively liable for the damage and the other parties are excluded from the liability').
83 Liu (2013) and Sands and Peel (2012, at 738–745) for a discussion of channelling under the nuclear liability conventions.
84 See Liu (2013, at 212) and Sands and Peel (2012, at 739).
85 Convention on Third Party Liability in the Field of Nuclear Energy, article VI(a), 20 July 1960, 956 U.N.T.S. 251.
86 Id., article I(a)(vi).
87 Id., article VI(c)(ii).
88 Convention on the Liability of Operators of Nuclear Ships, 25 May 1962, *American Journal of International Law*, 1963, Vol. 57(1), at 268.
89 Id., article II(2).
90 See Liu (2013, at 196–199); Sands and Peel (2012, at 746–747); and Wang (2011, at 87).

the ship'.[91] The application of all other legislation is pre-empted; no claims are possible other than those under the convention.[92] Claims against servants or agents of the owner are explicitly excluded.[93]

It is debatable whether this list of persons against whom no claim is possible still allows the possibility of claims against other parties. For example, some argue that claims against a cargo owner and operator would still be possible according to applicable national laws.[94] Additionally, the Hazardous and Noxious Substances by Sea Convention channels liability to the owner of the ship, defined as the person or persons registered as the owner of the ship or the person or persons owning the ship.[95]

### 8.5.2 *Analysis*

An argument often used to defend channelling is that it makes victims' lives much easier since they no longer have to investigate who precisely is the liable injurer in case of an accident with multiple injurers.[96] The statute indeed simplifies the victim's life by indicating that they can only sue the injurer to which liability is channelled. Thus, one could argue that channelling leads to a reduction of transaction costs.[97]

However, this hardly seems valid. The additional benefit of channelling for the victim is limited; the costs of discovering that it is the licensee of a nuclear power plant, for example, who may be primarily liable are not that high. Contrast this with the huge disadvantages for the victim: they no longer can possibly claim their damage from other parties who may have contributed to the loss as well. From a victim's perspective, one may well argue that joint and several liability is preferable. In that case the victim can simply sue any of the available injurers and claim full compensation.

One possible economic explanation for the phenomenon of legal channelling is the notion of the 'least cost avoider', already often referred to earlier. Calabresi, in his book titled, *The Costs of Accidents: A Legal and Economic Analysis*, held that the costs have to be allocated to the party who could reduce the costs as cheaply as possible.[98]

91 International Convention on Civil Liability for Oil Pollution Damage, article I(3), 29 November 1969, 972 U.N.T.S. 3.
92 Wang (2011, 87–88).
93 International Convention on Civil Liability for Oil Pollution Damage, article III(4), 29 November 1969, 972 U.N.T.S. 3.
94 Verheij (2007, at 141).
95 See International Convention on Liability and Compensation for Damage in Connection with the Carriage of Hazardous and Noxious Substances by Sea, article I(3), 3 May 1996, 35 I.L.M. 1415 (1996).
96 See Barboza (2010, at 32).
97 See Vanden Borre (2001, at 698–699).
98 Calabresi (1970, at 140–144).

One could argue that the legislature identified a particular operator (such as the licensee of a nuclear power plant) as the 'least cost avoider' and thus allocated liability to that particular person. However, the 'least cost avoider' was never meant to imply that if one particular party could be identified as the least cost avoider, that this would necessarily exclude liability of all others who could influence the accident risk, as is the case in legal channelling of liability. Such an interpretation of the least cost avoider also runs contrary to Calabresi's broader theory of tort law.[99]

There are, indeed, substantial disadvantages to channelling of liability.

Several scholars have argued that this regime of channelling is inefficient from an economic perspective, at least if one believes that an exposure to liability provides incentives for prevention.[100] In particular, the fact that channelling leads to sole liability of the operator, with the exclusion of liability suits against third-party contributors, is heavily criticised.[101] Indeed, one can imagine situations, such as nuclear accident cases, where another party has contributed to the loss as well; perhaps the person who may have delivered defective nuclear material that contributed to the loss. Exclusive channelling means that the victim no longer has the right to sue another party who could have influenced the risk of accident.[102] The effect is, of course, that the victim's claim may not be fully satisfied. One could criticise channelling from a distributive perspective. Moreover, the third party who has contributed to the loss should be exposed to liability in order to give them incentives for prevention. If the effect of the channelling is that the third party is no longer liable, it is clearly inefficient and overly incentivises risky behaviours.

Channelling may have this effect, especially in the nuclear case, since the liability of the nuclear power plant licensee (to which liability is channelled) is also limited because financial caps are introduced on the victim's compensation. Channelling requires the victim to exclusively sue the licensee of the power plant, where they are confronted with a financial cap. The victim has no opportunity to bring another lawsuit if, because of the cap, their damage was not fully compensated. A suit based on tort law against the licensee for the amount not covered by the cap is usually excluded in domestic law and a suit against a third liable party is usually excluded due to the channelling.[103]

Exclusive channelling in the international conventions means that the victim can, in principle, only file a law suit against the indicated person, e.g. the licensee (in case of nuclear accidents) or the tanker owner (in case of marine oil pollution).

99 See Section 8.1.1.

100 With respect to the channelling for oil pollution damage, see Faure and Wang (2006, at 187–189). As far as channelling of nuclear liability is concerned, see Vanden Borre (1999, at 13).

101 For a critical economic analysis of the channelling of nuclear liability, see Vanden Borre (1997, at 329–382; 2001, at 693–701).

102 Wang (2011, at 82).

103 Liu (2013, at 212).

In that sense, the channelling is 'exclusive' since a claim against other parties is (usually) not allowed.

However, exclusive channelling does not mean that liability is allocated in a final way. The licensee or operator who is held liable still has the possibility of a right of recourse against a third party who may be liable. In addition, it might be possible to pass on liability, e.g. on the basis of contract. This may be the case if, for example, defective materials were delivered to the licensee of a nuclear power plant. If such a shifting of the liability burden could take place, one could argue that the liability is simply transferred. Economists could argue that such a re-allocation complies with the principles of the Coase Theorem.[104] Indeed, an efficient allocation of resources nevertheless took place to the extent in which the ones who actually contributed to the loss are still held liable.

However, this private re-allocation of liability may not always be possible and the scope of recourse according to the conventions is in some cases quite limited. From that perspective, channelling of liability can hardly be considered as an efficient mechanism for the prevention of accidents or as an optimal tool for victim compensation.

The March 2011 Fukushima incident in Japan illustrates some of the undesirable consequences of channelling. The first reports on the Fukushima case made clear that the meltdown of the nuclear reactors may have been caused by the simple fact that the generators for the cooling system were located in the basement of the turbine buildings, which of course made them vulnerable to a tsunami.[105] Was this the result of negligent action by the operator, TEPCO, or rather the result of bad design or engineering by General Electric? In the latter case, a channelling of the liability to TEPCO would be problematic, since channelling would lead to an exclusion of liability of all other parties who may have contributed to the risk – in this particular case (at least potentially), General Electric. The Fukushima case suggests that channelling can be problematic in removing incentives for prevention to other parties who are able to limit or otherwise influence a risk.[106]

## 8.6 JOINT AND SEVERAL LIABILITY

Under joint and several liability, joint tortfeasors are held liable for all the damage to which their behaviour might have contributed.[107] Rules of joint and several liability give the victim a legal right to choose which operator to sue; they may claim full

[104] See Trebilcock and Winter (1997, at 232–235).
[105] See Yoshida (2011).
[106] Faure and Liu (2012, at 213–214). Japan did not follow the international conventions but introduced its own Nuclear Liability Act. This Act is, however, largely shaped on the basis of the same principles as the international conventions and equally contains a channelling of liability to the licensee of the power plant.
[107] Tietenberg (1989, at 306).

compensation from a single operator even when multiple operators could have contributed to the loss.[108] However, joint and several liability is controversial in the Law and Economics literature, since an injurer could in principle also be held liable for a portion of the damage not caused by their activity, thus potentially increasing their liability exposure and resulting in a reduction of activity levels in their non-injurious welfare enhancing activities.[109]

Joint and several liability can be seen as the reverse of proportional liability or channelling of liability discussed earlier.[110] Under joint and several liability, all of the joint tortfeasors are held fully liable for all the damage to which their behaviour might have contributed, as opposed to one party bearing all of the liability for all of the tortfeasors. However, if one of the actors were insolvent, inefficiency could arise since recourse could become impossible.[111]

Joint and several liability rules are transaction-cost-wise efficient means to relieve the burden of proof from victims.[112] Victims become enabled to collect damages, their whole damages, from just one of the contributing tortfeasors; thereafter, the tortfeasor who paid out damages could in turn exercise litigation against the other potential tortfeasors to recover the proportion of injuries that the payout firm did not cause.[113]

An argument in favour of joint and several liability is that it gives incentives for mutual monitoring by potential injurers.[114] However, in case of insolvency of one of the actors, inefficiencies may arise since recourse may become impossible.[115] Joint and several liability is debated since an injurer could in principle also be held liable for a part of the damage not caused by their activity and could thus potentially increase liability exposure.[116]

Rules of joint and several liability could be inefficient when attribution of liability is unproblematic, e.g. when there is only one feasible or obvious tortfeasor. Further, when there is only a single operator, the issue of attribution of liability would be wholly unproblematic.[117] The efficiency of joint and several liability is most robust when multiple (potential) tortfeasors are involved across different phases of the

[108] Joint and several liability can aid the judiciary when it is impossible to reasonably ascertain the relative contributions of different parties. See Richardson (2002).

[109] For this reason joint and several liability for environmental harm is opposed by Lucas Bergkamp (Bergkamp 2000, at 154–155; see also 2001, at 300–303).

[110] See Sections 8.3.3 and 8.5.

[111] See Kornhauser and Revesz (1989, at 832–837, analysing joint and several liability under full solvency) and Kornhauser and Revesz (1990, at 620–623, analysing instances of insolvency).

[112] See Bergkamp (2001, at 303).

[113] Id.

[114] See Tietenberg (1989, at 306).

[115] See Kornhauser and Revesz (1989; see also 1990).

[116] For this reason, joint and several liability in case of environmental harm is for example opposed by Bergkamp. See Bergkamp (2000b; see also 2001, at 300–303).

[117] See Gerard and Wilson (2009, at 1099).

project life cycle or are engaged in contemporaneously and multiply cooperating the activity site.

## 8.7 LATENCY AND RETROACTIVE LIABILITY

### 8.7.1 *Introduction*

We would now like to focus on a problem which has caused a lot of turmoil in the liability and insurance world of late. It has to do with the fact that, with the increasingly technological character of risks, time increasingly becomes a problem. Very often one can note that a long time lapse expires between the moment that a tort (e.g. an emission) occurs and the moment that the damage manifests itself. This problem of a long time lapse between the harmful event and the damage occurrence is known in the Anglo-American literatures as 'latency'; in Europe this problem is sometimes referred to as the 'long-tail risk'.[118] This long time lapse can, by the way, not only be caused by the technical feature that it takes a very long time before some risks manifest themselves. In some cases victims simply wait a long time with the filing of their lawsuit or, when they do, legal procedures may take a long time as well.[119]

We believe that this notion of time sheds a different light on a number of liability and insurance issues and causes a number of policy problems as well related to the financing of risks which had their origin in a distant past. Several problems may arise both for the liability issue itself, as well as for insurance and for the general question how long-standing risks should be financed. We will try to highlight some of these issues and also show that they are very much related.[120]

### 8.7.2 *Statutes of Limitations*

As far as the liability issue is concerned, a first point that always comes to mind when time issues are at stake is the statute of limitations. Without going into this issue in detail here one can easily argue that it nicely illustrates the balance of interests that has to be taken into account. On the one hand, the argument could be made that an unlimited liability in time might provide better incentives for the tortfeasor if they know that they can never get off the hook simply through a time lapse.

On the other hand, the problems of proving negligence and causation might become so large over time that the wrongfulness of the tortfeasor cannot be established anymore in a reasonable way. This, together with an argument of legal

[118] See e.g. with respect to the Netherlands Dommering-Van Rongen (1997, at 27–39).

[119] See generally on the economics of legal transitions, with applications to tort law, Kaplow (1986) and the dissertation by Haazen (2001).

[120] In this chapter we will address the latency issues which have some relevance for liability; in Chapter 11, we will look at some of these issues from an insurance perspective.

certainty, is often advanced to justify statutes of limitation.[121] For the insurer the argument can also easily be made that a liability which would be unlimited in time would be uninsurable.[122] Even if one therefore can argue that there are solid reasons for a statute of limitations one would nevertheless find that serious problems will arise as far as the financing is concerned. Indeed, the effect of a statute of limitations which has passed is that the tortfeasor no longer has to bear the financial consequences of their wrongdoing and victims remain uncompensated. This of course leads them to various attempts to delay the period of limitation as far as possible, e.g. by arguing that the statute of limitations only starts to run once the damage manifests itself and not when the harmful event occurred. In the end the uncompensated victim will turn to the government to claim compensation for the clean-up of polluted soil, for example, so that in the end society at large will pay for the consequences of wrongful acts which occurred in the past. The financial consequences are thus spread over the large community of taxpayers which is, by the way, often the consequence when no solvent debtor can be found.

We will, however, not focus on problems related to statutes of limitations in this chapter. We just use the example to show the relationship between liability, insurance, and financing of risk. A problem that we do want to discuss in further detail is that a time lapse can cause serious problems when the content of the liability rule or the standard of care has changed since the moment that the wrongful event took place. This problem, which is often referred to as retroactivity, raises the question of whether new standards of care (either legislative or jurisprudentially) should be applied to old situations.

### 8.7.3 *Examples*

Before providing an economic analysis of the retroactivity problem, we first would like to present a number of examples of cases which illustrate this problem.[123]

In some cases, there is an explicit introduction of retroactive liability by the legislator. One can, for instance, refer to the UK's Environment Act 1995, which instituted a strict retrospective liability for the remediation of contaminated sites.[124] Another well-known example is the heavily criticised US Superfund regime, instituted through CERCLA, which equally instituted a retroactive liability regime.[125]

[121] In economic terms the risk that the evidence deteriorates over time is qualified as a problem of 'error costs'. See Miceli (2000, at 383–394). See also Landes and Posner (1987, at 307).

[122] We will come back to the relevance of statutes of limitations for insurance in Chapter 11.

[123] For further detail see Faure (1998b, at 1–11). Many cases and examples are also presented in the dissertation by Haazen (2001).

[124] See Jones (1995, at 163).

[125] See for a summary of the most important criticisms on the Superfund regime, Revesz and Stewart (1995).

The problem of retroactive application of norms also arises in every instance where case law is developing new and more stringent standards of care for certain activities and applies these new norms to the existing situation. The problem is that in those cases the harmful event was not considered wrongful at the time when it took place, so that this case law in fact amounts to retroactivity.[126] Spier also showed that very often judges will apply a new standard of care to old situations. This was, for instance, the case in the Netherlands with respect to the new case law concerning traffic liability, which was also applied to cases which had their origin before the new case law and which therefore, in fact, were applied retroactivity.[127]

A last, interesting example concerns Dutch case law with respect to employers' liability for exposure to asbestos.[128] In the well-known case of *Cysouw* v. *De Schelde* it was clear that the employee Cysouw at some point during his services for the employer De Schelde had been exposed to a fatal asbestos crystal, which years later caused the fatal disease asbestosis. However, during a first period it was considered that the harmful consequences of exposure to asbestos were not known yet and that therefore it was not wrongful of the employer not to have taken precautionary measures to protect the employee. In a second period, when Cysouw still was employed, the effects of asbestos were known and the employer had not taken precautionary measures. Hence, it was crucial to find out whether Cysouw had inhaled the fatal crystal during the first period (in which case the employer would not have acted wrongfully) or in the second period (when there would be liability of the employer). The Dutch Supreme Court decided to shift this risk of uncertainty to the employer, who had the burden to prove that Cysouw did not receive the fatal crystal during the first period.[129] It will be hard if not impossible to deliver this proof.

### 8.7.4 *Time Lapse and Incentives to Prevent Accidents*

Let us now address the problem of how the law should, at first sight, deal with these issues of retroactivity, taking into account the just mentioned principles of efficiency and fairness.

[126] See generally on the retroactive effect of new case law Polak (1984, at 231–244) and see also the many examples of retroactivity in Dutch case law presented by Bolt and Spier (1996, 45–46); Haazen (2001); and Hartlief and Spier (1994, at 27–33).

[127] Bolt and Spier (1996, at 229).

[128] See in that respect also HR 17 November 1989, [1990] NJ, 572 (P.A.S.); HR 6 April 1990, [1990] NJ, 573 (P.A.S.); HR 15 June 1990, [1990] NJ, 716 (P.A.S.); compare Bier (1988, at 62–76); Geers (1988, at 148–169); Geers and Gevers (1977, at 951–959); and Van Dunné and Snijder (1991, at 64). See also Hartlief and Tjittes (1990b, at 282–288); Klosse (1993, at 1608–1613); and Kottenhagen-Edzes (1992, at 167–168); Spier (1993, at 33–38); Spier (1995, at 35–48); and Van Dunné (1995, at 19–34).

[129] HR 25 June 1993, [1993 NJ, 686: see with respect to this case and the problem of causal uncertainty also Faure (1993).

Looking at the efficiency aspect first, one can relatively easily state that a retroactive application of a new standard of care seems contrary to the principle that liability should give incentives for correct behaviour in the future. If suddenly a certain type of behaviour is considered to lead to liability ex post, whereas this was not the case ex ante, any finding of liability can then never affect the incentives of that particular tortfeasor for the future. Retroactive liability therefore does not seem to serve any purpose as far as the prevention of accidents is concerned. It has been shown in the European,[130] and also in the American, context that retroactive liability seems inefficient. Boyd and Kunreuther even held that retrospective liability may weaken the incentive to take precautions against future environmental costs.[131] From an economic perspective both legislators as well as the judiciary should therefore avoid retrospective liability as it cannot provide incentives for the prevention of environmental harm.

## 8.8 EMPIRICS

It seems interesting to briefly review some of the empirical literature that has reviewed whether liability rules had the deterrent effect they were supposed to have.[132]

### 8.8.1 *Deterrent Effect of CERCLA*

There is quite a bit of empirical evidence confirming that environmental liability does have a deterrent effect and indeed influences the behaviour of potential polluters. For example, Alberini and Frost found that waste generators do respond to the fact that they can 'be held liable for the cost of clean-up if the waste disposal site contaminates the environment after closure or abandonment and thus falls under the federal or state Superfund legislation'.[133]

A lot of research has also been devoted to the effects of the so-called Superfund liability under the US CERCLA. Most of these studies conclude that liability creates incentives, inter alia, towards precaution 'in managing hazardous wastes and

[130] See Faure and Fenn (1999, at 487–500).

[131] See Boyd and Kunreuther (1997, at 79–90).

[132] A caveat in advance, 95 per cent of the environmental litigation undertaken by the federal agencies may settle out of court, resulting in hundreds of millions of dollars a year in collected settlements (Bradshaw 2016, at 223). That said, this deprives case law of being as revealing as it might otherwise be (id., at 222), and thus other modes of impact must be used, such as reduction in accident rates. As important as litigation in liability is, it has been discovered that at least in the USA the empirical data on settlements has been missing from the scholastic record. A search of scholastic literature found only a handful of references to settlements (id., at 221).

[133] Alberini and Frost (2007, at 451, 466, 468–469).

discourag(ing) development of old industrial sites'.[134] At the same time, this research also shows that one has to be careful with interpreting the results.[135] As such, the mere fact that legislative duties to pay for clean-up costs would give incentives for prevention of waste generation does not necessarily mean that the overall judgment is that Superfund would be an efficient system. There is equal evidence that the administrative costs (a large part consisting of legal fees paid to the lawyers) of Superfund (especially litigation) can be spectacularly high as well.[136] Viscusi and Hamilton also found the cost of clean-up per case of cancer prevented to be 'in an excess of $6 billion', whereas 'the benefits of Superfund clean-up are highly concentrated at a very small percentage of sites, with most clean-up actions failing any reasonable efficiency test'.[137] The mere fact that liability provides incentives for prevention therefore does not necessarily imply that the system is efficient.[138]

Related and equally interesting research has pointed at the success of the liability provisions in the United States Oil Pollution Act of 1990 (OPA). A study by the Oil Companies International Marine Forum (OCIMF) holds that since the entry into force of the OPA, the volume of oil spilled from tankers into US waters has 'fallen from an average of 70,000 barrels per year to an average of 4,000 barrels per year – a decrease of 95%'.[139] The study holds that the introduction of so-called double hulls following the introduction of OPA had no apparent impact on improved pollution performance.[140] The reduction would be largely due to the liability and compensation regime of OPA, which holds vessel owners strictly liable for costs and damages resulting from oil spills.[141] This, so the study holds, serves as a real deterrent to pollution.[142]

And that sense of liability to the polluters was real; in another study, the vast bulk of out-of-court settlements in the USA from environmental enforcement efforts came from OPA enforcement proceedings (at $8,244 million), followed by CERCLA (at $1,175 million) and CWA efforts (at $954 million); thus we have evidence that the risk of liability was realised.[143]

[134] Sigman (2001, at 147).

[135] Id.

[136] See Gupta, Houtven, and Cropper (1995, at 83, 107; 1996, at 563–564, 581).

[137] Viscusi and Hamilton (1999, at 1012, 1025).

[138] For a summary of the statistical evidence on the deterrence effect of environmental liability, see Segerson (2007, at 257, 266).

[139] OCIMF 2003, at 1.

[140] Id.

[141] See Davis (2010, at 373–375) ('Liability for clean-up costs and damages under the Oil Pollution Act is without regard to negligence, and the only defenses are that the discharge was caused *solely* by an act of God, act of war, negligence on the part of the United States Government, or an act or omission of a third party').

[142] OCIMF 2003.

[143] Bradshaw (2016, at 234–237).

### 8.8.2 *Strict Liability versus Negligence*

Much research is also devoted to the question of whether environmental liability should be deterred through a negligence or strict liability rule.[144] Economic literature has often advanced strict liability for environmental pollution, since it provides the potential polluters optimal incentives for accident reduction.[145] Empirical research, for example, by Alberini and Austin, indeed confirmed that the imposition of strict liability in state environmental policies reduced unintended pollution releases.[146] Firms therefore show behavioural responses of avoiding liability 'when they are strictly liable for releases of hazardous chemicals into the environment'.[147]

However, the same authors also found the remarkable result that in states with strict liability, a greater spill severity and frequency could be found, which was associated with smaller production units and thus reduced assets, whereas this phenomenon was not found in states following negligence-based liability.[148] A first sight, this surprising result (more severe pollution cases under strict liability than under negligence) seems to deny the assumption of the literature that strict liability would provide better incentives for prevention. However, the same economic literature has equally indicated that strict liability could indeed lead to perverse results if polluters were potentially insolvent, meaning that the losses could be higher than their assets.[149] The fact that Alberini and Austin found that, under strict liability, firms organise themselves in smaller production units with reduced assets precisely confirms the assumption in the literature that strict liability is efficient only if a remedy for the insolvency problem can be found. The normative conclusion from this empirical research is thus not that the policymaker should not introduce strict liability for environmental pollution, but rather that if a serious insolvency risk exists, the introduction of strict liability should be accompanied with solvency guarantees, such as the introduction of compulsory insurance.[150] Otherwise, strict liability may exactly have the effect of driving polluters to reduce the assets that are exposed to liability,[151] and thus that a rule of negligence may be more robust in less-than-perfect conditions.

### 8.8.3 *Increased Liability and Liability Avoidance*

An interesting effect of environmental liability was discovered in empirical research as a result of the enlargement of the EU to Eastern Europe.

[144] For a summary of that literature, see Section 8.2.
[145] See Shavell (1980a, at 2–3). But see also Pozzo (1996, at 111).
[146] Alberini and Austin (2001, at 112).
[147] Id.
[148] Id.
[149] Shavell (1986, at 45). See generally Cooter (1984, at 1343–1523).
[150] See e.g. Jost (1996, at 259–260) and Polborn (1998, at 141–143).
[151] For an overview of the literature concerning the incentive impacts of environmental liability, see Earnhart (2004, at 100–101).

Potential buyers of property in Central and Eastern Europe could be held liable, also retrospectively, for cleaning up sites that were contaminated in the past.[152] Not surprisingly, research showed that this retrospective liability seriously limited the possibilities of privatisation in those countries, since potential investors were scared away by the foresight of having to pay for the pollution of the past.[153] Other research also confirmed that limited information to investors regarding the extent of past environmental contamination (and the related clean-up costs) also reduced the investors' willingness to pay for a particular enterprise in a bid.[154]

Specific empirical research has also been devoted to the compensation mechanisms after an oil spill. Hendrickx shows that '[c]lean-up operations have become more expensive', particularly as a result of pressure from environmental groups and public opinion.[155] However, he equally found that, '[f]or a higher proportion of spills, the polluter cannot be identified'.[156] He suspects that, as a result of the stricter liability of the tanker owner, they 'might have improved their skill of concealing their identity'.[157]

## 8.9 SUMMARY AND CONCLUSION

This chapter has covered a lot of concepts that likely felt familiar to most readers yet are now seen from a very different viewpoint. The Law and Economics literature has built a very solid research project on the rules of civil liability and when various forms might be robust.

While legal literature might be focused on the resolution of non-volitional obligations, from payment of damages to notions of justice, the Law and Economics literature since Calabresi has taken a different approach – that the goal of tort law is to reduce the costs of tortious acts across the whole of society, inclusive of the costs of risk avoidance, of victim damages, and of the institutional costs borne by society at large, such as the costs of the legal system. The shift is from tortfeasor as villain and victim as the sole injured party, to a perspective that all of society can undertake to reduce risks and that the costs of the injuries and of the private law system will eventually be borne by all, so public welfare is best served by reducing the costs across the whole of the system.

Law and Economics literature, based on its decision-making paradigm, views torts in two categories: (i) 'unilateral' torts, when only the tortfeasor is able to make decisions regarding how to encounter the risky activity, and (ii) 'bilateral', when both the tortfeasor and the victim are able to make decisions regarding how to encounter

[152] Bluffstone and Panayotou (2000, at 335–337).
[153] Id., at 336.
[154] Earnhart (2004, at 97–99, 104).
[155] Hendrickx (2007, at 257).
[156] Id.
[157] Id.

the risky activity. The literature also recognises that due to the way tort law has evolved in the courts, some behaviours that lead to risk are noticed by the court in evidence but that other behaviours are not taken into account, generally speaking. The accounted-for behaviours are called 'precautionary' and the not-accounted-for behaviours are called 'activity' and both are measured in 'levels'. One can have a high or low level of precaution and a high or low level of activity.

Robustness depends on context, especially for unilateral versus bilateral risks. We discussed how both rules of negligence and of strict liability would drive tortfeasors to efficient levels of precaution, but that only strict liability would also result in efficient levels of activity. Negligence provides that tortfeasors who can evidence a 'due care' level of precaution will not be found liable for damages, thus there are no costs for excess levels of activity. Under strict liability, tortfeasors pay for all damages, thus they receive robust incentives to constrain their activity levels to efficient levels of activity. The bilateral results were different, in that the choice of negligence resulted in a decrease of activity levels for the victim, whereas the choice of strict liability resulted in a decrease of activity levels for the tortfeasor. Thus, in bilateral contexts, a policymaker needs to carefully determine which party is better suited for policy needs to have their activity level constrained.

There are complications to the implementation of private rules of liability. One is causation. It is not always the case that there is a clearly identifiable and unique tortfeasor, both tortfeasors might be unknown and sometimes various tortfeasors might all be contributory to some degree. Ambient environmental risks might also be difficult to factor out of the causation links. There are various mathematical ways to approach these issues, but the key issue is that often the rule to assign causation will be somewhat inefficient due to the simple lack of full information conveyed through that method of apportionment.

Financial caps are another potential complication. In order to facilitate the uptake of critical technologies, governments might set limits on financial exposure for investors and operators. There might be ceilings, or financial caps, which limit how much might be recovered in damages. If the caps are effective in reducing the cost of damages below the non-capped level of expected damages, then the tortfeasor faces an unrealistic cost of damages that essentially creates a subsidy for the risky activity, encouraging its uptake. Assuming that precautionary levels are still efficiently set, the effect of these cap rules is to effect an increase in the activity levels, which could increase the incidence of accidents while simultaneously preventing payment of full compensation. In prelude to Chapters 11 and 12, if public policy is to support caps, then alternative means to provide equitable levels of compensation should be considered.

Litigation bears transaction costs and one means of reducing those costs for victims is to reduce the number of potential tortfeasors that they would need to pursue in trial to obtain eventual compensation in damages. Liability channelling is an approach to deem, per se in regulations, that a particular person is liable to all victims. For example, an operator of a nuclear plant might be channelled for all liabilities due to plant-caused injuries. So, victims would only need to bring litigation against the operator and would not need to chase other parties nor deal with the issues of joint and several liability. The operator might, in turn, then sue its suppliers and subcontractors or seek payment from insurance policies.

Another potential problem for environmental injuries is the timing of the incident of the risky act, of the injury event itself, and the timing of the discovery of the injury received. It could well be that these events are separated by many years or decades, as injuries might be unexpected, slowly accumulated, or distributed across a large area or number of victims. In such cases, it is possible that the tortfeasor has since gone bankrupt, folded operations and dissolved equity, or simply has become untraceable. In such cases, rules of civil liability are less robust without additional supports, as discussed in Chapter 9.

In conclusion, this theoretical model of civil liability rules has become well supported by empirical studies. Yet, complexity presents itself. Note the studies on strict liability and on negligence, that strategic behaviour from operators is stimulated by application of strict liability rules. The Law and Economics literature model of civil liability is a powerful model – one that enables policymakers to forecast the impacts of their potential liability rules in advance. But the application of that model must always be done with reference to strategic behaviour of the parties to remain effective.

# 9

# Environmental Regulation

In the previous chapter we have shown how liability rules can be used as a tool to implement environmental policy. We have demonstrated that specific problems may arise in applying liability rules to environmental harm. There may be many situations where it is impossible to apply rules of private law, such as liability rules. Private enforcement is for example only possible when there is a victim who can bring a lawsuit against an identifiable polluter, who is able to pay the compensation due. This may not always be the case.

For this and other reasons, ex ante public regulation on safety may be necessary to force compliance with the optimal standards that have been discussed in Chapter 4. It is this ex ante government intervention that is referred to as safety regulation, or sometimes just as regulation. In the environmental arena this is referred to as the command and control (CAC) approach.[1] The essence of this approach is that the government determines ex ante what can be expected from an operator and public sanctions will apply.

In the reality of environmental law and policy, public regulation plays a strong role. Especially at the origin of environmental law, most of it consisted of environmental standards laid down in regulation. Even though now there is a stronger shift towards a use of liability rules and market-based instruments, regulation still constitutes the body of environmental law in most legal systems.

The goal of this chapter is to put safety regulation into the Law and Economics framework. The next chapter will address the enforcement of regulation, more particularly via the use of the criminal law.

This chapter first addresses fundamental differences between the previously discussed liability rules and ex ante safety regulation. Both can provide incentives to comply with optimal standards, but the way they do so is different; it is important to understand these differences (Section 9.1). Next, the question will be addressed in

[1] Endres (2011, at 108) and Stewart (2007, at 150–151).

what kind of situations regulation may, from a public interest perspective, be supposed to be more effective than liability rules (Section 9.2). In some circumstance's regulation can, however, be ineffective. This is often the result if the contents of safety regulation are influenced by interest groups (Section 9.3). We refer to safety regulation as government regulation. However, that should not always be necessarily the case. In some cases, industry itself voluntarily imposes particular rules (self-regulation) or other private parties determine standards by which industry complies (private regulation) (Section 9.4). We examine the role of private interest in the articulation of regulatory frameworks (Section 9.5). Then, we discuss the toolsets enabled by private regulatory mechanisms and game theory to use public regulations to create private actors to reveal increased amounts of information enabling more efficient approaches to regulation (Section 9.6). Given specific weaknesses in (government) regulation, the question arises whether the policymaker should rely solely on one particular type of instrument or whether a combined use might be more appropriate (Section 9.7). Section 9.8 summarises and concludes.

## 9.1 DIFFERENCES BETWEEN LIABILITY RULES AND REGULATION

Without focusing on the different goals of tort law and regulation, we can notice that there are important differences in the way in which tort law and regulation work in providing incentives to parties in a potential accident setting to take optimal care.[2]

First, regulation needs to be defined. Cole wrote that, 'regulation is, generally speaking, a proactive alternative to the reactive tort system'.[3] According to Ogus:

> To speak about 'regulation' requires me to provide a definition of a concept which has different meanings both for lawyers and non-lawyers. Without entering into niceties, I take it to refer to obligations imposed by public law designed to induce individuals and firms to outcomes which they would not voluntarily reach. Regulation is largely enforced by public officials and compliance is aided by the threat or imposition of some sanction.[4] (Underscoring added.)

Consider the setting of the norms in both private tort law and in public regulations. Within private tort law, the norm to be followed, i.e. the efficient standard, is not defined ex ante by public regulation via a political or legislative process. One must first be legally injured before gaining standing to have a trial, which could then, ex post of the injury, render a set of behavioural standards for that activity that resulted in injury. Thus, a tort law standard will be set either by the parties themselves or a judge that determines the optimal standard to prevent the harm.

[2] Cane (2002).
[3] Cole (2011, at 3).
[4] Ogus (2009, at 333).

Under a negligence rule, it is the judge who through case law, and stare decisis where allowed, will define the due care standard required in the legal system. This will guide potential injurers who will comply with the due care standard in order to avoid liability.

Under a strict liability rule, it is the potential risk creators that do the weighing of costs and benefits in order to find out what the optimal care level is to prevent the harm. As a consequence of this, it means that parties are not obliged to follow this standard and that the standard is not imposed upon them by the government. Parties can even violate the standard as long as they are willing to pay the corresponding price, being the damages due to the victim in case an accident happens.

A consequence of private tort law is that since the norms are set by the private parties or by the judge, all the information costs to find out what the optimal standard is lay upon either the parties (under strict liability) or the judge (under negligence).[5]

The situation is completely different under public regulation. In that case, a regulatory authority will ex ante determine and set the standard that mandatorily has to be followed by all potential parties in a risky activity setting. The flexibility and freedom inherent in the tort system in searching for the optimal standard is missing in the regulatory approach. It is the government (or related public authorities of course) that will define the standard and which also forces potential risk creators (and sometimes potential victims) to follow the standard. As a consequence of this, in case of regulation, all the information costs are incurred by the government.

With this, we have already discovered a key difference between public regulation and tort law, being that the standards in regulation are set ex ante, before the accident happens. The standards in regulation also have to be followed irrespective of an accident. Hence, someone who violated a traffic light could not argue as a defence that they caused no harm. Tort law on the other hand works essentially ex post, being after an accident. Tort law is triggered by harm. As long as no harm occurs, tort law does not play a role and creates no standards. However, even though tort law is essentially an ex post system, the economic analysis of law does expect some measure of reasonable foreseeability prior to any accidents and standards for subsequent risky activities will be set in the early cases, thus ex ante standard setting will effectively be in place for later and subsequent events.

A second difference with tort law, is that private law extends beyond standard and norm setting to also include privately led enforcement.[6] It is in principle private parties, usually the victim themselves, which will bring enforcement of tort law, precisely because it is triggered by harm; if the victim will not come forward to make a claim then there will be no enforcement. Regulation, on the other hand is

5 This determination of a rule is clearly dependent on 'good facts' and good judgments from the engaged parties at trial, which is not at all guaranteed to exist.

6 For differences between enforcement regimes, see Hylton (2002).

enforced through public authorities. The police or other investigators will control whether regulatory norms are complied with, will take notice of violations, and will decide on enforcement strategies.

A third difference is of course in the differing sanctions. The sanctions in tort law are in principle private sanctions, that is to say the sanctions directly benefit the victim who receives restoration or damages. The sanctions in case of violation of regulatory law are, on the contrary, public sanctions. It is the government (an administrative or criminal court) that will impose the sanction and the benefits of the sanction accrue not to a private party (like a victim) but to the public state.

As a consequence of this, the fourth and probably most important difference between the two systems is that tort law is of course far more flexible. In that sense, the tort regime is sometimes characterised as a market system; the private parties or the judge fix the norms, enforcement and sanctioning are also private. There is also a lot of flexibility within tort law to adapt to changing circumstances. Regulatory law, on the other hand, is much more interventionist: the norms are set by the government, enforcement and sanctioning is public. There is no doubt that the regulatory approach involves a much greater degree of government intervention than tort law. Tort law merely supposes that there is a judge who either sets the due care standard (in case of a negligence rule) and enforces tort claims of victims or merely does the latter (in case of strict liability).

Although these differences may hold generally, there are of course some grey areas and overlaps. In some legal systems, the government may also use public law implementations of tort law to enforce regulation and there can be an overlap between public tort law and regulation. In some legal systems, the enforcement of regulatory norms is not always undertaken by government; some legal systems allow private enforcement of regulatory norms as well.[7] Still, as a general rule, the differences as just described will hold in most cases.

Given the fact that tort law relies more on the market and is less costly (one only needs a judge and one's self-determined budget for litigation costs, but the judiciary of course does much more than simply enforcing tort law) than regulation (where public costs need to be incurred to set the norms, to enforce them and to sanction them, plus an additional cost cycle to collect these public funds), then the natural preference of economists, all things being equal, will be with tort law.

Tort law is definitely the most flexible and less costly system. Hence, there should be persuasive arguments to shift to public regulation. Given the natural preference for tort law, one can understand why economists developed a list of 'criteria for public regulation' and not a list of 'criteria for tort law'.

Given the fact that public regulation requires a much greater degree of government intervention, one can also understand that this debate on market versus regulation has to a large extent been much politicised. The major advantage of

7 For an economic analysis of private enforcement, see Landes and Posner (1975).

the economic analysis of law, and more particularly of the contributions of Shavell, is that it has taken this debate out of the journalistic political arena and has provided clear economic criteria for when states and policymakers should consider the use of public regulations for environmental protections.

As we will show, these criteria are very balanced in shades of grey and do not provide a black or white answer in favour of or against regulation.

The reader should also note that this chapter will also show that a long-standing misunderstanding, being that all Law and Economics scholars would be in favour of market solutions and against regulation, is generally not correct. This chapter shows more particularly that Law and Economics scholars such as Shavell precisely point at the importance of regulation to provide incentives to take optimal preventive measures, more particularly in those cases where the market fails.

## 9.2 PUBLIC INTEREST CRITERIA FOR REGULATION

Let us now examine under what kind of circumstances liability rules may not suffice to deter environmental harm and a regulatory intervention may be necessary. The choice between regulation and liability rules was thoroughly examined by Shavell in 1984, in a paper in which he advances several criteria that influence the choice between safety regulation and liability rules.[8]

### 9.2.1 *Information Asymmetry as a Criterion for Regulatory Intervention*

Information deficiencies have often been advanced as a cause of market failure and as the justification for government intervention through regulation.[9] Also, for the proper operation of a liability system, information on, for example, the existing legal rules, the accident risk, and efficient measures to prevent accidents, is a precondition for an efficient deterrence. According to Shavell, the parties in an accident setting generally have much better information on the accident risk than that possessed by the regulatory body.[10] The parties themselves have, in principle, the best information on the costs and benefits of the activity that they undertake and of the optimal way to prevent accidents.

This 'assumption of information' will, however, be reversed if it becomes clear that some risks are not readily appreciated by the parties in an accident setting. These cannot always be easily assessed by the parties involved. Therefore, for every

8 Shavell (1980a, 1984a, and 1984b). Similarly, Epstein summarized these 'good reasons for imposing statutory duties' as the need to prevent serious or irreparable harms, to deal with actors potentially unable to pay litigious damages, and the need to have easy to understand safeguards (Epstein 2016, at 149).

9 See the basic article by Stigler (1961, at 213) and see Schwartz and Wilde (1979), as well as Mackaay (1982).

10 Shavell (1984a, at 359).

activity, the question that will have to be asked is who, either the government or the parties involved, could acquire the necessary information at the least cost.

Ogus warns that public regulatory systems tend towards modes of paternalism; often with insufficient consideration of justification for that paternalism.[11] He argues that the regulator presumes an advantage in knowledge over the risk taker, which might not be evident. On the other hand, Ogus similarly warns that systems of self-regulation often assume the reverse with similar lack of evidence.[12] Thus, in policy choice on public regulation, there is a need to clearly establish who has what information and if any material asymmetries exist, and if so, how best to include that knowledge in the design of the regulatory mechanism.

### 9.2.2 *Insolvency Risk*

If the potential damages can be so high that they will exceed the wealth of the individual injurer, liability rules will not provide optimal incentives.

The reason is that the costs of care are directly related to the magnitude of the expected damages; if the expected damages are much greater than the individual wealth of the injurer, the injurer will only consider the accident as having a magnitude equal to their wealth. They will take, therefore, only the care necessary to avoid an accident equal to their wealth, which can be lower than the care required to avoid the total accident risk.[13] This is a simple application of the principle that the deterrent effect of tort liability works only if the injurer has assets to pay for the damages they cause. If an injurer is protected against such liability, by insolvency or by indemnity, the problem of under-deterrence arises.[14]

Safety regulation can overcome this problem of under-deterrence caused by insolvency.[15] In that case, the efficient care will be determined ex ante by regulation and will be affected by enforcement instruments which induce the potential injurer to comply with the regulatory standard, irrespective of their wealth.

Therefore, a problem might still arise if the regulation were enforced purely by means of monetary sanctions. Again, if these were to exceed the injurer's wealth, the insolvency problem would remain. If a safety regulation is introduced because of a potential insolvency problem, the regulation itself should be enforced by non-monetary sanctions.[16]

[11] Ogus (2009, at 345).
[12] Id., at 346.
[13] Shavell (1984a, at 360).
[14] Shavell (1986).
[15] If insurance came into the picture, it could overcome the problems of under-deterrence, provided that the moral hazard problem, caused by insurance, can be overcome.
[16] Shavell (1985b).

### 9.2.3 *Missing Liability Litigation*

Some activities can cause considerable damage; but even so, a lawsuit to recover these damages may never be brought. If this were the case, there would of course be no deterrent effect of liability rules. Therefore, the absence of a liability suit would again be an argument to enforce the duty of efficient care by means of safety regulations rather than through liability rules.[17] There can be a number of reasons why a lawsuit is not brought, even though considerable damage has been caused.

Sometimes an injurer can escape liability because the harm is thinly spread among a number of victims. As a consequence, the damage incurred by every individual victim is so small that no victim has sufficient incentives to bring a suit; i.e. the costs of litigation may exceed the anticipated recoveries. In particular, this problem will arise if the damage is not caused to an individual but to common property, such as the surface waters in which each member of the population has a minor interest. In addition, a long time might have elapsed before the damage becomes apparent; in this case much of the necessary evidence may be either lost or not obtained. Another problem is that if the damage only manifests itself years after the activity, the injurer might have gone out of business.

A related problem is that it is often hard to prove that a causal link exists between an activity and a type of damage.[18] The burden of proof of a causal relationship becomes more difficult with the increasing passage of time since the damaging incident took place. Often a victim will not recognise that the harm had been caused by a particular tort, but might think that their particular ailment, e.g. cancer, had another non-tortious origin or might perhaps misassign fault in misunderstanding how they fell ill with cancer. For all these reasons, a liability suit might not be brought and hence safety regulation is necessary to ensure that the potential polluter takes efficient care.[19]

### 9.2.4 *Administrative Costs*

When examining the pros and cons of liability versus regulation, the administrative costs of both systems should also be compared. Liability rules are clearly costly in terms of time for both parties and in court fees. A part of these costs is borne by the whole community, such as the cost of the legal system or the fees for the judges. Regulation produces costs for the community, including the costs of making the regulation, setting the standards, passing the statutes, and of subsequent enforcement.[20]

17 Shavell (1984a, at 363).

18 See Kunreuther and Freeman (2001, at 304–305) and Landes and Posner (1984, at 417).

19 For alternatives to liability rules, see Bocken (1987, at 83–87) and Bocken (1988, at 3–10).

20 Shavell (1984a, at 363–364).

In this respect the liability system seems to have an advantage: the administrative costs of the court system are only incurred if an accident has actually happened. The main advantage of the tort system is that a lot of accidents will be prevented by the deterrent effect of being held liable and having to pay damages to the victim. In the case of safety regulation, the cost of passing the regulation and of enforcing it are always there, where there are accidents or not.

## 9.3 THE NEED TO REGULATE ENVIRONMENTAL POLLUTION

If one looks at the first criterion, that of information costs, it must be stressed that an assessment of the risks of certain activities, especially industrial activities, often requires expert knowledge and judgment. Small organisations might lack the incentive or resources to invest in research to find out what the optimal care level would be. Also, there would be little incentive to carry out intensive research if the results were automatically available to competitors in the market: this is the well-known 'free-rider' problem.

This problem can partially be countered by legal instruments granting an intellectual property right to the results of the research. However, the problem remains that it may not be possible for small companies to undertake studies on the optimal technology for preventing environmental damage. Therefore, it is often more resource efficient to allow the government itself to do the research on the optimal technology in a governmental environmental research institute. The results of this research can then be passed on to all of the parties in the market through the issuance of regulation. Hence, the setting of environmental standards in regulation can be seen as a means of passing on information on the environmental technology required to meet the set standards. It could be more efficient for the government to acquire information on the optimal emission standard than it would be for an individual firm, for instance, to find out what additional reduction in pollution would produce an optimal reduction of the expected damage from the emission. There are also undeniable 'economy of scale' advantages in regulation.

Also, the insolvency argument points in the direction of regulation. Pollution can be caused by individuals or firms with assets which are generally lower than the damage they can cause to a broader community by the pollution. In this respect it should not be forgotten that even a small firm could cause harm to a large number of individuals or to entire ecosystems. The amount of damage caused by this emission can readily exceed the assets of an individual company. Most firms have been incorporated as a legal entity and therefore their shareholders benefit from limited liability. Thus, the individual shareholders are not liable to the extent of their personal assets, as a creditor of the firm can only lay claim to part of all of the total assets purchased in a firm by the shareholders.

Also the chance of a liability suit being brought for damage caused by wrongful pollution is naturally very low. The damage is often spread over a large number of people, who will have difficulties in organising themselves to bring a lawsuit. In addition, the damage might become apparent only some years after the dangerous emission took place. This will bring proof of causation and latency problems, which will only make it difficult for a lawsuit to be brought against the polluter.

For these reasons it is clear that some form of government regulation of environmental pollution is necessary. To reformulate: this shows that liability rules alone cannot suffice to prevent environmental harm, but there might be publicly imposed, instruments other than the CAC-type regulation which can be used to reach this goal. Taxes are such an alternative. But also, these are publicly imposed and can thus be considered as 'regulation'. Another question is whether this necessarily implies that environmental law should solely depend upon regulation or whether liability can still fulfil a supplementary role.

## 9.4 SAFETY REGULATION IN PRACTICE

When Shavell's criteria for safety regulation are applied to environmental risks, one can easily note that a strong argument can be made that the standards for efficient care to be taken to avoid environmental damage should also be fixed ex ante by regulation, for the harms in environmental injuries are often not curable by purely financial modes of damages, so a focus should be on preventing accidents before they happen with the provision of ex ante guidance.

In many cases this regulation consists of licences or permits in which an administrative authority fixes an emission standard which must be followed by the potential polluter. These licences play a crucial role in environmental policy in most countries. That emissions are controlled through licences and that the quality and quantity of the emissions can be regulated by the conditions of these licences, is a cornerstone of environmental law. Since these licences are administrative acts, in most legal systems environmental law is considered to be a part of administrative law. Criminal environmental law usually only comes into the picture to sanction a violation of administrative regulations or emission standards in the licences.

Although environmental pollution can be generally controlled through these administrative licences, in individual cases damage to the environment can still occur. In those cases, liability under tort law comes into play and a question could be asked of the influence of regulation on the liability system and vice versa.[21] The complementary relationship between tort law and regulation will be discussed below in Section 9.7.

Although it is difficult to examine whether the environmental regulation is generally also effective in reducing environmental harm, some studies have attempted to examine the effectiveness of safety regulation in controlling

[21] Complementarities between tort law and regulation have been addressed in and Rose-Ackerman (1991, at 54–58; 1992a; and 1992b).

environmental harm. These studies do not address the specific quality of every environmental law but examine whether regulation has generally been more important in reducing environmental harm than liability rules. Dewees demonstrated that in North America the quality of the environment has improved substantially as a result of regulatory efforts, not so much in response to legal action in tort.[22]

This empirical evidence of the success of regulation, compared to tort law, has been stressed in the book of Dewees, Duff, and Trebilcock.[23] They hold that the large regulatory effort to improve the environment has met with considerable success when measured by the reduction of emissions, but that it is more difficult to argue that the environmental regulations of the 1970s in the USA equally had a considerable influence on the ambient environmental quality. They also stress that while environmental regulation is a determining factor in pollutant emissions and ambient concentrations, other non-regulatory factors such as economic growth and even the weather also influence environmental quality.[24]

## 9.5 PRIVATE INTEREST THEORY OF REGULATION

### 9.5.1 *Lobbying for Barriers to Entry or Lenient Standards*

Up to now we have assumed that governmental regulation is always made 'in the public interest'. Thus, the government always makes regulation to increase social welfare and to raise efficiency. This implies that the government would pass a regulation only if it was considered to be efficient in the terms of the criteria of Shavell mentioned above.

Reality is often different. Looking at legislation, one can often see regulation of activities for which such a method of control seems inefficient; in other cases, there is a proper argument for regulation, but the formulation of the regulation is inefficient.

Economists of the 'public choice' school have studied the phenomenon of regulation and have examined the reasons why some are inefficient.[25] In this public choice approach, microeconomic models are used to explain processes of regulation. A starting point is the assumption that the politician is also a *homo economicus*, who will have a preference for the introduction of regulation which will benefit those interest groups which would in turn support them in their political aspirations. From this point of view the politician is no longer someone who is serving the public interest, but a utility maximiser serving their own interests, by placing political services in the market of the voters and other stakeholders.

[22] Dewees (1992a) and Dewees (1992b).
[23] Dewees, Duff, and Trebilcock (1996).
[24] For an economic analysis, see Cooter (1982, at 97–101) and Landes and Posner (1981a).
[25] See in general Buchanan, Tollison and Tullock (1962) and Buchanan and Tullock (1962).

Starting point of the public choice analysis is that regulation is considered as the product of supply and demand on a political market. On the demand side we find the various interest groups who demand favourable regulation, and on the supply side the 'politically oriented preferences' of politicians who wish to favour interest groups which provide them political support. The product is environmental legislation favouring an interest group in exchange for political support. Thus, a welfare transfer (a so-called rent) can be transferred to the interest group. This rent-seeking behaviour will, according to the public choice literature be especially successful if the transaction costs for the group to bring together individuals to defend a common interest are relatively small and if the information costs incurred by the public at large to discover the rent seeking are relatively high.[26] Evidence of rent-seeking behaviour in environmental regulation in the USA was reported by Adler,[27] and similar stories can be found in Europe as well.[28]

These conditions for rent seeking may often be met in case of environmental regulation. The fact that a transfer to an interest group has taken place will often be disguised by arguing that environmental protection or victim protection is provided by the particular piece of legislation. Transactions costs are often low if only a few firms or NGOs come together to defend a common interest.

Indeed, the reason why this welfare transfer to interest groups can take place can be found in these two well-known economic phenomena of information costs and transaction costs.

The information costs are those incurred by the public at large in finding out the effect of the regulation. Because the wealth transferred to an interest group is derived from the general public, one individual will usually not realise that such a transfer to an interest group has taken place.

Most interest group legislation is claimed to protect the general public. This is often the case with regulation which is supposed to protect consumers (which often only protects certain producers),[29] or regulation which is supposed to protect victims (which often only protects the interests of insurance agencies for certain industries).[30]

The literature providing theoretical support for the rent-seeking argument in case of environmental regulation and empirical evidence is strong. Starting point for environmental regulation is often the political will to provide some action of environmental protection. Keenan and Rubin would argue that this demand for

[26] See McCormick and Tollison (1982, at 17); Olson (1982, at 26–27); Posner (1974, at 345).

[27] Adler (1996, at 26–34).

[28] Faure and Van den Bergh (1989a, at 308–330) or Faure and Van den Bergh (1989b).

[29] This has been proven with respect to Sunday closing regulation and 'unfair trade practices' statutes. See Van den Bergh (1986, at 185–205). See also the article of Jaffer and Kay (1986, at 169–183).

[30] This has been proven with respect to legislation concerning the liability for nuclear accidents. See Faure and Van den Bergh (1990, at 241–254).

regulation, which is not represented by a well-defined and active particular interest group, may be initiated by a 'shadow interest group'.[31] This is a group that would precipitate into being if an accident occurred. Potential victims of environmental pollution can thus be seen as members of this latent group. If a shadow interest group ceases to be a shadow group and becomes active, it will have all the characteristics of a normal interest group.

Knowing that shadow interest groups have the potential to become an effective lobby, rational politicians will, under certain circumstances, respond to these groups in the same way that they will respond to normal interest groups, even though the shadow groups have not yet organised.

If under these circumstances legislative intervention seems unavoidable, the theory of regulation suggests that the interest groups involved will accept a general principle of regulation but may strive to change its scope.[32] The industrial interest groups to whom the environmental regulation will be applied, may realise that regulation may enhance producer welfare while it simultaneously corrects, or at least reduces, an externality problem. This outcome has been stressed by Maloney and McCormick with respect to environmental quality regulation. They argue that the industry, realising that environmental regulation is unavoidable, will cooperate in the development of the regulation and try to change the contents to its advantage. A classic example is the introduction of so-called grandfather clauses, which stipulate that the regulation will not be applicable to firms or products which are already in existence. Hence, the regulation can create a new barrier for market entry and so protect the existing industrial practices and products.[33] In other cases, as far as standard setting is concerned, industry may lobby for lenient environmental standards to reduce the impact of new regulations against their own profits.

As indicated above, the efforts of industry may go in various directions: sometimes regulation will be used by using grandfather clauses to limit market entry;[34] in other cases there will be lobbying for more lenient environmental standards. With respect to the first type of lobbying we can refer also to the function of licences, which are considered a central instrument in environmental policy. Moore,[35] in 1961, pointed at the anti-competitive effects of licensing.[36]

The lobby for lenient standards may take place with the legislator. But since legislators often give standard-setting power to administrative agencies, this type of lobbying, e.g. to get lenient emission standards for an individual firm, will usually take place with the administrative agency. The behaviour of bureaucracies vis-à-vis

[31] Keenan and Rubin (1988, at 21–36).
[32] Pelzman (1976, at 211–240).
[33] Dewees (1983, at 53–71).
[34] Maloney and McCormick (1982, at 99–123).
[35] Moore (1961, at 93–117).
[36] See on the use of standards to seek competitive advantages also Hahn (1990a, at 149–175; 1990b, at 21–47); Huber (1983, at 1025); and Ogus (1994b, at 23–37).

industry capture risk is analysed by multiple authors such as Downing.[37] Rent seeking will not only take place during the standard-setting process, but can also play a role in case of zoning after a standard is set.[38]

### 9.5.2 *Influence of Private Interest on Instrument Choice*

The influence of private interest in environmental law has been addressed specifically in the literature with respect to the issue of instrument choice. Earlier, we indicated the variety of instruments that can be used to control environmental pollution, indicating that the literature suggests under what kind of circumstances a particular type of policy instrument would be optimal.

In practice these 'economic prescriptions' are not always followed.[39] One reason why emission taxes are seldom used in the USA, and policy still relies to a large extent on the CAC approach, might be that firms could prefer emission standards to taxes, because standards might serve as barrier to entry to new firms, thus raising the profits of existing firms. Charges on the other hand do not preclude entry by new firms and represent an additional cost to the existing firms on the market.[40] This basic point made by Buchanan and Tullock has been extended by other scholars, examining the implication of rent seeking for pollution taxation.[41]

The influence of lobbying on instrument choice has also been analysed in the many papers by Hahn,[42] Hahn and Noll,[43] Körber,[44] and De Grauwe,[45] Hahn points out that the policy instruments are almost never used in the way that is suggested by economic theory. Emission charges can be used as a revenue raising device with few direct effects on polluters, and many marketable permit approaches are not really designed to create markets. Through grandfathering, the rights of existing firms are often protected.

In addition, even if the economic prescriptions such as marketable pollution rights were followed, there is some evidence that emissions trading would be used as a loophole by which industry could forestall compliance.[46] Hahn also argues that the varying interest group attitudes in the USA and in Europe may account for the fact that European countries tend to rely more on the use of fees, whereas

37 Downing (1989, at 255–271).
38 Ault and Ekelund (1988, at 69–76); Fischel (1980, at 37–43 and 1985).
39 Hahn (1989a, at 195–211) and Hahn (1989b, at 135).
40 Buchanan and Tullock (1975, at 139–147) and see the comments by Coelho (1976, at 976–978) and Yohe (1976, at 981–982).
41 Brooks and Heijdra (1987, at 335–342) and Lee (1985, at 731–744).
42 Hahn (1989a, at 195–211; 1989b, at 135; and 1989c, at 95–114).
43 Hahn and Noll (1983, at 63–91).
44 Körber (1995, at 161–191).
45 De Grauwe (1995, at 111–168).
46 Hahn and Hester (1989, at 109–153).

marketable permits have only been introduced on a relatively broader scale in the USA.[47] Thus, the selection of an appropriate mix of policy instruments will to a large extent be determined by the way political choices are actually made in different countries.

### 9.5.3 *The Choice for the Level of Government*

The influence of interest groups will not only play a role as far as the contents of regulation is concerned, but also when the level of government where action will be taken is determined. Interest groups will choose the level of government where their influence can be largest. In the context of the EU this may explain why some industries will lobby in favour of environmental regulation at the European level. For new areas (where no national legislation exists) industrial lobby groups may encounter less countervailing power than at the local level where the environmental problems occur and NGOs may oppose lenient standards. Once standards are set at the central level in Brussels, Member States will have to comply. On the other hand, the industry of Member States which already have relatively stringent environmental standards, may have an incentive to lobby at the central level to make these stringent environmental standards compulsory Union-wide to force competitors from southern EU Member States to comply with these stringent standards as well and thus to create barriers to entry.[48] This may explain why a lot of environmental regulations emerge from Brussels also in cases where economic theory would predict that the problem may better be dealt with at the decentralised level.[49]

### 9.5.4 *Liability Law and Rent Seeking*

Finally, rent seeking can also occur in policy decision for liability rules applied to environmental accidents. Industry might lobby in favour of a financial cap on liability, thus transferring a rent from potential victims. Such caps can be found in conventions on marine oil pollution and nuclear liability.[50] The model conditions for efficient rent seeking will be found met: transaction costs for the nuclear industry are low, the information costs for the public are high, and the caps are often combined with other legal instruments which are supposedly aiming at 'victim protection', such as strict liability and compulsory insurance.[51]

47 Hahn (1989c, at 111).
48 Faure and Lefevere (1995a, at 321–326).
49 This is further discussed in Chapter 13.
50 The inefficiency of caps has been discussed in Section 8.4.
51 Faure and Van den Bergh (1990, at 241–254).

### 9.5.5 *Importance*

The interest group theory is important both for theoretical research and at the policy level.

First, theoretically it is important to stress that these theories have demonstrated that the traditional argument that regulation is necessary if the market fails to internalise externalities may not necessarily be true if the regulation provides results that are equally inefficient as a result of rent seeking compared with the market solution that might have emerged.

Second, most authors stress that it would be too one-sided to argue that environmental laws only serve the private interest. Even when there are strong incentives for rent seeking, many environmental statutes are still enacted in a struggle to protect the public interest.[52]

Third, in some cases the interests of industry and environmentalists coincide; hence, lobbying will not always result in industry opposing environmental regulation. This may more particularly be the case when industry observes that stringent regulation could create barriers to market entry not otherwise obtainable under trade laws.

Fourth, theoretically, a combination of public interest and private interest approach is highly useful to provide an understanding of how environmental regulations work. If the environmental policy instruments actually used do not correspond with the predictions of (public interest) economic theory, it might be helpful to look at the possible influence of private interest groups which might explain the existence of inefficient environmental regulation.

Fifth, the fact that environmental regulation is also susceptible to rent seeking which might lead to inefficiently lenient standards, may be an argument for combining regulatory standards with other policy instruments such as liability rules, which may be less susceptible to the influence of private interest.

## 9.6 SELF-REGULATION, PRIVATE REGULATION, AND MECHANISM DESIGN

Traditionally, lawyers assume law is divided into private law and public law and that the two function separately; indeed, that is the way law has been traditionally taught for centuries. But the literature of Law and Economics suggests that the two strands do not stand independently, as highlighted in the discussion on when civil liability rules fail to be effective and when public regulation could be frustrated, as seen in the previous chapter and earlier in this present chapter.

The way we presented safety regulation so far was based on the assumption that regulation would be issued by the government. That should not necessarily be the

[52] Adler (1996).

case. There may be arguments in favour of regulation (related to Shavell's criteria pointing at the weaknesses of liability rules), but in some cases there may equally be weaknesses in government regulation as well. Public regulations tend to face problems of regulatory capture, poor incentives for the regulated parties, problems of irregular (alternating over and under) enforcement, and problems of detection.[53] These issues can drive an argument in favour of alternative types of regulation.

However, there are yet three other perspectives, (i) that private parties could organise to self-regulate, (ii) a group of similar industrial actors could agree to have a third party audit them to an agreed-to standard and thereby enable private regulation, and (iii) public authorities could leverage game theory to use private rules to induce structures known as private regulatory mechanisms to create a synthetic approach to create incentives that both change private behaviour and provide information to public authorities. These modes of governance can be sought by an authority 'where problems confronting the regulator are particularly complex',[54] leaving the to-be-regulated party with superior access to necessary information on both optimising regulatory targets and modes of monitoring and enforcement. Indeed, the EU has been taking a serious look at these options since the early 1990s and they have become increasingly popular regulatory tools.[55]

Under the concept of self-regulation, self-regulation is 'understood narrowly as law formulated by private agencies to govern professional and trading activities':[56]

> When used in a legal context, the 'self' in 'self-regulation' is not used in the literal sense. Rather it connotes some degree of collective constraint, other than that directly emanating from government, to engender outcomes which would not be reached by individual market behaviour alone (Black, 1996). It is also normally taken to imply 'a fairly well established and generally recognised set of rules, whether customary or reduced to writing, in accordance with which the activity is regulated'.
>
> (Cane, 1987)[57]

In the case of operators engaged in an environmentally risky activity, the operators themselves would specify the applicable standards to which they will voluntarily comply,[58] followed by the operators then undertaking internal compliance efforts, e.g. personnel training or provision of compliance auditing, to ensure that their own firm remained in compliance with that agreed-to standard.

53 Van Zeben (2010, at 249).
54 Id., at 247.
55 Id., at 248
56 Ogus and Carbonara (2011, at 228).
57 Id., at 229.
58 Van Zeben wrote, '[s]elf-regulation may be seen as a "self-administered' form of C&C"' (Van Zeben 2010, at 247).

It has been held that such an approach can reduce the costs of centralised oversight and be more welfare efficient, as the actors closest to the necessary information are also those closest to the governed behaviour.[59] Such a system relies heavily on forms of non-governmental enforcement mechanisms: 'self-regulation involves a system of private ordering, without any form of state intervention; that is, without any imposition of rules by those with political power. Systems of private ordering are the basis for phenomena of spontaneous emergence of law and are sustained by extra-legal (or social) sanctions'.[60] As such, this would not be likely to work where such institutions are not in place.

It is much in this manner that firms provide quality control over their production lines. This is generally found to be effective when the producers' goals and the policymaker's goals are well aligned; e.g. when the policy goal will also increase profitability. Increasingly, the government relies on self-regulation, but specifies the conditions under which industry can regulate itself. This is referred to as conditioned self-regulation.

The primary potential benefits of self-regulation have five arguments: (i) principals will face reduced costs of regulation, (ii) a reduction in transaction costs between public regulator and private self-regulator/ee, (iii) lower costs in rule amendment or updating, (iv) a pass-through reduction in costs for downstream consumers, and (v) the creation of positive economic incentives for the private self-regulator/ee to enforce its own rules, as to continue beneficial conditions with public regulator and continuance of market competitive lower prices for its consumers.[61] These conditions are best met when (i) uncertainty is strong, (ii) the divergence between producers and consumers is small, and (iii) when the public regulator 'attaches a high weight to consumer surplus in the social welfare function'.[62]

In other cases, other private operators determine standards (such as standardisation institutions) and yet other private operators control compliance with those specified standards and certify that industry complied with the standards. This is usually referred to as private regulation. There are many instances of such private regulatory approaches in the market today, such as many of the food labelling initiatives or various movie or video game rating systems. Such approaches are effective when the information created by the audit and inspection is itself a good sought by consumers; e.g. an orange certified by a third party to be organically grown ensures consumer trust in the product and thus improves its overall marketability.

[59] Ogus and Carbonara (2011, at 229).

[60] Id., at 230. Nevertheless, they observe that such arrangements have been scholastically studied and found reliable and persistent in a number of non-environmentally focused rule sets, such as within the Maghribi traders or the mining camps of the American West (id.).

[61] Id., at 233.

[62] Id., at 234.

Or the government will in regulation explicitly require certification by private institutions or compliance with privately set standards. That shows that increasingly the line between government and self–private regulation becomes blurred and that hybrid forms of governance emerge. These private regulatory mechanisms can enable public authorities to achieve their environmental goals at lower transaction costs than more direct regulatory approaches.

A well-known example of private regulatory mechanisms is driver insurance for car drivers. The public authority can require all drivers to have third-party liability insurance; then at a low cost to the public bourse, the driver will provide data on their driving records to the insurer who can then assess the risk associated with issuing a policy to them. The Law and Economic literature observes that this creates what mathematicians call a strategic game. The driver wants to reveal data that lowers their insurance costs, so they begin to avoid risky driving behaviour. The insurance company doesn't want to pay out on policies, so it undertakes efforts to educate drivers and to collect accurate actuarial data on driving and car accidents. The state achieves two goals, ensured coverage of damages resultant from liability and an overall reduction in risky driving activities and thus likely fewer accidents at all, resulting in fewer payments. Thus, public welfare for safety and financial exposures is improved at a minimal of transaction costs to the state coffers. As Grossman, Clearley, and Cole wrote:

> Because insurance firms invest in acquiring precisely the information that establishes the probabilities and costs of accidents – information that is too costly for individuals to acquire on their own, for reasons having to do with economies of scale and cost spreading – insurance markets partially solve the problem connected with the tort system's inability on its own to gather and process that kind of information. Moreover, the insurance industry, along with legislative process, creates a system of incentives and fines, i.e. carrots and sticks, to induce potential injurers and victims to reduce the likelihood of harm over time and thus lower social costs.[63]

An example of the involvement of private regulation can be found in the EU timber regulation.[64] It requires EU traders who place timber products on the EU market for the first time to exercise due diligence. An important role in proving that timber has been sustainably harvested is played by so-called monitoring organisations. These organisations, to be recognised by the European Commission, are private entities which provide EU operators with operational due diligent systems.

Finally, industry often voluntarily imposes high standards on itself which go beyond the compliance with safety regulation; for a variety of reasons, mostly having to do with reputation and the expectation of a price premium. Large food chains may for example impose high standards upon their suppliers in order to avoid

63 Grossman, Clearley, and Cole (2006, at 9).

64 Regulation 995/2010 laying down the obligations of operators who place timber and timber products on the market.

reputation losses as a result of a food safety crisis.[65] Enterprises may engage in CSR in the environmental arena, referred to as corporate environmental responsibility (CER).[66]

In practice, those forms of governance are becoming increasingly important and therefore also deserve discussion.

## 9.7 COMBINATION OF VARIOUS INSTRUMENTS

### 9.7.1 *Optimality of Diverse Instrumentation*

Depending upon particular circumstances, all reviewed instruments have their specific strengths and weaknesses; no singular approach is all-sufficient. Environmental liability, for example, can provide excellent incentives to reduce pollution while still leaving industry with sufficient flexibility. The duty to compensate victims under liability prevents polluters from taking care below the required standard even without governmental intervention. Optimal standards are determined by the judge (under a negligence setting) or by the potential polluter themselves (under strict liability). Consequently, continuous incentives for adaptation and innovation to a changing environment are offered to reduce pollution (especially under strict liability). Liability rules are relatively cheap for the public at large, since no standards are determined ex ante through government agencies and enforcement takes place via private parties (the victims) and not via government.

However, liability rules will have these incentive effects only if the potential environmental tortfeasor has money at stake and only if the expected harm will not exceed that capital. Furthermore, liability will give rise to optimal behaviour only if victims can identify the polluters as the correct tortfeasor and establish causal relationships between the hazardous activities and the damages caused. If these factors cannot be ensured, as is often the case, there is a justification for regulation.

Yet regulation cannot be idealised either, since it is insufficiently flexible (too static), is not able to adapt quickly to changing circumstances, does not provide enough incentives for innovation, and (probably most importantly) can be subject to the influence of private interest groups, which gives rise to the setting of inefficient care levels.

Market-based instruments look promising and theoretically have many advantages over regulation. Yet legal and institutional design issues may reduce the efficiency of these so-called economic instruments: environmental taxes rarely if ever correctly set marginal environmental costs and even then, they are used only to a limited extent, and emissions trading may suffer from grandfathering and other design issues that

[65] See Fagotto (2015).
[66] See Lu (2017).

can reduce their effectiveness. These economic instruments are susceptible to lobbying that also affects instrument choice and design.

### 9.7.2 *Liability and Regulation: Exclusivity?*

According to Shavell's criteria, there is a strong argument to control the environmental risk through ex ante regulation or taxes. However, in individual cases there can still be damage to the environment. Then again, liability under tort comes into the picture and the question has been addressed in the literature how regulation influences the liability system and vice versa.[67]

A major point often stressed is that the fact that there are many arguments in favour of ex ante regulation of the environment does not per se suggest that the tort system should not be used any longer for its deterring and compensating functions. One reason for still relying on the tort system is that the effectiveness of environmental regulation is dependent upon enforcement, which may be weak. In addition, the influence of lobby groups on regulation, to which public choice theory has rightly pointed, can to some extent be overcome by combining safety regulation and liability rules. Safety regulation, such as emission standards in licences, can become outdated fast and often lacks flexibility, which equally merits a combination with tort rules.

Hence, from the above it follows that, although there is a strong case for safety regulation to control the environmental risk, tort rules will still play an important role as well.[68] This raises the question whether compliance with regulation will affect the liability issue.[69] We will address this point in the next sections.

### 9.7.3 *Violation of Regulation and Liability*

A topic to be considered is whether a violation of a regulatory standard should automatically be considered as a fault under tort law and thus lead to liability of the licensee.

Assuming that the licence sets the regulatory standard at the efficient care level, a violation of the regulatory standard should indeed lead to liability to give the licensee an incentive to spend on care. However, Shavell argues that the costs of following the regulatory standard are not the same for all injurers as some would face

67 The complementary relationship between tort law and regulation has been examined in detail by Arcuri (2001, 39–40); Burrows (1999, 227–242); Faure and Ruegg (1994); Kolstad, Ulen and Johnson (1990); Rose-Ackerman (1992a; 1995a; and 1996). Rose-Ackerman also compared US and European experiences in using regulation versus tort law in environmental policy. See Rose-Ackerman (1995a, 312–332 and 1995b).

68 For a recent different analysis, leading to the same result that liability and regulation should be combined, see Schmitz (2000, at 371–382).

69 For the intersection between public environmental law and tort law, see Lee (2016).

higher costs than others. This could be a more direct cost issue, such as older equipment, or something subtler such as access to patents and intellectual property for better environmental safety equipment. Thus, following the standard might be inefficient for some injurers. The injurers for whom following the regulatory standard would only be possible at high costs should not be held to follow this standard since it would create inefficiencies.[70] The question is whether this means that these injurers should not be held liable if they violate the regulatory standard, given that compliance reduces welfare due to inefficiency, and non-compliance could result in reduced welfare due to environmental injury. Either loss of welfare prevents availability of resources for other policy goals.

This problem can be compared with the reasonable person standard of common law or the civilian *bonus pater familias* standard, both from tort law. Although a detailed individualisation of standards of efficient care would be the optimal solution in a first-best world, this is often impossible given the costs of an individualised standard setting. Therefore, the legal system sets the required level of care at an average level, the *bonus pater familias* standard. The same can be said for regulation. If various groups can be identified at low costs, a separate standard for a certain group is efficient as long as the gains from selecting a further group outweigh the further administrative costs. In most cases, however, the regulator will not have the possibility of identifying atypical parties that might be able to avoid a loss at lower costs, for instance because they pose lower risks than normal. Therefore, a single regulatory standard will be used.[71]

Although one could, therefore, argue that a failure to satisfy the regulatory requirement should not necessarily result in a finding of negligence, so as to avoid some parties who pose lower risks taking wasteful precautions,[72] most legal systems generally consider a breach of a regulatory duty a fault.[73] One of the reasons for introducing safety regulation to prevent environmental damage is, as was mentioned earlier, that the regulator could possess better information to evaluate the efficient standard of care than the parties involved, due to its budget and temporal persistence.

Hence, the regulation passes on information to the parties on the efficient standard of care. The regulation also gives information to the judge who has to evaluate the behaviour of the injurer ex post in a liability case. The judge might lack the information necessary to find out whether in a particular case an injurer should not be held to follow the regulatory standard, for example because they posed a lower risk than usual. Therefore, particularly in environmental cases,

70 Faure and Van den Bergh (1987, at 109–110) and Shavell (1984a, at 365–366).

71 Cf. for the *bonus pater familias* standard, Posner (2003, at 171) and Shavell (1987, at 74).

72 Shavell (1984a, at 365–366).

73 Most legal systems indeed consider regulatory violation as negligence per se. See for instance Abraham (2002, at 379–398).

a judge will accept a finding of negligence as soon as a regulatory standard has been breached.[74] Thus, the statutory standards can be applied to define negligence.[75] Hence, one could argue that in this respect tort law could also be used to enforce regulations.[76]

### 9.7.4 *Compliance with Regulation and Liability*

A lot of attention is paid in the Law and Economics literature to the relationship between regulation and liability. That literature clearly recognises that the prevention of environmental harm can be achieved as a result of regulation.[77] A question arises whether following a regulatory standard could or should exclude an individual from incurring liability.

In environmental law this is particularly important, since the conditions under which an emission of pollutants is allowed are mostly laid down in a permit. These permits and their effects on liability can take various forms. In some cases, permits and regulations are fairly general, but in other cases they specify emission limits. It is especially in this latter case, i.e. when specifically allowed releases in a permit have been respected, that the industry often argues that as long as they follow the conditions of that licence, that no finding of negligence in tort law should be possible. This is often referred to as the 'justificative effect of a licence' or the 'regulatory compliance defence'.

The regulatory compliance defence is, however, rejected in several legal systems, such as in Belgium and in the Netherlands,[78] and also in the USA.[79] One can find a clear economic rationale for this rule. If compliance with a regulatory standard or licence were to automatically result in a release from liability, the potential injurer would have no incentive to invest more in care than the regulation asks from them, even if additional care could still reduce the expected accident costs.[80]

A first reason to hold an injurer liable (if the other conditions for liability are met), although they have followed the regulatory standard, is that indeed this standard is often merely a minimum but not an optimal or efficient level of safe guarding of the environment. The complete 'compliance defence' prevents any incentive to take

74 Faure and Van den Bergh have also argued that an advantage of this system is that it gives victims incentives to prove that the regulatory standard has been breached. This makes the victim an enforcer of safety regulation. They can claim compensation under the negligence rule as soon as a causal relationship between the violation of the regulatory standard and their damage is established (Faure and Van den Bergh 1987, at 110–111).

75 Rose-Ackerman (1992b, at 127).

76 For details see Kane (2002, at 427–467).

77 See this in Section 9.2.

78 For a comparative analysis of the question whether following a permit excludes criminal liability see Faure and Oudijk (1994, at 86–91).

79 See Abraham (2002, at 395).

80 Faure and Van den Bergh (1987, at 110) and Shavell (1984a, at 365).

precautions in excess of the regulated standard.[81] Exposure to liability will give the potential injurer incentives to take all efficient precautions, even if this requires more than just following the licence. This logic, by the way, holds both under negligence and strict liability. Since the regulatory standard cannot always take into account all of the efficient precautionary measures an injurer could take, testing the measures taken by the injurer, even though the regulatory standard was followed, will provide additional incentives. Allowing a regulatory compliance defence would also largely remove the beneficial inventive effects of strict liability. As we argued above, strict liability has the advantage that it provides the injurer with incentives to take all efficient measures to reduce the risk (prevention and activity level), even if regulatory conditions were followed.[82] A rule of complete regulatory compliance defence would prevent any precaution in excess of the regulated standard. If there is serious under-enforcement of standards, the role of liability as an incentive to take precautions remains an important policy tool.

A second reason is that exposure to liability might be a good remedy for the unavoidable capturing and public choice effects that play a role when permits are granted. If a permit always released an individual from incurring liability, all a plant operator would have to do is get a good permit with easy conditions from a friendly civil servant. That would then exclude any lawsuit for damages from a potential victim.

The capturing and public choice effects should be addressed also via direct tools. In this respect one can think about the liability, even under criminal law, of the licensor.[83] Liability of the licensor (and appropriate sanctions within administrative law) can provide incentives to civil servants to act efficiently when granting licences.[84] This, however, still requires tort law to take into account the fact that regulatory standards are not always set efficiently. If the optimal level of care is higher than the regulatory standard, liability will efficiently provide additional incentives.

Finally, tort law can also be seen as a 'stop gap' for situations not dealt with by the statute.[85] This makes clear that the exposure to liability notwithstanding, the permit is an important guarantee that the plant operator will take efficient care.

Therefore, simply following the conditions of a licence or – more generally – regulatory standards should not have a justificative effect in tort. The opposite may

[81] So Burrows (1999, at 242). Recently Schwartz added to the debate by discussing whether compliance with federal safety statutes should have a justificative effect in state tort cases. See Schwartz (2000, at 1–57).

[82] This outcome has been shown formally by Burrows (1999, 227–244) and Kolstad, Ulen, and Johnson (1990, 888–901).

[83] Faure, Koopmans, and Oudijk (1996, at 529–569).

[84] Note, however, that industry argues against such a liability of the licensor, claiming that this may entail the risk that licensors would be too reluctant in allowing emissions if this could give rise to their liability: Niezen, Raaijmaker, and Tervoort (2000, at 171).

[85] Arcuri (2001, at 43–44) and Rose-Ackerman (1992b, at 123).

only be true if it were clear that the administrative agency took into account all potential harm of all interested third parties when setting permit conditions. Indeed, theoretically, regulators and licensors are supposed to set standards in regulations and permits in a way that reflects political choices about the level of risks that maximises welfare. Hence, ideally, when setting objective pollution standards, regulators are supposed to weigh costs and benefits of different norms and choose the standard that delivers the highest social net benefit. In such case a judge in a civil liability suit should not be 'second guessing' efficient agency decisions. It is, however, rare that agencies will be able to take ex ante all these interests and possible damage into account when setting permit conditions. Hence, as a general rule, following licences or regulatory standards should not free from liability; the opposite would be the exception.

This logic is robust for both the negligence rule and a strict liability rule. Indeed, holding an injurer liable – notwithstanding their compliance with regulatory standards – will play an important role under a strict liability rule, since this will lead the injurer to take efficient care and adopt an efficient activity level, i.e. to take all efficient measures to reduce the potential accident costs, although this might require doing more (as far as precaution is concerned) than the regulation requires. Under a negligence rule this case law is also significant if the efficient care standard (which is assumed to be equal to the due care standard required by the legal system) is higher than the regulatory standard. The basic reason remains that efficient preventive measures can be taken above what is often prescribed in the norm. Requiring a potential polluter to take these efficient preventive measures thus increases social welfare.

Within the context of environmental liability, the justificative effect of licences is strongly supported by (of course) industry and by some authors. It is more particularly held that in environmental law, the damage will to a large extent depend upon prior zoning and planning decisions and will depend upon the framework of regulations and permits. One could imagine the situation where a government authority has balanced all the interests involved appropriately and has, on the basis of available information, taken an efficient decision, after having heard all parties involved, concerning the amount of environmental damage which would be allowed. In that case one could imagine that it would not be efficient that, for example, one of the parties who has been involved in the licensing process (and has hence been heard previously) would afterwards be allowed a liability suit for environmental damage to biodiversity although the damage consists precisely of the harm which has been foreseen as a result of the licence.[86] It is particularly in these situations that Rose-Ackerman argues that a judge in a civil liability suit should not be second guessing efficient agency decisions,[87] and that Bergkamp argues that

[86] Cf. Niezen, Raaijmaker, and Tervoort (2000, at 170–171).
[87] Rose-Ackerman (1992b, at 123).

the polluter should not 'pay double' – once because he has to follow regulatory conditions and once because he has to compensate the victim.[88] Bergkamp therefore argued that an EU environmental liability regime should contain a regulatory compliance defence.[89] This is, however, not the solution chosen in the ELD.[90] Although one should, once more, in principle not accept an adjudicated effect of prior regulatory decisions, as there may be exceptional situations where the regulatory decision can be such that all the interests involved have been weighed appropriately and that an efficient standard resulted from this balancing process. In that case it seems logical that when this efficient standard has been followed by the regulated, liability in tort is excluded.

This seems, however, more to be an exceptional situation than the general rule, and as such, should merit substantive review by any court considering such a liability defence.

### 9.7.5 *The Search for Smart Mixes of Instruments*

After having discussed the interdependencies between liability rules and regulation, it may be clear that neither public safety regulation, nor liability rules alone, can perfectly internalise environmental externalities. This is not only the case for safety regulation central to this chapter, nor for liability rules which were discussed earlier, but it equally applies to the market-based instruments (such as taxation and emission trading) which were central to Chapter 7. It is precisely since none of the instruments standing alone can be considered as being able to solve the problem of environmental pollution that there is a call from Law and Economics literature for 'smart mixes' of all of the legal tools, from both public and private law.[91]

Pigouvian-type taxes are very popular with economists and policymakers, as a tax is generally capable of affecting the total amount used of a given type of product and is also able to impact the choice between different product varieties. Yet due to inter alia monitoring and enforcement reasons, taxes appear to be less suited to addressing how a given product is used, when it is used, and where it is used.[92] Therefore, other instruments are needed to complement environmental taxes.

88 Bergkamp (1999).

89 Bergkamp (2000, at 5).

90 Directive 2004/35 of 21 April 2004 on environmental liability with regard to the prevention and remedying of environmental damage: Article 8(4) of the ELD stipulates that 'Member States may allow the operator not to bear the costs of remedial actions taken pursuant to this Directive where he demonstrates that he was not at fault or negligent and that the environmental damage was caused by: (a) an emission or event expressly authorized by, and fully in accordance with the conditions of an authorization conferred by or given under applicable national laws and regulations . . .'.

91 See Section 2.5.

92 OECD (2006).

There is an abundant Law and Economics literature on this optimal combination of various policy instruments that discusses the comparative benefits of various instruments in a given situation. Polinsky,[93] building upon Calabresi and Melamed,[94] argues that when the government has full information about the externality problem, only tax subsidies could control externalities efficiently and protect both parties' entitlements, even in a transaction-cost rich world. Yet in the presence of limited information, Polinsky claims that a tax is often inferior to the liability rules but that the property rights approach best protects entitlements,[95] thus drawing a distinction between remedies based on property rights and liability rules on the one hand and incentive-based mechanisms such as taxes and charges on the other.

Some attention has also been paid to the problem of combining tort recovery and effluent fees or tradable rights. Rose-Ackerman, for example, argued that incentive-based regulatory statutes should pre-empt tort actions: if fee schedules were set to reflect social costs, tort actions would be redundant or even counterproductive.[96] One the other hand, some have called for bounties to be awarded to private citizens who engage in environmental litigation on the behalf of the public interest, especially in support of environmental policies if it enables authorities to better survive fiscal budgets under austerity periods.[97] This underlines the usefulness of combining instruments to attain complementary benefits. If, on the other hand, both instruments in fact reach the same goal, applying two instruments may only lead to increased administrative costs or to over-deterrence. A rich body of Law and Economics literature examines the combined use of such instruments to realise complementary benefits.[98]

### 9.7.6 *Optimal Instrument Mixes in Practice*

In practice as well, environmental policy may be based on a combination of economic instruments and regulatory solutions.[99] In many legal systems, environmental pollution is controlled primarily via CAC regulation, but liability rules still apply, along with incentives for meeting optimal care levels even beyond regulatory standards.

Undoubtedly there is more potential in actual environmental policy to make optimal use of efficient combinations of policy instruments. Regarding climate change, for example, the EU chose emissions trading without employing other

93 Polinsky (1979).
94 Calabresi and Melamed (1972).
95 Brown and Holahan (1980, at 165–178) and Polinsky (1979, at 1–48).
96 Rose Ackerman (1992a, at 128).
97 Salzman, Ruhl, and Nash (2015, at 486–487).
98 See Gravelle (1987, at 115–131); Hansson and Skogh (1987, at 132–144); Skogh (1982, at 67–80; 1989a, at 87–101); and see more particularly Gunningham and Grabosky (1998).
99 See Gunningham and Grabosky (1998, at 422–453).

classic instruments such as taxation.[100] There is undoubtedly room to examine whether, also in the EU, environmental taxation could achieve (instead of or in combination with the ETS) similar or even better results than emissions trading. In this context it bears mentioning that the European Commission proposed to amend the rules on taxation of energy products and electricity,[101] in order to restructure and target their carbon emissions and energy content.[102] An interesting combination of environmental taxation and emissions trading can also be found in the UK in the form of the climate change levy that recycles money back to industry.[103] In Switzerland, by contrast, companies participating in an ETS are exempted from the domestic $CO_2$ tax. Since emission level will be contingent on individual firms' cumulative responses to incentives, the environmental effectiveness is less predictable.[104] Nevertheless, environmental taxation could be employed effectively in those sectors that are not subject to the EU ETS – not necessarily on the EU level but on the national level.

## 9.8 SUMMARY AND CONCLUSION

Public regulation for environmental law seems a 'no brainer' for most environmental lawyers. Yet, what we have attempted to do in the chapter is to highlight where private law has specific and identifiable shortcomings that either are problematic or wholly not functional, and thereby to provide solid theoretical support for the specific application of public law in those scenarios. Furthermore, we have illuminated how the literature of Law and Economics views the functional operation of private and public law as complementary, that they are best seen as two aspects of a joint mechanism to guide actors in their environmental behaviours. Such an approach relies on the mechanism design technique from game theory, and is often referred to in popular press as 'smart mixes'.

Liability rules are readily recognised for their limits. Perhaps most noteworthy is that you have no case until you are already injured, thus an argument exists that if your goal is to avoid accidents, civil liability rules are not optimal in that regard. Of course, the ability to learn from other cases and to form reasonable expectations of damages would provide incentives to avoid accidents. But the point remains that public regulations can interact and monitor behaviour prior to an actual accident. Also, private liability only works if the private tortfeasor has capital reserves against which to assess civil damages; death or dissolution, insolvency, and strategic forms of ownership can all greatly reduce the effectiveness of civil liability, whereas public regulation has a more diverse set of governance tools, including criminal law and

[100] See Section 7.2.3.
[101] Council Directive 2003/96/EC.
[102] European Commission (2011).
[103] Richardson and Chanwai (2003).
[104] Baldwin (2008, at 6).

incarceration, to effect its goals. Some privately caused harms affect too much of a community, spreading the injury across too many victims, for the case to be efficiently brought forward under normal modes of civil liability; public regulators might be able to more efficiently address the injury and its remedies. For these and other reasons, we found ample theoretical support in Law and Economics literature to engage public regulation to provide protection of the environment.

That said, public regulation is not free from its own problems. Agency capture and deflection of regulatory drafting are a major concern, as modelled under public choice theory. Public regulations that are ostensibly drafted to protect the community and the environment can also serve to create barriers to entry, providing a form of subsidy and market protection to pre-existing firms.

Another complicating issue for public regulation is the appropriate level of government to set the regulatory authority. Should the regulation be at the city, county, provincial, or national level? Might it in certain settings be more properly set above the national level, as within the EU? The Law and Economics literature, in a prelude to Chapter 13, does provide models for evaluating which levels are most appropriate, which is generally to determine which lowest level of governance might contain a sufficient number of the externalities, injuries, and stakeholders.

There is an exciting space, theoretically, in the domain of private regulatory mechanisms. These are programmes wherein public authorities design mechanisms that engage several private parties, all related to the environmentally risky activity, to create new interactions that both reveal more data and alter private behaviour to align with public regulatory goals. A common example of this technique is requiring private insurance for car drivers. Insurance companies request data on driving behaviour from drivers in exchange for sale of insurance policies, and drivers then begin to steward their driving to enable that data to support a lower cost of the insurance policy. Thus, the public authority has achieved better driving records without needing to increase its own enforcement costs, and at the same time has leveraged private insurance agencies to act as a private clearing house of both driving behaviour and of many private compensation settlements, reducing the public cost of litigation institutions. Similar designs can be created, using game theory and an understanding of the particular environmental problem to be addressed, to better enable budget-limited public environmental authorities to achieve more environmental goals by leveraging the assets and interests of the private parties that the authorities would otherwise need to regulate at public expense.

In conclusion, the literature of Law and Economics does not view the governance world as private versus public, but rather as a world of necessarily complementary public–private governance. Each domain has its own advantages and short fallings, and the literature has illuminated not only these differences but also how private law can support the function of public law and likewise how public law can support the function of private law. This is ever more so in the case of environmental law. Further, that sense of divide is seen as a false dichotomy, as the literature recognises that mechanism design can yield hybrid models that integrate the functions of both private and public law to enable private regulatory mechanisms, which enable public regulatory goals to be achieved at greater efficiencies.

The story of environmental Law and Economics is not a tale in defence of private law rights against public law regulation, but rather a harmonious tale of two systems that can be integrated to function as a more effective and efficient whole.

# 10

# Environmental Crime

## 10.1 INTRODUCTION

In this chapter we shall discuss the question why the criminal law is used at all to control environmental pollution. In addition, we shall discuss how the criminal law can be used in a way to deter environmental pollution and which type of sanctions would be optimal.

We explained that environmental law is usually structured in such a way that specific administrative requirements are imposed on industry and the allowed amounts and quality of polluting emissions are subject to prior approval via licences. Thus, administrative agencies decide on the permitted degree of pollution.

Environmental statutes usually provide that the violation of one of these administrative duties constitutes an environmental crime. Thus, it is a crime to operate a facility without a permit or to violate emission standards. Hence, one can already notice that the criminal law and administrative law are highly interweaved in environmental crimes.[1]

This chapter is structured as follows. We first indicate why environmental pollution should, from an economic perspective, be sanctioned through the criminal law at all (Section 10.2); we more particularly focus on differences between administrative law and criminal law in enforcing public environmental law (Section 10.3) and then focus on the question how environmental crime can be deterred, taking into account empirical evidence on penalties applied (Section 10.4). We then turn to optimal sanctions from an economic perspective (Section 10.5) and pay specific attention to corporate crime, as environmental pollution is often committed in the framework of corporate entities (Section 10.6). The chapter concludes by focusing on the different enforcement strategies to combat environmental crime (Section 10.7). Section 10.8 summarises and concludes.

[1] This point has been made extensively by Heine (1991, at 376).

## 10.2 WHY SHIFT TO PUBLIC ENFORCEMENT?

Of course, within the scope of this chapter, it is not useful to summarise the broad literature on criminalisation, an issue which has been extensively discussed both from a legal perspective,[2] as well as from a Law and Economics perspective.[3] For the sake of this chapter, it can just be argued that some of the arguments made in that literature in favour of criminal law do apply to the case of environmental pollution as well. However, one has to stress that much of the literature in fact provides arguments in favour of public enforcement or regulation rather than in favour of the criminal law.[4]

One argument in favour of public enforcement is that private law remedies will not sufficiently deter environmental injurers, as the incentives from liability rules poorly match the circumstances of ecological injuries.[5] The arguments are well-known: (i) environmental pollution often has no individual victim that could file a liability suit, (ii) causation may be difficult to prove, (iii) a long time lapse may make it impossible to recognise that, for example, health damage has been caused through environmental pollution, and (iv) procedural rules may complicate or prevent bring forward an environmental tort claim. These are arguments that are traditionally advanced in favour of public regulation.[6] This at least explains why public regulation and enforcement may be necessary from an economic perspective to cure the externalities caused by environmental pollution.[7]

A second reason traditionally advanced in economic theory in favour of public regulation, but also to explain the use of tools from criminal law, is the low probability of detection.[8] In many cases of environmental pollution, the probability of being caught may be very low, perhaps substantially below that of a reasonable expectation of detection. The result is that, according to the Becker model, the efficient sanction for deterring the potential polluter should be correspondingly higher.[9]

But given such a low probability of detections, the corresponding sanction needs to become multifold larger than the actual injury. In general, this effect cannot be achieved with tort law, since tort law in principle only forces the injurer to compensate the victim for the amount of damage suffered and no more.[10] This again shows

[2] See for example Ashworth (2000).
[3] Bowles, Faure, and Garoupa (2008); Faure and Visser (2004); and Ogus (2004a).
[4] See the arguments for public regulation reviewed in Sections 9.1 and 9.2.
[5] See, for example, Wilde (2002, at 307–310).
[6] See Shavell (1984a, 1984b).
[7] This is in-line with the criteria for safety regulation discussed in Section 9.2.
[8] Posner (1985) and Shavell (1985b).
[9] See also Skogh (1973) and Skogh and Stuart (1982).
[10] Although some legal systems, such as some jurisdictions in the USA, do allow for tort law sanctions beyond the actual damages, known as punitive damages, when recklessness or similar

the inappropriateness of civil law in cases where the probability of detection is too slight.

The low detection rate alone does not explain the need to use the criminal law to deter environmental pollution, but merely provides a supporting argument in favour of public enforcement. As we shall explain in the next section of this chapter, when combined with insolvency or similar challenges to enforcement, there is a risk of 'getting away with it'.

Before discussing that aspect, it should be stressed that these traditional economic arguments in favour of criminal law, or at least in favour of public enforcement, may equally provide arguments in favour of decriminalisation. It may be recalled that in the 1970s, many criminal law scholars were sceptical about the effectiveness of criminal law and argued that it ought to be used more moderately or not at all; this perspective was known as abolitionism. Although that once common view has now been abandoned, it is still believed that the very costly institution of criminal law should be reserved for those cases where other forms of civil and public deterrence cannot otherwise be achieved.

Perhaps the best way towards decriminalisation is to improve the effectiveness of civil law. Hence, if the main problem with tort law is that it limits compensation to the amount of harm done to the victim, one way of counterbalancing the low detection rate is to increase the amount of compensation payable by the injurer under tort law. That is precisely the idea behind the concept of 'punitive damages'.[11]

Another example, more specifically related to the issue at hand, refers to the argument that private law will often not be useful as a deterrent against environmental pollution, since when no one would be likely to bring a suit in tort; damage may be widespread to identify a cost efficient plaintiff, the whole community might have been victimised and thus several complexities emerge,[12] or the damage caused to collective goods that are not owned by any particular person, natural or artificial.

There are several potential options to improving the functionality of private law for environmental cases. One way of doing so is to allow the use of civil law also when no individual victim is harmed, but where a (high) level of social harm is caused by the tortious act. Another way of doing so is by allowing the state or other public authorities to act on behalf of the environment and to let them use tort law.

factors are engaged. But the very etymology of punitive damages reveals that it reflects a criminal law concept imported over to tort law.

[11] See Cooter (1982) and Landes and Posner (1981a). Nevertheless, punitive damages also seem to be applied, especially when the environmental harm is large (for example, with oil pollution) and where the probability of detection and conviction may in fact not be low at all. Punitive damages may therefore arguably be more necessary in the USA than in Europe, possibly also due to different patterns of criminalisation of environmental wrongdoing.

[12] When a whole community is hit by an environmental injury, issues of political process become options beyond the options of pursuing lawsuits. Which path is more cost efficient for the particular resources of that community is difficult to ascertain until a broader understanding of the situation is available.

Yet another way would be to grant non-governmental organisations or individuals the right to institute actions in tort; for example, to ask for an injunction to stop environmental pollution from occurring. Finally, class actions brought on behalf of a group of victims could be considered as a way to improve the functioning of private law, thus reducing the need for criminalisation.

## 10.3 ADMINISTRATIVE OR CRIMINAL LAW?

So far, we have presented the traditional economic arguments to explain why environmental pollution cannot merely be remedied via private law and why public enforcement is indicated. The main reason we gave was the low probability of detecting environmental crime and thus the high likelihood of responsibility evasion.[13]

However, this does not necessarily explain why one should have to use the criminal law. Indeed, the low probability of detection could well be compensated by imposing a high fine on the polluter. Fines have always been considered the preferred sanction in economic theory, for the simple reason that the costs of imposition are low and fines in fact only generate money for the public budget.[14]

Monetary sanctions can, in principle, have both a criminal and an administrative nature. Administrative procedure has the major advantage that it is usually less costly than the criminal procedure, ceteris paribus. Administrative fines can, within what is sometimes referred to as 'administrative penal law',[15] be imposed by administrative authorities after a relatively simple procedure and usually require a relative low threshold of proof. Compared with the criminal law, the costs of the administrative procedure are substantially lower. All things being equal, it can therefore be argued that if optimal deterrence can be achieved through fines, it seems desirable to use the less costly administrative law instead of the relatively more costly rules of criminal procedure.

Ogus and Abbot have argued that in the UK more use should be made of administrative fines (and other administrative sanctions for that matter) to enforce violations of environmental regulations.[16] A clear normative conclusion from this literature is therefore that in many more instances than is the case today,

13 Indeed, Steinzor has argued that the lack of effective detection and 'nonexistent enforcement' led to an acute regulatory failure, and thus 'until and unless the regulatory state is not just revived but greatly strengthened, a result that does not seem foreseeable in the near term, criminal prosecution is the best hope for people who believe that the government must redouble its efforts to preserve natural resources and protect the public health' (Steinzor 2016, at 213–214).

14 See for example Posner (1980) and Shavell (1985b).

15 The expression 'administrative penal law' may be confusing to some who consider 'penal' synonymous with 'criminal'. In the literature, this notion is used to refer to a system whereby administrative authorities impose penalties.

16 See Ogus and Abbot (2002a, 2002b).

administrative law should be used to deter environmental injuries, especially when the penalties consist of proportionate fines or other not-too-infringing administrative sanctions.

However, there are important reasons why not all efficient penalties necessary to deter environmental pollution can be imposed through administrative law and why criminal law therefore remains necessary.

Since the probability of detection of environmental pollution is in practice often very low, the optimal sanction to deter pollution would need to become very high to counterbalance. The likelihood that this optimal fine might outweigh the individual wealth of an offender is relatively high. Environmental polluters are often organised as corporate entities that benefit from limited liability.[17] Hence, there is always a risk that environmental harm may cause costs that are higher than the assets of the firm or, in the criminal law context, that the optimal fine (to outweigh a low detection rate) will be much higher than the assets of the firm. Indeed, the optimal monetary sanction required for deterrence so frequently exceeds the offenders' capital assets that non-monetary sanctions, such as imprisonment, become necessary.

Further, as noted by Steinzor, 'legal historian Lawrence Friedman identifies three goals of the criminal law: deterrence, punishment, and the setting of "moral boundaries" to show a society where the lines lies between good and bad'.[18] Thus, the application of criminal law to environmental transgressions could serve to set ex ante norms and strong incentives to deter such transgressions from occurring.

There is a clear economic reason why society does not want to impose very stringent sanctions, such as imprisonment or comparatively high fines, through an administrative proceeding. The reason is that the outcomes of the criminal trials, where the rules of evidence and discovery are developed with a different focus than those of administrative law, may be more cautiously rendered. This cautious aspect is important, because a task of criminal law is not only to apply optimal sanctions to be guilty, but to also avoid punishing the innocent. This is referred to as the goal of reduction of error costs.[19] The risk of error cost is a lot higher when very serious sanctions, such as imprisonment, can be imposed, rather than when only monetary sanctions are imposed. It is therefore understandable that less costly administrative proceedings are chosen in all cases where the consequences, and thus the risk of error cost, would not be too high in the event of a wrongful conviction. That logic partially explains why administrative law and its corresponding administrative procedures will be reserved for cases where relatively low penalties can suffice to provide deterrence.

The policy lesson from this economic literature is therefore rather straightforward: in cases where optimal deterrence of environmental polluters can be achieved

[17] See Cortenraad (1999) and Hansmann and Kraakman (1991).
[18] Steinzor (2016, at 234).
[19] See Miceli (1990).

through relatively modest sanctions, the use of less costly administrative penal law may be warranted instead of sanctions from criminal law.[20] However, in cases where the probability of detection is relatively low, social harm and the potential gain to the polluter is high and thus a more severe sanction is needed, it may become warranted to use the more costly criminal procedures in order to reduce the risk of error costs.

In reality, in many legal systems today, it is now possible to use either the criminal law, administrative penal law, or a mixture of both for environmental offences.[21]

## 10.4 HOW TO DETER?

### 10.4.1 *Raising Probabilities or Penalties?*

Since the first publications of Gary Becker,[22] and George Stigler in the 1960s,[23] a rich and abundant literature on the economics of crime and punishment has emerged. Those economic notions have also been introduced in the criminological literature on crime and punishment.[24] In that framework, a rational prospective offender is assumed to be a profit maximiser, who weighs the costs and the benefits of committing a crime and does not undertake illegal action unless the expected benefits of the crime exceed the expected costs. The bottom line of the economic theory is relatively simple – that it is assumed that the offender takes the decision to commit a crime or not, weighing costs and benefits.

Taking into account this point of view, the function of the criminal law can be stated relatively simply in this perspective as *increasing the expected costs from a regulation violating act to deter a prospective offender.*[25]

In calculating the expected costs, two important factors should be taken into account: first is the ability of authorities to catch and convict the offender $p$; the second is the expected maximum punishment S. The multiplication of these factors then constitutes the expected costs of a crime to the criminal. Assuming that these costs are C, then $C = p*S$. Criminal policy can therefore be attuned towards increasing either the probability of detection $p$ or the sanction.[26] Both can lead to an increase of the total costs C to a level where it exceeds the expected benefits to

[20] Nyborg and Telle would go further, that even warnings of potential sanctions or punishments may be efficient means of providing corrective incentives; thus, authorities can be more efficient with both fiscal budgets and political capital while retaining a firm grasp on preventing policy failure. See Nyborg and Telle (2004, at 2807–2808).

[21] For a discussion of the optimal use of criminal sanctions in addition to administrative penalties, see Garoupa and Gomez-Pomar (2004).

[22] See Becker (1962, at 1–13; 1968, at 169–217).

[23] Stigler (1970, at 526–536).

[24] For an interesting integration see Otto (1982).

[25] For an excellent summary of this economic theory of crime and punishment see Bowles (1982, at 54–105).

[26] In this sense, Nyborg and Telle's results reflect a clear signal of detection and a strong signal of imminent sanction, and thus their findings are complementary to Becker and Stiglitz and

the criminal and thus provides ex ante information to the potential criminal to include in their decision-making process. Given an expected negative outcome, a rational perspective would choose to avoid that activity.

A lot of attention is also paid to the costs of the criminal justice system, including (i) the costs to discover crime, (ii) the costs to catch the suspect, (iii) the costs of trail and conviction, and (iv) the costs to enforce resulting sanctions. These costs are important when the trade-off is considered between either raising the probability of getting caught or the maximum punishment.

Suppose for example that $S = 1000$ units and $p = 0.01$, then the expected costs of the crime to the criminal C are only ten units. By raising either the probability of getting caught or the expected maximum punishment by a factor of two, the new expected costs, $C_{new}$, for the criminal would double; $C_{new} = 2{*}C_{original}$.

The two ways to obtain these results, however, are not equally easy to achieve. Increasing the expected maximum punishment might demand less effort from the government than increasing and subsequently stabilising the probability of catching the offender; if for no reason other than enhanced policing is an immediate and costly budget item for the immediate class of legislators whereas the costs of years or decades of long incarceration would likely fall on future sessions of legislators equally removed in the future. Therefore, the point has been made in the literature that increasing punishment rather than the probability of catching offenders presents fewer transaction costs on present policymakers.[27]

Although one could formulate criticisms with respect to the above described model, it is important to note that from an economic point of view, the costs of crime control should be taken into account when decisions are made on how much to invest in deterring environmental pollution through the criminal law. Given the relationship between the detection rate and the optimal sanction, a reduction of the detection rate should, other things remaining equal, be compensated by a higher expected sanction to retain the same expected costs for the potential offender.[28]

Note that according to this model the behaviour of the potential polluter can be influenced by raising the expected costs of crime. This does not always necessarily mean that the expected sanction should at least reflect the environmental harm.[29] Criminal law does not necessarily react to environmental harm, but to the violation of environmental statutes. As explained below, criminal law can react to the violation of regulations which prescribe or prohibit certain behaviour, irrespective of the

warnings won't reduce the overall effectiveness of the regulatory regime; see Nyborg and Telle (2004, at 2813).

[27] See for instance Adams and Shavell (1990, at 337); Polinsky and Shavell (1991, at 618); and Posner (1973, at 223–231).

[28] Polinsky and Shavell (1979, at 880–891).

[29] Given that the expected costs to the polluter is the number reflected in the product of the expected sanction and the likelihood of detection, it becomes critically important to have an accurate gauge on how likely detection really would be in the field.

question whether actual harm was caused. The criminal laws are addressing behaviour that gives rise to risk of harm in order to prevent those circumstances and their harms from happening. Sometimes that risky behaviour may actually hurt the environment, but in other cases there is merely an infringement of behavioural standards established in administrative laws, without the actual harm being caused. Thus, the expected sanction should reflect that modelling perspective, not necessarily the harm caused or not caused, although one certainly could call the violation of standards a form of a social injury, given Shavell's perspective on governing activity levels for risky activities.

### 10.4.2 *Empirics*

Data on detection and prosecution of environmental crime show that in fact the likelihood that a violation ends up in court and is sanctioned is extremely low. For the Flemish region in Belgium, based on data of the environmental inspectorate, it was found that the average probability of being apprehended and prosecuted for a violation is *less than 1 per cent*,[30] meaning that less than 1 in 100 firms that are in violation of the regulatory standards will be detected and prosecuted.[31]

Not only is that probability to be inspected very low,[32] but many detected violations are not prosecuted either. In the Flemish region, the prosecutor dismissed 62 per cent of violations established by the environmental inspectorate.[33] Similar data comes from the UK, where on average the prosecution rate for detected pollution incidents is less than 5 per cent;[34] however, serious incidents have a much higher prosecution rate.[35] Similar data comes from Germany, where older studies indicated that around 50 per cent of all environmental violations were dismissed by the public prosecutor.[36]

The pattern of lacking consequence continues once the case gets to the court. A study on the fines imposed by the courts within the competence of the Court of Appeals of Ghent in the Flemish region in the period 1990–2000 found that an average fine of €5,000 was imposed both in the first instance and on appeal.[37] A later study referred to average fines imposed for violations in the textile sector of €2,869 in

30 This implies in a simplistic Beckerian model, that the sanction needs to be at 100-fold of the benefit to the violator to set incentives under the model; this type of sanction exceeds normal tort law and administrative law ranges of function.

31 Svatikova (2011, at 115), available at: http://repub.eur.nl/res/org/9747/ (then search 'Economic Criteria for Criminalization: Optimizing Enforcement in Case of Environmental Violations' and follow hyperlink).

32 Billiet and Rousseau (2005).

33 Faure and Svatikova (2010, at 73).

34 See Bell and McGillivray (2005, at 295–296).

35 Svatikova (2011, at 123).

36 See Meinberg (1988) and Lutterer and Hoch (1997).

37 Billiet and Rousseau (2003, at 131).

the first instance and €7,175 on appeal.[38] For the Netherlands, average fines imposed through the criminal system were reported ranging from €1,351 to €2,342.[39] Overall, these are not fees that would capital cripple most corporate polluters, more likely the costs might even be tax deductible in many systems as long as the fees are not criminal in character, reducing even further the Becker effect of deterrence.

If one looks at these average fines imposed by criminal courts in Western Europe and multiplies this with the probability of being detected and prosecuted of about 1 per cent, this would lead to estimations in expected sanctions for the Flemish region varying from €87.70 to €176 to €181.[40]. Thus, the cost of environmental pollution facing a potential Flemish firm is approximately the cost of a nice dinner at a nice restaurant; certainly a cost, but not a substantial cost for firms with substantial revenues.

The European experience, with low expected sanctions for environmental crime would, at first blush, be different in the USA, where strict sentencing guidelines apply, to which the judge should, in principle, adhere.[41] The fines imposed for environmental crime indeed seem on average to be higher in the USA, compared with the low amounts in Europe.[42] However, Barrett found in a study on the application of sentencing guidelines for environmental crime that 'the sentences imposed in the majority of these cases reflected the reluctance of judges to impose significant incarceration for violations of environmental laws'.[43] Others even held that these sentencing guidelines led to negative outcomes for deterrence.[44] Since judges consider the guidelines unreasonable, this results in the opposite effect of lenient sentencing of environmental criminals.[45] According to some US scholars, significant violations are in fact sentenced too leniently, which may undermine the deterrent value of environmental enforcement and may trivialise environmental law itself.[46]

The simple summary here is that if policymakers seek guidance from the Law and Economics literature on how to reduce criminal acts of environmental harm, they probably need to look at the Becker model with new eyes and reconsider the resources spent on detection and the efforts spent on trials and enforcement.

38 Id.
39 See Schoep and Schuyt (2008).
40 Rousseau (2007a). See also Rousseau (2007b; and 2010, at 203).
41 For an economic critique of these sentencing guidelines, see generally Easterbrook (1983, at 289).
42 Several studies refer to median fines in the range of $50,000 to $100,000. For a summary see Firestone (2003, at 138–143).
43 Barrett (1992, at 1421).
44 Babbitt, Cory, and Kruchek (2004, at 62–63).
45 Id.
46 See for further empirical evidence on the deterrent function of environmental sanctions, Shimshack (2017).

### 10.4.3 *The Harrington Paradox*

Given these low numbers of prosecutions and sanctions, and hence correspondingly low expected sanctions, one could even ask the question why would firms comply at all with environmental regulations, since at first sight a violation seems always more profitable. This phenomenon has been referred to in the literature as the Harrington Paradox, following research by Winston Harrington, who established that given low expected sanctions one would expect more environmental criminality than can be observed in practice.[47]

However, here again one should come back to a general warning that one always has to interpret numbers with caution. Indeed, there may well be good reasons why firms comply with environmental regulation notwithstanding the Harrington Paradox.

One reason for compliance is that one could argue that of course not all cases are prosecuted before a criminal court, but that does not necessarily mean that nothing happens. There can in many cases also be good reasons to dismiss a case, simply because the conditions for criminal liability are not fulfilled; for example, because wastes were illegally deposited, but no perpetrator could be identified. Also, in cases where conditions for criminal liability are fulfilled, other mechanisms than the criminal prosecution may exist which could expose the potential polluter to expected costs. Prosecutors can, in some legal systems, also propose a financial payment to the perpetrator and hence deal with the case themselves, in order to avoid the high administrative costs of the criminal prosecution.[48] This may hence add something, but probably not a lot, to the expected sanction.

More powerful is probably the possibility for some environmental agencies to impose administrative fines in lieu of criminal sanctions.[49] This exists for example in legal systems in countries such as Austria and the Netherlands, which have, in addition to the criminal law, the possibility of administrative fines.[50] German research shows that the likelihood that these administrative fines (referred as *Geldbußen*) are imposed for administrative violations (referred to as *Ordnungswidrigkeiten*) is substantially higher than the likelihood of a prosecution in the criminal court.[51]

Therefore, a simple hypothesis is that in systems which allow administrative fines in addition to criminal prosecution, one can add substantially to expected costs and thus to deterrence. The simple reason is that in those systems a dismissal in the

47 Harford and Harrington (1991, at 392). See generally Harrington (1988, at 289–290, providing a counter analysis of the phenomenon).

48 OECD (2009, at 85) (using the Netherlands as an example).

49 See in this respect also the discussion on the choice between administrative or criminal law in the previous section.

50 Faure and Heine (2005, at 21–22).

51 Lutterer and Hoch (1997, at 190–191).

criminal procedure does not necessarily mean that nothing happens, as an administrative fine could still be imposed, thus adding to deterrence.[52]

A second point is that there may be other costs beyond the mere sanctions imposed by the courts that could deter potential violators. In that respect, one could, for example, refer to the mere fact that in cases of a criminal prosecution, the captains of industry may be confronted with the unpleasant experience of having to appear in court for several days, which can constitute a more expensive set of costs (loss of time and thus opportunity costs) to them than the actual sanction would cost them.[53] The mere fact of having to appear in court, and especially being convicted by a criminal court, could lead to a 'shaming' and hence to a loss of reputation for entrepreneurs; it could lead to challenges of their positions as executives or as board members.[54]

However, US empirical research by Karpoff et al. showed that whereas the stock value of publicly traded firms could fall after the announcement of a bad environmental outcome, such as an oil spill or criminal prosecution, these 'stock price effects are approximately equal to government-imposed penalties, clean-up costs and private settlements'.[55] It is therefore possible to conclude that a criminal conviction will not cause an additional reputational loss and that the mere fact of being labelled as a 'criminal' does not lead to additional costs.[56]

A third reason why the low prosecution rates of environmental violations in Western Europe should be interpreted with caution is that the prosecutor could in fact engage in regulatory dealings,[57] whereby the prosecutor only agrees to dismiss the case after evidence of compliance by the firm.[58] Some argue that this so-called soft approach in many cases leads to compliance by firms.[59]

A problem with this approach is, however, that since the economic gain resulting from a violation of environmental statutes can be substantial, a firm that, after detection, only risks having to do what it had to do according to the law anyway has nothing to lose by choosing to violate the standards until they are caught so doing; the time value of delayed expenditures may actually make this a revenue positive gambit for the firm. Violation, for instance by delaying an investment in

52 See Firestone (2003, at 147–158, discussing enforcement options available to the US EPA and the enforcement choices applied to different parties). Also, in the USA, the EPA has the choice to enforce environmental law administratively or criminally. Id. Empirical evidence shows that a substantial portion of cases are prosecuted administratively. Id., at 156.

53 For example, after the Exxon Valdez ran aground in 1989, a five-month trial followed and subsequent appeals carried the ordeal out for nearly two decades before the Supreme Court finally rendered the ultimate decision. Totenberg (2008), available at: www.npr.org/templates/story/story.php?storyId=48308288

54 See generally Braithwaite (1989, discussing the deterrent effect of shame).

55 Cohen (2001, at 213), citing Karpoff et al. (1998).

56 Id.

57 Fenn and Veljanovski (1988, at 1055, 1068).

58 Toy and Leffler (2001, at 23).

59 Billiet and Rousseau (2005, at 18–19).

environmental prevention equipment, can thus lead to substantial interest savings, basically without additional risks.[60] A substantial problem of under-deterrence might be a logical consequence of the incentives provided.

There may be a fourth reason why many firms comply notwithstanding low expected sanctions under the criminal law. This is related to the fact that companies base their ex ante decision on being in compliance on their subjective perception of the probability of being detected and prosecuted and the sanctions that can be imposed.[61] They may hence not be aware of the low expected sanction in reality; thus, the firms might be using a misguided higher expectation of detection and being sanctioned, and thus rationally choosing with those assumptions to remain in compliance.

Rousseau found strong empirical backing for this phenomenon: when firms had to pay a monetary sanction during the previous two years, they were on average more in violation in a second period than firms that did not have to pay a fine in the first period. The interpretation is clear: those who did not have to pay a fine before overestimated the expected fine and complied. Firms that were fined had learned of the true probabilities for expected sanctions and, being now aware that the risks were low, were no longer as deterred as they had been previously.

This has an important policy implication: fining a polluter with too low a fine can have a perverse learning effect: firms will then be informed about the low expected sanction, whereas those who were not confronted with these low sanctions may still wrongly believe that expected sanctions are higher than they actually are and thus be more induced towards compliance. The policy implication seems to be that if the agency or court decides to fine a polluter it is better not to impose any fine at all than one too low, since otherwise one would destroy wrong, subjective perceptions of potential perpetrators that fines are higher than they actually are.

## 10.5 OPTIMAL SANCTIONS

Building on the basic economic theory of crime,[62] we can take the main conclusions from this literature and extend it to the field of environmental crime.

When optimal deterrence can be achieved equally through fines and prison sanctions, fines should be preferred since they have fewer transaction costs to impose than prison sanctions.[63] As was indicated above, many economists have for that reason shown themselves to be opponents of prison sanctions, simply because the

[60] This was argued with respect to the situation in the Netherlands by Nentjes and Hommes (1990, at 3).

[61] Rousseau 2007b, at 17 and 19 (noting that firms that are aware of the monetary restrictions are generally more likely to violate, implying that fears of sanctions may actually be more powerful than the sanction itself).

[62] See the earlier discussion on Becker, Stigler and others in Section 10.4.

[63] See, among many others, Polinsky and Shavell (1979, 1991); and for a summary Bowles (1982).

costs of implementation of those sanctions are much higher than the budgetary costs of imposing fines for the same level of impact in changed behaviours. That is why the procedural tool of fines has been advanced as the ideal sanction in case of corporate crimes such as environmental crime.[64]

This approach to prefer fines over incarceration has, however, been criticised by Coffee,[65] as well as by Shavell,[66] who argued that fines can only work as an effective deterrent if there is no insolvency problem. As we have argued earlier, in the case of a low probability of detection and an insolvency risk, non-monetary sanctions will have to be applied.[67]

These two lessons from economic theory seem to be followed in legal practice as well: the available criminological studies report that the fine is the most commonly used sanction; prison sanctions for environmental crime are rare and tend to be limited to cases of fraud or serious environmental harm.[68]

A result of economic theory is that optimal sanctions in the case of environmental crimes depend upon a variety of elements, as discussed in Section 10.4.1. Optimal sentencing policy would consist of applying fines as long as possible, in the light of the insolvency risk, and to combine them in a differentiated manner with non-monetary sanctions when necessary.[69]

In reality, sentencing practice can be very different. This is more particularly the case in the USA where strict sentencing guidelines apply, to which the judge in principle must adhere. At first glance in contrast to the economic model, the sentencing guidelines also provide quite often of incarceration as the main penalty in case of violation of environmental regulations; although the legislators may have acted on both Becker's model and public choice theory by simply setting the sanctions high enough to overcome lower expected rates of detection and enforcement by the judiciary, to appease voters' desires for environmental policy action.

Barrett concluded in a study on the application of sentencing guidelines for environmental crime that 'the sentences imposed in the majority of cases reflected the reluctance of judges to impose significant incarceration for violations of environmental laws'.[70] Also, others have held that the sentencing guidelines lead to negative outcomes as far as enforcement and deterrence are concerned. Research by Babbitt et al. showed that the practice of lenient sentencing of environmental criminals, as a refusal to apply the guidelines, was well documented. Since the judiciary feels that the guidelines 'over criminalise' environmental violations, they may systematically

64 Posner (1980).
65 Coffee (1980).
66 Shavell (1985b).
67 Polinsky and Shavell (1979) and Segerson and Tietenberg (1992).
68 See, for the situation in Europe generally, Heine and Meinberg (1988); Meinberg (1988); and for the situation of Belgium, Billiet and Rousseau (2003).
69 See Cooter and Ulen (2012, at 452).
70 Barrett (1992, at 1421).

sentence (even significant) violations too leniently, which may undermine the deterrent value of environmental enforcement and may trivialise environmental law itself.[71]

Frank Easterbrook has strongly opposed this idea of strict sentencing guidelines, arguing that 'there is no correct price for crime in the same way that there is no correct price for apples'. He holds that the price of (environmental) crime depends upon a variety of elements, indicated above, which enable the judge to determine the optimal penalty in a differentiated way.[72] Easterbrook therefore supports discretionary sanctioning powers for judges, arguing that this will allow the judge to differentiate the sanctions in a more precise manner, taking into account the relevant economic criteria.

The economic lessons as formulated by Easterbrook seem to be followed in Europe, where if sentencing guidelines exist at all, they seem to provide sufficient flexibility for the judge to differentiate sanctions according to the economic criteria. The Department for Environment, Food and Rural Affairs (DEFRA) in the UK published a 'Review of Enforcement in Environmental Regulation', which provides for sentencing guidelines but at the same time holds that this should not impose a rigid tariff but should merely provide a more systematic framework for more effective and consistent sentencing decisions.[73]

As far as non-monetary sanctions are concerned, there are, especially in modern environmental statutes, a variety of measures that can be imposed upon the convicted polluter, such as a duty to restore the harm committed or an order to compensate pollution victims (independently of the latter's private law rights). Even though these measures are usually treated as non-monetary sanctions in legal doctrine (because they are different from a fine), many of these arguably have a monetary implication as well. In some cases, these measures can even go so far as an order to shut down a plant or to repair the damage that has been caused. In some cases, the legislator also provides the judge with the power to order the publication of the judgment in the mass media.

Even though the application of these special sanctions still varies between different legal systems, one can certainly note their increasing use. For example, if a polluter is prosecuted for illegally depositing waste, he will often be required also to clean up the waste he has discharged. In some legal systems, these orders can be enforced by means of a so-called penalty payment that will be due if the duties are not fulfilled within the time limit laid down in the judgment.

These specific duties seem to be effective penalties and lead to deterrence. The costs of soil clean-up can be substantial and thus provide additional deterrence. The publication of a judgment can lead to serious reputational loss.

71 Babbitt, Cory, and Kruchek (2004, at 63).
72 Easterbrook (1983, at 295 and 325).
73 Parpworth (2007, at 21).

One particular sanction which is increasingly gaining popularity in the fight against white-collar crime generally, but ever-more in the area of environmental crime, is the forfeiture of illegal gains. From a legal perspective, this forfeiture of illegal gains rests on the notion that 'crime should not pay'.[74] The gains obtained by the crime should be removed from the criminal in order to put them back in the status quo ante.[75] Bowles, Faure, and Garoupa showed that the forfeiture of illegal gain can be efficient at providing additional deterrence in case of a low detection rate and low effective fines.[76] However, early empirical studies by German criminologists showed that the risk of removal of illegal gain had hardly any effect on potential criminals in their decision whether or not to commit the crime.[77] Meanwhile, the possibilities of removing illegal gain, as well as the practical application in the environmental area, has spectacularly increased since these early studies of 1992–1993.[78] The additional deterrent effect, and therewith the effectiveness of the removal of illegal gains, in the case of environmental crime may well have substantially increased.

## 10.6 CORPORATE ENVIRONMENTAL CRIME

In the case of environmental pollution, the crime is often committed, not by an individual actor acting directly in their private person, but by persons acting on behalf of a company cum artificial person. Many of the serious cases of environmental pollution have been committed within corporate entities. Therefore, unavoidably, the question arises whether the corporation, the employee or both should be held liable.

From an economic point of view, designating the liable party is unimportant as long as sanctions are freely transferable and the parties are fully informed. With transferable sanctions, either the corporation charges the liable employee for the fine that it paid, or the employee asks the corporation for reimbursement of the fine that they paid. According to this line of reasoning, it is unimportant whether the fine is imposed on the corporation or the individual and the corporation governs these matters. This is an application of the Coase Theorem.[79]

74 That crime should not pay the polluter is at first glance related to the principle of environmental law that the polluter should pay for any and all harms caused; however, it is entirely possible that in certain scenarios, perhaps in an act of Kaldor-Hicks efficiency, pollution might be welfare enhancing, thus, one needs to be cautious in developing policy goals. See also discussion on elasticity in Section 7.7.

75 For an overview of these legal foundations see Faure (2005), and for a comparative overview see Kilchling (1997, 2002).

76 Bowles, Faure, and Garoupa (2000, 2005).

77 See Perron (1993) and Smettan (1992).

78 For an overview of the practice in Belgium and the Netherlands, see Faure and De Roos (1998).

79 Coase (1960).

However, this Coasean solution to penalties within corporate entities may not always work in practice. One problem is that monetary sanctions are not always freely transferable between the employer (the corporation) and the employee, sometimes because the law prohibits paying someone else's fine. This is, for example, the case in Germany.[80] A contractual transfer of the fine may thus not always be possible. Therefore, in countries with rules like Germany, it does matter at whom the penalty is directed.[81]

However, the literature equally indicates that even though there are strong arguments for corporate criminal liability,[82] there are reasons to apply criminal liability to individuals within the corporation as well.[83] Non-monetary sanctions were one of the key reasons given to support the implementation of environmental criminal law,[84] but because non-monetary sanctions are hard to apply to corporations (how does one incarcerate an artificial person?), they must also be applied to individual employees as well.

Polinsky and Shavell have made a strong economic argument in favour of the individual criminal liability of the employee. One of the arguments they make is that monitoring by firms may often be imperfect; another problem is that if employees only face fines, they may not be induced to exercise socially optimal levels of care and they might even be reimbursed by their employer. Therefore, Polinsky and Shavell argue that non-monetary sanctions on employees should be used in addition to fines applied on corporations.[85] Also, in the area of environmental crime, it is held that when the employee cannot bear the full burden of the optimal penalty, the government might still be able to impose the optimal penalty on the company.[86]

This leads to the conclusion that corporate liability (leading to fines and non-monetary sanctions applicable to corporations) should be combined with the individual criminal liability of employees. However, some criticism has been formulated against corporate criminal liability, stressing even more the need to have individual liability on the part of the employee.

Wheeler has argued that, in general, criminal statutes should not be used to regulate product safety.[87] His arguments against criminal law are mainly arguments against punishing the corporation and are, to a certain extent, of interest for environmental crime as well. One of his points is that a civil lawsuit may be as much of a deterrent as criminal sanctions.[88] Another is that criminal law may lead to costly

[80] See Faure and Heine (1991, at 43–44).
[81] Segerson and Tietenberg (1992, at 61–63).
[82] Friedman (2000) and Kahan (1998).
[83] See further on organisational liability for environmental crimes, Miller and Justice (2017).
[84] See Section 10.3.
[85] Polinsky and Shavell (1993) and Kornhauser (1982).
[86] Cohen (2001, at 208–209).
[87] Wheeler (1984).
[88] Powerful counter-arguments have been produced by Shavell (1984a, 1984b), who showed that in specific circumstances, tort law may lack a deterrent effect.

over-deterrence and that the costs of detecting, investigating, prosecuting, and sentencing are much higher than the benefits of marginal deterrence. His argument that the existing market forces in place, such as private tort actions and civil regulatory systems, can better regulate product safety than criminal law may well hold true for the field of product liability. However, it is less convincing with regard to the area of environmental crime, precisely for the reasons given in favour of public regulation for environmental protections, as covered at length in Chapter 9.

Another criticism of the use of corporate criminal liability has been formulated by Arlen. She argues that the traditional argument in favour of what is referred to as vicarious liability, is seen as an indirect means of sanctioning wrongful employees, assuming that corporations subject to criminal liability will in turn sanction the wrongful employee. This regime can, however, according to Arlen, lead to potentially perverse incentives for the following reason: if a corporation is able to monitor its employees optimally, it will have to increase its level of corporate enforcement expenditures. This might reduce the number of agents who commit crime by increasing the probability of detection and thus reducing the costs of crime. On the other hand, the increased enforcement expenditures may also increase the probability that the government will detect those crimes, whereby the corporation's expected criminal liability for those crimes is increased. This means that additional enforcement by the firm only increases the firm's expected criminal liability. Thus, vicarious liability could lead to the perverse incentive that the corporation will reduce the monitoring of its employees in order to avoid the detection of its own corporate environmental crimes.[89]

## 10.7 ENFORCEMENT STRATEGIES

### 10.7.1 *Deterrence or Cooperation?*

In enforcement literature, not necessarily restricted to economic theory, a lot of attention has been paid to the type of strategy which has to be followed to induce compliance by polluters.[90] The literature makes a distinction between two enforcement styles.

The economic approach is qualified as the deterrence style, based on the idea that the authorities should be hard on polluters and should prosecute in all cases, preferably resulting in well-enforced sanctions. A deterrence model, therefore, does not rely on agency discretion.

A cooperation enforcement style relies more heavily on negotiations between the polluter and the agency, whereby the agency, through persuasion and by providing information, tries to bring the polluter to compliance. Within this cooperation

89 Arlen (1994).

90 See in that respect also the recent contributions by Holley and Sinclair (2017) and Silberman and Hindin (2017).

model, punishment is not the appropriate instrument, but rather a method of last resort if other instruments (of persuasion and information) have failed.[91]

First, the cooperation model does not fit into an economic approach to enforcement. The classic Becker model assumes that the application of strict and deterrent sanctions, in combination with enforcement efforts to increase the detection rate, will provide incentives for the polluter towards compliance. If a cooperation model merely results in the risk that the polluter would, after being detected, still have to invest in abatement technology which they already had to do on the basis of a permit, deterrence will fail. Some economists therefore hold that the cooperation model, which was followed in the Netherlands in the 1990s, stimulates violations of environmental regulation since companies who comply after a first warning do not encounter any negative consequences of their violation.[92]

Second, another problem with the cooperation model is that when a cooperative strategy has failed and the administrative agency has to change its position to a deterrence style, the cooperation and strong links between polluter and the agency may have made it difficult or even impossible to change to a deterrence approach when necessary.

Third, the cooperation strategy has the inherent risk that powerful and knowledgeable companies will de facto be able to control and 'capture' the agency. See, for example, a study of environmental law enforcement in Denmark, which showed that cooperative enforcement was undermined by capturing.[93] There is hence always the danger that the cooperation model will lead to situations of collusion and corruption,[94] as a result of which compliance will fail.

However, notwithstanding these limits of the cooperation model, many have also pointed to the limitations of the deterrence approach itself.

It has been argued that a strict deterrence approach that does not take into account that as a result of practical difficulties compliance could be vexing bearing on impossible, and the corporation may choose to refuse to comply because the deterrence approach is felt to be unreasonable.[95] Enforcement agents may be unwilling to act as 'policeman' in an adversarial relationship with the polluter.[96]

The cooperative strategy even receives some support from economists. It would indeed be too simple to reject the cooperation style entirely because of the danger of capture. An advantage of the cooperation model is that through persuasion, education, and information companies can be led towards compliance.[97] One reason to follow the cooperation model can be related to the high costs for the enforcing

[91] Van Rooy (2006, at 228–233).
[92] Nentjes and Hommes (1990, at 1–7).
[93] May and Winter (1999).
[94] Garoupa and Klerman (2004).
[95] Hawkins (1984).
[96] Aalders (2003) and Aalders and Wilthagen (1997).
[97] Fenn and Veljanovski (1988).

agency in bringing a case to court.[98] Those high costs may also explain why, in some cases, there is a seemingly high tolerance of non-compliance by the enforcing agency; this can be a strategic response by the agency to a difficult enforcement environment.[99] This may hence provide a rationalisation of 'regulatory dealing' between the agency and the polluter. Especially in cases where administrative authorities are well informed and small- and medium-sized enterprises are not, a cooperative strategy could lead to a situation where the controlling agency in fact assists the enterprise towards compliance with environmental regulation.[100]

This type of result, of education towards compliance, was confirmed in an experimental study which found that there are substantial learning effects in the sense that compliance with the desired pollution reduction can be substantially higher in a second period when the firm was informed in a prior period about the content of their obligations.[101] These results indicate that firms can understand and adapt their behaviour to elaborate regulatory contracts after a suitable learning period. This seems also to correspond with criminological research in the Netherlands which has confirmed that many violations of environmental regulation do not take place wilfully, but rather as a result of a lack of information or knowledge. In these cases, more particularly where first offenders are concerned, a cooperative enforcement style could probably be effective.[102]

Summarising, there may not be such a strict distinction between the deterrence and cooperation styles. Proponents of the cooperative approach realise that coercion is also necessary in a cooperation model. Braithwaite therefore proposes a successful enforcement strategy that starts with informal and less intrusive enforcement options (persuasion, warnings) and then moves towards more punitive options (fines or criminal prosecution) when cooperation has failed.[103] This is an administrative law approach that Galle has entitled, 'carrot, stick, and salience'.[104]

In a powerful study, Lofton attributes the difference in enforcement styles between the USA, which has a strongly deterrence-based enforcement style, and the UK, which has followed a cooperative strategy, to differences in cultural values and attitudes on social regulation.[105] Given the strong opposition of US business to environmental regulation, Lofton argues that only coercion or the threat of coercion would have worked to ensure compliance with environmental regulation in the USA. Introducing a cooperative approach, which has worked in the UK, into the US context, would according to Lofton, have had disastrous consequences for

98 Ogus and Abbot (2002b, at 293).
99 Heyes and Rickman (1999).
100 See Johnston (2001).
101 Alpizar, Requate, and Schram (2004).
102 Huisman (2001) and Huisman and Van de Bunt (1997).
103 Braithwaite (2002).
104 Galle (2013, at 108–109).
105 Lofton (2001).

environmental quality in the USA. He therefore argues that varying enforcement styles are largely based upon cultural differences. Hence, one can understand that, given the different cultural attitude of industry to environmental regulation in the USA, the shift from traditional CAC to a more flexible system of industry self-regulation is described as a 'dangerous journey' by some US commentators.[106]

### 10.7.2 *Targeting and Risk-Based Enforcement*

In addition to this literature on enforcement styles, partially empirical literature on the effectiveness of specific enforcement approaches does provide more insights.

First, it can be recalled that an overview of the empirical literature shows that studies generally find a deterrent effect from increased inspections and government enforcement actions, but less so from increasing penalties.[107] However, a problem is of course that, as was already pointed out by Stigler, the marginal costs for increased monitoring can be high. Also, various empirical studies show that even in the absence of frequent prosecutions, inspections deter future violations.[108]

Several suggestions have been formulated and experiments executed to increase the effectiveness of monitoring and at the same time reduce monitoring costs.

Arlen and Kraakman suggested a system whereby firms are required to self-report a violation of pollution standards; voluntary reporting would be rewarded with lenient treatment, whereas prosecutors would focus enforcement efforts on violations which are not self-reported. Thus, the most severe sanctions would be reserved for offenders who failed to report or who submit false reports.[109]

Innes has also shown that there may be substantial economic benefits from stronger incentives for environmental self-reporting, including saved avoidance costs, reduced enforcement costs, and an increased frequency of appropriate remediation.[110]

One lesson from the work of Harrington, whose paradox we discussed earlier, is that it may be effective to divide firms into different classes on the basis of their compliance behaviour and to focus enforcement efforts correspondingly.[111] This idea of targeted monitoring, whereby monitoring costs are mostly spent on those known to have a tendency to be in non-compliance, has been worked out, also empirically, by many. Friesen found that by targeting enforcement efforts on specific segments of the regulated community, greater compliance with environmental regulations could be achieved.[112] Also Heyes and Rickman showed that,

[106] Steinzor (1998).
[107] Cohen (2000 and 2001, at 209).
[108] For an empirical study of the petroleum sector in Canada, see Eckert (2004).
[109] Arlen and Kraakman (1997); Cohen (2001, at 207).
[110] Innes (2001).
[111] Harrington (1988); Harford and Harrington (1991); and Harrington and Heyes (2001).
[112] Friesen (2003).

given limited agency assets to spend on inspections, an enforcement agency may engage in 'regulatory dealing', using tolerance in some contexts and increasing compliance for other types of violations.[113] They show that accepting a certain degree of tolerance with specific violations does not at all mean that the enforcement agency (in their study, the USA's EPA) is 'going soft' on pollution; it may rather be the result of a strategic choice to maximise the available budget and thus enforcement efforts.[114]

Rousseau showed that the Flemish Environmental Inspection Agency uses targeting to select firms it will routinely inspect and bases this selection on past compliance behaviour and on firms' capacity. Firms are inspected more frequently as long as the environmental problem persists. Once it is solved, firms only receive routine inspections. Hence firms move relatively easily back to the 'good' group. Rousseau argues that higher deterrence could be achieved by lowering the probability of escaping from the 'bad' group, which is effectively equal to one in Flanders. Thus, the deterrence potential of targeting could even be better exploited.[115]

## 10.8 SUMMARY AND CONCLUSION

In many ways, the models from the Law and Economics literature on environmental criminal law are similar to the models drawn for public law and regulations, as one would expect. The arguments presented in Chapter 9 continue to hold for this chapter on environmental criminal law. But we also join the models from Law and Economics on criminal law, as we noted with Becker's and Stigler's analysis.

Fundamentally, the key issues here are the ability to deal in non-monetary sanctions, the need to improve the reliability of the environmental criminal law system to actually result in full adjudication from discovery of the crime to sentencing and punishment, as well as the effective determination of the sanction given the known rate of prosecution likelihood.

The ability to address environmental aggressors with something beyond financial punishment is a strong tool offered by environmental criminal law. Strategic behaviour or insolvency can frustrate the effectiveness of administrative financial sanctions. And while administrative sanctions might include tools such as revocation of licence or claims on property, there is always extra gravitas in the loss of freedom; thus, the potential risk of incarceration provides a strong incentive when the financial tools fail.

It remains unclear how to best deal with corporate entities, but many states look through the corporate entity to reach the human decision makers inside. For those

[113] Heyes and Rickman (1999).
[114] See also Heyes (2002).
[115] Rousseau (2007c).

parties, it then becomes a calculus, per Becker and Stigler, of expected costs; what is the likelihood of being punished and how severe would that punishment be, the product of those two factors needs to exceed the 'benefits' of violating the environmental standards.

While environmental law has made great progress in the last fifty years, environmental criminal law remains less often implemented around the globe. It is clear from the Law and Economics literature that sound theoretical models support the use of environmental criminal law alongside other public law efforts.

# 11

# Insurance for Environmental Damage

## 11.1 INTRODUCTION

Up to this point, we have discussed a variety of legal instruments which can be used to prevent environmental harm or which – at least – can provide a potential polluter with appropriate incentives to reduce environmental risk. However, notwithstanding the use of liability rules, economic instruments, regulation, or voluntary compliance instruments, environmental damage can nevertheless occur. Therefore, in this and the next chapter, we will focus on the question through what kind of instruments environmental damage may be compensated.

The liability rules we discussed in Chapter 8 may have a compensatory effect, although we equally stressed that from an economic perspective, prevention instead of compensation is the primary function of liability rules. Only under strict liability will the injurer be forced to compensate the damage and even then, compensation may be endangered if the injurer is insolvent.

In these two chapters, we will discuss other compensation mechanisms beyond the more conventional damages for liability mechanism. In this chapter, we will first focus on the traditional compensation mechanism, insurance, and see which problems may arise if (liability) insurance is applied to environmental pollution. In the next chapter, we will address a variety of alternative compensation mechanisms and consider whether these can – under circumstances – better compensate environmental harm than traditional insurance.

First, we apply traditional insurance theory to environmental liability (Section 11.2) and then discuss traditional problems, or rather conditions for insurability such as the need to remedy moral hazard (Section 11.3) and adverse selection (Section 11.4) and the necessity to raise capacity (Section 11.5). Issues of causal uncertainty and joint and several liability are discussed in Section 11.6. We then argue that in case of potential insolvency there are strong arguments to mandate financial guarantees to cover environmental harm (Section 11.7). Section 11.8 summarises and concludes.

## 11.2 INSURANCE THEORY APPLIED TO ENVIRONMENTAL LIABILITY

### 11.2.1 *The Utilitarian Approach*

The literature distinguishes two theoretical foundations for risk shifting.

The first, and the most traditional economic approach, is to consider risk shifting as a remedy for risk aversion.[1] Individuals (and institutions) may have an aversion more particularly to risks that occur with a low probability and high damage.[2] Given wealth restraints and the limited marginal utility of increasing wealth, individuals suffer disutility from the risk of being exposed to the possibility of losing a large amount of wealth. Since risk aversion creates disutility for individuals and organisations, social welfare increases if risk is removed from individuals with risk aversion.[3]

Second is a sensitivity based on scale of capital and budget versus the scale of the risks involved. Economists speak of risk neutrality, risk aversion, and risk preferring; these reflect three different types of economic actors. Risk-neutral individuals hold absolute numbers and expected sums of the same in the same regard; that is, they see $50 as a 50/50 chance at $100. The risk-averse individuals prefer to avoid risk; for them, $50 is more than a 50/50 chance at $100. The risk-preferring see the inverse, they prefer a 50/50 chance at $100 over a guaranteed $50.

However, the degree of risk aversion or preference often depends not only on the type and the size of the risk, but also on the comparative capital of the concerned individual.[4] For example, an individual who only possesses €50,000 may be highly averse to a 1 per cent risk of losing €100,000. However, if the same individual possessed several millions, there would be no risk aversion and hence also no demand to hedge particular risks. This starting point is quite important as it explains that the demand for risk shifting by firms exposed to environmental risks will depend upon the type of risk (low probability, high damage or rather the reverse) and on the capital budget situation of the firm concerned.

Therefore, the demand for risk shifting will be high in a situation where both the risk to which the firm is exposed is relatively high (in the sense that a high damage can occur when the risk materialises) and the firm's capital budget is limited. The latter may more particularly be the case when the potential costs to the firm if the risk materialises would be larger than the capital of the firm.

This simple economic logic is also related to the fact that risk shifting is not a costless exercise.[5] Therefore, a willingness to pay for risk shifting will only occur in case of risk aversion, wherein the costs of shifting risks are more affordable than the costs of bearing the direct risk. This also shows that the attitude to risk and the

[1] See Shavell (2004, at 258–259).
[2] Kahneman and Tversky (1979, at 263, 281).
[3] Shavell (2004, at 259).
[4] Guiso and Paiella (2008, at 1122).
[5] Biener, Eling, and Wirfs (2015, at 144–145).

related demand for risk shifting is not binary (in the sense of all or nothing), but of course has a gradual nature.

It should, however, be stressed that in the Law and Economics literature also, other justifications for corporate insurance have been identified beyond risk aversion. A key aspect of corporate law is the low cost to enter by purchase of stock and likewise the low cost of exit by sale of shares; shareholders can readily avoid undesirable risks by careful choice and stewardship of their investment portfolios. Mayers and Smith indicated that the corporate form provides an effective hedge since it allows shareholders to eliminate risk through investment in a diversified portfolio.[6] Since risk reduction is not considered as the most obvious basis for a specific demand for insurance by corporations, Mayers and Smith identify a few other reasons for corporations to demand insurance.[7] One possibility is that corporate insurance contracts allow an allocation of risk to the claimholders of the firm who have a comparative advantage in risk bearing.[8]

It may also be that sometimes the risk aversion of key personnel overlaps with the firm's sense of risk preferences. Another potential motive is to ensure that boards and key executives seek to reduce down-side risk on their own performance, as measured by the firm's financial reports, to both enhance their own career development and to reduce the risk of derivative lawsuits or other functional complaints from shareholders.[9] The rise of risk management as a subject matter in business schools and in corporate practice can be seen as salient financial advantages and enablement of 'best practices' defences in avoiding corporate litigation on these issues.

### 11.2.2 *The Transaction Cost Approach*

Operators often wish to benefit from services offered by insurance companies that can reduce transaction costs.

Insurance could reduce information and transaction costs. Insurance may also lower the expected transaction costs of bankruptcy and provide real service efficiencies in claims administration.[10] Insurers offer the services of administrating claims at much lower costs than corporations would be able to do themselves.[11] This is related to the specialisation of insurers in claims handling, but also to economies of scale.[12]

The advantage for traders is that the contractual conditions in the insurance policy (aiming at the reduction of moral hazard) in fact replace the need for traders

6 Mayers and Smith Jr. (1982, at 282).
7 Id.
8 Id., at 283–284.
9 This is, in a sense, an application of public choice theory to corporate executives and board members, at least those that serve more directly in the view of the voting shareholders.
10 Id., at 284–286.
11 Skogh (1989b, at 727).
12 Cummings (1977, at 539).

to contract in detail, for example, concerning the allocation of risk.[13] This explains why there is a demand for risk shifting also by actors who suffer no risk aversion.[14]

### 11.2.3 *Applied to Environmental Insurance*

A distinction can be made between two types of insurances. There are insurance policies that individuals take to protect themselves against the future losses that they may suffer themselves, either in their income or in their property.[15] Fire insurance is a typical example.[16] These types of insurance policies are referred to as first-party insurance.[17]

Insurance policies can also be taken for the risk that one has to compensate damage suffered by a third party.[18] These are therefore referred to as third-party insurances.[19] A liability insurance is a typical example of a third-party insurance. In that case the potential injurer takes insurance against the risk they run of having to compensate potential victims.[20]

In the case of environmental damage, both first-party and third-party insurance can be relevant. First-party insurance can be taken by either potential victims or operators for the environmental damage that they would suffer themselves. Operators could take liability insurance to cover the damage suffered by a third party. Victims (or operators) in some cases also take first-party insurance which is not always specifically geared to environmental damage. It could consist of a general accident insurance or property insurance, which could serve to cover environmental risks as long as those are not excluded from the insurance policy.[21]

Hence, one can argue that also with respect to environmental liability these general principles will apply:

- Insurance can provide protection for risk-averse injurers.
- By accepting a certain loss in the form of the payment of a premium the future risk in case an accident happens can be removed from this injurer.
- This arrangement will be utility maximising for the particular injurer and may reduce transaction costs, since ex ante it has been decided who will intervene in case an accident occurs.
- The insurance company will be able to provide coverage if they can aggregate similar risks in risk groups and thus spread the risk among their insured via the law of the large numbers.

13 Id.
14 Faure and Porrini (2017, at 177).
15 Faure and Bruggeman (2008, at 11–14).
16 Id.
17 Id.
18 Id.
19 On those different types of insurances for environmental liability, see Faure (2002, at 31–41).
20 Faure and Bruggeman (2008, at 11–14).
21 For details see Richardson (2002, at 371).

For every insurance scheme, equally for environmental liability insurance, it is crucial that the insurer possesses accurate information on the likelihood or probability that the event will occur and on the possible magnitude of the damage should an accident occur. These expectations, on (i) probability, and (ii) magnitude of the loss, are essential for the insurer to be able to calculate their 'actuarially fair' premium. The premium to be paid by the insured will include several charges: (i) loading costs for administrative expenses, (ii) a profit margin, and (iii) potentially other charges required by local statutes.

In this respect environmental liability insurance is not necessarily different than any other type of insurance. However, it is important to stress that one crucial element in insurance is of increased importance for environmental policies, which is the scientific assessment of both the risk of the injury and of the potential scale of damages in what is usually a bundle of non-market-provided ecological services. The complexity of these services and the scarcity of market-based cost and value data could frustrate actuarial efforts that underlay insurance markets; nevertheless, to frustrate is not the same as to make impossible, and exotic environmental liability policies do exist on the market, such as the liability insurance policies offered for commercial carbon capture and storage (CCS) operations.[22]

This is not only necessary in order to make an accurate estimation of the premium to be charged, but also to set aside a reserve in case the accident for which insurance coverage was sought occurs. This information is necessary to deal with the two following phenomena which may endanger the insurability of the environmental risk, being the control of moral hazard and adverse selection.

A conclusion of this simple introduction to the working of liability insurance is that an insurer needs information concerning the probability that a certain event (the fact that their insured will be held liable) will occur and they will need information on the possible magnitude of the damage. The product of the multiplier p and the multiplicand D ($AFP = p*D$) constitutes the actuarially fair premium.

The reason an insurer could take over this risk is the law of large numbers: a larger group of insureds with a similar risk can be brought together by an insurer into a risk group, and thus risk spreading enables risk stability across a group and enables less risk as a statistical whole.

If the insurer ideally has ex ante perfect information on the predictability of the probability and the magnitude of the damage, we call the particular risk insurable. It is precisely on the basis of statistics that the insurer will require information on the likelihood that the risk will occur with a particular insured; statistics may also provide information on the possible magnitude of the damage.

[22] Zurich has offered two different CCS-related insurance policies since 2009. SwissRe and ACE have been reported to have similar insurance products in development (Aldrich, Koerner, and Solan 2011, at 10).

Both those data requirements may, however, be a problem in the case of environmental (liability) insurance. Several elements may negatively influence the ex ante predictability of the risk.[23] The ex ante information on the predictability of the risk is often low, given the tendency to be environmental risks of a new character. Reliable statistics may sometimes be missing both with respect to the probability of the event occurring and with respect to type and scale of the damage. As far as natural resource damage is concerned an additional problem lies in the fact that generally accepted measurement techniques to quantify environmental damage may be lacking. Hence, there may not be a feasible situation for the 'law of large numbers' to be applied.

However, the predictability of the liability risk is a crucial element to guarantee the insurability of environmental liability. The question therefore arises whether the predictability of the liability risk can be increased, even in the absence of reliable statistics, or whether in that case the particular risk should be judged as uninsurable.

The Law and Economics literature has indicated that uncertainty concerning the probability or the damage is an element with which the insurer can – in principle – take account ex ante. If there is uncertainty, because of a lack of reliable statistics, this should not necessarily lead to the conclusion that a particular risk is uninsurable. We are then dealing with the concept referred to as 'insurer ambiguity', addressed by Kunreuther, Hogarth, and Meszaros.[24] They argue that the insurer can react to this uncertainty concerning either the probability of the event or the magnitude of the damage by charging a so-called risk premium to account for this unpredictability. An insurer can in principle also deal with a 'hard to predict' event, by charging an additional premium. Although theoretically the additional risk premium is the answer to insurer ambiguity, in practice the insurer will at least need some information to make more than an educated guess concerning the risk premium it has to charge. Given the fact that an insurer finds themselves in a competitive environment, market forces may well drive the insurer to engage in liability insurance even when an appropriate risk premium cannot be charged.

Whether this will in practice actually be done is hard to predict. We have to remind that insurance business in many countries is to a large extent highly regulated. This might limit the possibilities of insurers anyhow to engage in extremely risky activities by charging high premiums. The direct link between tarification and provisioning is indeed the subject of insurance supervision. Moreover, since many insurers are traditionally conservative and prudent, they might be inclined to be quite cautious with providing cover if uncertainty should be considered too large.

[23] Monti rightly points out the fact that there may be both factual and legal uncertainty (Monti 2001).

[24] Kunreuther, Hogarth, and Meszaros (1993, at 71–87). We will come back to the importance of 'insurer ambiguity' when dealing with the insurability of retrospective liability.

An important condition to ensure the availability of environmental liability insurance is that the insurer needs to obtain ex ante information in order to be able to reasonably predict the probability of an environmental harm occurring. That is necessary in order to be able to calculate premiums. Ideally predictability requires statistics. As environmental risks are often novel and emergent, there may not be a lot of historical data on the basis of which reliable statistics could be built. However, as an alternative to statistics, mathematical modelling can be used to predict the likelihood of environmental harm in the future.

Other conditions need to be fulfilled as well in order to insure environmental risks: the classic problems of moral hazard (Section 11.3) and adverse selection (Section 11.4) need to be controlled. The magnitude of environmental harm can be large. That begs the question how sufficient capacity can be generated to cover environmental harm when it occurs (Section 11.5).

## 11.3 MORAL HAZARD

### 11.3.1 *Definition*

Moral hazard is the phenomenon that the strategic behaviour of the insured injurer (and every insured for that matter) will change as soon as the risk is removed from the insured to the insurer. This is precisely the essential contradiction in liability insurance. The disutility the injurer suffers because of their exposure to risk was precisely needed to give them correct incentives for care taking.

If risk is fully removed from the injurer and shifted to the insurer, the injurer will indeed miss the incentive for care taking that was exactly given to them by the deterrent effect of having to pay compensation in case of an accident. This, in turn, frustrates the goals of tort law as understood in the Law and Economics literature, and thus rends tort law less effective in preventing accidents and injuries. Pauly has demonstrated this behaviour of the injurer is not immoral but completely rational, since they simply react to varying costs for their behaviour.[25] For the insurer, of course, the problem arises how nevertheless incentives can be given to the insured to behave in exactly the same way as if no insurance were available. The goal here is the optimal control of moral hazard.

### 11.3.2 *Remedies*

#### 11.3.2.1 Monitoring

In the literature, two ways of controlling the moral hazard problem are indicated.[26] The first is a control of the insured and an appropriate adaptation of the premium;

[25] Pauly (1968, 531–545).
[26] See Shavell (1979, at 541–562).

the second is exposing the insured partially to risk. A first-best solution would be a capacity for a detailed control of the insured.[27] In that case the premium conditions would be exactly adapted to the behaviour of the insured and the premium would reflect the care taken by the insured.

In an optimal world this should give the insured incentives to behave exactly as if no insurance were available and the premium would reflect the true accident risk. Of course, this first-best solution is only possible in the ideal world where control by the insurance company would bear few costs and information on the behaviour of the insured would be readily available. In practice this is of course not true. There are, however, some means for a control of the insured, and a differentiation of premium conditions is possible according to certain groups of risk. This can either be an ex ante screening with a higher premium for certain high-risk groups or an ex post premium increase or change of policy conditions based on previous loss experience. This is the so-called experience rating.[28] Much of insurance legislation is also aimed at reducing moral hazard.[29] Think in this respect of the prohibition, contained in many insurance laws, to insure accidents which are caused with intent.

### 11.3.2.2 Exposing the Insured to Partial Risk

A second-best solution is partially exposing the insured to risk. This is considered second best because insurance should ideally be aimed at transferring risk from the injurer. Exposing the insured to risk will mean that some degree of risk aversion will remain. On the other hand, the advantage is that the insured injurer will still retain some incentives for care taking despite being partially insured. This exposure to risk can be either at the lower level of damage or at the higher level. One could indeed think of a system with a deductible whereby a lower threshold applies, or one could introduce an upper limit on coverage whereby the insured bears their own loss in case the damage exceeds the insured amount.

### 11.3.2.3 Combination

In practice, one will of course see a combination of both systems of the control of moral hazard. Usually there is some degree of differentiation within the policy conditions, a deductible and an upper limit on coverage. The methods used depend upon the information costs, but also on the value of the insurance policy.[30]

[27] Spence and Zeckhauser (1971, at 380–391).

[28] Although not yet in broad practical application for environmental law, there are efforts to enable various data protocols, from shared social networks to blockchain-protected data files, to better enable such observation and feedback to the insurers at substantially lower transaction costs that would need to be paid for conventional informational gathering.

[29] See Rea (1993, at 145–162; 1998, at 342–348).

[30] Marshall (1976, at 880–890).

An insurer will more readily tend to invest resources in making a nicely tailored insurance policy for a company that pays a substantial premium than in case of insureds paying smaller fees, such as retail consumers and small businesses.

If moral hazard is controlled optimally through the use of the above devices, the insured will again behave as if no insurance coverage were available, with the benefit that the disutility of risk is effectively transferred from them. The incentives for care taking are in that case no longer given by liability law, since the threat to have to pay compensation to a victim is shifted under contract law to the insurance company. In case of insurance the care taking of the injurer is achieved through an appropriate adaptation of the contractual policy conditions to the behaviour of the individual insured.

This evidences that liability insurance has an important social function. Under liability insurance the insurer has to guarantee that the insured will take efficient care and thus have an incentive to avoid accidents. This makes clear that an appropriate control of moral hazard is not only in the interest of the individual insurer, but also of society. If there was no efficient control of moral hazard, insurance would on the whole do worse than good by over-incentivising the undertaking of risky activities and likely lead to higher incidences of environmental injury.

### 11.3.3 *Moral Hazard in Environmental Insurance*

#### 11.3.3.1 Monitoring via Policy and Licence Conditions

These general principles concerning the control of moral hazard apply to insurance for environmental risks as well.[31] The ideal and first-best method of control is to monitor the environmental behaviour of the insured as much as possible, and react to this behaviour by requiring specific preventive measures through the policy conditions and by responsively adapting the premium. Such an approach to monitoring of the risk may be costly. On the other hand, in environmental insurance the economic amounts and environmental welfare values at stake are larger than more routine commercial insurance policies. Hence, this may merit investments in information gathering for the particular policy. Some classification based on prior experience is possible as well. It is, hence, essential for the insurer of the environmental risk to obtain accurate information on the risk ex ante and during the performance of the insurance policy and preferably at the lowest costs possible.[32]

The insurer can of course rely on existing mechanisms to control the 'ecological reliability' of their insured. Given our discussion on regulation, most of those parties

[31] See Richardson (2002, at 354) and Wagner (2009, at 386–392).

[32] See on the importance of information for the insurer of the environmental risk, Endres and Schwarze (1991, at 1–25).

carrying those environmental risk insurance policies are licensed operators. Hence, an absolute minimum would be that the insurer takes steps to ensure those mechanisms are functioning properly; for example, by checking whether insured operators in fact do possess valid licences and that those operators do conform their continued regulatory compliance in support of the insured activity. In addition, the insurer could require expressly in the policy conditions that the operator follows the conditions of the licence and could make insurance coverage even dependent upon that. In other words, the insurer could make use of the fact that a decision concerning the optimal way to reduce environmental harm has already been made by the administrative agency and possibly been laid down in the administrative licence. Properly tailored regulation can therefore assist the risk differentiation by the insurer.[33]

Given the informational advantage of the regulator, ex ante regulation can have the major advantage that (as most insurers do) the insurer can primarily require the operator to comply with regulatory standards.[34] Violation of regulatory standards by the insured will often be a cause for refusal of coverage or for a recourse action by the insurer.[35] This shows again the importance of a smart collaboration between the regulator and the insurer whereby, on the one hand, the regulator informs the insurer about minimum safety standards (laid down in regulation) and, on the other hand, the insurer becomes a de facto enforcer of regulatory standards. The promulgation of ex ante regulatory standards can thus facilitate risk differentiation by the insurer and in that way contribute to an important extent to the insurability of the environmental risk.

#### 11.3.3.2 Risk Differentiation

As far as the operation of an industrial facility or plant is concerned, the insurer could check whether the operator formally complies with the conditions of the licence and also use devices which may ensure that the insured will reduce environmental harm in an optimal way.

One possibility is to check whether the operator has a controls process to avoid harm by installing an environmental management system which has adequate warnings, or by whether there are regular eco-audits. The insurer could even require that the results of regular eco-audits are made known to them, and could stipulate in the insurance policy that coverage may be suspended if the audit raises concerns on risky behaviour. Hence, audit- and self-reporting systems as well as external controls which are sometimes required anyway can be used by the insurer to control the 'ecological reliability' of their insured. Thus, the insurer acts in their own interest by

33 Richardson (2002, at 360–366).

34 Id.

35 Id.

obtaining information on the risks they cover at relatively low costs and at the same time exercise their social functions in a responsible way by stimulating ecological behaviour and reduction of environmental harm from the insured.

The insurer could take one step further and, especially at the design stage of plants, require implementation of design features to prevent environmental risks. From an insurance point of view, monitoring is much easier and therefore less costly if one knows that a clean production technology is used by the insured from the outset which eliminates or reduces the possibility of harmful events. If insurers were to engage at this early state of planning, they could combine an optimal control of moral hazard with taking up their social responsibility.

#### 11.3.3.3 The Need for Specialisation

All these examples show that there are a variety of techniques the insurers may use to control moral hazard in case of environmental risks. However, these examples also make clear that such a control is only possible if the insurer has adequate information on the risks they are covering. For a run-of-the-mill insurer who covers traffic liability, fires, and professional liability and occasionally takes one insurance policy of environmental liability as well, this may be a problem.

Information may be acquired at lower costs if the insurer is willing to specialise in the environmental risk. This specialisation may give the insurer adequate information on the appropriate techniques to reduce the environmental risk. In the end, this specialisation may provide the insurer a comparative advantage. At the same time specialisation may be the only way in which some of the complex environmental risks can be insured anyhow, controlling the moral hazard in an optimal way.

## 11.4 ADVERSE SELECTION

### 11.4.1 *The Problem*

Insurance is based on a statistical system of loss spreading; therefore, the insurer needs a minimum number of similar risks they insure. At the same time risk pools have to be constructed as narrow as possible, meaning that the average premium in the risk pool should correspond with the risk of most of the members in the particular pool.

Would this not be the case, then the average premium would be relatively high for low-risk members which would then leave the group. In that case the well-known phenomenon of adverse selection could emerge, which has been described in the seminal paper of Akerlof on the market for 'lemon' used cars.[36] Adverse selection

[36] See Akerlof (1970, at 488–500).

will, in other words, arise if potentially responsible parties fail to disclose their true risk profile appropriately, which may endanger the narrowing of risk pools.[37]

Adverse selection is, however, not incurable. The appropriate remedy for both moral hazard and adverse selection is risk differentiation.

### 11.4.2 *The Cure*

It follows from the economic principles of liability insurance that an adaptation of the policy conditions to the individual risk is essential to control both moral hazard and adverse selection.

Priest claimed that the adverse selection problem once caused an insurance crisis in the USA and that its cure required an appropriate differentiation of risk.[38] If the insurance policy requires preventive action from the insured party and provides for a corresponding reward in the premium, then this method should give optimal incentives to the insured for accident reduction. Thus, risk pools should be constructed as narrowly as possible so that the premium reflects the risk of the average member of that particular pool.[39]

A further differentiation of the risk is only efficient as long as the marginal benefits of this further differentiation outweigh the marginal costs of such a differentiation and that search entails its own set of transaction costs, all limiting how far risk differentiation can proceed.[40]

Risk differentiation certainly does not mean that insurers would have to use an individual tariff in each case.[41] The possibilities for individual differentiation will inevitably also depend upon the value of the particular insurance policy. For mass insurance products with a low premium, risk differentiation can only take place in general categories. In professional liability insurance of enterprises, however, the benefit of detailed differentiation, rewarding an enterprise for preventive action, may well outweigh the costs.

It is thus not difficult to make an economic argument in favour of effective risk differentiation as a remedy for a growing liability risk. If good risks are not rewarded for preventive action, either they will not have an incentive for prevention or they

37 See also Wagner (1996, at 105–106).

38 Priest (1987, at 1521–1590). Priest has been criticized by Viscusi, who claims that there were other reasons for the product liability crisis in the USA than adverse selection on its own (Viscusi 1991, at 147–177).

39 Abraham (1988, at 949–951).

40 Generally, the question is whether the benefits of particularisation outweigh their costs, which has to be addressed in tort law when a standard of care is defined (Posner 1998), but also when legal rules are made (Ehrlich and Posner 1974, at 257) or standards are set (Ogus 1981, at 210–225; Ogus 1994b, at 25–37).

41 On the costs of risk differentiation, see Bohrenstein (1989, at 25–39); and Wils (1994, at 449–467).

will leave the risk pool, and consequently the risk pools will be unravelled, as described by Priest.[42]

## 11.5 CAPACITY

An important condition for the insurability of any risk is not only that the risk should be predictable; in addition the insurer must also have sufficient capital capacity in order to have money available once the risked event materialises.[43] The economic principle is simple – that the total amount of premiums generated by the pool of insured should be large enough to cover the potential risk when it materialises.[44] This is more difficult when the number of insured is small and, as with environmental risks, the potential damage could be quite substantial. However, one should not judge too quickly that the large magnitude of the potential damages makes the risk uninsurable. There are quite a few techniques that insurers can use to make risks with a large potential magnitude insurable also.

That may more particularly be a problem when there is only a relatively small number of insureds interested in the product that the insurer wishes to sell. One problem is that there may be a relatively small number of operators interested in environmental insurance for highly specialised risks, such as offshore drilling installations. Another problem is that there are high barriers to enter the insurance market, created by the need for expert knowledge in environmental risks and for creating sufficient capacity. That may limit the insurability of environmental risks. It could therefore lead to the situation that the total pool of insured is relatively too small and that hence not enough insurance capacity can be generated to cover the loss when it occurs.

A first possibility is to use co-insurance. This simply amounts to the possibility of many insurers jointly covering one particular project. If there were one specific site to be covered, four insurers could decide to cover the risk together with each covering 25 per cent, thus being able to generate higher capacity.

Another solution to deal with the capacity problem is reinsurance. Through reinsurance an insurer effectively shifts a part of their risk to a reinsurance company in exchange for a reinsurance premium.[45] Large environmental risks (for example related to oil drilling) could be reinsured through the international reinsurance market, thus creating higher capacity.

A third possibility is pooling by insurers. This has to be distinguished from pooling by operators, which is usually qualified as a risk-sharing agreement.[46] In case of

42 Priest (1987, at 1521–1590).

43 In simple words, insurers need to hold sufficient financial resources to meet the claims they can expect. See Richardson (2002, at 332–333).

44 Id.

45 Id.

46 Id.

pooling by insurers, insurance companies decide to cover a particular risk on a non-competitive basis for an entire sector.[47]

A risk where pooling by insurers typically takes place is the nuclear risk.[48] Insurance of nuclear risks is provided through the so-called nuclear pools.[49] Since those risks were considered to be very large, the major national insurance companies in every nuclear country decided in the 1950s to pool their resources on a non-competitive basis in order to be able to provide coverage for them.[50] These pools provide cover for the third-party liability and to some extent first-party insurance for the damage caused to the nuclear power plant as well.[51]

Pooling is not only used in nuclear liability insurance, but also with other risks, for example with environmental liability insurance.[52] Environmental pools exist in many countries.[53]

However, pooling between insurance companies may be problematic from an insurance perspective, since insurance companies pool their resources on a non-competitive basis and thus exclude the normal competitive process.[54] The competition authorities in the EU have increasingly paid attention to those pools, especially examining the compatibility of pooling by insurers with European competition policy.[55] A study that has been executed on behalf of the European Commission has also examined the amount of co(re)insurance pools currently available in Europe.[56] The study identified a total of fifty-one pools, many of which focus on catastrophic risks, such as nuclear, environmental, and terrorism related risks.[57]

The literature related to particular new environmental risks, such as CCS, has also pointed at the possibility of pooling by insurance operators and has in that respect argued that antitrust waivers for participating parties may be necessary.[58] Antitrust waivers may perhaps be too strong a suggestion. Even within the boundaries set by competition policy it should be possible to on the one hand enjoy the benefits of cooperation from pooling and on the other hand still have the benefits of competition, more particularly when not just one insurance pool covering

47 See e.g. Faure and Van den Bergh (1990, at 250–251).
48 Id.
49 Id.
50 Id., at 250–251.
51 Id.
52 Id.
53 See generally id.
54 Id.
55 See in that respect especially Commission Regulation (EU) No. 267/2010 of 24 March 2010 on the application of article 101(3) of the TFEU to certain categories of agreements, decisions, and concerted practices in the insurance sector.
56 European Commission and Ernst & Young, 'Study on Co(Re)Insurance Pools and on Ad-Hoc Co(Re) Insurance Agreements in the Subscription Market' July 2014, available at: http://perma.cc/M27F-QTM9
57 Id.
58 See in that respect Trabucchi and Patton (2008, at 9).

environmental risks would be created, but rather different pools between which competition would still exist.[59]

## 11.6 CAUSAL UNCERTAINTY AND JOINT AND SEVERAL LIABILITY

There are a few aspects in the development of liability law which may endanger the insurability of environmental risks. The first has to do with the tendency in some case law to shift the risk of causal uncertainty to operators; the other has to do with the phenomenon of joint and several liability.

### 11.6.1 *Joint and Several Liability*

Joint and several liability is often considered an expansion of traditional tort liability.[60] According to some scholars, such an expansion of liability is dangerous since it could endanger the insurability of liability risks.[61] This fits into the idea that domestic tort liability should remain within limits of insurability because stretching the boundaries of tort liability could potentially lead to an insurance crisis.[62]

Within that context, a question has been asked: what is the effect of joint and several liability on the insurability of liability risks? From an insurance perspective, some have warned against joint and several liability because the insurer is no longer merely insuring the risk created by their insured individual with whom contractual relations governs behaviour, but also the risk caused by all others beyond any sense of contractual privy.[63]

Joint and several liability then amounts to a system where insurers can no longer accurately calculate premiums,[64] and may have difficulties in correctly calculating the amount of reserves to be set aside.[65] This problem especially arises in the case where no recourse is possible because other contributing tortfeasors cannot be found or are insolvent and therefore judgment proof. One important condition for insurability is that the insurer needs to be able to predict the risk.[66] Under joint and several liability with insolvency of contributing partners, there is a risk that insurers may not only cover the damage caused by their insured, but de facto

[59] For a further discussion, more particularly of raising capacity for CCS related risks, see Faure and Partain (2017, at 161–163).
[60] See inter alia Trebilcock (1987, at 929, 959).
[61] See Abraham (1988, at 942) and Katzman (1988, at 75).
[62] This argument has especially been strongly defended by Priest (1987, at 1521).
[63] See Cousy (1995, at 235).
[64] Since they are no longer merely insuring the risk caused by their insured, but potentially by others as well.
[65] Faure and Hartlief (2003, at 127).
[66] See Ben-Shahar and Logue (2012, at 197).

cover the entire market,[67] and civil liability under joint and several liability could become unpredictable and hence uninsurable.[68]

### 11.6.2 *Causal Uncertainty*

Largely based on deepest pocket or victim protection arguments, a tendency can be found in case law to shift the risk of causal uncertainty to enterprises.[69] Given the focus here on insurance, that strategy will also mean that this risk will then be shifted to their insurance agency.

From an insurance point of view, a tendency to institute a joint and several liability rule could endanger the insurability of risks. In such a case, a specific manufacturer would be required to compensate for damage which, on the whole, was probably never caused by the insured firm. Taking the example we discussed earlier, it would mean that an insurer would have to compensate 111 cancer victims for whom the nuclear power plant has to pay compensation, whereas only in 11 cases was the cancer caused by the radiation emitted by the power plant. Such a tendency will undoubtedly lead to uninsurability, as has been convincingly shown by Abraham relating to insurance for Superfund clean-ups in the USA, where liability is equally joint and several.[70] In case of causal uncertainty only a proportionate liability rule can guarantee insurability: with a proportionate liability rule the insured firm will only be held to compensate damage which originated from its activities, something for which the insurer can ask preventive measures and a corresponding premium.

At the risk of repeating in summation, the danger of shifting the burden of causal uncertainty to the enterprise is that the insurer of the specific employer or producer will be required to compensate for damage which, on the whole, had probably not been caused by the insured party.[71] Unless a proportionate liability rule is followed, it is not possible to cover a risk if that would mean that the insurer would not only cover the damage of their own insured parties but also the damage that might possibly have been caused by another party.

The problems are largely caused by a hidden redistributive agenda: the wish to provide victim protection no matter what it may cost. These tendencies may be far more problematic from an insurability point of view than the shift towards strict

[67] See Wansink (1993, at 7–12) for a point made by the Dutch insurance expert Wansink who held that joint and several liability leads to an insurer de facto covering the liability insurance for the entire market, which according to him amounts to uninsurability of the risks.

[68] See inter alia Bergkamp (2000b, at 154–155), for an argument that joint and several liability may be unfair and may lead to over-deterrence.

[69] This issue has been discussed in Section 8.3.

[70] Abraham (1988, at 942–988).

[71] Id., at 959–960 and Katzman (1988, at 89–90).

liability itself. Indeed, whereas we argued that strict liability as such is insurable, this is no longer true if the risk of causal uncertainty is shifted to the enterprise.

## 11.7 COMPULSORY FINANCIAL GUARANTEES

In the Law and Economics literature, several criteria have been advanced to analyse where mandatory financial security may be robust recommendations.

The most important reason for introducing compulsory insurance is insolvency. Insolvency may pose a problem of under-deterrence. If the expected damage largely exceeds the injurer's assets, the injurer will only have incentives to purchase insurance up to the amount of their own assets.[72] They are only exposed to the risk of losing their own assets in a liability suit.[73] The judgment proof problem may therefore lead to under-insurance and thus to under-deterrence.[74]

Jost has pointed out that, in these circumstances of insolvency, compulsory insurance might provide an optimal outcome.[75] By introducing a duty to purchase insurance coverage for the amount of the expected loss, better results will be obtained than with insolvency whereby the magnitude of the loss exceeds the injurer's assets.[76]

However, the literature has equally formulated a few conditions and warnings when introducing compulsory financial security.[77]

First, one is warned is that the moral hazard problem should be controlled and contained. If moral hazard cannot be controlled, the regulator should even consider a prohibition of liability insurance.[78]

Second, if one were only to introduce compulsory insurance (as compared to mandatory financial security, which is broader), this should only be done when no restrictions on the insurance market exist. If high concentration exists, premiums would be too high and this could equally reduce the incentives of insurers to control the moral hazard risk.

Third, from a policy perspective, it may not be wise to limit the duty to provide financial security to insurance. If the policymaker were to introduce compulsory insurance, it would become totally dependent on insurance to fulfil the duty to insure. This could create an undesirable situation whereby insurers would become

72 Jost (1996, at 259).

73 Id.

74 Id.

75 A similar argument has been formulated by Polborn (1998, at 141–146) and by Skogh (2000). Skogh has also pointed out that compulsory insurance may save on transaction costs.

76 See also Kunreuther and Freeman (2001, at 304–316).

77 For a summary of those warnings see Faure (2006, at 149–168). See also Richardson (2002, at 360–366).

78 See Shavell (1986, at 43–58).

de facto licensors of the industry, which could be problematic from a policy perspective.[79] Insurers under compulsory insurance de facto become surrogate regulators, which at least has the advantage that it provides them strong arguments for effective risk management.[80] That may hence be a strong argument towards a flexible approach, i.e. not to limit the provision of mandatory security necessarily to insurance, but to allow the market itself to suggest a wide variety of financial and insurance instruments, as long as they can guarantee compensation when the accident happens.

## 11.8 SUMMARY AND CONCLUSION

Insurance is an industry that most modern consumers have familiarity with, but the literature of Law and Economics has provided models so that we can examine how to robustly choose when to use it as part of a broader effort to address the problems of environmental damages.

Insurance has two basic theoretical motivations. First, for those parties holding a risky asset to purchase a commodity that reduces the overall expected risk of the two assets, being the original asset and the asset of the insurance policy. This is often discussed as a strategy to deal with risk aversion, the preference to avoid risk instead of being risk neutral. Another motive is related to the scale of capital; actors with smaller pools of capital can gain conditional access to larger pools of capital by acquiring an insurance policy for specific conditions. Insurance is also theoretically viewed as a means to reduce transaction costs in the event of certain outcomes; providing investors with less costs across a broader range of potential outcomes.

Insurance policies are available in various forms on the market, but two of the main types of policies for environmental accidents are first-party (damage to self and own assets) and third-party (damage to other parties and their assets) liability insurance. Both systems of insurance require a sufficiently large pool of reasonably similarly risked parties that are engaged in similar activities, where the risk of damages from those activities is readily rendered into reliable probability forecasts. This is not always the case, as either there might be too few parties to assemble a sufficiently large population (see Section 12.2 for other options in that case), or the activity itself might be too novel or unexplored to be well defined for actuarial purposes.

Perhaps the most interesting, if not also the most important, contribution from the Law and Economics literature is the perspective brought on moral hazard and on adverse selection problems. Moral hazard contains the idea that if you assume the risk for someone else, then they no longer face the costs of those risks and

[79] See Monti (2001, at 51–79).
[80] Richardson (2002, at 362–363).

thus are more likely to undertake those risks; in short, moral hazard means possession of an insurance policy could lead to increased levels of risk taking under that policy, that the safety of the policy could increase risky behaviours. For environmental concerns, this is a serious issue; that by providing assurances of being able to cover costs of damages might actually increase the likelihood of injury and thus of the damages. In environmental injuries, where often environmental damage cannot be truly reversed by remedy, moral hazard is a dangerous consideration. One potential cure, as discussed, is to allow some portion of the risk to remain with the insured client. Another cure is to provide monitoring of the behaviour of the insured client. Both could be combined in a form of a private regulatory mechanism, much as is common with car insurance policies.

The flip side of moral hazard is that actors with low-risk profiles or deeper pools of capital might not seek insurance, leaving behind other actors lacking such access to capital or those with higher risk levels. Then the costs of insurance would increase, given the absence of the safer and preferred customers. That could in turn result in a second wave of exits from the insurance market, resulting in worse poor risks remaining left in the insurance pool. And again, one would expect the costs of insurance to rise, ad infinitum, until only the most risky were left and no one would be able to afford the resultant policies. This is adverse selection in a nutshell; to prevent this problem legal rules need to consider regulatory requirements to ensure a sufficiently broad pool is generated for the insurance agencies to be able to economically supply the market with insurance.

Market capacity to supply the necessary volume of insurance policies and to be able to pay them out when needed can be reinforced with several tools, including forms of co-insurance, reinsurance, and pooling.

We also discussed ramifications of civil liability rules on insurance, such as causal uncertainty and of joint and several liability, which could leave insurance payouts being delivered for the wrong company. The problem facing the insurance agencies is that the risk may become uninsurable and thus require some form of public support.

Compulsory financial guarantees are attractive policy options, in that it would require insurance to be prepaid to ensure that it would be available when needed, freeing the public regulator and the public community from worrying if funds will be available in a time of need. As such, compulsory financial guarantees could obviate the worries on insolvency and like concerns. However, this policy step cycles back to moral hazard and might create de facto regulators out of the insurance agencies. In fact compulsory insurance cures (to some extent) adverse selection by forcing everyone (bad and good risks) into the pool, but it does create other problems.

In conclusion, insurance is an interesting product that addresses many concerns to ensure that damages can be paid when necessary, but insurance also remains tricky in that it can create moral hazards, resulting in more injuries and thus damages. Again, it bears repeating that while some injuries, like a wrecked car, might be remedied by cash pay-outs, this is not often the case for material environmental injuries. Thus, the creation of moral hazard for environmental insurance policies, both first-party and third-party, is a serious concern. Rules need to be carefully considered to secure that the insurance coverage in consideration remains economically viable for both the insurance agency, considering adverse selection, and market capacity.

# 12

# Compensation for Environmental Damage

## 12.1 INTRODUCTION

In the previous chapter we have presented insurance as a mechanism that can fulfil two functions: on the one hand it can provide a protection to potential victims of environmental harm in case of insolvency of potential polluters and thus guarantee an effective compensation; on the other hand, it can equally promote prevention of environmental harm via the risk differentiation to control moral hazard. It was mentioned that as long as insurance companies can reasonably predict environmental harm, insurance can to a large extent be employed to cover environmental risks. However, there are specific limits of insurance. These are on the one hand related to limited information of insurers (especially in case of new environmental risks) and on the other hand, limited capacity (that may especially play a role in case of catastrophic environmental harm).

We will now focus on a few other mechanisms than insurance that could equally be employed to cover environmental harm. We will first discuss the possibilities offered by self-insurance (Section 12.2); next we will discuss risk sharing between operators as an alternative to insurance (Section 12.3) and briefly discuss alternatives such as guarantees, deposits, and bonds (Section 12.4). Yet, another alternative is to create a compensation fund to cover environmental risks (Section 12.5). One could theoretically still think about other compensation mechanisms, such as a direct compensation of environmental harm by the government, or an intervention of the government as reinsurer of last resort. These will, however, remain undiscussed within the scope of this chapter.[1] Section 12.6 summarises and concludes.

[1] For a further discussion, more particularly related to compensation for damage resulting from $CO_2$ storage sites, see Faure (2016b, at 466–471).

## 12.2 SELF-INSURANCE

### 12.2.1 *Theory*

Self-insurance is a mechanism whereby larger players in the market do not take insurance coverage at all but run the risk themselves.[2] In fact, self-insurance can take two different forms.

One possibility is pure self-insurance, which in fact is nothing else than major companies booking a financial reserve for future losses.[3] In a technical sense, this cannot be considered as 'insurance' for the simple reason that there is no risk spreading, no risk distribution, and hence no loss spreading after an incident happens.[4] Self-insurance in that sense is merely a reserve for potential losses whereby operators use their balance sheet to guarantee payment in case a major accident would happen. Reserves do allow for a risk spreading in time but not between various parties exposed to a risk.

Another possibility is the creation of a so-called captive insurance agency.[5] A captive is in fact an insurance company that is created by the company that uses the captive's insurance policies.[6] Many large oil and gas operators have created their own insurance companies.[7] A reason for doing so is that they can satisfy a local statutory duty in the countries where they maintain operations to show financial coverage but avoid a costly transfer of capital to a third party, namely an insurance company.

### 12.2.2 *Evaluation*

Self-insurance, either via reserves, captives, or by using the capital market, foreseeably has its strengths and weaknesses.

The advantage from the industry's perspective is that it is a relatively low-cost solution; operators can take care themselves of providing guarantees for future losses and do not have to bear the transaction costs of dealing with a third-party insurance agency.[8] Especially for major operators, forcing them to shift risks to an insurance company may make little sense, especially in cases where the capital depth or credit rating of the operator is in fact stronger than that of the insurance company.[9]

2 EPA, Geological Sequestration of Carbon Dioxide 18 (July 2011).
3 Id.
4 See Faure and Hartlief (2003, at 144).
5 See e.g. Bawcutt (1991); see also Dowding (1997).
6 See Bergkamp, Herbatchek, and Jayanti (2013, at 118, 128–129).
7 Id.
8 Id.
9 Id.

Using self-insurance, at least partially, has an advantage in curing the so-called moral hazard risk that will always emerge in case of insurance: by taking a substantial risk retention the operator will still be exposed to risk, limiting its exposure to moral hazard.[10]

The disadvantages of self-insurance (no matter what form it takes) may also be obvious: self-insurance is not necessarily a waterproof guarantee against insolvency.[11] That would only be the case if regulation could guarantee that the money set aside for covering the environmental damage would only be used for that specific goal. Self-insurance could lead to an externalisation of risk in case of insolvency.[12] Smaller operators without strong balance sheets or credit rating could simply run the risk of liability and if the risk materialised they would simply pass on the costs to the tax payer.[13] Self-insurance can only be considered an effective financial security if guarantees can be provided that the reserves set aside will actually be used for the potential losses for which they were earmarked. Otherwise the risk would also exist that e.g. in case of insolvency the trustee in bankruptcy could simply collect the assets, and money may not be available to compensate victims.

Self-insurance could be a valuable strategy for major players that could potentially create environmental risks, such as large energy companies with substantial balance sheets. For smaller- and medium-sized players, self-insurance could only play a role as a deductible, in addition to other hedging strategies. If self-insurance would be offered by operators as a financial guarantee, serious controls should therefore be imposed to verify the viability of the self-insurance as a reliable guarantee.[14] This is why, for example in the financial security provided for offshore installations in the North Sea, self-insurance is accepted, but is subject to serious repeated controls of the balance sheets of the operators who rely on self-insurance.[15]

## 12.3 RISK-SHARING AGREEMENTS

### 12.3.1 *Theory*

A risk-sharing agreement or a pool is a system whereby operators mutually agree to share each other's losses. It resembles insurance, but there are, as will be explained in more detail, a few differences. The fundamental difference is the lack of a third party; as insurance involves a third party (the insurance company), whereas in a risk-

[10] See Shavell (1979, at 541–562).
[11] Richardson (2002, at 373).
[12] Id.
[13] Id.
[14] See for the financial security under the (European) ELD, Bergkamp, Herbatchek and Jayanti (2013, at 128).
[15] For a detailed account of this so-called OPOL (Offshore Pollution Liability Agreement) mechanism, see Faure and Wang (2015, at 25–36).

sharing scheme the operators are both insured and insurer; there is hence no involvement of a third party.[16]

Unlike in the case of commercial insurance, where ex ante information about the probability of a certain risk and its magnitude should be available to allow the calculation of an ex ante charged premium, in a risk-sharing agreement policy, each member's capital contribution can be agreed upon beforehand and only actually paid ex post and only on the condition that an event actually occurs.[17] This characteristic makes it possible for a risk-sharing agreement to deal with uncertain risk, for which the statistical data about the occurrence are rare or the probability and size is less predictable. As long as a risk differentiation can be made among the members, a risk-sharing agreement can be feasible, since an ex ante charging of premiums is no longer necessary. Only the relative contribution of each member to the risk has to be determinable.

Another difference between a risk-sharing agreement and insurance concerns the costs. In an insurance policy, the risk is shifted to the insurer at the price of a premium.[18] The premium is not recoverable by the insured no matter whether the insured risk is materialised or not. In a risk-sharing agreement, a member only contributes if an accident happens; the duty to compensate can either be postponed or the contribution can be carried over to the following year if there is no accident.[19] A member can also recover their contribution by stopping creating the risk and leaving the pool.[20]

### 12.3.2 *Case Study: Pools for Vessel-Induced Pollution (P&I Clubs)*

One example of a mutual risk-sharing agreement from the maritime area is provided by the so-called Protection and Indemnity Clubs (P&I Clubs). A P&I Club is a non-profit mutual insurance association which is established by ship owners and charterers to cover their third-party liabilities related to the use and operation of ships.

The essence of the P&I Club is that the ship owners are members of the club. Hence, they are, in principle, not considered clients (as with an insurance company) but rather as members, thus having a very close relationship to the club. Different from traditional insurers, P&I Clubs underwrite on a cost but not profit basis, which means that it follows the equation that 'calls plus investment income should equal claims plus expenses plus reinsurance premiums'.[21] The amount of each advance is based on the ship owners' claims history, the size of the fleet, the club's anticipated

16 Doucette (2001, at 533).
17 Id.
18 Id.
19 Richardson (2002, at 373).
20 Id.
21 Id., at 98.

needs, and the strength or profitability of the insurance market.[22] In other words, the clubs try to tailor the premiums to the risks the vessels are exposed to.

It is worth noting that a P&I Club provides more services than a pure insurer and operates as a mixture of an insurance company, a law firm, and a loss adjuster. Besides offering an insurance coverage, a P&I Club can also provide a worldwide network of correspondents and representatives to give on-the-spot assistance to the ship owner when required, give Letters of Undertaking to offer a security when members' vessels are arrested, and assist in claims handling and settlement.[23]

In a P&I Club, the ship owners make contributions to a risk pool defined by an ex ante agreement. Different from traditional insurance, under which premiums need to be paid ex ante, the contribution/premium for P&I Clubs is 'an agreement that each member should bear his aliquot share of the losses of the year covered by the policy'.[24] The premium is levied through calls. Before the beginning of each year, club managers estimate the claims and expenses for the year and decide a proportion of the total to be called up as an 'advance call'. The remaining proportion will be collected via supplementary calls.[25] The clubs have made it clear that estimation of supplementary calls does not prevent them from levying a higher or lower amount.[26] The members are 'obliged to pay the supplementary call to the extent the advanced call is insufficient to cover the claims'.[27] In a catastrophic year, if the total claims exceed the amount that is 'recoverable in respect of that claim under the Group Excess Reinsurance Policies', payment can be paid from the Catastrophe Reserve Fund. In the case that this fund is insufficient, an overspill call will be levied.[28] In this way, the P&I Clubs combine an ex ante payment with a retrospective payment. The advance call is announced at the beginning of each policy year, but the payment can be made by instalments during the year. Supplemental and overspill calls are collected ex post.

### 12.3.3 *Policy Analysis*

The existence and function of P&I Clubs demonstrates that risk-sharing agreements can serve the goals of both providing incentives for prevention and providing compensation to victims. Risk sharing can provide an interesting alternative when commercial insurance fails to emerge due to the lack of information (especially with newly emerging environmental risks) or high associated costs.

[22] Ronneberg (1990, at 29); Hazelwood and Semark (2010, at 95).
[23] Ronneberg (1990, at 25–29).
[24] *Williams* v. *The British Marine Mutual Insurance Company* (1886), 6 Asp MLC 134, at 136.
[25] Hazelwood and Semark (2010, at 104).
[26] Id.
[27] Zhu (2007, at 171–180).
[28] Id., at 105.

However, this does not mean that risk-sharing agreements can always emerge. The size of the pool is essential for the establishment of risk-sharing agreements. A large number of members can better spread the risks and make a large amount of compensation available.[29]

However, a large size may affect the capacity of members to conduct mutual monitoring. Under this situation, it is crucial to adopt measures to ensure the risks created by different members are comparable,[30] or to conduct risk differentiation.[31] In addition, in case the potential amount of members to the pool would be quite high, the administrative costs of running the pool might be large, as a result of which pooling may lose some of its relative attractiveness, compared to insurance.

The theoretical advantages of a risk-sharing agreement (strong incentives for mutual monitoring) are only materialised if a risk differentiation is possible in the sense that higher risks pay effectively a much higher contribution than lower risks. Especially with 'low probability, high damage' events, the relative difference between high and low risk operators may be too small to provide incentives for risk reduction.

If the operators can at least rely on the fact that all members will have to comply with minimum safety regulations, their additional task of mutual monitoring will be relatively limited. That may hence be an important lesson at the policy level: if the policymaker would like to stimulate risk sharing by operators, it can play an important role in providing a facilitative strategy; it could provide minimum safety standards, thus reducing the need for very intensive mutual monitoring. In the absence of minimum safety standards, there will always be a risk of negative redistribution and adverse selection, since the risk-sharing agreement will then be most attractive for the bad risks as a result of which the good risks will not be willing to join.

## 12.4 GUARANTEES, DEPOSITS, AND BONDS

### 12.4.1 *Theory*

When an operator might find themselves constrained for capital, other parties could provide a financial guarantee to the operator.[32] Such a financial guarantee could be

[29] Mathematically speaking, at some point the number of parties seeking to coordinate may become too large for a P&I Club style of organisation; however, such a larger population of similarly focused industry members is likely to find that such a larger population now fits the statistical character favoured by conventional forms of insurance.

[30] For example, the nuclear pool in the USA relies on the common public regulation and on self-regulatory institutions such as the Institute of Nuclear Power Operations (INPO) to ensure the comparability of risks.

[31] For example, P&I Clubs have established measures to evaluate the risks of vessels and decide the premiums accordingly.

[32] Faure and Van den Bergh (1990, at 241, 252).

provided by a mother company or another third party that would presumably have a stronger financial capacity than the operator. It could also be provided by a financial institution such as a bank. In particular cases the guarantee could take the form of a letter of credit.

All of those guarantees have a simple theoretical basis: a presumably stronger third party (either a corporate entity or a financial institution) basically puts its balance sheet at risk by guaranteeing that it will cover the liabilities of the operator in case a particular risk would materialise.[33] Of course, a guarantee would only provide security to victims if a third party, the guarantor, would directly accept obligations towards the authorities or potential victims to compensate in case of harm.[34]

The advantage for the stakeholders may be that a guarantee from both an operator and a third party could provide more resilience and reliability than when only the operator's assets are at stake. Operators would find themselves using these types of guarantees when regulatory authorities determine that public reliance on self-insurance would be insufficient. However, the costs of entering into those guarantees can be quite high for the operator.[35] If it would be a guarantee by a related corporate entity that should not necessarily be the case, but it may be different if guarantees would have to be provided by a bank. Compared with insurance, one can hold that if insurers specialise in environmental risks they may have more information for an appropriate risk differentiation and premium setting as a result of which the costs of insurance could be lower than the costs of a bank guarantee.

### 12.4.2 *Deposits, Funds, and Bonds as Alternatives to Guarantees*

An alternative is to require the operator to provide a deposit, ex ante, into a guarantee account.[36] The idea would be that a direct guarantee is provided by depositing a sum of money corresponding to the potential environmental damage in order to cover future losses.

Trust funds, stand-by trust funds, and escrow accounts are also comparable instruments.[37] In all those cases (although there are differences) money is set aside to serve for a specific purpose in the future.

Yet another alternative is to use the capital market and more particularly bonds, whereby the interest rate on the bond reflects the accident rate.[38] Investors could consider buying a warrant-creating bond in favour of the operator of their choice.[39] For example, if during the period of the bond (say one year) no accident were to

33 Id., at 253, 271.
34 See Bergkamp, Herbatchek, and Jayanti (2013, at 127).
35 Id., at 260.
36 Id., at 252.
37 Id.
38 Id.
39 Id.

happen, the amount of the guarantee provided by the bond would be paid with interest. If, however, the risk were materialised the bond posted would be used to cover the damage.[40] This would be a form of a private regulatory mechanism that relies on both price-setting markets and information-revealing games between the operator and the bond buyer.[41]

### 12.4.3 *Evaluation*

The enthusiasm in the sector for the just mentioned deposits will logically be relatively small. The obvious reason is that it leads to an immediate immobilisation of capital for losses that may not even materialise in the future. It hence leads to a large liquidity problem. If the deposit should be large enough to cover all potential losses, it would be substantial and could create liquidity problems for the operators involved and may for that reason not be very popular. Also, bank guarantees may not be an attractive alternative. The reason is that they are often considered relatively expensive, compared to insurance.[42]

Corporate guarantees can in some cases be used. The problem is, however, that corporate guarantees do not always provide a good protection from potential claims of the operators' creditors.[43] A guarantee would only provide security to victims if a third party (guarantor) would directly accept obligations towards the authorities or potential victims to compensate in case of harm.[44] Whereas this may be a scenario that could be used – e.g. to guarantee compliance with obligations to clean up polluted sites, given that environmental damage can have a widely varying character – it is not likely that those type of guarantees would be provided specifically for environmental risks.

One instrument that is mentioned in some literature and is based on the use of capital markets is bonding.[45] A problem with any use of capital markets, including bonding, is that most of the so-called catastrophe bonds (CAT bonds) are always

40 See for an explanation of the working of these CAT bonds also Tyran and Zweifel (1993, at 431–444).

41 Private regulatory mechanisms were discussed in Section 9.4.

42 They are held not to provide additional security for the competent authority. See Havercroft and Macrory (2014, at 49); available at: http://hub.globalccsinstitute.com/sites/default/files/publications/179798/legal-liability-carbon-capture-storage-comparative-perspective.pdf [http://perma.cc/R8W4-QFR2].

43 A problem is that a guarantee provided, e.g. by a related company, is usually not specified for a particular goal and will therefore generally support the activities of an affiliated company. However, when that company runs into insolvency, the guarantee will be used to deal with all claims of the mass of creditors. There is no guarantee that the proceeds would only be used to satisfy the claims of victims of environmental damage. In concurrence with the other creditors, victims may not be able to enforce their claims.

44 See Bergkamp, Herbatchek, and Jayanti (2013, at 127).

45 See Wilson, Klass, and Bergan (2009, at 4580). For a further detailed analysis of the feasibility of bonding schemes, see generally Gerard and Wilson (2009, at 1097, 1099).

used for catastrophes which are essentially sudden events.[46] CAT bonds usually have a short period of cover, within which either the catastrophe happens and hence the bond is lost, or nothing happens and the profit on the bond is made.[47] CAT bonds are, however, typically not used for long-term risks.[48] Since many environmental risks have a potential long-tail, bonding may not be an appropriate instrument to cover environmental risks. It could at best be used for sudden damage that would appear immediately during the operation of a particular installation, but is less suited for environmental damage that would only appear e.g. years after a particular installation has been closed.

The EPA found that the relative financial risk to the government from corporate guarantees remains high.[49] The US EPA Guidance Document, drafted to provide regulatory guidance on these matters for CCS projects, discusses guarantees and deposits under several headings. Use of corporate guarantees is to be limited to instances of self-insurance. Further reducing the role of such guarantees, the EPA would only permit a corporate guarantee to be used in limited forms of corporate ownership.[50]

Trust funds are considered useful by the EPA for those activities that are relatively well-defined with regards to risks and costs, but not for those activities of uncertain frequency and costs.[51] The relative financial risk to the government may be low, but the costs of a trust fund can be high.[52]

## 12.5 COMPENSATION FUNDS

### 12.5.1 *Various Types of Funds*

#### 12.5.1.1 The Rise of Compensation Funds

A question that inevitably arises when issues of environmental damage are discussed is whether traditional liability law, combined with insurance, is at all able to provide for compensation for environmental damage. Issues of fault or negligence have been avoided in many legal systems by a trend towards strict liability. However, we already

[46] Josen 2015, available at: http://derivativetimes.blogspot.com/2012/06/catastrophe-bonds-fear-of-unknown.html [http://perma.cc/X38D-A3QS].
[47] Id.
[48] Id.
[49] Id., 45.
[50] The guarantee must be offered by a parent corporation to benefit a corporate subsidiary in which it owns at least 50 per cent of the subsidiaries' voting stock and has been in business for at least five years. See US EPA, Geological Sequestration of Carbon Dioxide. Underground Injection Control (UIC) program. Class VI Financial Responsibility Guidance, Washington DC, EPA (July 2011), 17.
[51] Id., at 21.
[52] The US EPA Guidance Document equally contains recommended specifications concerning inter alia the wording of the trust documents. Id., at 26–27.

indicated that strict liability alone will of course not guarantee a compensation for environmental damage, given the insolvency problem. This will create a demand for insurance. However, it is well known that many problems may arise with the insurance of environmental damage.[53] Therefore, in many legal systems the question has been asked whether compensation for environmental damage should be provided through compensation funds.

Well-known, and often criticised, in this respect is of course the Superfund, introduced through CERCLA in the USA.[54] Also in several European legal systems pleas can be heard in favour of installing compensation funds to cover environmental damage. In the Netherlands this has been proposed in the literature.[55] The idea of compensation funds is now often introduced in policy documents by various EU Member States formulating reforms of environmental law. In this respect we can point at the Interuniversity Commission for the Reform of Environmental Law that proposed the introduction of a compensation fund in the Flemish Region,[56] but also at a Dutch study performed on behalf of the Ministry of the Environment proposing the introduction of an environmental compensation fund in the Netherlands.[57]

One cannot escape the impression that often – especially at the political level – funds are advocated as a miracle solution for all problems of environmental damage whereby no clear definition is given of the specific funds. This can be misleading since the term fund is often used for a variety of private or public financial arrangements – some of which have been discussed previously in this chapter – that may be quite different. We will briefly sketch the kind of funds that might play a role when environmental damage is discussed.

This short overview will make clear that usually very different goals are achieved by these various funds.

### 12.5.1.2 Limitation Fund

In US literature the idea of a fund is sometimes used to refer to a funding tool in response to a situation whereby mass damage is caused by similar products or services. The problem that usually arises in these cases of serial damage (e.g. with toxic torts) is that the liable enterprise may be willing to agree to a settlement with the victims on the condition that they can offer a certain sum to all the victims whereby they can reach a final settlement for the damage caused by the specific tort.

[53] See generally on the limits of insurability, Faure (1995b, at 454–462).

[54] Interesting papers analysing Superfund can be found in Revesz and Stewart (1995).

[55] See Hulst (1993); Knottenbelt (1990); Kottenhagen-Edzes (1992, at 297–298); and Van (1995).

[56] See Bocken et al. (1996, at 31–32) and Interuniversitaire Commissie voor de Herziening van het Milieurecht in het Vlaamse Gewest (1995, at 943–985).

[57] Gilhuis and Verschuuren (1994). For comments see Hulst (1995, at 167–173), as well as De Putter and Verschuuren (1995, at 96–99).

In a certain sense the manufacturer then raises a fund that will have to be used to compensate all victims.

It could be called a limitation fund since the enterprise agreeing to such a settlement usually wishes to limit its liability to the amount brought into the fund. In this case no risk spreading with other (potential) manufacturers takes place, since only the liable manufacturer finances the fund. Examples of such a limitation fund can be found in the area of civil liability for oil pollution damage. Article V of the Convention of Brussels on Civil Liability for Oil Pollution Damage provides for the possibility for the liable tanker owner to provide for a limitation fund that should compensate victims.[58] As reward for the payment of a particular sum the duty to compensate is usually limited to the amount made available: a limitation fund.

It has also been argued in the Netherlands that such a fund solution would make compensation of health damage caused by exposure to toxic substances a lot easier.[59] A problem that will, however, inevitably arise with environmental damage is latency. It is essential in a limitation fund solution that latecomers are excluded. Therefore, this might not be the ideal solution for environmental damage. The goal of a limitation fund in these cases is not so much to provide a remedy against disappearing perpetrators, but to have an adequate instrument to divide the available proceeds among the victims in case of serial damage.[60]

There could however be one role for such a limitation fund. If one fears that a certain activity may cause harm in the future, at the start of the operation the enterprise involved in the activity could be asked to pay a substantial amount ex ante, which should become available in case environmental damage occurs. If the damage occurs the liability would then be limited to the amount the injurer had to pay. As we have just explained in the previous section, this regime has been proposed in the Flemish Decree on Environmental Policy.[61] The advantage of such a regime for the enterprise is obvious. It will have certainty with respect to the amount to be paid, which is never the case when it is subjected to full unlimited liability. In addition, the amount reserved for compensating environmental damage (through either insurance, a payment in cash, a bank guarantee or any other financial guarantee to be approved by the agency) can be paid back after the operations if no environmental damage occurred. Hence, the money is not lost as is the case with insurance premiums paid.

58 But in that particular case the liability itself has also been limited.

59 See the inauguration address of Dommering-Van Rongen (1996).

60 This was the reason that the European Directive on Product Liability also incorporated the idea of a limitation fund in article 16, which gave Member States the option to limit liability in case of serial damage to an amount which may not be less than 70 million ECU. However, only a few Member States have used this option.

61 See Bocken et al. (1996, at 31–32). It is based on earlier work of inter alia Smets (1991, at 397–423).

From society's point of view, the advantage is that there is at least certainty that an amount of money deemed adequate to compensate environmental damage will be available in case an accident happens.

#### 12.5.1.3 Advancement Fund

A second arrangement referred to as a fund is the advancement fund. The prepayment or 'advancement construction' is a remedy for long-lasting civil procedures concerning liability- and insurance coverage issues that can last much longer than the life of the victim. Especially in the case of asbestos victims, it has been argued that it is highly unfair that victims' relatives only receive compensation after the death of their relative because the process of compensation runs longer than the remaining lifespan of their relative. Therefore, an advancement fund has been created in the Netherlands as remedy for asbestos victims.[62]

Examples of these advancement funds can also be found in environmental legislation. In Belgium the Act of 10 January 1977 installed an advancement fund for damage caused by groundwater extraction.[63] Again it is uncertain whether this advancement fund can play a large role in case of environmental damage.

The reason why compensation funds are sometimes defended with respect to environmental damage is not so much related to long-lasting procedures, but more to the uninsurability of certain environmental risks or to the fact that no individual injurer can be identified. If these are the problems to be solved, an advancement fund is no adequate remedy.

#### 12.5.1.4 Guarantee Fund

Guarantee funds are well known as instruments to protect victims against the possible insolvency of a liable injurer or their insurer. The advantage of a guarantee fund is that it only intervenes for the so-called excess risk, being the risk for which in the specific case for various reasons no insurance coverage is available.

However, it is essential that a guarantee fund only intervenes if other compensation mechanisms such as insurance have failed. The possible role of a guarantee fund for compensating environmental damage will be discussed below.

#### 12.5.1.5 A General Environmental Fund

A fourth alternative could be the environmental fund that would generally operate as a substitute for liability and insurance. Usually when the phrase 'compensation fund' is used in the context of compensation for environmental damages, it refers to

[62] For a critical analysis see Faure and Hartlief (1996b, at 37–43).
[63] For a detailed discussion, see Bocken (1984, at 368ff.)

a general environmental fund and not the other types of compensation funds previously discussed in Sections 12.5.1.[64] However, if these compensation funds were to be used as alternative for the liability system, inevitably the question will arise how they can be financed in an adequate way. Therefore, we shall now focus on basic differences between compensation funds on the one hand and liability combined with insurance on the other hand as devices to provide compensation for damage.

### 12.5.2 *Case Study: The Gulf Coast Claims Facility (GCCF)*

#### 12.5.2.1 Historical Experience

On 16 June 2010, following the massive accident and subsequent oil spill and leakage from the BP Macondo wellsite on the 20 April 2010, BP established a fund of $20 billion with an open-ended commitment should the amount turn out to be insufficient. That fund, the US Gulf Coast Claims Facility (GCCF) was administered by Kenneth Feinberg and two appointed independent trustees. Hence, someone other than the defendant (BP) held the funds.

On 23 August 2010, the GCCF began to accept claims and issued its Protocol for Emergency Advance Payments, which established procedures for emergency advance payments for individuals and businesses to apply for compensation to cover the loss of earnings or profits, removal and clean-up costs, real or personal property damage, loss of subsistence use of natural resources, and physical injury or death caused by the spill.[65]

During its brief existence the GCCF was able to compensate a large number of victims and to do this quicker and at lower cost than the conventional tort system.

According to a study commissioned by the US Department of Justice, within eighteen months, the GCCF processed over 1 million claims, paying out a total of more than $6.2 billion to over 220,000 individual and business claimants.[66] Approximately, 99.8 per cent of the number of claims and 96.8 per cent of the amounts paid related to lost earnings or profits.[67] During the period of sixteen months, 3,000 employees were working for the GCCF in thirty-five offices at an approximate cost of US$40 million per month.[68] By reducing administrative costs, more money was

[64] For an overview concerning the current use of various compensation funds, see Bocken (1987, at 83–87; 1988, at 3–10; and 1990, at 11698–11714).

[65] GulfCoast Claims Facility Protocol for Emergency Advance Payments, GulfCoast Claims Facility, s II (F), 23 August 2010.

[66] BDO Consulting (commissioned by the US Department of Justice), 'Independent Evaluation of the GulfCoast Claims Facility: Report of Findings and Observations', 5 June 2012, at 62, available at: www.justice.gov/opa/documents/gccf-rpt-find-obs.pdf, last accessed 24 August 2015; See also Feinberg (2012, at 167, 174).

[67] Ibid, at 62.

[68] Interview with Kenneth Feinberg, special administrator of the GCCF, in Haifa on 16 June 2013.

available for victim compensation.[69] Generally in the USA in mass damage class actions, one-third of the available compensation goes to plaintiffs' lawyers. In comparison the expenses of running the GCCF are fairly modest.[70] Thus, the GCCF scheme has the potential to solve disputes faster than US mass tort litigation and is capable of producing the additional benefit of fast compensation, whereby preventing follow-on damage.[71]

The GCCF-route was entirely voluntary. The GCCF allowed for three types of payments: a quick payment,[72] an interim payment,[73] and a final payment.[74] Once the GCCF-route was opted for, in some cases payment by the GCCF excluded compensation from the court (in the case of the so-called quick and final payments); in other cases, such as with interim payments, the claimants were not excluded from potential court-based compensation.[75]

The prospect of receiving fast compensation serves to trigger individual claims because a victim knows that their efforts will not be in vain and compensation will come early enough to prevent an imminent bankruptcy, for example. The GCCF mechanism also fares positively with regards to the costs incurred for individuals, thus reducing rational apathy. Victims simply have to fill in the claims form. Online and at local claims centres, victims were provided with help on how to fill in these forms. Substantial amounts could be paid out rapidly; most victims were paid in less than three years after the incident.[76] Another positive characteristic of the procedure from the victims' point of view is the fact that it was left to their choice whether they wanted of allow this fast procedure or sue BP individually. Emergency advance payments could, furthermore, be obtained, which would be deducted from the final payments.

[69] Interview with Kent Syverud in Saint-Louis on 5 March 2013. The interview took place within the framework of a report drafted for the European Commission on Civil Liability and Financial Security for Offshore Oil and Gas Activities; available at: http://ec.europaeu/dgs/energy/tenders/doc/2013/20131028b3-978-1 final_report.pdf

[70] Interview with Kenneth Feinberg, in Haifa on 16 June 2013.

[71] The mere fact that initially it was signalled to the victims that $20 billion were available undoubtedly had an attractive effect on the amount and number of (perhaps some fraudulent) claims (Feinberg 2012, at 146). This is also shown by the anecdotal evidence that originally more than 1 million claims were handed in, whereas finally 'only' approximately 500,000 claimants received compensation. Id., at 174. Arguably, the system was able to filter out some of the frivolous complaints.

[72] This implied filling out a form without any further documentation of damage and receiving within two weeks a cheque for $5,000 for individuals and $25,000 for businesses (id., at 168), with a corresponding obligation not to sue BP.

[73] Based on past damage, while retaining their right to sue and to return to the GCCF (id., at 169).

[74] This would cover past, present, and future damage on the condition of a full release, promising not to sue and no right to return to the GCCF (id., at 171).

[75] Id., 167–72; Gilles 2012, 419.

[76] Interview with Kenneth Feinberg, in Haifa on 16 June 2013.

The decisions on the compensation claims of the victims were made by the special administrator Kenneth Feinberg and his team.[77] This is clearly a strength in the design. The manager of the GCCF used alternative dispute resolution (ADR) techniques inter alia to present a draft of the protocol for advanced payments to potential victims at many meetings that took place in various locations in the USA where victims were located.[78] Hence, victims were involved in drafting the protocol which clearly stipulated the conditions under which payment would take place, and victims could have a voice in the formulation of this protocol, thus adding to the legitimacy of the procedure.

The protocol aimed to ensure that the administrators of the GCCF would make payments according to the clearly specified criteria. This method enabled the administrator of the fund to verify the validity of the claims rapidly, equally allowing them to turn down many unjustified claims. Hence, this is a positive aspect regarding the required degree of accuracy in harmonising the procedure and making it predictable. It is a welcome fact that the procedure was easy enough to put victims in a position not to involve a lawyer. Therefore, principal–agent situations of that kind could be avoided.

The GCCF has been disapproved of in various legal publications, particularly questioning whether it led to better outcomes than in a comparable tort case.[79] However, positive mention has been made of the GCCF in this literature when it comes to inter alia speed, low costs, and cost certainty.[80] The GCCF is said to have the ability to 'forestall the potentially devastating effects on families and local areas directly impacted'.[81] Compared with the lengthy and costly litigation, such private funding may have the advantage of 'distributing funds to affected claimants more quickly and at less cost to the claimants'.[82]

#### 12.5.2.2 Conditions for an Effective Rapid Claims Handling Mechanism

Particular polity considerations are to be taken into account when attempting to develop a rapid claims management system for particular victims regarding the accuracy, the players involved, and the interrelation between various systems – all under the benchmark of the goals of tort law. To avoid opportunistic behaviour by both the potential tortfeasors and the victims, these mechanisms need to be carefully designed by paying attention to efficient risk differentiation. This implies that

77 For an overview of the organisation of the GCCF, see Feinberg (2012, at 204).

78 Id.

79 See Mullenix (2011, at 819, n.50). See Ewenczyk (2013, at 267); MacDonell (2012, at 796, n.33); Thomas (2012, at 567, 570) reports how the outcome of the symposium 'Remedies for Big Disasters: The BP Gulf Oil Spill and the Quest for Complete Justice' has overall been negative regarding the evaluation of the GCCF.

80 See e.g. Greenspan and Neuberger (2012, at 97).

81 Id, at 99.

82 Id.

tortfeasors need to be exposed to the risk that they create and (in case of multiple tortfeasors) in proportion to their contribution to the accident risk. Close attention needs to be paid to the incentives of victims and enforcers. This leads to the following guidelines for disaster-based ADR mechanisms.

A facility could be created which rapidly pays the damage to a specific category of victims, for which substantial follow-on harm can be prevented, which leads to large societal benefits. Cases would need to be classified as those involving high risk of substantial follow-on damage and those in which time is less of an issue. The ADR mechanism will hence in particular be of importance for cases in which time is of essence. The additional benefit stemming from fast solutions shifts the cost–benefit analysis more clearly to ADR rather than court litigation than in the case of disputes where time is not of essence.

Sufficient funds to finance such a system have to be guaranteed. The first-best option is to have the liable tortfeasor themselves pre-finance the rapid compensation to the victims (as in the case of the GCCF), to avoid that obstacles in the procedures to take recourse reduce the deterrent effect of the enforcement system. Only when this would be impossible could one imagine pre-financing by the facility (such as in Belgium) and an ex post repayment by the liable tortfeasor or their insurer. In Belgium a system involving pre-financing by the collectivity of insurers is in place. As mentioned, this is only the second-best option. A model (as in Belgium) based on ex ante financing by the fund needs to ensure that liability will ultimately be allocated to the tortfeasor. Therefore, for example, in a model as in Belgium to the extent that the operator would not have pre-financed the facility, the facility would be subrogated in the rights of the victim, thus claiming back the compensation from the persons liable for the incident to create a correct allocation of the risk.

Out-of-court dispute resolution procedures may not only base the decision on legal criteria, but equally on equity considerations. With a view to avoiding that this sets the wrong incentives to tortfeasors, for instance in that they systematically underestimate the probability of needing to pay compensation, the following guideline holds: eligibility of claimants and assessment of damages should in principle take place on the basis of criteria of tort law,[83] to guarantee a correct allocation of the risk to the tortfeasor and to serve compensation goals. In one way or the other a claim verification would need to take place, verifying that under normal rules of tort law those claims would be compensated as well (thus avoiding moral hazard on the side of the victim). However, the example of the GCCF indicated that the marginal benefits of claims verification should outweigh its marginal costs. One could imagine a role of the court in the verification process. In that case verification should, however, only be marginal and not include a second guessing of the results

[83] Which can either be the common law of torts (as in the Belgian case) or a special statue such as the US OPA (in the case of the GCCF).

obtained by the facility. The latter could lead to additional costs and a loss of the advantages of speed.

When timeliness is more critical to plaintiffs than monetary amounts, in such urgent cases then there may be more support for lighter procedural requirements to facilitate out-of-court solutions. It is crucial that sufficient account is taken of the composition of the entity that will apply the out-of-court solution. This ensures balanced decision making. As seen in the US's GCCF, victims can become involved in the design of the procedure. In addition to the tortfeasor being exposed to the costs of the harm, one can imagine exposing them, at least to some extent,[84] to the costs of administering the complaints handling. In such a context it is even more crucial that measures are taken to avoid capture or a bias in the decision making.

Rather than dealing with all claims in one collective procedure, benefits can be seen in an assessment on a case-by-case basis, which guarantees that each victim is satisfied individually. There are various techniques which increase victims' satisfaction with an out-of-court procedure and at the same time mitigate problems of biased decision making. Victims can, for instance, be involved in the whole process of setting up a compensation mechanism, as was done in the case of Deepwater Horizon. One can design procedures in which the victim's side may be involved even more. Additionally, one could smartly design appeal options that would increase accuracy and be a tool to control the quality of the decision making. A case-by-case approach has the inherent advantage that an occurrence and spreading of errors can be avoided to a large extent.

Finally, there is a benefit in such a facility being presented as optional, in that it allows victims to choose the way that best satisfies their preferences. However, a complex system also entails the danger that victims face large information costs in finding out the beneficial route. At the same time, if many victims opted for the wrong route due to a lack of information, this may again negatively impact the tortfeasor's incentives to take optimal care.

### 12.5.3 *Funds versus Insurance*

Before addressing the above-mentioned funds in further detail, it is interesting to compare generally funds with insurance according to their ability to adequately differentiate risks and the potential costs.

#### 12.5.3.1 Risk Differentiation

If both funds and insurance were in theory available, there are not many reasons to assume why a compensation fund would provide better protection against insolvency than the private insurance markets.

[84] An allocation of the full costs of the out-of-court entity to the tortfeasor may equally lead to over-deterrence, which should also be avoided.

Insurance is, as mentioned above, in principle able to differentiate risks as insurers are specialised in risk differentiation and risk spreading. Insurers therefore possess techniques to determine in what way their insured contribute to the risk. This assumes that the insurance markets are competitive. In the absence of competition on insurance markets, either the supply of insurance coverage could be too limited or premiums could be excessively high, which could justify a preference for a compensation fund.[85] But if insurance markets are competitive, insurers can be assumed to be better able to deal with classic insurance problems such as moral hazard and adverse selection than the administrators of a compensation fund. One cannot see as a matter of principle why a government agency that would run a compensation fund would have better information on risks than an insurer.

This might, however, be different if highly technical risks are involved where operators of certain facilities are in a much better position than the insurance company to monitor each other. One could argue that a risk-sharing agreement between nuclear plant operators could lead to an optimal monitoring between the operators, since they possess much better information on prevention, and good and bad risks than an insurance company would.[86] Also in maritime insurance the P&I Clubs, which are based on a mutual risk sharing between tanker owners, play a crucial role.[87] With respect to these highly specialised matters one could therefore argue that the operators themselves might in some cases be better suited than an insurance company to control moral hazard, since they are better able to process information on the particular risk.[88] However, the given examples show that with these risk-sharing agreements no use is made of a government-run compensation fund. These would thus rather be arguments in favour of the risk-sharing agreements discussed earlier and not necessarily for a compensation fund.

#### 12.5.3.2 Costs

Comparing insurance with compensation funds, one should also address the comparative costs of both instruments. Insurance will generally be cheaper because liability insurance policies are not concluded for one activity, but for a whole set of risks. There is one insurance policy with transaction costs that are incurred once and an administrative structure within an insurance company that will be forced to an adequate cost reduction by competitive pressures.

The costs of risk spreading might also be lower with an insurance company than with a compensation fund. Insurers are indeed specialised in methods for acquiring information on differentiation of risks. In addition, it has been argued in the

85 Faure and Van den Bergh (1995, at 65–85).

86 See Faure and Skogh (1992, at 499–513) and Faure (1995, at 21–43).

87 See Coghlin (1984, at 403–416).

88 These 'joint compensation systems' are also discussed in the EU Commission's 'Green Paper on Remedying Environmental Damage', COM (93) 47 final, 14 May 1993.

literature that insurance provides for a reduction of transaction costs between contracting parties, because parties can ex ante agree on a distribution of risks and losses in case of an incident.[89] The comparison will also depend upon the type of compensation fund under discussion.

In most cases one immediately thinks of a compensation fund run by a regulatory authority. If that is the case, one can of course refer to the literature on the negative effects of bureaucracies to argue that such a publicly operated compensation fund should not necessarily provide compensation at lower costs than the private insurance market. This can be reduced if the fund is administered privately, but in that case a competition with other funds has to be organised to provide incentives for cost reduction.

One could only think of cost advantages of a fund if one did not refer to a fund as one that would replace the liability and insurance system, but would be a limitation fund, such as the one proposed by the Interuniversity Commission, whereby potential injurers make an ex ante reservation for potential future losses.

### 12.5.4 *A Compensation Fund for Environmental Damage?*

So far, we have sketched that in general there are very few reasons to expect that a compensation fund would provide better compensation than a private insurance market. This is especially the case if one assumes that one or more identifiable polluters can be found. If environmental damage can be remedied though liability, it is unclear why funds would have advantages compared to insurance. However, this does not mean that there may be no role for compensation funds with respect to environmental damage at all. Most fund solutions therefore typically refer to the situation that a polluter cannot be identified or is insolvent.[90]

#### 12.5.4.1 Guarantee Fund

A compensation fund may well be used to guarantee compensation in case of insolvency of the injurer or their insurer. In that case a fund does not replace the liability and insurance system, but only intervenes in a particular case when the injurer or their insurer was found insolvent. This combined use of the liability system, insurance, and a guarantee fund for the insolvency risk has the advantage that the incentives of the liability system will remain untouched and that the fund will only have to intervene in the event of insolvency.

However, the question arises whether such a fund could at all be used separately from compulsory insurance (in the broadest sense). Indeed, if insolvency of the injurer is the problem one fears, it seems more logical to discuss the introduction of

[89] This argument has been made by Skogh (1989b, at 726–732).
[90] See e.g. Smets (1997, at 223–248).

a duty to insure instead of immediately advancing a fund solution. If one looks at the use of guarantee funds now, one can note that they are usually used to provide for the cases that an insurance company goes bankrupt. This merits the question whether it is at all useful to provide for a duty to insure for environmental damage.[91] As we have noticed, so far only a few countries have introduced compulsory environmental liability insurance.[92] However, it is important to stress that if one wishes to provide a protection against the insolvency of the injurer, it is more appropriate to focus on a variety of financial mechanisms that force a potential polluter ex ante to provide for compensation for future losses instead of focusing on an ex post fund solution.

Generally, one can doubt whether it is useful to focus on a guarantee fund that should e.g. intervene in case of insolvency of an insurer instead of focusing on other ex ante compensation mechanisms to provide coverage.

#### 12.5.4.2 Restoration Fund

There is one other situation where insurance cannot intervene and a compensation fund could prove to be useful. This relates to the situation where no individual enterprise can be identified as liable for the harm caused.[93] Since there is no individual injurer who is liable, there is logically also no insurer who will be bound to compensate.

One can think of a deterioration of a specific habitat through acid rain. These are typically the cases where liability is not a suitable instrument. One could consider a compensation fund for these specific cases where no individual injurer can be found. However, the compensation fund should then be limited to those situations, so that liability rules and insurance can still exercise their preventive effects in all other cases where an injurer can be found.

Still the question will have to be answered who shall contribute to such a fund. Ideally this would be funded by all contributors to the risk. However, different than in case of traffic accidents, it is not easy to identify ex ante what kind of activities contributed to the loss. If it is generally possible to argue that e.g. sulphur dioxide ($SO_2$) emissions caused the loss, economists would advocate a Pigouvian tax on $SO_2$ emissions to finance the fund. One reason, however, why environmental taxes are still relatively scarce in practice is that it will often be hard to determine to what proportion this specific activity contributed to the risk and hence to determine the optimal marginal tax rate. If this is not possible, the only alternative is that the government will pay for the restoration of the specific site, either directly or by

91 See on that point Section 11.6.

92 For instance Germany. See Wagner (1991b, at 249–260; 1992, at 261–272; and 1996, at 97–146).

93 Other causes of failure of traditional liability and insurance are discussed by Bocken (1991, at 133–145).

financing a compensation fund that has to finance the clean-up activity. However, since it is in both cases the taxpayer who will have to provide the financial means, one can question whether the instalment of a compensation fund has any added value, apart from the fact that one is certain that specific public funds will be reserved for compensation of environmental damage.

## 12.6 SUMMARY AND CONCLUSION

This chapter has focused on financial tools beyond conventional insurance, to cover self-insurance, risk-sharing agreements, forms of deposits, and various types of compensation funds. The common element in these cases is that the capital either remains solely with the actor or remains closer to the actor than in the necessary payments to a third party in conventional insurance – that is to say, they are less costly on capital budgets.

Traditionally the term self-insurance meant to book a financial reserve to cover certain future risks. In the late 1970s, the term began to include the concept of 'captives', wherein a company would own its own insurance agency and write its own policies. Depending on corporate structure, this may well mean little more than a financial record within a singular entity. Were insolvency to hit, or other forms of closure or dissolution, then those funds might not remain available to provide for damages.

Risk-sharing agreements are contractual agreements between similarly placed firms to agree to pay-up in capital, based on a pre-agreed ratio, to cover any of the co-parties' capital needs to cover emergencies and damages. In a sense, it is self-insurance by contract among 'friends', with a slightly better chance of being able to pay in future time periods due to the diversification of the risk across the group and the likelihood that at least some of the parties will remain sufficiently capitalised at that time.

Various forms of deposits and guarantees involve a third party holding the capital of the risky first party until a certain event or time period has been successfully reached. However, the financial structures normally undertaken involve taking loans to cover the deposit, so that the costs of the loan are tax deductible expenses and the firm retains the bulk of its capital in its business operations. In effect, this type of structure can create substantial moral hazards.

Compensation funds can be created in two basic manners, the first is to have the actor pay while undertaking the risky activity in some form, while the second is to have public funds cover the cost of the funds. In the first case, the actor could pay on a daily basis, on a mass emitted basis, or on any other type of tolling fee, so that the payment is in some sense proportional to the risk created for the environment. Those funds would then be collected by a public agency to support any later claim (s) for compensation in damages. The alternative is for public funds to cover the costs. Compensation funds are particularly useful when it can be established that certain activities are risky to the environment, but additionally those same risks will be difficult to track back to particular risk takers. They are Pigouvian in theory, if set correctly under the requirements of marginal analysis.

In conclusion, these tools provide a different set of risks and benefits than those proffered by conventional insurance tools. What might be optimal may well be a smart mix of the various tools, but policymakers will need to keep the concerns on insolvency, on moral hazard, and on adverse selection in mind when developing requirements for both insurance and these alternative means of assuring funds for compensation in damages.

# 13

# Environmental Federalism

## 13.1 INTRODUCTION

This volume has addressed a great many legal instruments that could be employed to prevent environmental harm from occurring or to compensate ex post for environmental harm. To some extent the question was equally addressed which actor would be best suited to make the appropriate rules. Especially when discussing regulation (in Chapter 9), attention was paid to the different roles of the legislator and the judiciary, and an argument was made in favour of a supplementary role for the judiciary (via liability rules) to reinforce the function of public regulation.

However, the question was not addressed at which level of governance the different rules should be promulgated. The implicit assumption was that these rules and policy instruments would emerge within a simplistic notion of a state possessing a singular – flat – level of governance. However, a typical feature of environmental harm is that it crosses borders in a manner that engages multiple distinct jurisdictions. That border-straddling nature of the injury therefore justifies the question how economics can be employed to address this question of the optimal level of governance. This concept is also known as a question of subsidiarity within the EU.[1]

This question has been addressed in a literature which is known as the economics of federalism. The search for the optimal level of governance often leads to substantive debates; different policies have emerged across the EU, the USA, China, and India, given their various forms of and time periods of experience with federalism.[2] The advantage of this economics of federalism is that it provides an academic

[1] Livermore references that the concept of subsidiarity in the present question of federalism and appropriate vertical distribution of authority was from the Catholic Church, in an Encyclical issued by Pope Pius XI in 1931 (Livermore 2017, at 646).

[2] For example, the USA formalised its current federal form in its Constitution, as ratified in 1789; its notions of federalism in environmental law can be dated back to over a hundred years ago, when Justice Holmes found that a state has a sovereign interest in the air above its territory, that the quality of the air is a basic attribute of state sovereignty (Cole 2011, at 18).

framework for analysis, allowing to address questions of the optimal allocation of jurisdiction based on criteria of welfare maximisation.

This chapter will proceed as follows. After this introduction the starting points for the analysis will be presented (Section 13.2); next, criteria for centralisation will be presented (Section 13.3) and the consequences of the analysis for environmental standard setting will be discussed (Section 13.4). Finally, a policy perspective will be presented following from this literature (Section 13.5). Section 13.6 summarises and concludes.

## 13.2 STARTING POINTS[3]

### 13.2.1 *Tiebout's Model of Federalism*

The question whether regulation should be promulgated at central (European or federal) level or at a more decentralised level (or, to put it in a more balanced way, what kind of environmental regulations should be set at which level) has been addressed in the economics of federalism. This discussion builds on a body of economic theory that began to emerge in the postwar era of the late 1940s and 1950s, thus these models have existed and been examined for a number of decades.

In 1956, Tiebout developed a seminal theory on the optimal provision of local public goods.[4] He imagined a scenario wherein local governments within a common federal nation competed as if they were firms creating public goods.[5] His model enabled a solution to the 'free-rider' problem in providing public goods by observing that communities compete in the provision of public goods and that residents could respond by 'voting with their feet' to create better alignment of provided goods with taxpayer willingness to support the provision of those goods. The seven conditions of the theory are:[6]

(i) that local voters can readily relocate to other communities within the same federal nation,
(ii) that each local voter has full awareness of the circumstances and options within each jurisdiction,
(iii) that there are sufficiently many communities from which to select a community,
(iv) the local voters face no employment consequences of relocating,

3 This part of the chapter shall be largely based on the inauguration address of Roger Van den Bergh, in which the economic literature providing criteria for (de)centralisation is discussed (Van den Bergh 1994, at 337).
4 Tiebout (1956, at 416). For a discussion see Rose-Ackerman (1992b, at 169–170).
5 Van Zeben (2012, at 7).
6 Id., at 7, citing with reference to Tiebout (1956, at 419).

(v) that the public services of each community create no externalities or other diseconomies for the other communities,

(vi) that like private firms each producer of public good faces an optimal number of residents in the community at which point the preferred public goods could be produced at the lowest average cost, and

(vii) communities with populations smaller than the optimal size of population per the previous assumption will make efforts to attract new residents to better attain those lower average costs of public good production.

Tiebout argued that when all those conditions hold true,[7] voters will react to their knowledge of options in different communities to choose their most preferred community, respectively per each voter, leading to overall allocative efficiency across the federal nation.

For example, if in one community, the majority of the citizens have a high preference for sporting facilities and in another community a majority of citizens have a preference for opera, the first community will probably construct sporting facilities, whereas the second will probably provide an opera house. If someone living in the second community preferred sporting facilities to the opera house, they could then move to the first community, which apparently provides services which better suit their preferences. A well-informed citizen could move to the community that best matches their preference; i.e. that community that provides the local services sought by that citizen-on-the-move. This so-called voting with the feet competition between local authorities will lead citizens to cluster together according to their preferences.

In practice, one can notice that different communities do indeed offer a variety of different services. Thus, a citizen can influence the provision of local public goods not only by participating in decision-making procedures, such as by voting, but also by choosing within which communities to engage in those decision-making procedures by relocating their abode to those communities.[8]

Further, by having communities compete with each other, and the efforts put into communicating the information about the effectiveness of each community's approach to public goods, deliberative information is created for all of the communities to evaluate their future policies and public goods.[9]

7 It is well recognised that the seven elements are restrictive in nature, but certain areas do functionally reflect these requirements, for example certain areas in the USA, as well as other areas that might reflect partial satisfaction or no satisfaction of these requirements. We make no argument herein that these are by any means commonly assumed conditions, merely that this model is very useful for analysing federal systems.

8 See generally on the possibilities of citizens taking action, the well-known treatise of Hirschman on exit, voice, and loyalty (Hirschman 1990).

9 Livermore (2017, 640).

Theorists have developed models that evaluate the benefits of federal approaches in comparison to more centralised modes of governance.

In 1972, Oates formally integrated Samuelson's earlier models on public goods, Arrow's framework for theoretically distinguishing public and private goods, and Musgrave's work on public finance to create his formal model, known as the Decentralisation Theorem.[10] This theorem holds that local creation and distribution of public goods will be Pareto superior to similar efforts higher up in a federal structure, as long as there are no notable spill-over effects.[11]

Similarly, in 1980, Brennan and Buchanan found that centralised states can be modelled as monopolies producing public goods, with the well-known welfare problems of monopoly production.[12] They argued that a decentralised or federal approach to governance could be modelled as principal/agent model, wherein either the voters are principals with responding levels of governance as agents, or national-level governance as principal with responding levels of subsidiary governance as agents; both forms of the model worked to reduce the welfare losses of monopolistic production of public goods.[13]

Thus, the economic theories of federalism share ideas that public goods are desired by voters and that some form of competition between producers of those public goods reduces welfare loss for the public as a whole. In other words, the models support the notion of a market in public goods in contrast to a Leviathan monopolistic producer of the same goods.

### 13.2.2 *Competing Legal Orders*

This basic idea applies not only to community services, but also to fiscal decisions,[14] and environmental choices.[15] In addition, this idea of citizens moving to the community that provides services which best correspond to their preferences, can also be applied with respect to legal rules. A competition between legislators will lead to legal systems competing with each other to provide legislation that corresponds best to the preferences of citizens.[16]

The model holds that lawmakers in various nation states will create a competitive market for the supply of law.[17] Thereafter, citizens would cluster together in states that provide legal rules that correspond to their preferences. Well-informed citizens

[10] Van Zeben (2012, at 6).
[11] Id.
[12] Id., at 9; with reference to Brennan and Buchanan (1980).
[13] Id.
[14] See e.g. Inman and Rubinfeld (1994, at 147); Kirchgässner and Pommerehne (1993); and Oates (1972).
[15] See Oates and Schwab (1988, at 333–354).
[16] For a sociological perspective on the consumption of legal rules by individuals, see Partain (2015).
[17] Ogus (1999b, at 405–418).

who may be dissatisfied with the legislation provided, could move (voting with the feet) to the community that provides legislation that corresponds best to their preferences. This idea, assuming that different legal systems offer different legal rules, thus explains the variety and differences between the legal systems.[18]

It also shows that differences between the various legal rules of different countries should not necessarily be judged as negative.[19] The idea of competing legal systems can probably best be seen 'in action' in international private law, where actors can choose the legal systems that best suits their needs in a choice of law regime.[20]

Frey and Eichenberger have proposed an extreme form of this competition between legal orders by suggesting the emergence of Functional Overlapping Competing Jurisdictions (FOCJ), whereby citizens could choose different governmental unities for different functions of government.[21]

This system, assuming that a competition between legal orders leads to allocative efficiency in the provision of legal rules, works only if certain conditions are met. One condition is that citizens have adequate information on the contents of the legal rules provided by the various legislators, in order to be able to make an informed choice. In addition, exit is often costly or legally prohibited,[22] so people may stay even if the legal regime does not suit their needs optimally.[23] A location decision is made under the influence of a set of criteria, whereby the legal regime may not be decisive.[24] Usually the job location and residence are so important that in reality there is often little left for people to choose.[25]

[18] Van den Bergh (1998, at 134). Also, the Hotelling market model may be seen as antecedent to this result. See Hotelling (1929).

[19] Indeed, the argument for preservation of the legal diversity is central both to the function of the 'market for legal rules' and a market of ideas; the conception of a right to that legal diversity underlays the arguments presented by Partain (2015).

[20] Although the choice for a particular legal regime may not always be related to the quality of the legal system but e.g. to the quality of the court or arbitration system. The latter explains, according to Ogus, the popularity of English law in choice of law clauses in contracts (Ogus 1999b, at 408).

[21] Frey (1996, at 315–327). See also Frey and Eichenberer (1996, at 335) and Casella and Frey (1992, at 639).

[22] The complexities of emigration law and of immigration law exceeds the scope of this present volume on environmental law. But the present analysis can be readily applied in large areas lacking the legal issues of emigration and immigration, because we have ready access to such large federal zones as the EU, the USA, or Canada. Free movement is a right and is commonly exercised in those regions. Nevertheless, it is ever clearer that people will emigrate from states with undesirable legal rules to immigrate to states with more desirable rules, often at great financial cost and risk of life.

[23] As Ogus states, there should be no barriers to the freedom of establishment and to the movement of capital (Ogus 1999b, at 407).

[24] That is one of the reasons why Frey and Eichenberger argue in favour of FOCJ: the choice for one legal or institutional regime should not be exclusive; there may be 'overlapping' jurisdictions depending upon the different functions (Frey and Eichenberger 1996, at 316–318).

[25] Rose-Ackerman (1992b, at 169).

### 13.2.3 *Bottom-Up Federalism*

Taking the Tiebout model result that policies should begin in decentralised versions as a starting point, and assuming that competition between decentralised legislators will lead to an optimal provision of legal rules, the central question is: why centralise?

Van den Bergh therefore criticised a part of the discussion in the European legal literature which seemed to focus on the question why there should be decentralisation (referred to by Van den Bergh as 'top-down federalisation'). According to Tiebout's model, that is the wrong question. Van den Bergh's counter-model forecasts a 'bottom-up federalisation', which begins by assuming that in principle the local level should be optimal, since the local level would be likely to possess the best information on local problems and on the preferences of its local citizens.

Only when there is a good reason, should decision making be moved to a higher level. Economic theory has indeed suggested that there may be a variety of reasons why the local level is not best suited to take decisions and where central decision making can lead to more efficient results.[26]

We will now apply these criteria for centralisation to environmental policy.

## 13.3 CRITERIA FOR CENTRALISATION

### 13.3.1 *Transboundary Externalities*

The transboundary character of the problem to be regulated is presented in economic theory as an argument in favour of centralisation from two different angles. In preview, the earlier discussion on Pigou's externalities and Coasean approaches to mediating or solving those problems presumed a singular court or jurisdiction within which to operate; notionally the arguments heretounder are similar – centralisation would facilitate addressing externalities by bringing them into one 'court'.

One aspect is that in case of transboundary externalities, states will have an incentive to impose stringent regulations upon their own citizens if the consequences of harmful actions are only felt outside their own territory. Transboundary externalities may thus create inefficiencies in the absence of central regulation.[27] Public goods resulting from the joint contribution to an environmental benefit (such as reducing climate change) will suffer from a classic prisoner's dilemma and from free-riding behaviour. States will benefit from the abatement taken by others even if they do not abate themselves. That explains why global public goods

[26] For an application of economic theory to the re-allocation of competences within the EU, see Van den Bergh (2016). For application to wildlife and environmental law within the USA, see Lueck (1995, at 655–660).

[27] Revesz (2000, at 67).

are undersupplied and why central regulation (thus international environmental law) is necessary.[28]

A second argument is that if the problem to be regulated crosses the borders of competence of the regulatory authority, the decision-making power should be shifted to a higher regulatory level, preferably to an authority which has jurisdiction over a territory large enough to deal with the problem adequately.[29] 'Economic theory provides a straightforward but difficult-to-implement answer to regional problems: to draw 'optimal' jurisdictional boundaries'.[30]

This argument in favour of centralisation could play a role with respect to environmental problems. It can be argued that these are certainly often transboundary.[31] In many regional organisations or federal states, one can therefore also notice that the transboundary character of a problem is often used as an argument for shifting decision-making powers to the central level. For example, in the European context, much of the European legislation deals with transboundary problems and the same is to a large extent the case in the USA as well.

However, some have warned that the argument that centralised powers are necessary to deal with transboundary problems should not be accepted too easily.

First, Esty and Geradin have powerfully argued against an 'all or nothing' approach, meaning either all powers resting with the local authorities or shifting all powers to the central level. They have argued that the transboundary pollution problems can be dealt with via legal instruments other than centralisation, in other words via instruments which do not involve a change of the national environmental laws of a particular country.[32] One possibility is the external application of (domestic) high-standard country laws. Another one is the national enforcement of domestic laws with cross-border monitoring. In other words: the transboundary character of the externality may be an argument for cooperation, not necessarily for homogeneity of legal rules. However, Esty and Geradin admit that these alternative approaches have serious limitations as well and might not be effective remedies in all cases.[33]

Second, Cohen argued that Coasean bargaining between the polluting and the victim state may lead to negotiated agreements between them.[34] Therefore, Cohen argues that there is no a priori reason to centralise regulatory decision making.[35]

[28] Barrett (2007, 238–239).

[29] Esty (1996).

[30] Rose-Ackerman (1995b, at 38).

[31] See equally Oates and Schwab (1988), who also argue that as long as the effects of pollutants are confined within the borders of the relevant jurisdictions, local authorities will make socially optimal decisions of environmental quality.

[32] See Esty and Gerardin (1998, at 5–46). See also Esty and Geradin (1997, at 265–336), in which they provide an interesting overview of the various legal instruments to deal with harmonisation and apply this in the NAFTA and in the European context. See also Trebilcock and Howse (1998, at 5–37).

[33] Esty and Geradin (1998, at 34–35).

[34] See also Van den Bergh (1999).

[35] Cohen (1996, at 167–171).

There might, however, be several reasons why the ideal solution from Coase's world might not be possible to solve transboundary pollution problems. First, although there are some indications in international environmental law on this point, it might not be certain what the legal rule is: right to pollute or polluter pays. This uncertainty concerning the assignment of property rights might endanger negotiations. Second, adequate information is needed both on the consequences of pollution and on the possible abatement techniques.[36] Third, there might be no strategic behaviour. Finally, parties need to have the possibility of enforcing a negotiated agreement.

However, some federal environmental law (in the USA) or environmental directives (in Europe) deal with local problems that do not cross national borders. The question therefore arises whether there is another economic rationale for centralisation in those cases where the effects of pollutants are confined within the borders of specific states.

### 13.3.2 *Race to the Bottom*

Centralisation has also been advanced as a remedy to the prisoner's dilemma associated with a race-to-the-bottom scenario, which envisions that governments could use lenient regulation as a competitive tool to attract industry.[37]

The validity of this race-to-the-bottom argument is strongly debated among Law and Economics scholars, who tend to stress the benefits of competition between states and point out the dangers of centralisation.[38] Others point at the potentially destructive effects of this interstate competition and hence attach more belief to the race-to-the-bottom rationale.[39]

Is there empirical evidence that industry will relocate as a result of lenient environmental law?[40] North-American research has already showed that effects of environmental regulations on location decisions of industry are 'either small, statistically insignificant or not robust to tests of model specification'.[41] Although more evidence somewhat relaxes these earlier findings, it certainly does remain valid in the area of environmental law.[42]

For example, as far as the old EU Member States are concerned, it is doubtful whether they would engage in a game in which they would strive for low-level environmental law in order to attract industry. Elements other than environmental law may be far more important in the location decision of businesses. Also, as far as

[36] Id., at 168.
[37] See e.g. Rose-Ackerman (1992b, at 166–170).
[38] See especially Revesz (1992 and 1996).
[39] See e.g. Esty (1996) and Esty and Geradin (1998).
[40] This topic is renewed in the next chapter from a developing state perspective; see Section 14.3.
[41] Jaffe et al. (1995).
[42] Faure and Johnston (2009, at 246–250).

environmental law is concerned, it is more likely that these democratic states would wish to protect victims of environmental pollution instead of corporate interests, thus engaging in a race for the top.[43] This story may only have changed after EU enlargement to include Central and Eastern Europe, the result of which is now many Member States with substantially lower environmental standards have entered into the EU.

Although the argument in favour of centralisation (to counter a race to the bottom) has thus increased, one can expect, paradoxically, the contrary. The reason is that many West-European companies have moved to the East, also benefitting from lower environmental and labour standards. Such firms would, if anything, have an incentive to favour environmental regulatory decentralisation, so that they could continue to take advantage of lax environmental standards in those newer Member States.[44]

### 13.3.3 *Improving Trade*

In some literature the question of centralisation is not only addressed from the angle of the Tiebout-type fiscal federalism arguments, but rather from the perspective that harmonisation of law would be necessary to avoid trade distortions. It is an argument that plays a role in many federal jurisdictions and that has especially played an important role in Europe to justify centralisation in order to impose harmonised legislation. Simply stated, the argument is that complying with legislation imposes costs on industry. If legislation is different, these costs would therefore differ as well and the conditions of competition within the common market would not be equal. The argument apparently assumes that total equality of conditions of competition is necessary for the functioning of the common market. 'Levelling the playing field' for European industry is the central message.

There are, however, some problems with this traditional European argument, which in fact claims that any difference in legislation between the Member States could endanger the conditions of competition and therefore justifies the harmonisation of legal rules. The latter argument seems particularly weak.[45] From an economic point of view, there can be differences in marketing conditions for a variety of reasons, and if the conditions of competition were indeed totally equal, as the argument assumes, there would also be no incentive for trade.[46]

Also, Europe has developed an elaborate set of rules that guarantees, inter alia, a free flow of products and services and thus contributes to market integration without

43 Ogus (1999b, at 48); Vogel (1995, at 13).

44 Faure and Johnston (2009, at 267–271).

45 Spier and Haazen (1999, at 478).

46 This issue was noted early on by Adam Smith and David Ricardo in their theories of trade. Smith called this concept the theory of advantages in trade, Ricardo the model of comparative advantages, and they discussed the matters of Portuguese and British trades in wine and textiles.

the necessity of harmonising all rules and standards.[47] In this context, the case law of the European Court of Justice with respect to the free movement of goods versus environmental protection springs to mind. This shows that the goal of market integration can be achieved through other less comprehensive instruments than total harmonisation, which can remove barriers to trade just as effectively.[48]

Hence, one should make a distinction between the political ideal of creating one common market in Europe on the one hand and the (economic) race-to-the-bottom argument on the other hand.[49] It has equally been shown that harmonisation of all-legal rules is not necessary to facilitate transboundary trade.

Differences in regulatory standards can of course impose costs upon enterprises,[50] but companies are not deterred from cross-border sales even when this means that they have to adapt to local legal rules. The idea that full harmonisation of law would be necessary to increase competition within the internal market was even strongly rejected by business organisations.[51] Empirical evidence indeed shows that a lack of cross-border trade is not related to the differences in legal rules, but to other causes.[52]

### 13.3.4 *Reduction of Transaction Costs*

An argument strongly linked with the market integration argument is that the current differences between legal rules lead to substantial administrative costs.[53] The assumption simply states that uniform rules are easier to apply than differentiated legal rules, as a result of which substantial savings on costs are available.

At first sight, this argument is seductive: uniform rules reduce information costs because the study of the different legal systems in the Member States is no longer necessary.

There are, however, several problems with the simplicity of this argument. One problem is that the argument suggests that the costs of harmonisation would be nil or at least very low. Many scholars have pointed at the fact that introducing a new legal concept within a particular legal culture in fact imposes high costs; according to some, even prohibitive costs.[54] As a result of the many differences between legal cultures and traditions in different statesthe costs of those legal transplants may

47 See generally on the potential conflict between free trade and environmental protection, Esty (1999).

48 Esty and Geradin (1997, at 296–299); Ogus (2004b, at 177–179).

49 See also Revesz (1997a, at 1331), who equally argues that these are separate points which should be distinguished.

50 See Vogenauer and Weatherill (2006).

51 Ott and Schäfer (2003, at 236).

52 Thommes, Faure, and Heine (2014) and Van den Bergh (2007, at 202–203).

53 See inter alia Lando (1993).

54 Legrand (1997).

indeed be extremely high.[55] Van Dam also pointed at the diversity in national legal cultures and the correspondingly high costs of harmonisation in Europe.[56]

A second, related problem is that not only are the administrative costs of harmonisation neglected, but so are the benefits of differentiation. Law and Economics scholars point at the fact that varying legal rules should not be considered as problematic as long as they reflect varying preferences of citizens.[57] Uniformity hence always creates a cost related to the loss of differentiation.

### 13.3.5 *Providing a Minimum Level of Protection*

Some may argue that harmonisation should not merely be based on economic arguments, but that a minimum level of protection (in other words of environmental quality) should be provided.

In that case centralisation seems, at first sight, contrary to basic economic logic. From an economic point of view, the environmental quality to be provided could differ according to differing preferences of citizens.[58] Again from an economic point of view, there is no reason for centralisation if the externalities are local and no prisoner's dilemma exists. This economic argument in favour of differentiation and decentralisation according to the preferences of citizens is also valid for the whole body of environmental law, doubly so for environmental quality standards. This corresponds with the Tiebout framework of competition between legal orders, where citizens are free to choose the environmental quality that corresponds optimally with their preferences. The economic arguments therefore lead to an environmental federalism in which the norms of environmental quality between Member States could differ as long as there are no transboundary effects and no race-to-the-bottom risks.[59]

Only if one were to leave the economic logic, could an argument be made that centralised (federal) law should guarantee all the citizens within the jurisdiction a minimum level of environmental quality. In that case it would, contrary to economic logic, no longer be the democratic or market preferences of citizens that would prevail, but rather a smaller group of politically connected policymakers that would set basic environmental quality standards within the jurisdiction. Ogus wrote that the preferences of citizens for lower standards at lower costs may sometimes be overruled if it could be held that these low standards would infringe widely held

55 See Majone (2008) and Legrand (2008).

56 Van Dam (2007).

57 Van den Bergh (2000, at 435) and Ogus (1999b, at 405).

58 Developed by Ogus (1994b, at 25–30, and more generally in 1999b, at 413).

59 However, since firms are in a competitive environment a Member State which chooses to impose a high level of protection (and thus high costs on firms) will have to compensate this with e.g. lower taxes on wages in order to avoid the exit of business.

perceptions of human rights.[60] In the environmental context this point could take the form of guaranteeing all citizens a basic environmental quality.

Still the problem with this argument is that it is not clear whether today environmental law within particular states would be of such a bad quality that it would violate human rights. If that were the case, human rights could indeed be called upon to provide protection to victims, but that does not necessarily require centralisation.[61] The problem is that if this argument were taken further than providing a 'minimum' environmental quality, the question then arises how one could agree on a similar environmental quality within the particular jurisdiction. However, if one were to argue (for ecological reasons) in favour of a harmonised environmental quality within a federal jurisdiction, then this unavoidably also has consequences for the question which types of standards will have to be harmonised.

## 13.4 CONSEQUENCES FOR ENVIRONMENTAL STANDARD SETTING

### 13.4.1 *Introduction*

We can now come back to the different types of standards that are used in environmental policy and that we have identified earlier in Chapter 4. We made the distinction between the two main types of standards, on the one hand target (or ambient quality) standards and on the other hand emission standards (or emission limit values). The question then arises which type of standard would have to be harmonised in order to reach either free trade or basic environmental quality. We will show that the choice between those goals has consequences for the types of standards one should harmonise.

### 13.4.2 *Environmental Quality Standards*

If it is a policy decision to guarantee a similar environmental quality to all citizens in the particular jurisdiction, irrespective of individual preferences, quality standards should be harmonised. This idea can also be found in the rhetoric in some federal jurisdictions.[62] This clearly shows the difference between the economic and the legal approach. From an economic perspective the quality standards could be

[60] 'Rights may, in this instance, justifiably "trump" efficiency' (id., at 418). See also Cohen (1996, at 170), who calls for minimum quality standards at centralised level for reasons of 'equity, justice, or pure paternalism', and Stewart, who states that geographically uniform standards ensure every individual a minimum healthy environment even though such uniformity is economically inefficient (Stewart 2000).

[61] See further on the role of human rights in protecting victims against environmental pollution, Section 5.7.

[62] See for instance the considerations proceeding the Wild Birds Directive, which states, 'whereas conservation is aimed at the long-term protection and management of natural resources as an integral part of the heritage of the peoples of Europe'. The European heritage was not the only

differentiated, taking into account individual preferences.[63] The idea of guaranteeing an environmental quality can be realised only through harmonised quality standards, to which the environmental components in the federation should, in principle, correspond. These quality standards, also referred to as target standards, should then of course be the standards of an ideal environmental quality to be achieved and not merely standards that function as a 'red flag', as has sometimes been the case.

This type of policy assumes that the federal level would not only set quality standards, but also has powers to monitor whether these quality standards are actually achieved. In this respect there is a large difference between two major jurisdictions: the USA and Europe. Europe largely lacks the possibility of controlling environmental quality within the Member States, whereas, to the contrary, the Federal Environmental Protection Agency in the USA does possess those powers.

### 13.4.3 *Emission Limit Values*

If it is accepted that in a federal jurisdiction a basic environmental quality should be guaranteed through harmonised quality (target) standards, the next step is to ask how these standards can be achieved. The quality standards will be influenced by the specific emissions coming from various sources. However, according to the theory of optimal specificity of legal rules,[64] the costs of meeting a certain level of environmental protection (in other words the target) may well vary according to location-specific circumstances.[65] In the words of Esty and Geradin, 'Differential standards are more economically efficient than total harmonisation because they better match regulatory requirements to localised needs'.[66]

Take the example of Europe. The local conditions in Belgium or Germany may be totally different from those in Portugal or Greece. Hence, the emission limit values, which are needed to reach a similar environmental quality within the Union, will have to take these differences into account.[67] The inevitable conclusion is that where the environmental quality (target) to be reached may be uniform, the emission limit values will need to be tailored to location-specific circumstances and will therefore be differentiated.[68] An obvious consequence of this is that firms

justification for the Wild Birds Directive. Since birds tend to fly, the transboundary character of the issue comes into the picture as well (Van den Bergh, Faure, and Lefevere 1996).

63 See Ogus (1994a, at 208).

64 Ehrlich and Posner (1974, at 257–286); Ogus (1994a, 168–171 and 1994b, at 23–37).

65 Kolstad (1987, at 386–399) and Faure and Lefevere (1995, at 321–326).

66 Esty and Geradin 1998, at 43.

67 Esty and Geradin rightly argue that an intervention to eliminate differences in standards which reflect natural locational advantages would not be a good policy (Esty and Geradin 1997, at 271).

68 Revesz rightly states: 'The harmonisation argument cannot be used, as it has in the European Union, to justify both uniform ambient standards and uniform emission standards' (Revesz 1997a, at 1339–1340; 2000, 50–51).

operating in less polluted Member States can face less stringent emission limit values and can therefore market their products at lower prices. Thus they benefit from a competitive advantage.[69]

Again, this should not be a problem as long as these differences do not pose a race-to-the-bottom risk.[70]

### 13.4.4 *Policy*

This favoured approach of harmonised target standards with differentiated emission limit values has not been followed either in the USA or in Europe. As the discussion on standard setting in Chapter 4 made clear, in Europe various directives explicitly refer to the setting of emission limit values at the central level. The problem with setting harmonised emission limit values is that this runs counter to the idea of achieving a uniform environmental quality. Harmonised emission limit values will lead to differentiated environmental quality.

This issue shows that it is often difficult for a policy maker to choose between pursuing a purely environmental policy (in which case the goal to achieve harmonised environmental quality would be achieved via differentiated emission limit values) and trade policy as well. Since in federal jurisdictions facilitating interstate trade often has priority, emission limit values will be centralised in order to facilitate interstate trade.

## 13.5 POLICY PERSPECTIVE

It follows from the previous analysis that the economics of federalism comes to balanced conclusions on when it might be necessary to shift decision making concerning environmental law to a higher level, i.e. to centralise. If there is a danger of transboundary externalities, the recommendation from the economic literature is clear: centralisation is indicated to remedy the market failure caused by the transboundary externality. The same is true if there is empirical evidence of a race to the bottom, also referred to as a pollution haven.

The difficulty with the latter argument is, however, that it is not always clear whether there is a (healthy) competition between legal orders or a race to the bottom. Instead of racing to the bottom, states could equally race to the top, which is not necessarily welfare maximising either. To the extent that the race to the top actually creates barriers to entry it is not necessarily desirable. It is for that reason that the recommendations from the economic literature are quite balanced.

69 Esty and Geradin (1997, at 271 and 306).

70 If there is a race-to-the-bottom risk, interjurisdictional differences will still lead to inefficiencies (Rose-Ackerman 1995b, at 40–41).

The economic literature also points at the importance of not only formally harmonising legal rules where centralisation would be indicated, but also to make sure that enforcement of these central rules takes place at the local level as well. In some jurisdictions such as Europe, where powers to regulate are largely centralised but implementation is left to the Member States, that creates serious problems. Implementation and enforcement problems could then lead to a situation whereby transboundary externalities or a race to the bottom persist. That is a strong argument in favour of not only allocating powers to regulate, but also equally to enforce to the central level as well.[71]

We already noticed that in some jurisdictions, namely in the EU, but in some cases in the USA as well, harmonisation efforts in the domain of environmental law do not necessarily fit into the economic theory of centralisation. If certain legislative action cannot be set to promote public interest, public choice scholars would ask whether the legislation favours special interest groups.

In particular cases special interest groups representing industry might, understandably, lobby in favour of a harmonisation of setting emission limit values at the centralised level of governance.[72] Interest groups in areas which are already heavily regulated may have incentives to extend their strict (national) regulations to the European level, forcing foreign competitors to follow the same strict regulation with which they already comply. The result is that industry will lobby to erect barriers to entry. In addition, green NGOs could be pleased with this lobby and might support the demand to transfer strict national standards into a central standard.[73] Thus, industry in heavily regulated (and probably polluted) areas can (supported by green NGOs) force their very stringent emission limit values upon their (southern) competitors, although these states probably would not need these stringent environmental limit values if the policy goal were one of reaching uniform environmental quality.

This is precisely what happened in Europe in respect of the IPPC Directive. A strong lobbying exercise in favour of emission limit values at the community level was undertaken by German industry, inter alia.[74] They argued that industries in other Member States should bear the same costs which German producers already had to bear (as a result of strict domestic standards).[75] Thus it becomes clear that the 'harmonisation of conditions of competition' argument is used to serve the interests of industries in heavily regulated areas to erect barriers to entry. Their competitors operating in southern Member States with more lenient environmental standards

71 For a refined analysis distinguishing between norm-setting, implementation, and enforcement as far as the allocation of powers is concerned, see Van Zeben (2014).

72 See also Esty and Geradin (1997, at 303).

73 These 'alliances' between environmentalists and domestic producers are also discussed by Vogel (1995).

74 See Faure and Lefevere (1996, at 13).

75 Esty and Geradin (1997, at 307).

may indeed not have the possibility to comply with these more stringent environmental standards. The southern Member States therefore understandably lobbied in favour of harmonised ambient quality standards with domestic emission limit values.[76] Hence, environmental law can be used to limit market entry and environmental law is abused to serve private interest goals.

This European example shows that sometimes the decision on the optimal level of governance in environmental policy is not taken on the basis of economic criteria. Lobbying by interest groups may sometimes favour either the central or the decentral level, depending on where the interest group expects to have the most influence on the regulator. The example equally shows that lobbying will not always have to result in lower environmental standards. Interest groups in areas that are already heavily regulated may have incentives to extend their strict (national) regulations to the central level, forcing foreign competitors to follow the same strict regulation with which they already comply.

In the USA, President William J. Clinton signed an executive order that agencies should complete an analysis, akin to an EIA, of the impact of new policies on the existing US federal system.[77] Each agency should determine the benefits and costs of centralisation and of national uniformity.[78]

This leads to the conclusion that the 'harmonisation of conditions of competition' argument, as presented in European rhetoric, can be problematic, from both the economic and ecological points of view, and in fact serves the interests of industrial groups in heavily regulated areas.[79] It can actually be in their interests that 'conditions of competition' are harmonised.

## 13.6 SUMMARY AND CONCLUSION

This chapter is in many ways a chapter that reaches interesting abstractions on the nature of power, rights, and of constitutionalism, all in the interests of environmental law.

We began with a discussion on Tiebout, who argued that when people with the same preferences cluster together in communities, that competition between local authorities will, under certain restrictive conditions, lead to allocative efficiency. This implies a market in jurisdictions, that voters can move to choose locations with policies that reflect their own preferences; while this is valid in much of the

[76] Id.

[77] Livermore (2017, at 670). The reference is to Exec. Order No. 13.132, 64 Fed. Reg. 43,255 (4 August 1999). Livermore does note that many agencies have failed to undertake this effort. Id.

[78] Id.

[79] This is not to say that there is no risk of regulatory capture resulting in inefficient standards at the level of the Member States. Compare (in the US context) Rose-Ackerman (1992b, at 166, 173). However, in Europe, it is especially the non-transparent Brussels bureaucracy which is feared from a public choice perspective.

developed world, it often retain substantially high transaction costs as both physical relocation and the legal procedures of emigration and immigration are all rich in transaction costs. But we can test these ideas where those costs are lower, in the federal zones of the EU and of the USA.

Van den Bergh's counter-model forecasts a 'bottom-up federalisation', wherein the default assumption is that the best level of governance is at the most local level available, unless it is otherwise demonstrable that the particular environmental issue cannot be sufficiently resolved at that level of government, e.g. the more 'trans-boundary' an issue becomes, the higher the level of government it may take to properly address the issue, but the quest to determine the right level should begin at the lowest level and cease at the lowest functional answer.

Another point that we addressed is the issue of centralisation, of whether all actors should be required to comply with a singular jurisdiction-wide regulatory requirement to prevent an environmental problem (centralisation), or should they be allowed to individually discover their own most efficient method of preventing the environmental problem (decentralisation). By retaining governance at the lowest level possible, decentralisation is made more feasible and thus the cures to prevent environmental injuries would remain more efficient, if possible, to remain decentralised. But the correct level of governance and of centralisation will depend greatly on the particulars of each type of environmental threat or injury and cannot be readily generalised for a universal answer. Concerns of race to the bottom, race to the top, of managing the transaction costs of compliance, and of ensuring minimal levels of environmental protection were all discussed in turn.[80]

It is clear that the consequences of these decisions on setting environmental standards is substantial. Furthermore, the Law and Economics literature highlights the importance of not only formal harmonisation of legal rules where centralisation would be indicated, but also of the need to match that the enforcement of these centralised rules takes place at the local level as well.

Much of legal analysis, and often of economic analysis, assumes a simpler world of a single government per jurisdiction, but the real world is often structured with vertical separation of governance operations. The question of optimal federalism remains in theoretical development, but we have shown that early insights from the Law and Economics literature do provide useful guidance in how to coordinate legal rules for environmental protection across the various levels of governance.

80 This tension in environmental law, of race to the bottom or race to the top, has antecedents from other areas of law. Justice Brandeis is believed to have coined the phrase 'race to the bottom' in the corporate law case of *Louis K. Leggett Co.* v. *Lee* (288 US 517) (1933). However, the actual quote is somewhat different: 'Companies were early formed to provide charters for corporations in states where the cost was lowest and the laws least restrictive. The states joined in advertising their wares. The race was one not of diligence, but of laxity. Incorporation under such laws was possible, and the great industrial states yielded in order not to lose wholly the prospect of the revenue and the control incident to domestic incorporation' (Id., at 558–560, underscoring added).

# 14

# The Role of Environmental Law in Developing Countries

## 14.1 INTRODUCTION

For the final substantive chapter of this book we will pay attention to the role of environmental law in developing countries or, even more generally, to the relationship between economic development and environmental protection, as that of course precisely constitutes the core of sustainable development.

At first blush, one may (wrongly) think that economic development goes hand in hand with environmental pollution. It might even seem that there is some intuitive support for this line of thought. After all, where states are in a natural state without any industrial development, the threats to the natural environment are also limited. Yet pre-industrial societies do interact with nature and have impacts on sustainability. Herding tribes can hunt prey to extinction.[1] Irrigation brings both agriculture and the problems of salt and mineral deposits. Regional overpopulation and the resultant impacts on local ecologies have crashed more than a few pre-industrial communities. As we can see from many archaeological settings, acquiring sustainable technologies has long been a key challenge for civilisation across our human history.

However, there is a literature indicating that, under particular conditions, economic developments (measured in growth of GDP) can actually increase environmental quality.[2] That literature is of crucial importance, especially for developing countries, which would otherwise fear that investments in environmental protection might jeopardise their fights against poverty. This literature is known is the Environmental Kuznets Curve and will be discussed in Section 14.2.

Following the previous chapter on environmental federalism there is equally a literature devoted to the North–South divide, and more particularly to the question

[1] See the examples of the 'Tragedy of the Commons', and the potential remedies, in Section 3.1.

[2] For a summary of the literature, see Faure (2011).

whether states will necessarily compete with lower environmental standards. It relates to the race to the bottom and pollution haven hypothesis discussed earlier. There is an interesting counter hypothesis, powerfully developed by Michael Porter (and thus known as the Porter hypothesis) arguing that both countries and firms can in fact generate benefits by investing in environmental protection. There is increasing proof of a positive relationship between investments to comply with stringent environmental law, innovation, and profitability. That literature again constitutes an important lesson for developing countries as it shows that countries (and firms) could benefit from investing in environmental innovation (Section 14.3).

Finally, there is a fascinating Law and Economics literature that has paid attention to the question what type of environmental law and policy developing countries exactly need. They argue that fundamental conditions (such as a well-functioning administration with sufficient capacity and free of corruption) are often not fulfilled in developing countries. For that reason, this literature examines whether in developing countries other instruments should be employed for environmental policy than in the North. Also, that literature provides very interesting insights (Section 14.4).

Expanding on this topic by reference to a field-tested approach, we provide an example from public interest litigation in India to show how a particular instrument, litigation of private liability rules, to make public regulatory environmental policy more robust might seem odd from a theoretical perspective but may well match the particular institutional context of that specific country (Section 14.5). Section 14.6 summarises and concludes.

## 14.2 ENVIRONMENTAL KUZNETS CURVE

### 14.2.1 *Concept*

The idea of the Environmental Kuznets Curve (EKC) is named after the Nobel Prize winner Simon Kuznets, who wrote on the relationship between income inequality and income levels in a country.[3]

Since the 1980s, scholars have also applied this concept to environmental pollution, examining the empirical relationship between measures of environmental quality and national income.[4] This literature shows an inverted u-shaped relationship, meaning that in a first phase of economic development (at low income levels) increasing economic development led to increasing environmental degradation. However, there is a certain turning point (the top of the inverted u-curve) where income levels have increased to such a point that a demand for higher environmental quality emerges and where hence increased economic welfare leads to

[3] Kuznets (1955).

[4] See especially Grossman and Krueger (1993 and 1995).

increased environmental improvements. This work has especially become known through the World Bank, which referred to it in its World Development Report 1992. The normative lesson that was drawn from this literature was that developing countries would have an interest in fighting poverty and increasing income levels, since this would also lead to higher levels of environmental quality.

This vision has strongly been voiced by Beckerman, who was involved in drafting the World Development Report 1992.[5] Beckerman holds, 'it is fairly clear that the best way to improve the environment of the vast mass of the world's population is to enable them to maintain economic growth' and 'the strong correlation between incomes and the extent to which environmental protection measures are adopted demonstrates that, in the longer run, the surest way to improve your environment is to become rich'.[6]

### 14.2.2 *Explanation*

The EKC is at first glance surprising since the dominant view may be that more economic development (industrialisation) will automatically lead to more environmental pollution. The EKC shows that in the beginning of industrialisation and economic development, environmental damage may occur or increase, but that there is a point beyond which environmental pollution peaks and later increasing levels of income would lead to decreased levels of pollution and corresponding higher levels of environmental quality. There is empirical evidence in support of the EKC, but the difficulty is of course identifying the precise causality behind the relationship. Simply stating that increasing income levels in the end lead to less pollution is too simple. Strand presents five theoretical reasons why the EKC may work; why higher income levels in a country could lead to lower pollution levels:[7]

1. When incomes grow, there may be a tendency for a larger share of total demand to consist of services rather than manufactured goods. This could explain why environmental and resource burdens decrease as incomes grow.[8]
2. General technological process leads to greater efficiency in the use of energy and materials. This idea is also strongly related to the work of Michael Porter, holding that environmental improvement does not necessarily come at the expense of competitiveness. Porter showed that, to the contrary increased environmental performance will also lead to an

5 Beckerman (1992).
6 Id., at 491.
7 Strand (2002, at 6–8).
8 This recalls Engel's law, holding that as incomes rise the percentage budget on foodstuffs will decline even if more expensive foods are purchased, that expanding budgets enable purchases of goods beyond immediately necessities and that these income-based findings on environmental services reflect this earlier observation (Engel 1857).

increased competitiveness of nations and industries.[9] This has been known as the 'Porter hypothesis', showing that not only countries but also companies may benefit from investments in environmental protection since it could increase their competitiveness.[10]

3. The increase of income can also lead to changing preferences of the population; once the basic needs are satisfied the population may value a clean environment, especially since it wants to enjoy free time and recreate in a clean environment. In the words of Arrow et al., 'People spend proportionally more on environmental quality as their income raises'.[11]
4. With increasing economic development an educated population may pressure for democratic reform and democratic societies tend to be more environmentally friendly.
5. Given different levels of income between countries, increasing income may lead to an environmentally burdening production to move to low income countries. This environmental dumping to pollution havens may reduce pollution levels in the rich countries which are able to relocate polluting activities to lower income countries.[12]

### 14.2.3 *Policy Consequences*

Some argue that this EKC literature, indicating that after a turning point increasing income levels lead to higher environmental quality, gives at least some room for optimism in the sense that economic development is apparently accompanied by such technological progress that environmental degradation, at least for traditional environmental quality variables such as air and water quality can be successfully reduced.[13]

However, looking at the EKC literature in this simple way, one could be tempted to deduce from this literature the (simplistic and therefore wrong) conclusion that the best way for a nation to promote environmental protection would be to promote economic growth.[14] Empirical evidence after all shows that higher income levels go hand in hand with increased environmental protection.[15] In the words of Dasgupta et al., 'In developing countries, some policy-makers have interpreted such results as conveying a message about priorities: grow first, then clean up'.[16] Given those

9 Porter and Van der Linde (1995).
10 We discuss the Porter hypothesis further in Section 14.3.2.
11 Arrow et al. (1995, at 92).
12 On which more in Section 14.3.
13 Strand (2002, at 18).
14 This has been qualified by Ayres as 'false and pernicious nonsense' (Ayres 1995).
15 See also Esty and Porter (1998, 2001).
16 Dasgupta et al. (2002, at 147).

assumptions, one might reasonably conclude that regulatory instruments such as environmental law could only to a limited extent influence environmental quality, since this quality would to a large extent be dependent upon other factors, more particularly economic development and per capita income levels.

However, more refined empirical studies have shown that this conclusion would be too unbalanced, as environmental law itself plays a complex role in the EKC. Panayotou has shown that, as far as the case of ambient $SO_2$ levels are concerned, policies and institutions can significantly reduce environmental degradation at low income levels and speed up improvements at higher income levels.[17] Cole et al. have also shown that 'developed countries have "grown out of" some pollution problems', but 'this is by no means an automatic process. Pollution levels have fallen only in response to investment and policy initiatives'.[18] Also Arrow and his co-authors conclude that 'economic liberalisation and other policies that promote gross national product growth are not substitutes for environmental policy'. Indeed, 'economic growth is not a panacea for environmental quality',[19] since 'in most cases where emissions have declined with raising income, the reductions have been due to local institutional reforms such as environmental legislation and market-based incentives to reduce environmental impacts'.[20] Dasgupta et al. also show that the primary reason to make the EKC lower and flatter (and hence reach quicker the turning point towards decreasing pollution with raising income levels) is related to the primary role of environmental regulation. Richer countries have the capacity to regulate pollution more strictly, which is an important explanation for the EKC.[21]

Dan Esty and Michael Porter have empirically examined the hypothesis to what extent a nation's regulatory regime could influence environmental quality, beyond the effects of income levels as suggested by the EKC literature. The result of this powerful research, based on an examination of regulatory intensity and environmental quality in a great number of developed and developing countries, is that economic development and environmental protection go hand in hand with the improvement of a country's institutions and more particularly the environmental regulatory regime.[22] They find that not only the rigour and structure of environmental regulations have a particular impact on environmental performance, but also the enforcement; this result is similar to the point made earlier on Becker's and Stigler's findings on enforcement of environmental regulations and criminal environmental enforcements.[23] The empirical evidence suggests that a country can

[17] Panayotou (1997). See also de Bruyn (1997), who equally argues that environmental policy, fostered by international agreements, explains why $SO_2$ emissions curb downward at high income levels.

[18] Cole, Rayner, and Bates (1997, at 412).

[19] Arrow et al. (1995, at 93).

[20] Id., at 92.

[21] For the reasons see Dasgupta et al. (2002, at 152–153).

[22] See Esty and Porter (2005).

[23] Becker (1962) and Stigler (1970). See analysis in Section 10.4.

benefit environmentally not only from economic growth, but equally from developing the rule of law and strengthening its governance structures.[24]

Interestingly, Esty and Porter also found evidence that countries that adopted a stringent environmental regime relative to their income were able to speed up economic growth rather than retarding it.[25]

### 14.2.4 *Importance*

The policy results of the above lessons are (i) economic growth provides several mechanisms that enable superior environmental outcomes, and (ii) enhanced environmental rules and developments of effective regulatory institutions act to accelerate both economic and environmental benefits. Indeed, Esty and Porter empirically evidenced that strengthening the regulatory structure also encourages the promotion of environmental quality.[26] The evidence presented by Esty and Porter provides yet another confirmation of the so-called Porter hypothesis: countries that adopt stringent environmental regimes should not be afraid that such efforts would endanger their competitive position, since the evidence shows that this may speed up economic growth rather than retard it; to wit, to the contrary, it would likely be those states that do not adopt such environmental legal frameworks that could find themselves facing the competitive risk of slower economic development.

These studies also provide strong support for increasing effective regulatory capabilities in developing countries. The international community can play a valuable role in lowering and flattening the EKC by financing appropriate training, policy reforms, information gathering, and public environmental education.[27] Drafting effective environmental regulation for developing countries requires also that policymakers should pay enough attention to the legal, economic, political, and social situations in which environmental regulation must function.[28]

## 14.3 POLLUTION HAVENS AND THE PORTER HYPOTHESIS

### 14.3.1 *Race to the Bottom or Top?*

In the chapter concerning environmental federalism, the race-to-the-bottom argument in favour of centralisation of environmental standards was explained. The idea is that jurisdictions might engage in a race to the bottom to attract foreign investments. As a result of this, a type of prisoner's dilemma could arise, whereby countries

[24] Esty and Porter (2005, at 424).
[25] Id., at 425.
[26] This is also argued by Binder and Neumayer (2005).
[27] See Dasgupta et al. (2002, at 163–164).
[28] See Faure, Goodwin, and Weber (2010); see also McAllister, Van Rooij, and Kagan (2010).

would fail to enact or enforce effective legislation. Jurisdictions are thus supposed to compete against each other with lenient environmental legislation to attract industry.[29] The result would be an overall reduction of environmental quality below efficient levels. This would correspond with the traditional result from game theory that a prisoner's dilemma creates inefficiencies and reduced outcomes for all parties.

Subsequent work has shown that the race to the bottom is in fact not a necessary result.[30] Oates and Schwab showed that there are conditions under which local environmental regulation will provide the efficient level of pollution control, that if: (i) all of the citizens of a jurisdiction work in the polluting industry; (ii) each suffers equally from pollution; (iii) labour is fixed in the jurisdiction; (iv) capital is perfectly mobile but also competitively supplied; and, finally, (v) local governments choose the environmental policies that maximise the utility of the median voter, then local pollution taxes will be socially optimal.[31] However, this result is not robust with respect to variations in the underlying assumptions.

Local governments could pursue goals other than maximising aggregate utility and the alternative to the race to the bottom may be a race to the top, where local pollution regulations are too stringent. Such a race to the top could also lead to overregulation at local level, which could equally create inefficiencies.[32] David Vogel has argued that a race to the top could occur in environmental legislation as well. This would be the result of coalitions between environmental NGOs (favouring stringent environmental protection for ecological reasons) and industry groups in highly regulated countries (favouring stringent regulation to create barriers to entry).[33] Ogus argues that firms may benefit from being located in a jurisdiction with high standards since this may generate technological improvements and thus competitive advantages; that may also explain a race to the top.[34]

### 14.3.2 *Porter Hypothesis: Weak and Strong Versions*

The race-to-the-top argument of course fits into the Porter hypothesis. In contrast to the traditional economics paradigm that environmental regulation imposes an additional cost in firms and thus may damage firms' competitiveness in the market,[35] Porter basically argues in many publications that firms that move beyond environmental compliance will automatically not only make more investments in environmental protection but become more innovative generally.

29 See Revesz (1992).

30 Van Zeben provides a summary and review of literature finding that the concept discredited. See Van Zeben (2012, at 12–13).

31 Oates and Schwab (1988, at 333).

32 See Revesz (1997a, at 1337); Revesz (1997b, at 536–540).

33 See Vogel (1995; 2004).

34 Ogus (1999b) and see Van den Bergh, Faure, and Lefevere (1996, at 141–142).

35 Jaffe et al. (1995, at 133).

The innovations needed to reach higher environmental standards would, according to Porter, also provide other benefits to the firm. In particular, Porter and Van de Linder believe that regulation can exert substantial influence on firms' environmental innovation in at least six aspects.[36] Consequently, this further innovation would provide strategic gains to the firm, as a result of which those firms that strive for higher standards of environmental protection in the end would also be more profitable.[37] Porter has defended his hypothesis not only with respect to individual corporations, but also with respect to states. He holds that increased environmental performance will lead to increased competitiveness, of both nations and industries[38].

An overview of literature shows that the empirical evidence broadly supports the Porter hypothesis. Ambec et al. distinguish between a 'weak' and a 'strong' version of the Porter hypothesis. The weak version only indicates that properly designed environmental regulation may spur innovation.[39] The strong version implies a relationship between environmental regulation and the business performance of a firm.[40] The authors conclude that the evidence for the weak version of the Porter hypothesis (that stricter environmental regulation leads to more innovation) is fairly clear and well established.

When we look at the empirical evidence on the strong version of the Porter hypothesis (that stricter regulation enhances business performance) the record shows that while earlier studies found that environmental regulation has a direct negative effect on business performance,[41] more studies have found clear empirical support for the strong form of the Porter hypothesis.[42]

### 14.3.3 *Empirical Evidence of a Race to the Bottom*

The empirical evidence on the race to the bottom is inconclusive;[43] Jaffe et al. summarised the empirical literature as finding only that that the effects of environmental regulations are 'either small, statistically insignificant or not robust to tests of model specification'.[44] In their review, Jaffe et al. suggested that the stringency of environmental regulations might have some effect on new firms in their decision to

36 Porter and Van der Linde summarised these six aspects (Porter and Van der Linde 1995, at 99–100).

37 This has inter alia been defended in id., at 97–118. For a summary see Faure and Johnston (2009, at 205–274).

38 See Porter (1991).

39 Ambec et al. (2013, at 9).

40 Id.

41 Id.

42 Id., at 16.

43 For an overview of the early empirical evidence, see Engel (1997, at 315–350), who argues that the empirical evidence shows a race to the bottom, which is, however, denied by Revesz (1997b).

44 Jaffe et al. (1995, at 157–158).

locate for the first time,[45] but would not induce existing firms to relocate.[46] They pointed out that other criteria such as tax levels, public services, and the unionisation of the labour force have a much more significant impact on the location decision than environmental regulation. Many other studies have shown that pollution control costs are not major determinants of relocation and that there is little evidence of a pollution haven hypothesis.[47]

After all, if this pollution haven hypothesis were correct, one would have to see decreasing environmental quality in developing countries, whereas to the contrary, major urban areas in China, Brazil, and Mexico have all experienced significant improvements in air quality over periods of economic development.[48]

Many economists remained somewhat sceptical of the empirical finding that environmental regulations were not a major determinant of industrial location,[49] and more empirical work evidences an inverse relationship between the stringency of air quality regulations and the level of capital flows in pollution intensive industries.[50] The US Clean Air Act (CAA) distinguishes between relatively pristine 'attainment' areas and more heavily polluted non-attainment areas by imposing more stringent pollution standards on areas in non-attainment. Research found that even controlling for other observable factors that might influence capital movements, industrial plant growth is significantly higher in less stringently regulated attainment areas than in non-attainment areas.

Studies on industrial locations in the USA find an estimated cost to an area of being out of attainment with federal standards of between 0.7 and 1.3 new plants per year,[51] a large percentage loss given that the average county in the sample studied gets only 0.4 new plants per year.[52] List et al. have also examined the effects of air quality regulation on the destination choice of relocating plants. Also, that study shows that more stringent (air) pollution regulations play a critical role in the siting decision of relocating plants. Their results 'provide strong evidence that air quality regulations matter'.[53]

Levinson, however, argues that notwithstanding large differences between US states in hazardous waste disposal taxes, there has not been any pollution haven

45 See Esty and Geradin (1998, at 12–15).

46 For the importance of distinguishing first location decisions from relocation decision, see List, McHone, and Millimet (2003).

47 For a summary see Dasgupta et al. (2002, at 159–160).

48 Id., at 160–162.

49 For example, Xing and Kolstad (1995), argued that the laxity of environmental regulations in a host country is a significant determinant of foreign direct investment by the US chemical industry.

50 See Becker and Henderson (2000, at 379) and Greenstone (2002, at 1175).

51 These studies allow for the fact that attainment status is endogenous with respect to plant location decisions, and carefully compares places that are similar in all respects except attainment status.

52 List et al. (2003, at 948).

53 List, McHone, and Millimet (2003, at 658).

effect. He provides a variety of explanations, the most important one being that these state hazardous waste disposal taxes do not impose large employment losses on industries that generate waste.[54]

Other empirical work has tackled the problem of controlling a fuller range of variables (besides just environmental regulatory stringency) that affect firm locational choice.Millimet and List,[55] working with a more detailed dataset and again employing a propensity score matching estimator, found that even at the very local county level,[56] location-specific attributes such as unemployment levels and the overall level of manufacturing employment significantly impact the effect of environmental regulatory stringency. Millimet and List found that the cost of strict environmental regulations is lower both for counties with high unemployment, because they have relatively abundant, cheap labour, as well as for counties with a greater concentration of employment in manufacturing, because such counties generate agglomeration economies for manufacturing firms.

In sum, the new empirical literature on the race to the bottom has found that within the USA, environmental regulations have statistically significant, large effects on industrial location.[57] Further, these effects were either missed entirely or seriously underestimated in earlier studies.[58] However, it should be stressed that most of this empirical research focuses on competition between US states; the situation may be different in Europe where there is less evidence (at least as far as the old Member States are concerned) of a race to the bottom.

### 14.3.4 *Empirical Evidence of Races to the Top*

However, there is also evidence of races to the top, aiming at strengthening the international competitiveness of domestic firms. Some other (competing) states may mimic the strict regulatory standards and the reason is that jurisdictions which have developed strict standards can force foreign producers to meet their domestic standards, since otherwise market access may be denied.

The best evidence probably comes from California, which used the possibility to enact stricter emission standards than the other states (thus the phenomenon is now referred to as the California Effect), whereby other states subsequently followed the California example.[59] Many more examples of this 'California Effect' exist, which in

54 Levinson (2000).

55 Millimet and List (2004, at 239).

56 US county levels.

57 Levinson (2003, at 96).

58 Results of a meta-analysis of literally hundreds of studies by Jeppesen, List, and Folmer (2002, at 21), show that the odd earlier results showing that the locational decisions of polluting and non-polluting industries were similarly influenced by environmental regulations may have been due to the failure of earlier studies to control for variables such as factor composition and mobility and lobbying power.

59 See Vogel (2001, at 336).

fact leads to the opposite of a race to the bottom, being the imposition of strict environmental standards which are subsequently 'exported'.[60]

'California Effects' can in some cases also be found in the transatlantic relationship. These were basically situations whereby regulatory trade measures by the (then) EC led to a strengthening of domestic regulatory standards in the USA and Canada.[61] This once more shows that there is no straightforward answer on whether jurisdictions engage in a race for the bottom or rather a race for the top, since all depends on particular facts and circumstances.

Looking at the case of the EU, there also seems relatively little evidence that the traditional EU Member States were engaged in a race to the bottom. Some high standard countries in Europe were rather involved in a race to the top than in a race to the bottom.[62] The case of the IPPC Directive precisely proves that point:[63] Northern European countries were strongly in favour of imposing strict emission standards (based on best available technologies) with which their industry presumably already could comply at the European level in order to create a 'level playing field'. Less developed Member States such as Spain and Portugal were concerned over the potential costs to industry of having to use best available techniques as a result of the directive. The directive now clearly is to the advantage of industries in countries such as Germany, that already have strict facilities specific emission limits. They prevailed at the European level, leading to a harmonisation of European emission limit values. De facto, this forces the foreign competitors in the South to follow the same strict regulation with which the industry in the North already complied.[64]

This example shows that, as was indicated in the literature, a race to the top can equally lead to political policies overriding industrial and economic efficiencies.

## 14.4 OPTIMAL ENVIRONMENTAL REGULATION FOR DEVELOPING COUNTRIES

Law and Economics scholarship pays a lot of attention to the question of optimal rules for developing countries.[65] Schäfer formulated a few highly interesting observations concerning the choice between rules and standards for developing countries which may also have important implications for environmental law.[66] Schäfer's main claim is that a rule-based system may be preferable in developing countries,

60 Id.
61 See on this issue extensively, Princen (2002).
62 See Van den Bergh, Faure, and Lefevere (1996, at 141–142) and Faure (2001, at 272).
63 Council Directive (EC) 76/464 *Official Journal* 1976 L 129/23.
64 See Faure (2010).
65 See further Faure, Goodwin, and Weber (2010).
66 Schäfer (2006).

since the concentration of decision making at the centre of the state may be an economic answer to the lack of human capital.

Schäfer's claims concerning the superiority of rules versus standards for developing countries have received support as well from Kenneth Dam.[67] Dam shows that the claim of some scholars that the common law which relied rather on vague notions and a strong involvement of the judiciary is not necessarily superior to statutory law. Dam equally claims that rule of law ideas suggest that the independence of the judiciary, separation of powers, and strong regulation in particular areas are crucial to economic development.

### 14.4.1 *Lacking Administrative Capacity*

We will now review Law and Economics literature that has analysed sources of the poor quality of environmental legislation in developing countries and that has equally addressed some remedies.

A general problem is that environmental legislation that comes into being in developing countries (whether on the initiative of the particular developing country or initiated by international organisations) seems to take the local situation insufficiently into account, especially as far as the lacking administrative capacity is concerned.

Advanced environmental instruments, such as public participation, integration of environmental permits, decentralisation, and environmental impact assessment are, from a western theoretical model, undoubtedly effective and useful instruments for a solid environmental policy. However, in order to be effective these instruments presuppose the existence of a solid administrative structure that can guarantee the implementation of those more sophisticated instruments.

It is not only the lacking capacity that may be a problem in that respect. Many instruments, such as EIAs, but also the delegation of powers to the executive, are based on a model of cooperation with administrative authorities. This cooperation may work well in western models which assume that all public authorities cooperate in the execution and implementation of regulation in the public interest. There are of course limits to how well this works in various developed states, but there are many checks and balances which guarantee that civil servants and public authorities are accountable to the public at large.

However, in countries where corruption is an institutionalised system, legislation which relies heavily on a cooperation with (decentralised) public authorities (e.g. through a permit systems) runs a large risk of going off course. From this it follows that in addition to the lacking capacity, also the corruption problem can lead to a lacking implementation of environmental law in developing countries. It is more

67 Dam (2006).

particularly the combination of insufficient capacity and corruption problems that can be disastrous for the implementation of environmental law.

The examples provided above make clear that often environmental legislation in developing states was developed on the basis of Western examples, which has been demonstrated to have been ineffective in practice. The sources of this ineffectiveness have been studied at length.[68] Some have pointed at problems of enforcement and implementation. However, one lesson from the literature seems to be that more particularly where administrative capacity (or in economic terms, human capital) is lacking, a solution may be found at the normative level in a shift from standards towards rules.

It should therefore not be surprising about the ineffectiveness of environmental law in developing countries, especially when standard based Western environmental laws are copied by developing countries. Legal instruments that may work well in Western legal systems can work in those systems because some fundamental conditions (such as the absence of corruption and the presence of a solid administrative infrastructure) are present to guarantee the effectiveness of the particular legal instruments. If those basic conditions are not met ex ante, one can argue that the ineffectiveness of environmental law is already incorporated in the way in which the environmental legislation is written. In that light it is not so much the enforcement problems that are the source of the ineffectiveness, but it is rather the inadequate design of the legislation that contributes to the enforcement problem.

The analyses by Schäfer and Dam may suggest some solutions which seem equally relevant for the area of environmental law. The key of an alternative approach is of course that it should take into account the specific problems, requirements, shortcomings, but in some cases also strong points of the particular country in which the environmental instrument has to be implemented. Rather than imposing Western-type standard-based environmental laws that suppose that Western-style administrative institutions are available to guarantee an effective implementation of modern environmental instruments, we suggest it may be more suited to take into account the existing local administrative institutions and the particular environmental concerns of developing countries, and to shape both substantive and procedural environmental law taking into account these problems.

### 14.4.2 *Corruption*

When it appears that the effectiveness of environmental law is challenged from corruption problems, two theoretical solutions are possible.

The first and theoretically best solution is probably to fight the corruption problem in developing countries itself. Thereby one would hope that by remedying

[68] See for example for the case of China the interesting doctoral dissertation by Van Rooy (2006). See also Xu and Faure (2016).

the corruption an effective environmental law based on a Western model with an independent public authority that acts in the public interest could be put into place. This is the first-best and ideal solution and of course an ideal that should as such not be given up.[69] Many international organisations have spent much time and effort fighting the corruption within administrative structures in developing countries.[70] However, it may take a very long time before this first-best and ideal solution can be fully implemented. During the past thirty years, since the start of the development of environmental law in developing countries, there has not been an enormous amount of progress in that respect; of course, there are always a few positive exceptions.

An alternative, second-best, approach would therefore be to accept the existence of corruption problems and to attempt to create environmental laws that are less 'corruptible'. This is an approach that has generally been advanced as a solution to corruption problems by Ogus.[71] Ogus deals with the problems of corruption generally and not only with respect to developing countries or with respect to environmental problems. However, his findings are quite important for the development of environmental law in developing countries.

Starting point for Ogus is that the phenomenon of corruption will as such be difficult to remedy.[72] Therefore, he argues that an attempt could be made to develop legislation that is less sensitive to corruption problems. This is also precisely the motivation of the approach encouraged by Schäfer: the use of imprecise standards leaves ample space for discretionary decisions, creating possibilities for corruption.[73] Precise and per se rules could reduce the potential for opportunistic behaviour by bureaucrats.[74]

These general insights can also be applied to the domain of environmental law. Ogus provides the example of the difference between general norms, whereby the legislator leaves a large room of discretion to the executive and provides very precise rules in the legislation itself.[75] When there is a distrust with respect to the public authorities that would have to execute the legislation, because of corruption problems within those institutions, the optimal solution would probably not be to grant

69 Van den Heuvel (1982, at 121–136).

70 See Huther and Anwar (2001).

71 Ogus (2004c, at 229–246).

72 The result is that also in countries such as Indonesia programmes aiming at the redistribution of subsidised rice to poor households are likely to fail. Olken showed that on average 18 per cent of the rice disappeared, as a result of which the welfare losses from corruption were larger than the potential welfare gains from the redistributive intent of the programme (Olken 2006, at 853–870).

73 Legal English, particularly as received in the UK, contains two possible meanings for 'leave', one based in 'leave' as departure or left behind, and another based in Norman-French 'laissez' meaning to permit. While the intent here is the first, the second potential reading is equally viable.

74 Schäfer (2006, at 116–119).

75 See Ogus (2007).

executive powers to those public authorities. In the field of environmental law this can play a role as far as the standard-setting problem is concerned. When corruption problems exist, it can be feared that the standard that will be incorporated by ministerial actors would be set inefficiently low.[76] If one would wish to prevent this danger of suboptimal standard setting from the beginning, an obvious remedy may be to lay down relatively strict standards in the legislation itself (or in general rules) by which administrative authorities have to abide. Earlier, we already indicated that it may be important to create legislation that minimises the scope of discretion for administrative authorities, given limited administrative capacity.[77] This proposal can also be supported as a remedy to cope with corruption problems. Very precise and clear rules at the level of the legislator from which the public authorities cannot deviate seem to be a better remedy for corruption problems than using very vague and open norms that would precisely grant a large scope of discretion to public authorities.

From the same perspective one should, when corruption problems exist, also be careful with 'modern' environmental legal techniques, such as environmental agreements or so-called covenants, whereby governments and (groups of) enterprises make agreements with respect to the reduction of environmental pollution.[78] When it cannot be expected that in the drafting of these environmental agreements the public authorities will act in the public interest, but one to the contrary has a reasonable expectation of 'capture' by the involved industry of the authorities, it is not very likely that the use of these agreements will generate optimal outcomes.

The existence of potential corruption problems may also have an effect for the choice of environmental instruments. Instruments that have large financial interests at stake and that grant a large scope of discretion to corrupt civil servants should of course be avoided. Preference should be given to clear and precise rules in legislation from which individual civil servants cannot deviate.

From this perspective one should also point at the importance of a complementary role of liability rules. This means that following the conditions of a permit should in principle not have any justificative effect as far as liability is concerned; there should in other words certainly not be a so-called regulatory compliance

[76] In this respect we refer to a level which is lower than would be required when the operator would use the best available techniques not entailing excessive costs or other standards based on cost–benefit analysis.

[77] In developed countries, we can see similarly tight standards in criminal law settings when legislators seek to establish punitive measures that are stronger than what the legislators would expect judges to impose if left to broader guidance. A 'three strikes' rule or a 'high minimum' sentencing guideline are examples of this type of policy. Recall, however, that these types of sentencing guidelines are for the developed world usually considered as inefficient, as they do not allow enough flexibility for an appropriate adaptation of the penalty to the facts of the case and the perpetrator. See Section 10.5.

[78] See on these environmental agreements generally ELNI (1998) and Orts and Deketelaere (2002).

defence. This would have as effect that even if an operator received a very favourable permit as a result of corruption, there would still be the possibility for victims to hold the enterprise liable for the environmental damage caused. The literature has often held that liability rules can thus play an important complementary role to back up regulatory failure. Allowing private liability rules, independent of compliance with public regulation, can thus be an important instrument to prevent successful lobbying by industrial pressure groups with corrupt civil servants.

Of course, this supplementary role of liability rules can only be effective when citizens are capable of bringing their claim with an independent judiciary that has the possibility of condemning the liable enterprise to pay compensation to the victims. Given the fact that in some developing countries corruption problems not only exist with civil servants but also with the judiciary, one should in those circumstances not expect too much of a remedy from this supplementary role of liability rules.[79]

Finally, one could also doubt whether environmental taxation, the instrument most favoured by economists, is well suited in a context of corruption. If corrupt civil servants would be the ones that fix the tax and subsequently collect it as well, one has to fear that taxation will amount to nothing else than a financing of the civil servant. Even though that may have some incentive effects as well, it is to be feared that the well-known environmental taxes will in those circumstances not lead to optimal results and may even be counterproductive.[80]

In a legal system where it is not possible to rely on independent civil servants working in the public interest, it may therefore be more suited still to use the traditional CAC instrument of environmental law instead of using environmental taxes that may be much more sensitive to corruption problems.

[79] A potential work-around, however odd it might be to suggest it, would be to take a Coasean-type approach to better facilitate negotiations as if mediated through corruption, by enabling the weaker party to symmetrically respond to the effects of corrupt communication. This recognises that corruption is an effort to overcome certain transaction costs of policy formation by spending resources to bypass the 'agreed to' procedural rules of a given community. As Dan Farber once somewhat seriously yet humorously commented, if bureaucrats or operator executives needed to reside in the zones affected by their decisions or activities, it would likely improve the overall environmental quality of the impacted area: 'According to economists, firms have little reason to take into account the cost of externalities – that is to say, the harms their activities may impose on others. The traditional solutions are damage remedies or taxes to transfer the financial cost to the industry, or regulation to force industries to limit their harmful activities. Why not try a more direct solution? Why not require owners and managers to expose themselves to the same risks?' (Farber 2015).

[80] However, as seen in Japanese and Korean environmental law, fees for environmental damages are established by the environmental ministries but certain procedural enforcement rules are carried out by the tax authorities; e.g. when an environmental fee is not timely paid. This separation of policy development and judgment, versus the subsequent enforcement activities, may alleviate some of the concerns herein.

### 14.4.3 *Environmental Federalism in Developing Countries*

The previous analysis clearly also has consequences for the important question whether environmental standards should be developed at a central or rather at a decentralised level.

First, building upon Schäfer's distinction between rules and standards, it can be stressed that rules allow for the concentration of human capital precisely in cases where, as in developing countries, human capital is much lower than in developed countries.[81]

Second, building upon what was mentioned in the previous section, one can easily argue that a level of decision making has to be chosen where it is most likely that standards will be set in the public interest. Of course, it is impossible to argue in a general way whether this will be the case at the central or at the decentralised level. Corruption is indeed possible at all levels of government.

However, as far as the specific area of creating environmental standards is concerned, one could argue that it may be more likely that environmental standards will be created in the public interest after a reasonably transparent decision-making process when this takes place at the central level, far away from lobbying efforts by local lobby groups. A well-known problem with decentralisation to for instance local governments is that these can be very sensitive to lobbying more particularly industrial interest groups. The latter can point at the socio-economic interests represented by the particular industry for the local community. Local governments are sometimes too strongly influenced by the financially strong local industry.[82] This will make it quite difficult for (sometimes corrupt) local governments to set environmental standards in the public interest.[83]

If this were a generalised fear it might be justified to centralise rather than to decentralise competences for environmental standard setting. This runs counter to the tendency in some developing countries, again such as Indonesia, where also, as a result of support by international organisations, governments have increasingly moved to decentralisation.[84]

However, one has to stress again that in this respect no generalisations can be made. In every particular case it will have to be examined at which level in that particular legal system it can be expected that environmental standards will be set in the public interest. It is indeed well possible that in specific cases the reverse may be

[81] Schäfer (2006, at 116–119).

[82] Van Rooy formulated this as follows with respect to the situation in China: 'Most of the studies looking at the external context find fault with the decentralized environmental governance structure that has enabled local governments to choose short-term economic concerns over pollution control' (Van Rooy 2006, at 112).

[83] In the literature especially Dan Esty warned for that reason for public choice distortions at state level and argued therefore in favour of standard setting at the centralised federal level. See Esty (1996, at 597–598) and see Esty and Geradin (1998, at 32).

[84] See Niessen (2006, at 143–181).

true. That may be the case where local governments are able to set efficient environmental standards after a balanced and transparent decision-making process, whereas to the contrary at central level well-organised industrial lobby groups will be capable of obtaining inefficient environmental standards from corrupt politicians.

In sum, depending upon the amount of corruption at the different levels of government and the influence of industrial lobbying, a decision concerning the optimal level of standard setting will have to be made. Moving the decision-making competencies to the central level does only make sense if the corruption risk is lower at central level and/or if a transparent decision making at central level can better guarantee that environmental standards will be set in the public interest.

### 14.4.4 *Indicators*

The previous analysis leads to a few remarkable conclusions. It seems that when the particular situation of some developing countries and more particularly the lack of human capital and corruption problems are taken into account, different suggestions are formulated for an optimal environmental policy than what is suggested by traditional literature with respect to optimal instrument design in environmental policy.

That literature advises policymakers to use flexible market-oriented instruments and to use more consensualism, for instance via environmental agreements.[85] An adaptation of environmental standards to location-specific circumstances, to be implemented by a strong decentralised authority, is often considered to be optimal policy design.[86] However, this literature which is mostly created by Western scholars interested in environmental policy (lawyers, economists, and other social scientists), always formulates these suggestions on the basis of a few assumptions, such as the presence of an effective administrative authority acting in the public interest and the absence of corruption. In developing countries these conditions are, as discussed above, often not fulfilled.

This does not mean that corruption problems or a lacking administrative capacity should simply be accepted as a fact of life. Of course, valuable attempts to remedy these problems should be made. However, we argue that as long as these problems have not been fundamentally tackled it would be naïve to introduce environmental legal instruments that simply overlook the functional difference that may in fact require alternative local legal mechanisms. Although remedies against those problems will remain important, as long as these problems continue to exist it seems wiser to develop environmental laws that take into account those problems instead of simply assuming that the law will, via an unknown mechanism, be able to remedy them.

85 See inter alia ELNI (1998) and Orts and Deketelaere (2002).
86 For an excellent summary of this literature, see Gunningham and Grabosky (1998).

This approach leads to a few policy conclusions which seem contrary to the suggestions made in Western legal doctrine as far as the development of a modern, flexible, and market-oriented environmental law is concerned.[87] One consequence is that approaches based on consensualism seem dangerous because they are very sensitive to corruption problems. Also, the introduction of market-oriented instruments such as tradable emission rights and environmental taxes may be less suited for particular developing countries, since these instruments presuppose the existence of a strong administrative infrastructure (tradable emission rights) or because they may be quite sensitive to corruption problems (environmental taxes). Also, the traditional policy advice of flexibility and adaptation of standards to location-specific circumstances via a decentralised standard setting seems less adapted to the situation of developing countries, both from the perspective of a lacking administrative capacity as well as from the perspective of corruption.

The message seems to be that if one takes into account these problems, the legislator should create clear and strict norms either in the environmental statute itself or via general rules. In any event the scope of discretion for administrative authorities should be as limited as possible. This will make the environmental standard setting less sensitive to corruption problems and will also avoid instruments that rely heavily on administrative capacity when the resources are lacking.

## 14.5 EXAMPLE: INDIA

India has made considerable strides in environmental protection in recent years, and the responsibility for this improvement is generally attributed to its Supreme Court.[88] For example, the Supreme Court introduced the concept of the polluter pays principle into Indian law and has also actively encouraged public interest litigation by extending the rules of locus standi.[89] The Court is thus a particularly interesting player in environmental regulation.

Over the course of the 1980s, the Court began to show a real interest in environmental matters and has since become extremely active in forcing the clean-up of India's environment.[90] By encouraging public interest litigation in the area of pollution, the Court has ordered the cleaning of the Ganges River and has required the entire bus fleet in Delhi to convert to liquefied natural gas in an attempt to

[87] However, some have also been critical of so-called market-based instruments as they are used in modern environmental policy, arguing that it may undermine environmental morality. See Frey (1997) and Frey (1999, at 395–417).

[88] Lokur (2006); see also Dias (1994, at 245–262, noting that judicial activism has filled a lot of gaps in Indian environmental law); Raja and Rathinam (2005a, 2005b, and 2006).

[89] See *Indian Council for Enviro-legal Action & Ors* v. *Union of India*, (1996) 3 S.C.C. 212 (India); see also Lokur (2006, at 17, discussing the Indian Supreme Court's intervention on air pollution); Sathe (2001, at 70–72).

[90] See Mehta (2006, at 142, arguing that despite the Indian Supreme Court's effort, the executive branch fails to enforce existing environmental laws).

improve the notoriously poor air quality in the capital.[91] In taking on such an active role of environmental protector, the Indian Supreme Court has effectively moved from adjudication to administration and the distribution of resources, tasks usually reserved to the executive.[92]

Unsurprisingly, this usurpation of power by the courts in the cause of a cleaner environment has not gone without criticism.[93] On one level, there is scepticism about the effectiveness of the Court's activist approach and environmental public interest litigation as developed by the Court. The interventions of the Supreme Court can arguably be seen as a second-best solution, given the inadequacy of the legislature and the executive in securing the effective implementation of environmental law in India.[94]

Some have argued, however, that the interventions of the Supreme Court have inhibited the development of a responsible and independent bureaucracy.[95] If this is the case, notwithstanding the good intentions of the Court, the overall impact has been negative, since the Court's activism has only created ad hoc, temporary solutions instead of acting to reinforce the actions of a consistent administration.[96] There is indeed reason for pessimism as to the general efficacy of the environmental public interest litigation as developed by the Indian Supreme Court: the impact of environmental pollution on public health in India is still dramatic,[97] and India scores poorly in environmental performance indicators when compared with other middle-income developing countries such as Brazil.[98]

Perhaps, as Rajamani suggests, the Court's actions should be viewed as 'chemotherapy for the carcinogenic body politic',[99] where a sustainable and long-term solution to environmental degradation nonetheless requires action by the

91 See Rajamani (2007, at 315–316): 'The phenomenon of endless judicial oversight in public interest cases leads one to query whether the judiciary is merely substituting judicial governance for executive governance in areas flagged for its attention by pubic interest litigants.'). The exercise of public interest environmental jurisdiction also raises concerns with respect to access, participation, effectiveness, and sustainability, as well as the danger of judicial excessiveness or over-activism. Id., at 318. Another case in which the Supreme Court took the lead is assessed in Perez (2002). The article concerns the struggle to prevent the construction of a national port in a small fishing village at the Dahanu region north of Bombay. As the port was likely to have a negative effect on particular environmental conditions, the Court developed a very innovative institutional structure to monitor the 'ecologically fragile' Dahanu region. Id., at 12. However, the author points out that several studies have found high levels of non-compliance with India's judicial orders. Id., at 24.

92 Divan and Rosencranz (2002, at 21).

93 Id., at 21.

94 See Dam (2004, at 601–605).

95 See Rajamani (2007, at 315).

96 See Cha (2005, at 227).

97 Rajamani (2007, at 312).

98 See, e.g. Esty and Porter (2005, at 397–399, comparing India's high urban particulate concentration per city population vis-à-vis developed nations).

99 See Rajamani (2007, at 295, quoting Baxi [2002, at xvi]).

administrative authorities, who possess better information than Supreme Court justices on how to set effective environmental standards.[100]

Yet India remains interesting because it demonstrates how some degree of success can be achieved in the short term by playing to the relative strength of a country's institutions. In India, where the legislative and the executive branches were unable to set or enforce environmental standards in an effective manner, innovative lawyers used liability rules and broad legal standing, in conjunction with a strong and independent judiciary, to achieve remarkable results.

This flexibility of approach underlies our main argument. Whereas Law and Economics provides that administrative law is best suited for the setting of environmental standards, given the superior ability of agencies to weigh costs and benefits in the public interest and the lack of expertise and information of judges in determining an optimal environmental solution, the inability of the legislative and executive level to act in such an optimal manner required a 'second-best' alternative. Instead of simply lamenting the lack of action on the part of the administration, environmental lawyers persuaded the judiciary of the need for courts to act in the public interest and provided them with the information to make decisions. While this approach is not ideal, as the criticisms clearly show, it has provided some measure of environmental protection where none could be expected from other branches of government.

The success of environmental public interest litigation in India also corresponds with the indicators that we sketched earlier.

First, the judicial activism was a response by the Indian judiciary to calls from concerned citizens within India; it answered a need identified by Indians, using a method that relied upon the system of legal norms in place.

Second, while independently opting for the path of judicial activism, the Indian Supreme Court adopted certain legal transplants from the common law (such as extending locus standi), but the transplant was guided by local needs and knowledge. Its success was predicated upon a strong and independent judiciary being in place. Although standards would ideally have been set at the level of the legislature, the problems of capacity and capture at the level of the executive determined that the judiciary was, given the specific context of India, the institution best able to provide environmental protection.

The main actor concerned – the Supreme Court – is a centralised body far removed from the localities. This centralisation of policy making corresponds with the suggestion that decisions be made at the level of governance where capacity is strongest and where actors are most independent, in this case, the central level of the judiciary.

[100] Note that meanwhile the situation in India has somewhat changed as from 2011 a National Green Tribunal (NGT) has been created. For details see Paloniitty and Eliantonio (2018, 109–110).

## 14.6 SUMMARY AND CONCLUSION

Perhaps what is most important from this chapter is the conclusion, from empirical data, that economic development is not an adversary of environmental protection, but rather that the two appear to be mutually reinforcing in many cases. Furthermore, there is no fundamental theoretical reason from a law and economics perspective that economic growth and environmental protections need be adversarial, especially if the lessons of Pigou, Coase, and Calabresi are well respected along the way.

Since its suggestion in the early 1990s, Environmental Kuznets Curve (EKC) supposition holds that beyond an early stage of economic development, that increasing levels of per capita income will be associated with improving environmental qualities or services – that economic development favours environmental protection. There are various assumptions of why this empirical relationship is found: (i) wealthier citizens are better educated and seek better environmental conditions, (ii) wealthier citizens seek to consume higher quality environmental services, (iii) higher level economies shift towards increasing proportions of service based economies, which are lighter on environmental impacts, or (iv) the Porter hypothesis, that greener technologies are actually more efficient in a capitalist sense and thus higher per capita income should be associated with greener economies. Another alternative is that as per capita incomes rise, countries seek to outsource their dirtier components to other countries. It is not yet clear why the EKC works, but evidence appears to hold that it does.

Perhaps it is the simplest of all economic arguments, that as a country expands its economic frontiers, and as less of its income is trapped in Engel's income, more Pareto improvements will include a variety of welfare improvements, and environmental protection is generally such a welfare improvement; that is, when people can afford a choice, they are likely to prefer a cleaner environment. Thus modes of economic growth that enable such choices will result in such improvements.

The strong version of the Porter hypothesis, that green economies are competitive economies, implies that a race to the top might actually take place globally; that in order to become more efficient at economic growth, policymakers will choose policies to make their nations comparatively advantaged in green industries. We discussed the empirical findings that supported this outcome. We also discussed the econometric studies to determine if the reverse were true – are there countries experiencing a race to the bottom to offer competitive costs to attract foreign investment; we found that the literature had not found strong evidence of such a race to the bottom.

We discussed the role of rules and of standards for developing economies trying to protect their environments. We noted that there were debates on whether either were more robust for developing economies. The preponderance of the scholastic discussions appears to support the establishment of 'clear and strict norms' over flexible or market-based methods, given the higher transaction costs facing their legal institutions and to resist the challenges of lobby capture.

In conclusion, the literature of Law and Economics supports the idea that economic growth is likely to coincide with improvements in the protection of the environment as per capita incomes grow. Porter has further demonstrated, based on his models and supported by empirical studies, that the creation of rules to protect the environment is likely to result in the overall economy becoming more competitive. Whether it is the chicken or the egg, the literature sees both economic growth and environmental protection as complements.

# 15

# Epilogue

## 15.1 OUR MOTIVES

One of our motivations to write this book was to show the importance and usefulness of the Law and Economics approach to environmental issues.

For us, applying Law and Economics to environmental issues may be self-evident, but we noticed scepticism from colleagues and friends, during casual conversations, who in fact held a wrong conception of Law and Economics as if it would only be interested in the business-oriented side of law, equally assuming that economic concepts, such as efficiency and welfare maximisation would be irreconcilable with environmental protection. To them, the worlds of environmental protection and Law and Economics seemed like two worlds apart.

To some extent these opinions were the result of lacking information or misconceptions concerning the actual focus of Law and Economics. For example, there is no preconceived political neo-liberal agenda behind the economic approach to law.

With this book we wanted to explain the mysterious world of Law and Economics to the environmental community, showing that Law and Economics is an academic methodology which has no preconceived political agenda. It consists of applying the rich world of microeconomics and its concepts and methodology to many world problems, including the environment.

The idea that Law and Economics would only apply to economic or business law may have been true before Ronald Coase wrote his famous 'problem of social cost' article in 1960. In that distant past, economists were indeed mostly interested in the more economic aspects of law, such as market regulation or competition policy. But since the revolution brought by Coase, the new Law and Economics was created, as well as a revolution in institutional economics, expanding the domain of economic analysis potentially to all domains of the law, including environmental issues.

## 15.2 AN EFFECTIVE METHODOLOGY FOR ENVIRONMENTAL LAW RESEARCH

The major part of this book consisted in applying the well-known areas of Law and Economics analysis related to torts, regulation, crime, and federalism to the area of environmental law. Even though environmental problems pose very specific problems and challenges, we hope to have shown that the methods of Law and Economics are useful tools to explain the way in which environmental law and policy is built up and functions.

Law and Economics has enabled us to shed a better light on the wide variety of different legal and policy instruments that can be found in the real world, and the way in which these instruments function. And, as noted by Hsu, the notions of efficiency in economic models has great overlap with the notions of fairness in law.[1]

We do not claim that Law and Economics is the only or exclusively suitable methodology for explaining environmental law and policy. A lot of valuable information can undoubtedly also be found in other literatures belonging to the adjacent domains of environmental economics,[2] and environmental governance,[3] amongst many other literatures.

However, one important feature of the environmental Law and Economics methodology is that it assumes, as a starting point, that legal rules and instruments affect the behaviour of stakeholders confronted with environmental problems (traditionally qualified as either polluters, victims of various third parties); that legal rules will lead to behavioural changes; and that those reactions can be studied within the frameworks of game theory and microeconomics to better ensure that policy goals are efficiently achieved. At its core, environmental Law and Economics is a research programme to enable the broadest achievement of environmental and other welfare enhancing policy goals by making the most efficient use of the available political and capital resources.

That legal rules affect behaviour, and can thus be employed to reach particular policy goals, may be more debated by lawyers when it is applied to more traditional fields, such as traffic or medical liability. Some doubt that the behaviour of a car driver could be influenced by the applicable liability regime. However, this scepticism is less prevalent in the domain of environmental Law and Economics, as most of the legal rules in this domain affect commercial enterprises for which it is easier to accept the assumption that changes in a legal regime, with economic impacts, may affect their behaviour.

1 Hsu (2004, at 345–346).
2 See inter alia Endres (2010).
3 See inter alia Abbot (2009); Breton et al. (2009); Winter (2006); and Wurzel, Zito, and Jordan (2013).

## 15.3 LEGAL MODELS AND POLICY VERIFICATION

One major advantage of the Law and Economics method generally is that it allows verification of whether particular instruments used by the policymaker (be it a legislator or the judiciary) could actually achieve the goals desired by the policymaker.[4]

In the environmental area one of the most important questions for the policymaker is undoubtedly 'what works?' In other words, can we verify to what extent a particular legal or policy instrument also reaches the goals desired by the policymaker? That is of course to an important extent an empirical question. That constitutes yet another important change in Law and Economics compared to the way in which the methodology was originally developed forty to fifty years ago. Whereas Law and Economics traditionally was merely theoretical and strongly based on assumptions on how individuals and enterprises would react to different legal settings, the 'empirical revolution' now provides a wealth of information to the policymaker concerning the degree to which the instruments implemented did indeed have the desired effects, or perhaps other unintended effects. Again, the insights gained from empirical and experimental Law and Economics are still young, but the development in the domain is in full evolution and can lead to valuable insights for policymakers.

The buzzword nowadays is indeed often that policy making should be 'evidence-based'. That of course necessitates an idea of how particular legal and policy instruments work out in specific contexts in practice. It is only from the successes or failures of particular policy measures (including experiments) that the policymaker can learn and obtain information, enabling an improvement of policy making.

## 15.4 SUSTAINABLE DEVELOPMENT

The idea that economic thinking and environmental protection can be reconciled is also at the core of the concept of sustainable development, one of the leading principles of environmental policy.[5]

The entire goal of the search for optimal instruments of environmental policy, central to this book, was precisely to show that economic development can take place with respect for the environment on the condition that environmental law and policy are designed in a smart way. There is, as we showed in the last chapter, also an important lesson for developing countries: economic growth should not necessarily lead to more environmental pollution, nor should environmental protection retard

4 Hsu (2004, at 350–352), with particular reference to the mathematical character of economic, and thus of Law and Economic, models.

5 See Section 5.2.

economic growth, and policymakers should be aware that there is a strong alternative to this binary choice paradigm.

But a crucial condition for this sustainable development to succeed is that an appropriate institutional environment be created in which legal and policy instruments can be developed and enforced, aiming precisely at the internalisation of negative externalities related to environmental pollution.

## 15.5 AN EVOLVING METHODOLOGY

Law and Economics has changed. The models are no longer those developed forty to fifty years ago, based on the rational choice theory and largely theoretical. Insights from cognitive psychology and from empirical studies have allowed a further refinement of the Law and Economics method, immensely increasing the practical value of the methodology.

Even though the traditional starting point for the Law and Economics approach was and still is the so-called rational choice theory, as it was used to develop the initial models in the 1970s and 1980s, the methodology of law and economics Law and Economics has also developed in a dynamic manner. As a result of the insights from cognitive psychology, the domain of behavioural Law and Economics developed, implying that the insights from behavioural studies have equally been incorporated into traditional Law and Economics.

We demonstrated that for the environmental arena, the insights from behavioural Law and Economics may have interesting consequences. For example, when it comes to choosing appropriate instruments, behavioural research has warned that some of the so-called market-based instruments (such as emission trading or environmental taxes) that were traditionally favoured by environmental economists, may have as a negative side effect that environmental protection would be reduced to merely paying a price (for an emission allowance or tax), thus potentially negatively affecting environmental morale. To some extent the insights from those behavioural studies are promising and interesting, but it may be too early to relate strong policy recommendations on these insights, for example as far as the choice between different instruments is concerned. However, behavioural Law and Economics does generate new insights on a daily basis and it therefore remains important to keep a close eye on those developments as they may also have an important bearing on environmental law and policy.

## 15.6 AN EVOLVING 'LAW OF THE ENVIRONMENT'

Law and Economics has changed, but undoubtedly the case for environmental law and policy has also changed. By and large, environmental law was (of course with country-specific differences) created in the same decades when Law and Economics emerged. In that period, the legal instruments of environmental policy were largely limited to instruments of an administrative nature. Permitting, and introducing specific conditions in the permits, may have been the most important policy tool. Most of environmental law was administrative law – public law backed up with criminal sanctions and supplemented to a limited extent with liability rules; although there were substantial hurdles for pollution victims in private enforcement. Environmental law was also clearly the business of the government. The government rather one-sidedly made rules imposing those largely as a straitjacket upon industry.

Because, inter alia, that model of governance did not always lead to the desired environmental results, many changes in environmental law have occurred.

Even though many legal systems still rely on permitting, some countries have replaced permits with more general rules and, more importantly, other instruments have been introduced, qualified as 'incentive' or 'market-based'. Pigouvian taxes or Dales' ideas concerning emission trading were probably considered as wild ideas by economists and not ripe for implementation, but since then, increasingly a variety of market-based instruments have been introduced at many policy levels with the aim of achieving better environmental protection at lower costs. Market-based instruments shift responsibility to attain particular environmental goals to industrial operators.

In some cases, this has gone a step further, introducing self- or private regulation as well as hybrid forms of co-regulation or conditioned self-regulation (whereby the government creates the conditions for self-regulation to emerge). Those tendencies fit into the context of responsive regulation,[6] whereby environmental law-making is no longer (only) seen as the business of government, but where stakeholders (industry, but also others such as environmental NGOs) are included in a cooperative process. The fundamental idea behind this change in policy perspective is that including stakeholders in the decision making (co-regulation) and instruments (incentive-based) may lead to a higher 'responsibility-isation' of the actors involved to reach particular environmental policy goals, thus potentially leading to better compliance.

## 15.7 EVOLUTION IN ENVIRONMENTAL POLICIES

Also, in that respect developments at policy level are still in full evolution. The policy changes are to an important extent also related to the changes in the nature of the environmental problems.

Whereas the major worry in the early environmental law mostly concerned so-called point source pollution, coming from particular well-identified industrial sites, more modern environmental problems such as desertification, deforestation, pollution of the oceans, environmental disturbance caused by nanoparticles of genetically

[6] Ayres and Braithwaite (1992).

modified organisms, and certainly climate change may be of a totally different nature. Many of those problems are by nature transboundary and do not always allow a clear identification of a causal chain between emissions by particular operators and specific environmental consequences. Those new problems have led to the introduction of new instruments.

Policymakers equally realise that there is not one single legal or policy instrument that may be suited to dealing with all pollution problems. Given the inherent benefits but also weaknesses in each of the different instruments, policymakers now search for an optimal combination of a variety of instruments, which (given the nature of the specific pollution problem) may in combination tackle that problem in an optimal manner. The question therefore arises how these so-called smart instrument mixes can be found.

Another challenge is the rise of austerity budgets, limiting the funding of environmental authorities to achieve their environmental goals;[7] here too, we see a role for environmental Law and Economics to assist in delivering on those environmental goals against those tighter budgets.

## 15.8 CONCLUSION

The goal of this book was to show the importance and usefulness of Law and Economics as a methodology to better understand environmental law and policy. Its literature has developed into a very appendant and rich domain with lots of developments and evolutions, both at the theoretical as well as at the empirical level. We hope, in alignment with Hsu, that a result of sharing this approach to environmental law 'can refocus environmental law on the environment'.[8]

Our main goal was to share the lessons learned from Law and Economics in application to environmental policy. The concept of a handbook does not allow an in-depth discussion of all of the nuances and most developments. In some cases, important aspects could only be touched upon without developing those issues in full detail. Readers interested in further exploring particular areas can consult the detailed list of references as a source of further reading.

Environmental law and modern Law and Economics have one feature in common: both are featured by integration. Environmental law is no longer limited (as it probably was at the origin) to administrative law. Environmental law now consists of a portfolio of public law, various private law domains (liability rules, contract law, property law), and also criminal law, tax law, and even human rights law. All of those different legal domains were, each with their own particular features, brought together to improve environmental quality.

7 Salzman, Ruhl, and Nash (2015, at 490).
8 Hsu (2004, at 308).

The same type of integration equally features in Law and Economics. Environmental Law and Economics is no longer just an application of microeconomic concepts to environmental issues. Yes, environmental Law and Economics integrates insights from environmental economics, but also insights from political science, public choice, cognitive psychology, and environmental governance literature. Given the complex nature of environmental problems, such an eclectic, holistic, or integrated approach is necessary to better understand environmental problems in all of their complexities.

Even though a substantial part of this book deals with positive analysis, using economic methods to explain and understand existing legal and policy instruments, the methodology also has important normative policy consequences.

Precisely because Law and Economics has become more empirical and 'evidence-based', it also can provide important policy advice to the legislator and the judiciary. Traditionally, lawyers may have opposed a normative use of economic concepts, arguing that economic analysis is based on a notion of efficiency which is a '*Fremdkörper*' for legal analysis.

To an important extent, the lessons provided in this book do not necessarily rely on any specific interpretation of concepts such as efficiency or welfare maximisation. It rather focuses on the positive question of which instruments may actually affect the behaviour of stakeholders in solving specific environmental problems.

The answer to that question undoubtedly has very important consequences. Moreover, environmental Law and Economics, to an important extent, goes beyond efficiency by equally addressing, for example, issues of distribution and environmental justice. The toolkit provided by Law and Economics also allows, for example, analysis of whether particular especially vulnerable groups would be more negatively affected by a specific policy measure (such as building a dam) than others.

In sum, with this book we hope to have shown that Law and Economics has over the past fifty years developed a rich methodology, allowing analysis of environmental law and policy and enabling robust policy advice, based not only upon theoretical predictions, but equally on empirical studies.

We do realise that environmental issues are so complex that we may not have been able to deal with all issues in full depth. Our book is therefore rather an invitation to further explore the rich Law and Economics literature and to apply it also to new and yet undiscovered issues in environmental policy.

# References


Aalders, M., 'Self-Regulation and Compliance with Environmental Law from a Global Perspective', in Niessen, N. & Bedner, A. (eds.), *Towards Integrated Environmental Law in Indonesia*, Leiden, CNWS, 2003, pp. 21–36.

Aalders, M. & Wilthagen, T., 'Moving beyond Command and Control: Reflexivity in the Regulation of Occupational Safety and Health and the Environment', *Law & Policy*, 1997, Vol. 19(4), pp. 415–443.

Abbot, C., *Enforcing Pollution Control Regulation: Strengthening Sanctions and Improving Deterrence*, Oxford, Hart, 2009.

Abelson, P., *Cost Benefit Analysis and Environmental Problems*, Farnborough, Saxon House, 1979.

Abraham, K., 'Environmental Liability and the Limits of Insurance', *Columbia Law Review*, 1988, Vol. 88(5), pp. 942–988.

Abraham, K. S., 'The Relation between Civil Liability and Environmental Regulation: An Analytical Overview', *Washburn Law Journal*, 2002, Vol. 41, pp. 379–398.

Ackerman, B. & Stewart, R. B., 'Reforming Environmental Law: The Democratic Case for Market Incentives', *Columbia Journal of Environmental Law*, 1988, Vol. 13, pp. 171–199.

Ackerman, B. A., Rose-Ackerman, S., Sawyer, J., & Henderson, D., *The Uncertain Search for Environmental Quality*, New York, Free Press, 1974.

Ackerman, F. & Heinzerling, L., *Priceless: On Knowing the Price of Everything and the Value of Nothing*, New Press, 2000.

Adams, M., 'New Activities and the Efficient Liability Rules', in Faure, M. & Van den Bergh, R. (eds.), *Essays in Law and Economics: Corporations, Accident Prevention and Compensation for Losses*, Antwerp, Maklu, 1989, pp. 103–106.

Adams, M. & Shavell, S., 'Zür Strafbarkeit des Versuchs', Goldammer' Archiv für Strafrecht, 1990, pp. 337–86.

Adler, J.H., 'Rent-Seeking behind the Green Curtain', *Regulation*, 1996, Vol. 19(4), pp. 26–34.

Ahebwa, W., Van der Duim, R., & Sandbrook, C. H., 'Private-Community Partnerships: Investigating a New Approach to Conservation and Development in Uganda', *Conservation & Society*, 2012, Vol. 10(4), pp. 305–317.

Akerlof, G., 'The Market for "Lemons": Quality, Uncertainty and the Market Mechanism', *Quarterly Journal of Economics*, 1970, Vol. 84(3), pp. 488–500.

Alberini, A. & Austin, D., 'Liability Policy and Toxic Pollution Releases', in Heyes, A. (ed.), *The Law and Economics of the Environment*, Cheltenham, Edward Elgar, 2001, pp. 92–115.

Alberini, A. & Frost, S., 'Forcing Firms to Think about the Future: Economic Incentives and the Fate of Hazardous Waste', *Environmental & Resource Economics*, 2007, Vol. 36(4), pp. 451–474.

Albrecht, J., 'The Use of Consumption Taxes to Re-launch Green Tax Reforms', *International Review of Law and Economics*, 2006, Vol. 26, pp. 88–103.

Aldrich, E., Koerner, C., & Solan, D., 'Analysis of Liability Regimes for Carbon Capture and Sequestration: A Review for Policymakers', Energy Policy Institute (2011).

Allen, D. W. & Lueck, D., 'Risk Preferences and the Economics of Contracts', *The American Economic Review*, 1995, Vol. 85(2), pp. 447–451.

'The Nature of the Farm', *The Journal of Law and Economics*, 1998, Vol. 41(2), pp. 343–386.

Alpizar, F., Requate, T., & Schram, A., 'Collective versus Random Fining: An Experimental Study on Controlling Ambient Pollution', *Environmental and Resource Economics*, 2004, Vol. 29(2), pp. 231–252.

Ambec, S., Cohen, M., Elgie, S., & Lanoie, P., 'The Porter Hypothesis at 20: Can Environmental Regulation Enhance Innovation and Comparativeness', *Review of Environmental Economics and Policy*, 2013, Vol. 7(1), pp. 2–22.

Arcuri, A., 'Controlling Environmental Risk in Europe: The Complementary Role of an EC Environmental Liability Regime', *Tijdschrift voor Milieuaansprakelijkheid*, 2001, pp. 39–40.

Arlen, J., 'The Potentially Perverse Effects of Corporate Criminal Liability', *Journal of Legal Studies*, 1994, Vol. 23, pp. 833–867.

Arlen, J. & Kraakman, R, 'Controlling Corporate Misconduct: An Analysis of Corporate Liability Regimes', *New York University Law Review*, 1997, Vol. 72, pp. 687–779.

Arrow, K. J., 'A Difficulty in the Concept of Social Welfare', *Journal of Political Economy*, 1950, Vol. 58(4), pp. 328–346.

'The Origins of the Impossibility Theorem', in Maskin, E. & Sen, A. (eds.), *The Arrow Impossibility Theorem* (Kenneth J. Arrow Lecture Series), New York, Columbia University Press, 2014, pp. 143–148.

et al., 'Economic Growth, Carrying Capacity and the Environment', *Ecological Economics*, 1995, pp. 91–95 (reprint from *Science*, Vol. 268, pp. 520–521).

Ashworth, A., 'Is the Criminal Law a Lost Cause?', *Law Quarterly Review*, 2000, Vol. 116, pp. 225–256.

Ault, R. W. & Ekelund, R. B., 'Rent-Seeking in a Static Model of Zoning', *American Real Estate and Urban Economics Association Journal*, 1988, Vol. 16, pp. 69–76.

Ayres, R. U., 'Economic Growth: Politically Necessary but Not Friendly', *Ecological Economics*, 1995, Vol. 15(2), pp. 97–99. See http://engscisoc.pbworks.com/f/Ayres.pdf

Ayres, I. & Braithwaite, J., *Responsive Regulation: Transcending the Deregulation Debate*, Oxford, Oxford University Press, 1992.

Babbage, Ch., *Passages from the Life of a Philosopher*, London, Longman and Co., 1864.

Babbitt, C. J., Cory, D. C., & Kruchek, B. L., 'Discretion and Criminalisation of Environmental Law', *Duke Environmental Law and Policy Forum*, 2004, Vol. 15, pp. 1–64.

Ball, S. & Bell, S., *Environmental Law*, London, Blackstone Press Ltd., 1991.

Baldwin, R., 'Regulation Lite: The Rise of Emissions Trading', *Regulation & Governance*, 2008, Vol. 2(2), pp. 193–215, available at: www3.interscience.wiley.com/journal/119423171/issue, also as Law Society Economy Working Papers, 3/2008, available at: www.lse.ac.uk/collection/law/wps/wps.htm.

Barbier, E. B., Burgess, J. C., Swanson, T. M., & Pearce, D. W., *Elephants, Economics and Ivory*, London, Earthscan, 1990.

Barboza, J., *The Environment, Risk and Liability in International Law*, Nijmegen, Martinus Nijhoff Publishers, 2010.

Barde, J.-P., 'Environmental Policy and Policy Instruments', in Folmer, H., Gabel, H. L. & Opschoor, H. (eds.), *Principles of Environmental and Resource Economics: A Guide for Students and Decision-Makers*, Aldershot, Edward Elgar Publishing, 1995, pp. 218–220.

Barral, V., 'The Principle of Sustainable Development', in Krämer, L. & Orlando, E. (eds.), *Principles of Environmental Law*, Cheltenham, Edward Elgar, 2018, pp. 103–114.

Barrett, J. J., 'Sentencing Environmental Crimes under the United States Sentencing Guidelines: A Sentencing Lottery', *Environmental Law*, 1992, Vol. 22, pp. 1421–1449.

Barrett, S., 'An Economic Theory of International Environmental Law', in Bodansky, D., Brunnée, J., & Hey, E. (eds.), *The Oxford Handbook of International Environmental Law*, Oxford, Oxford University Press, 2007, pp. 231–261.

Baumol, W. J. & Oates, W. E., 'The Use of Standards and Prices for Protection of the Environment', *Swedish Journal of Economics*, 1971, Vol. 73, pp. 42–54.

*Economics, Environmental Policy and the Quality of Life*, Prentice Hall, Angelwood Cliffs, 1979.

Bauw, E., *Buitencontractuele aansprakelijkheid voor bodemverontreiniging*, Deventer, Kluwer, 1993.

Bawcutt, P. A., *Captive Insurance Companies, Establishment, Operation and Management*, Oxford, Woodhead-Faulkner, 1991.

Baxi, U., 'Introduction' in Sathe, S. P., *Judicial Activism in India*, 2002, p. xvi.

Becker, G. S., 'Irrational Behavior and Economic Theory', *Journal of Political Economy*, 1962, Vol. 70, pp. 1–13.

'Crime and Punishment: An Economic Approach', *Journal of Political Economy*, 1968, Vol. 76, pp. 169–217.

*The Economic Approach to Human Behavior*, Chicago, University of Chicago Press, 1976.

Becker, R. & Henderson, J. V., 'Effects of Air Quality Regulations on Polluting Industries', *Journal of Political Economy*, 2000, Vol. 108, pp. 379–421.

Beckerman, W., 'Economic Growth and the Environment: Whose Growth? Whose Environment?', *World Development*, 1992, Vol. 22, pp. 481–496.

Bell, S. & McGillivray, D., *Environmental Law*, 6th ed., Oxford, Oxford University Press, 2005.

Bell, R. & Russell, C., 'Environmental Policy for Developing Countries', *Issues in Science and Technology*, 2002, Vol. 18, pp. 63–70.

Ben-Shahar, O. & Logue, K. D., 'Outsourcing Regulation: How Insurance Reduces Moral Hazard', *Michigan Law Review*, 2012, Vol. 111, pp. 197–248.

Bergkamp, L., *De vervuiler betaalt dubbel*, Antwerp, Intersentia, 1999.

'The Commission's White Paper on Environmental Liability: A Weak Case for an EC Strict Liability Regime', *European Environmental Law Review*, 2000a, p. 5.

'The Proper Scope of Joint and Several Liability', *Tijdschrift voor Milieuaansprakelijkheid*, 2000b, pp. 153–156.

*Liability and Environment: Private and Public Law Aspects of Civil Liability for Environmental Harm in an International Context*, The Hague, Kluwer Law International, 2001.

Bergkamp, L. & Van Bergeijk, A., 'Scope of the ELD Regime', in Bergkamp, L. & Goldsmith, B. J. (eds.), *The EU Environmental Liability Directive: A Commentary*, Oxford, Oxford University Press, 2013, pp. 51–79.

Bergkamp, L., Herbatchek, M., & Jayanti, S., 'Financial Security and Insurance', in Bergkamp, L. & Goldsmith, B. J. (eds.), *The EU Environmental Liability Directive: A Commentary*, Oxford, Oxford University Press, 2013, pp. 118–138.

Betlem, G., 'It's No Use Crying over Spilt Chemicals', *Maastricht Journal of European and Comparative Law*, 1995, Vol. 2, pp. 289–305.

Biener, Ch., Eling, M., & Wirfs, J. H., 'Insurability of Cyber Risk: An Empirical Analysis', *The Geneva Papers on Risk & Insurance*, 2015, Vol. 40, pp. 131–158.

Bier, L., *Aansprakelijkheid voor bedrijfsongevallen en beroepsziekten*, Deventer, Kluwer, 1988.

Bigano, A., Proost, S., & Van Rompuy, J., 'Alternative Environmental Regulation Schemes for the Belgian Power Generation Sector', *Environmental & Resource Economics*, 2000, Vol. 16, pp. 121–160.

Billiet, C. M. & Rousseau, S., 'De hoogte van strafrechtelijke boetes: een rechtseconomische analyse van milieurechtspraak (1990–2000) van het Hof van Beroep te Gent', *Tijdschrift voor Milieurecht*, 2003, Vol. 2, pp. 120–134.

Billiet, C. & Rousseau, S., 'De zachte rechtshandhaving in het bestuurlijke handhavingspoor: de inspectiebeslissing en het voortraject van bestuurlijke sancties. Een rechtseconomische analyse', *Tijdschrift voor Milieurecht*, 2005, pp. 2–33.

Binder, S. & Neumayer, E., 'Environmental Pressure Group Strength and Air Pollution: an Empirical Analysis', *Ecological Economics*, 2005, Vol. 55, pp. 527–538.

Birnie, P., Boyle, A., & Redgwell, C., *International Law & the Environment*, 3rd ed., Oxford, Oxford University Press, 2009.

Blackman, A., 'Columbia's Discharge Fee Programme: Incentives for Polluters or Regulators?', *Journal of Environmental Management*, 2009, Vol. 90, pp. 101–119.

Bluffstone, R. & Larson, B. A. (eds.), *Controlling Pollution in Transition Economies: Theories and Methods*, Cheltenham, Edward Elgar, 1997.

Bluffstone, R. A. & Panayotou, Th., 'Environmental Liability and Privatisation in Central and Eastern Europe: Towards an Optimal Policy', *Environmental & Resource Economics*, 2000, Vol. 17(4), pp. 335–352.

Bocken, H., 'Van fout naar risico', *Tijdschrift voor Privaatrecht*, 1984, pp. 329–415.

'Alternatives to Liability and Liability Insurance for the Compensation of Pollution Damages', *Tijdschrift voor Milieuaansprakelijkheid*, 1987, pp. 83–87.

'Alternatives to Liability and Liability Insurance for the Compensation of Pollution Damages', *Tijdschrift voor Milieuaansprakelijkheid*, 1988, pp. 3–10.

'Systèmes Alternatives pour L'indemnisation des Dommages Du à la Pollution', *Revue Générale des Assurances et des Responsabilités*, 1990, pp. 11698–11714.

'Deficiencies of the System of Liability and Liability Insurance as a Mechanism for the Indemnification of Environmental Damage Suffered by Individual Victims', in Bocken, H. & Ryckbost, D. (eds.), *Insurance of Environmental Damage*, Brussels, Story Scientia, 1991, pp. 133–145.

Bocken, H., Lambrecht, W., Boes, M. et al., 'The Flemish Draft Decree on Environmental Policy: An Outline', in Bocken, H. & Ryckbost, D. (eds.), *Codification of Environmental Law, Proceedings of the International Conference*, The Hague, Kluwer Law, 1996, pp. 31–32.

Boer, B., 'Environmental Principles and the Right to a Quality Environment', in Krämer, L. & Orlando, E. (eds.), *Principles of Environmental Law*, Cheltenham, Edward Elgar, 2018, pp. 52–75.

Bohm, P., 'An Approach to the Problem of Estimating Demand for Public Goods', *Swedish Journal of Economics*, 1971, Vol. 73, pp. 55–66.

Bohrenstein, S., 'The Economics of Costly Risk Sorting in Competitive Insurance Markets', *International Review of Law and Economics*, 1989, Vol. 9(1), pp. 25–39.

Böhringer, C., Koschel, H., & Moslener, U., 'Efficiency Losses from Overlapping Economic Instruments in European Carbon Emissions Regulation', *Journal of Regulatory Economics*, 2008, Vol. 33(3), pp. 299–317.

Bolt, A. T. & Spier, J. (eds.), *De uitdijende reikwijdte van de aansprakelijkheid uit onrechtmatige daad*, NJV Preadvies, Zwolle, Tjeenk Willink, 1996.

Bond, V., 'The Cancer Risk Attributable to Radiation Exposure: Some Practical Problems', *Health Physics*, 1981, Vol. 40, pp. 108–111.

Bongaerts, J. C. & Kraemer, R. A., 'Water Pollution Charges in Three Countries: Control through Incentives', *European Environmental Review*, 1987, Vol. 1(4), pp. 12–19.

Borrini-Feyerabend, G., Collaborative Management of Protected Areas: Tailoring the Approach to the Context, IUCN, September 1996, available at: http://portals.iucn.org, last accessed 29 November 2014.

Bowles, R., *Law and the Economy*, Oxford, Martin Robertson, 1982.

Bowles, R., Faure, M., & Garoupa, N., 'Economic Analysis of the Removal of Illegal Gains', *International Review of Law and Economics*, 2000, Vol. 20, pp. 537–549.

'Forfeiture of Illegal Gain: An Economic Perspective', *Oxford Journal of Legal Studies*, 2005, Vol. 25, pp. 275–295.

'The Scope of Criminal Law and Criminal Sanctions: An Economic View and Policy Implications', *Journal of Law and Society*, 2008, Vol. 35(3), pp. 389–416.

Boyd, J. & Kunreuther, H., 'Retroactive Liability or the Public Purse?', *Journal of Regulatory Economics*, 1997, Vol. 11(1), pp. 79–90.

Boyle, A. & Anderson, M. R., *Human Rights Approaches to Environmental Protection*, Oxford, Clarendon Press, 1996.

Bradford, T., 'Cost Benefit Analysis and Demand Curse for Public Goods', *Kyklos*, 1970, Vol. 23, pp. 775–791.

Bradshaw, K., 'Settling for Natural Resource Damages', *Harvard Environmental Law Review*, 2016, Vol. 40, pp. 211–251.

Braithwaite, J., *Crime, Shame and Reintegration*, Cambridge, Cambridge University Press, 1989.

'Rewards and Regulation', *Journal of Law and Society*, 2002, Vol. 29, pp. 12–26.

Brans, E., 'Fundamentals of Liability for Environmental Harm under the ELD', in Bergkamp, L. & Goldsmith, B. J. (eds.), *The EU Environmental Liability Directive: A Commentary*, Oxford, Oxford University Press, 2013, pp. 31–50.

Brennan, G. & Buchanan, J. M., *The Power to Tax: Analytic Foundations of a Fiscal Constitution*, Cambridge, Cambridge University Press, 1980.

Breton, A., Brozio, G., Dalmazzone, S. & Garrone, G. (eds.), *Governing the Environment: Salient Institutional Issues*, Cheltenham, Edward Elgar, 2009.

Bretsen, S. N. & Hill, P. J., 'Water Markets as a Tragedy of the Anticommons', *William & Mary Environmental Law & Policy Review*, 2009, Vol. 33(3), pp. 723–783.

Brooks, M. A. & Heijdra, B. J., 'Rent-Seeking and Pollution Taxation: An Extension', *Southern Economic Journal*, 1987, Vol. 54(2), pp. 335–342.

Brown, J. P., 'Toward an Economic Theory of Liability', *Journal of Legal Studies*, 1973, Vol. 2(2), pp. 323–349.

Brown, J. P. & Holahan, W. L., 'Taxes and Legal Rules for the Control of Externalities When There Are Strategic Responses', *Journal of Legal Studies*, 1980, Vol. 9, pp. 165–178.

Brown, Jr. G. M. & Johnson, R. W., 'Pollution Control by Effluent Charges: It Works in the Federal Republic of Germany, Why Not in the US?', *Natural Resources Journal*, 1984, Vol. 24, pp. 929–966.

Brüggemeier, G., 'Liability for Water Pollution under German Law: Fault or Strict Liability', in Van Dunné, J. (ed.), *Transboundary Pollution and Liability: The Case of the River Rhine*, Lelystad, Vermande, 1991, pp. 85–91.

Buchanan, J. M. & Tullock, G., *The Calculus of Consent*, Ann Arbor, University of Michigan Press, 1962.

Buchanan, J. & Tullock, G., 'Polluters' Profits and Political Response: Direct Controls versus Taxes', *American Economic Review*, 1975, Vol. 65, pp. 139–147.

Buchanan, J., Tollison, R. & Tullock, G. (eds.), *Toward a Theory of the Rent Seeking Society*, Ann Arbor, University of Michigan Press, 1962.

Buchanan, J. M. & Yoon, Y. J., 'Symmetric Tragedies: Commons and Anticommons', *The Journal of Law and Economics*, 2000, Vol. 43(1), pp. 1–14.

Burrows, P., 'Combining Regulation and Liability for the Control of External Costs', *International Review of Law and Economics*, 1999, Vol. 19, pp. 227–242.

Burtraw, D. & Palmer, K., 'SO2 Cap-and-Trade Programme in the United States: A "Living Legend" of Market Effectiveness', in Harrington, W., Morgenstern, R. D., & Sterner, Th. (eds.), *Choosing Environmental Policy: Comparing Instruments and Outcomes in the United States and Europe*, Washington, DC, Resources for the Future, 2004, pp. 41–66.

Buzbee, W. W., 'Regulatory Strategy Diversity in United States Environmental Law', in Paddock, L. C., Glicksman, R., & Bryner, N. (eds.), *Decision-Making in Environmental Law*, Cheltenham, Edward Elgar, 2016, pp. 164–175.

Calabresi, G., *The Costs of Accidents: A Legal and Economic Analysis*, New Haven, Yale University Press, 1970.

'Optimal Deterrence and Accidents', *Yale Law Journal*, 1975a, Vol. 84, pp. 656–671.

'Concerning Cause and the Law of Torts: An Essay for Harry Kalven, Jr.', *University of Chicago Law Review*, 1975b, Vol. 43(1), pp. 69–108.

Calabresi, G. & Melamed, D., 'Property Rules, Liability Rules, and Inalienability: One View of the Cathedral', *Harvard Law Review*, 1972, Vol. 85(6), pp. 1089–1128.

Cane, P., 'Tort Law as Regulation', *Common Law World Review*, 2002, Vol. 31, pp. 305–331.

Carson, R. L., *Silent Spring*, Boston, Mariner Books, Houghton Mifflin, 1962.

Casella, A. & Frey, B., 'Federalism and Clubs: Towards an Economic Theory of Overlapping Political Jurisdiction', *European Economic Review*, 1992, Vol. 36(2–3), pp. 639–646.

Cha, J. M., 'A Critical Examination of the Environmental Jurisprudence of the Courts of India', *Albany Law Environmental Outlook Journal*, 2005, Vol. 10, pp. 197–228.

Chelius, J. R., 'Liability for Industrial Accidents: A Comparison of Negligence and Strict Liability Systems', *Journal of Legal Studies*, 1976, Vol. 5, pp. 293–309.

Coase, R. H., 'The Problem of Social Cost', *Journal of Law and Economics*, 1960, Vol. 3, pp. 1–44.

Cocker, A. & Richards C., *Valuing the Environment, Economic Approaches to Environmental Evaluation*, London, Bellhaven Press, 1992.

Coelho, Ph. R. P., 'Polluters' Profits and Political Response: Direct Control versus Taxes: Comment', *American Economic Review*, 1976, Vol. 66, pp. 976–978.

Coffee, J. S., 'Corporate Crime and Punishment: A Non-Chicago View of the Economics of Criminal Sanctions', *American Criminal Law Review*, 1980, Vol. 17, pp. 419–476.

Coghlin, T. G., 'Protection and Indemnity Clubs', *Lloyd's Maritime and Commercial Law Quarterly*, 1984, Vol. 11, pp. 403–416.

Coglianese, C. & Nash, J., 'The Law of the Test: Performance-Based Regulation and Diesel Emissions Control', *Yale Journal on Regulation*, 2017, Vol. 34, pp. 33–90.

Cohen, M., 'Commentary', in Ehrling, E. & Van den Bergh, R. (eds.), *Law and Economics of the Environment*, Oslo, Juridisk, 1996, pp. 167–171.

Cohen, M. A., 'Empirical Research on the Deterrent Effect of Environmental Monitoring and Enforcement', *Environmental Law Reporter*, 2000, Vol. 30, pp. 10.245–10.252.

'Criminal Law as an Instrument of Environmental Policy: Theory and Empirics', in Heyes, A. (ed.), *Law and Economics of the Environment*, Cheltenham, UK/Northampton, MA, Edward Elgar, 2001, pp. 198–216.

Cole, D. H., 'The "Stern Review" and Its Critics: Implications for the Theory and Practice of Benefit-Cost Analysis', *Natural Resources Journal*, 2008, Vol. 48, pp. 53–90.

'Property Creation by Regulation: Rights to Clean Air and Rights to Pollute', in Cole, D. H. & Ostrom, E. (eds.), *Property in Land and Other Resources*, Cambridge, MA, Lincoln Institute of Land Policy, 2011, pp. 125–155.

Cole, D. H. & Grossman, P. Z., 'When is Command-and-Control Efficient? Institutions, Technology, and the Comparative Efficiency of Alternative Regulatory Regimes for Environmental Protection', in Helfand, G. E. & Berck, P. (eds.), *The Theory and Practice of Command and Control in Environmental Policy*, Oxon, Routledge, 2018, pp. 115–166.

Cole, M. A., Rayner, A. J., & Bates, J. M., 'The Environmental Kuznets Curve: An Empirical Analysis', *Environment and Development Economics*, 1997, Vol. 2(4), pp. 401–416.

Conniff, R., 'The Political History of Cap and Trade: How an Unlikely Mix of Environmentalists and Free-Market Conservatives Hammered out the Strategy Known as Cap-and-Trade', *Smithsonian*, 2009, available at: http://smitsonianmag.com/science-nature/Presence-of-Mind-Blue-Sky-Thinking.html.

Cooter, R. D., 'Economic Analysis of Punitive Damages', *Southern California Law Review*, 1982, Vol. 56, pp. 97–101.

Cooter, R., 'Prices and Sanctions', *Columbia Law Review*, 1984, Vol. 84, pp. 1343–1523.

Cooter, R. E., 'Expressive Law and Economics', *Journal of Legal Studies*, 1998, Vol. 27, pp. 585–608.

Cooter, R. & Ulen, T., *Law and Economics*, 3rd ed., Illinois, Glenview, 2000.

Cooter, R. D. & Ulen, T., *Law and Economics*, 4th ed., Boston, MA, Addison Wesley, 2004.

*Law and Economics*, 5th ed., Boston, Addison Wesley, 2008.

Cooter, R. & Ulen, Th., *Law and Economics, International Edition*, 6th ed., Boston, Pearson, 2012.

Cortenraad, W. H. F. M., *The Corporate Paradox, Economic Realities of the Corporate Form of Organisation*, Boston, Kluwer Academic, 1999.

Cousy, H. A., 'Recent Developments in Environmental Insurance', in Abraham, F., et al. (eds.), *Recent Economic and Legal Developments in European Environmental Policy*, Leuven, Leuven University Press, 1995, pp. 235–237.

Cummings, J. D., 'Economies of Scale in Independent Insurance Agencies', *Journal of Risk and Insurance*, 1977, Vol. 44(4), pp. 539–553.

Dales, J., *Pollution, Property and Prices: An Essay in Policy*, Toronto, University of Toronto Press, 1968.

Dam, K. W., *The Law-Growth Nexus: The Rule of Law and Economic Development*, Washington, DC, Brookings Institution Press, 2006a.

Dam, S., 'Green Laws for Better Health: The Past That Was and the Future That May Be – Reflections from the Indian Experience', *Georgetown International Environmental Law Review*, 2004, Vol. 16(4), pp. 593–615.

Dasgupta, S., Laplante, B., Wang, H., & Wheeler, D., 'Confronting the Environmental Kuznets Curve', *Journal of Economic Perspectives*, 2002, Vol. 16, pp. 147–168.

Davis, R. K., 'Recreation Planning as an Economic Problem', *National Resources Journal*, 1963, Vol. 3, pp. 239–249.

Davis, C. M., *Maritime Law Deskbook*, Burlington, WA, Compass Publishing, 2010.

Deacon, R. T., 'Deforestation and the Rule of Law in a Cross-Section of Countries', *Land Economics*, 1994, Vol. 70(4), pp. 414–430.

De Alessi, M., 'Private Conservation and Black Rhinos in Zimbabwe: The Savé Valley and Bubiana Conservancies' 1999, available at: www.cei.org, last accessed 26 March 2015.

De Boer, J., 'Risicoaansprakelijkheid voor gevaarlijke stoffen en milieuverontreiniging', *Nederlands Juristenblad*, 1993, p. 225.

De Bruyn, S. M., 'Explaining the Environmental Kuznets Curve: Structural Change and International Agreements in Reducing Sulphur Emissions', *Environment and Development Economics*, 1997, Vol. 2(4), pp. 485–503.

De Geest, G. (ed.), *Encyclopedia of Law and Economics*, 2nd ed., Cheltenham, Edward Elgar, 2012.

De Grauwe, P., 'Political Economy of the Choice of Environmental Policy Instruments in the EC', in Abraham, F., Deketelaere, K., & Stuyck, J. (eds.), *Recent Economic Legal Developments in European Environmental Policy*, Leuven, Leuven University Press, 1995, pp. 111–168.

Demsetz, H., 'Toward a Theory of Property Rights', *American Economic Review*, 1967, Vol. 57(2), pp. 347–359.

Depoorter, B., 'Horizontal Political Externalities: The Supply and Demand of Disaster Management', *Duke Law Journal*, 2006, Vol. 56, pp. 101–125.

De Putter, P. & Verschuuren, J., 'Een milieuschadefonds in Nederland?', *Milieu en Recht*, 1995, Vol. 5, pp. 96–99.

De Sadeleer, N., *Environmental Principles: From Political Slogans to Legal Rules*, Oxford, Oxford University Press, 2002.

'The Precautionary Principle and Climate Change', in Farber, D. A. & Peeters, M. (eds.), *Climate Change Law*, Cheltenham, Edward Elgar, 2016, pp. 20–31.

De Sepius, J., 'The European Emission Trading Scheme Put to the Test of State Aid Rules', NCCR Trading regulation working paper 2007/34, available at: http://papers.ssrn/com/so3/papers.cfm?abstract_id=1088716.

Dewees, D. N., 'Instrument Choice in Environmental Policy', *Economic Inquiry*, 1983, Vol. 21, pp. 53–71.

Dewees, D., The Comparative Efficacy of Tort Law and Regulation for Environmental Protection, *Geneva Papers on Risk and Insurance*, 1992a, pp. 446–467.

'Tort Law and the Deterrence of Environmental Pollution', in Tietenberg, T. H. (ed.), *Innovation in Environmental Policy: Economic and Legal Aspects of Recent Developments in Environmental Enforcement and Liability*, Aldershot, Edward Elgar, 1992b, pp. 139–164.

Dewees, D., Duff, D., & Trebilcock, M., *Exploring the Domain of Accident Law: Taking the Facts Seriously*, New York, Oxford, 1996.

Diamond, P., 'Single Activity Accidents', *Journal of Legal Studies*, 1974, Vol. 70(1), pp. 107–164.

Dias, A., 'Judicial Activism in the Development and Enforcement of Environmental Law: Some Comparative Insights from the Indian Experience', *Journal of Environmental Law*, 1994, Vol 6(2), pp. 243–262.

Divan, S. & Rosencranz, A., *Environmental Law and Policy in India*, 2nd ed., India, Oxford University Press, 2002.

Dodson, G., 'Co-governance and Local Empowerment? Conservation Partnership Frameworks and Marine Protection at Mimiwhangata, New Zealand', *Society & Natural Resources*, 2014, Vol. 27, pp. 521–539.

Dommering-Van Rongen, L., *Schade Vergoeden door Fondsvorming*, Deventer, Kluwer, 1996.

Dornau, R., 'The Emissions Trading Scheme of the European Union', in Freestone, D. & Streck, C. (eds.), *Legal Aspects of Implementing the Kyoto Protocol Mechanisms*, Oxford, Oxford University Press, 2005, pp. 412–425.

Doucette, J. E., 'Wading in the Pool: Interlocal Cooperation in Municipal Insurance and the State Regulation of Public Entity Risk Sharing Pools – A Survey', *Connecticut Insurance Law Journal*, 2001, Vol. 8, pp. 533–547.

Douma, W. Th., Massai, L., & Montini, M. (eds.), *The Kyoto Protocol and Beyond: Legal and Policy Challenges of Climate Change*, The Hague, TMC Asser Press, 2007.

Dowding, T., *Global Developments in Captive Insurance*, Brussels, FT Energy, 1997.

Downing, P. B., 'A Political Economy Model of Implementing Pollution Laws', *Journal of Environmental Economics and Management*, 1989, Vol. 8, pp. 255–271.

Driesen, D. M., 'The Ends and Means of Pollution Control: Toward a Positive Theory of Environmental Law', *Utah Law Review*, 2017, Vol. 2017(1), pp. 57–113.

Drupsteen, Th. G., *Milieurecht*, 2nd ed., Zwolle, Tjeenk Willink, 1991.

Dubin, J. A. & Rothwell, G. S., 'Subsidy to Nuclear Power through Price-Anderson Liability Limit', *Contemporary Economic Policy*, 1990, Vol. 8(3), pp. 73–79.

Duvic-Paoli, L. A., 'Principle of Prevention', in Krämer, L. & Orlando, E. (eds.), *Principles of Environmental Law*, Cheltenham, Edward Elgar, 2018, pp. 161–173.

Earnhart, D., 'Liability for Past Environmental Contamination and Privatisation', *Environmental & Resource Economics*, 2004, Vol. 29, pp. 97–122.

Easterbrook, F., 'Criminal Procedure as a Market System', *Journal of Legal Studies*, 1983, Vol. 12, pp. 289–332.

Eckert, H., 'Inspections, Warnings, and Compliance: The Case of Petroleum Storage Regulation', *Journal of Environmental Economics and Management*, 2004, Vol. 47, pp. 232–259.

Eggertson, T., 'Analyzing Institutional Successes and Failures: A Millennium of Common Mountain Pastures in Iceland', *International Review of Law and Economics*, 1992, Vol. 12(4), pp. 423–437.

Ehrlich, I. & Posner, R., 'An Economic Analysis of Legal Rule-Making', *Journal of Legal Studies*, 1974, Vol. 3, pp. 257–286.

Eichner, T. & Pethig, R., 'EU-Type Carbon Emissions Trade and the Distributional Impact of Overlapping Emissions Taxes', CESifo Working Paper No. 2579, 2009.

Ellerman, A. D., 'The US SO2 Cap-and-Trade Programme', in *Tradable Permits: Policy Evaluation, Design, and Reform*, Paris, OECD, 2004, pp. 71–97.

'US Experience with Emissions Trading: Lessons for $CO_2$ Emissions Trading', in Hansjürgens, B. (ed.), *Emissions Trading for Climate Policy: US and European Perspectives*, Cambridge, Cambridge University Press, 2005, pp. 78–95.

Ellerman A. D., 'Are Cap-and-Trade Programs more Environmentally Effective than Conventional Regulation', in Freeman, J. & Kolstad, Ch. D. (eds.), *Moving to Markets in Environmental Regulation: Lessons from 20 Years of Experience*, Oxford, Oxford University Press, 2007, pp. 48–62.

Ellerman, A. D., Joskow, P. L., Schmalensee, R., Montero, J. P., & Bailey, E., *Markets for Clean Air: The US Acid Rain Program*, Cambridge, Cambridge University Press, 2000.

Ellickson, R., 'Alternatives to Zoning. Covenants, Nuisance Rules, and Fines as Land Use Controls', *University of Chicago Law Review*, 1973, Vol. 40(4), pp. 681–781.

ELNI, *The Role and Effects of Environmental Agreements In Environmental Policies*, London, Cameron May, 1998.

Endres, A., *Environmental Economics: Theory and Policy*, Cambridge, Cambridge University Press, 2010.

*Environmental Economics: Theory and Policy*, Cambridge, Cambridge University Press, 2011.

Endres, A. & Schwarze, R., 'Allokationswirkungen einer Umwelthaftpflicht-versicherung', *Zeitschrift für Umweltpolitik und Umweltrecht*, 1991, Vol. 14, pp. 1–25.

Endres, A. & Staiger, B., 'Ökonomische Aspekte des Umwelthaftungsrecht', in Ahrens, M. & Simon, J. (eds.), *Umwelthaftung, Risikosteuerung und Versicherung*, Berlin, Erich Schmidt Verlag, 1996, pp. 79–93.

Engel, E., *Die Production und Consumptionverhältnisse des Konigreich Sachsen*, 1857.

Engel, K. H., 'State Environmental Standard Setting: Is There a "Race" and Is It "to the Bottom"?', *Hastings Law Journal*, 1997, Vol. 48, pp. 271–398.

Epstein, R., 'A Theory of Strict Liability', *Journal of Legal Studies*, 1973, Vol. 2, pp. 151–204.

'Nuisance Law: Corrective Justice and Its Utilitarian Constraints', *Journal of Legal Studies*, 1979, Vol. 8(1), pp. 49–102.

Epstein, R. A., 'From Common Law to Environmental Protection: How the Modern Environmental Movement Has Lost Its Way', *Supreme Court Economic Review*, 2016, Vol. 23(1), pp. 141–167.

Epstein, R., Gregory, Ch., & Kalven, H., *Cases and Materials on Torts*, 4th ed., Boston, MA, Little, Brown and Company, 1984.

Eskridge Jr. W. N., 'Politics without Romance: Implications of Public Choice Theory for Statutory Interpretation', *Virginia Law Review*, 1988, Vol. 74, pp. 275–338.

Estep, E., 'Radiation Injuries and Statistics: The Need for a New Approach to Injury Litigation', *Michigan Law Review*, 1960, Vol. 59, pp. 259–304.

Esty, D., 'Revitalising Environmental Federalism', *Michigan Law Review*, 1996, Vol. 95, pp. 570–653.

'Economic Integration and the Environment', in Vig, N. & Axelrod, R. (eds.), *The Global Environment: Institutions, Law and Policy*, Washington, DC, CQ Press, 1999, pp. 190–209.

Esty, D. C., 'Red Lights to Green Lights: From 20th Century Environmental Regulation to 21st Century Sustainability', *Environmental Law*, 2017, Vol. 47(1), pp. 1–80.

Esty, D. & Geradin, D., 'Market Access, Competitiveness and Harmonisation: Environmental Protection in Regional Trade Agreements', *Harvard Environmental Law Review*, 1997, Vol. 21(2), pp. 265–336.

Esty, D. & Gerardin, D., 'Environmental Protection and International Competitiveness: A Conceptual Framework', *Journal of World Trade*, 1998, Vol. 32(3), pp. 5–46.

Esty, D. C. & Porter, M. E., 'Industrial Ecology and Competitiveness: Strategic Implications for the Firm', *Journal of Industrial Ecology*, 1998, Vol. 2(1), pp. 35–43.

'Ranking National Environmental Regulation and Performance: A Leading Indicator of Future Competitiveness', The Global Competitiveness Report 2002 (2001), pp. 78–100.

'National Environmental Performance: An Empirical Analysis of Policy Results and Determinants', *Environment and Development Economics*, 2005, Vol. 10, pp. 391–434.

European Commission, 'Proposal for a Council Directive Amending Directive 2003/93/EC Restructuring the Community Framework for the Taxation of Energy Products and Electricity', Brussels, COM(2011) 169/3.

European Group on Tort Law, *Principles of European Tort Law, Text and Commentary*, Vienna, Springer, 2005.

Ewenczyk, A., 'For a Fistful of Dollars: Quick Compensation and Procedural Rights in the Aftermath of the 2010 Deepwater Horizon Oil Spill', *Journal of Maritime Law and Commerce*, 2013, Vol. 44(3), p. 267.

Farber, D., 'Addressing Externalities: A Modest Proposal – How to Make Health and Safety a Personal Priority for Industry Officials', Legal Planet, University of California at Berkeley, 19 October 2015, available at: http://legal-planet.org/2015/10/19/addressing-externalities-a-modest-proposal/

Fagotto, E., *Industry Food Safety Standards: Public and Private Interests in Food Safety*, diss., Rotterdam, Erasmus University Rotterdam, 2015.

Faure, M.G., *(G)een Schijn van Kans: Beschouwingen over het Statistisch Causaliteitsbewijs bij Milieugezondheidsschade, Inaugural lecture Maastricht November* 1993, Antwerp, Maklu, 1993.

Faure, M., 'Eerstingebruikneming in het milieurecht: een rechtseconomische analyse', in Raes, K. & Willekens, H. (eds.), *Economische verklaringen van het recht*, The Hague, VUGA, 1994, pp. 147–178.

'Economic Models of Compensation for Damage Caused by Nuclear Accidents: Some Lessons for the Revision of the Paris and Vienna Conventions', *European Journal of Law and Economics*, 1995a, Vol. 21, pp. 21–43.

'The Limits to Insurability from a Law and Economics Perspective', in *The Geneva Papers on Risk and Insurance*, 1995b, pp. 454–462.

'Economic Aspects of Environmental Liability: An Introduction', *European Review of Private Law*, 1996, Vol. 4(2), pp. 85–110.

'Harmonization of Environmental Law and Market Integration: Harmonizing for the Wrong Reasons?', *European Environmental Law Review*, 1998a, Vol. 7(6), pp. 169–175.

Faure, M. G., 'Is aansprakelijkheid 'met terugwerkende kracht' efficiënt en verzekerbaar?', *Aansprakelijkheid en Verzekering*, 1998b, pp. 1–11.

'The Harmonisation, Codification and Integration of Environmental Law: A Search for Definitions', *European Environmental Law Review*, 2000, Vol. 9, pp. 174–182.

'Regulatory Competition vs Harmonisation in EU Environmental Law', in Esty, D. C. & Geradin, D. (eds.), *Regulatory Competition and Economic Integration*, Oxford, Oxford University Press, 2001, pp. 263–286.

'Environmental Damage Insurance in the Netherlands', *Environmental Liability*, 2002, pp. 31–41.

'Gewinnabschöpfung und Verfall auf ökonomischen Prüfstand', in Arnold, J. et al. (eds.), *Menschengerechtes Strafrecht: Festschrift für Albin Eser zum 70. Geburtstag*, Munich, Beck, 2005, pp. 1311–1330.

'Economic Criteria for Compulsory Insurance', in *The Geneva Papers on Risk and Insurance*, 2006, Vol. 31, pp. 149–168.

Faure, M. G., 'Optimal Specificity in Environmental Standard-Setting', in Dias Soares, C., Milne, J. E., Ashiabor, H., Kreiser, L., & Deketelaere, K. (eds.), *Critical Issues in Environmental Taxation: International and Comparative Perspectives*, Vol. III, Oxford, Oxford University Press, 2010, pp. 730–745.

'Does Environmental Law Matter?', in Faure, M. G. & Smits, J. (eds.), *Does Law Matter? On Law and Economic Growth*, Antwerp, Intersentia, 2011, pp. 385–416.

'In the Aftermath of the Disaster: Liability and Compensation Mechanisms as Tools to Reduce Disaster Risks', *Stanford Journal of International Law*, 2016a, Vol. 52(1), pp. 95–178.

'Liability and Compensation for Damage Resulting from $CO_2$ Storage Sites', *William & Mary Environmental Law & Policy Review*, 2016b, Vol. 40(2), pp. 387–476.

Faure, M. & Betlem, G., 'Applying National Liability Law to Transboundary Pollution. Some Lessons from Europe and the United States', in Faure, M. & Song, Y. (eds.), *China and International Environmental Liability. Legal Remedies for Transboundary Pollution*, Cheltenham, Edward Elgar, 2008, pp. 129–191.

Faure, M. & De Roos, Th., *De berekening van het wederrechtelijk verkregen voordeel uit milieudelicten*, The Hague, SDU Uitgevers, 1998.

Faure, M. G. & Fenn, P., 'Retroactive Liability and the Insurability of Long-Tail Risks', *International Review of Law and Economics*, 1999, Vol. 19(4), pp. 487–500.

Faure, M. G. & Fiore, K., 'An Economic Analysis of the Nuclear Liability Subsidy', *Pace Environmental Law Review*, 2009, Vol. 26(2), pp. 419–447.

Faure, M. & Grimeaud, D., 'Financial Assurance Issues of Environmental Liability', in Faure, M. (ed.), *Deterrence, Insurability, and Compensation in Environmental Liability: Future Developments in the European Union*, Vienna, Springer, 2003, pp. 7–255.

Faure, M. & Hartlief, T., 'Gevolgen van de uitbreidende werkgeversaansprakelijkheid: beleidsconsequenties voor verzekeraars?', in Faure, M. G. & Hartlief, T. (eds.), *Verzekering en de Groeiende Aansprakelijkheidslast, een juridisch, gezondheidskundig en economisch onderzoek naar ontwikkelingen met betrekking tot de Aansprakelijkheidslast en de consequenties voor verzekeraars naar aanleiding van de werkgeversaansprakelijkheid voor bedrijfsongevallen en beroepsziekten*, Deventer, Kluwer, 1995, pp. 283–337.

'Towards an Expanding Enterprise Liability in Europe? How to Analyze the Scope of Liability of Industrial Operators and Their Insurers', *Maastricht Journal of European and Comparative Law*, 1996a, Vol. 3, pp. 235–270.

'Een Asbestfonds als alternatief voor de aansprakelijkheid van de werkgever?', *Tijdschrift voor Sociaal Recht*, 1996c, pp. 37–43.

'Remedies for Expanding Liability', *Oxford Journal of Legal Studies*, 1998, Vol. 18, pp. 681–706.

*Insurance and Expanding Systemic Risks*, Paris, OECD, 2003.

Faure, M. & Heine, G., 'The Insurance of Fines: The Case of Oil Pollution', in *The Geneva Papers on Risk and Insurance*, 1991, Vol. 39, pp. 39–54.

Faure, M. G. & Heine, G., *Criminal Enforcement of Environmental Law in the European Union*, The Hague, Kluwer Law International, 2005.

Faure, M. G. & Johnston, J. S., 'The Law and Economics of Environmental Federalism: Europe and the United States Compared', *Virginia Environmental Law Journal*, 2009, Vol. 27(3), pp. 205–274.

Faure, M. & Lefevere, J., 'Protecting Drinking Water Quality against Contamination by Pesticides: An Alternative Regulatory Framework', *Review of European Community and International Environmental Law*, 1995, Vol. 4(4), pp. 321–326.

Faure, M. G. & Lefevere, J. G. J., 'The Draft Directive on Integrated Pollution Prevention and Control: An Economic Perspective', *European Environmental Law Review*, 1996, Vol. 5, pp. 112–122.

Faure, M. G. & Liu, J., 'The Tsunami of March 2011 and the Subsequent Nuclear Incident at Fukushima: Who Compensates the Victims?', *William & Mary Environmental Law & Policy Review*, 2012, Vol. 37, pp. 129–218.

Faure, M. G. & Luth, H. A., 'Behavioural Economics in Unfair Contract Terms. Cautions and Considerations', *Journal of Consumer Policy*, 2011, Vol. 34, pp. 337–358.

Faure, M. & Oudijk, J.C., 'Die strafgerichtliche Überprüfung von Verwaltungsakten im Umweltrecht, ein rechtvergleichender Überblick der Systeme in Deutschland, den Niederlanden und Belgien', *Juristenzeitung*, 1994, Vol. 49, pp. 86–91.

Faure, M. G. & Partain, R. A., *Carbon Capture and Storage: Efficient Legal Policies for Risk Governance and Compensation*, Cambridge, MA, MIT Press, 2017.

Faure, M. & Philipsen, N. (eds.), *Access to Justice in Environmental Matters*, The Hague, Eleven International Publishing, 2014.

Faure, M. & Porrini, D., 'Göran Skogh on Risk Sharing and Environmental Policy', in *The Geneva Papers on Risk and Insurance*, 2017, Vol. 42(2), pp. 177–192.

Faure, M. & Ruegg, M., 'Environmental Standards Setting through General Principles of Environmental Law', in Faure, M., Vervaele, J., & Weale, A. (eds.), *Environmental Standards in the European Union in an Interdisciplinary Framework*, Antwerp, Maklu, 1995, pp. 39–60.

Faure, M. & Skogh, G., 'Compensation for Damages Caused by Nuclear Accidents: a Convention as Insurance', in *The Geneva Papers on Risk and Insurance*, 1992, pp. 499–513.

*The Economic Analysis of Environmental Policy and Law: An Introduction*, Cheltenham, Edward Elgar, 2003.

Faure, M. G. & Svatikova, K., 'Enforcement of Environmental Law in the Flemish Region', *European Energy & Environmental Law Review*, 2010, Vol. 19(2), pp. 60–79.

Faure, M. & Ubachs, S., 'Environmental Taxation in the Netherlands: A Dutch Treat?', in Kreiser, L. A. (ed.), *Critical Issues in International Environmental Taxation: Insights and Analyses for Achieving Environmental Policy Goals through Tax Policy*, Chicago, CCH, 2002, pp. 301–329.

'Comparative Benefits and Optimal Use of Environmental Taxes', in Milne, J., Deketelaere, K., Kreiser, L., & Ashiabor, H. (eds.), *Critical Issues in Environmental Taxation, Vol. I: International and Comparative Perspectives*, Richmond, Richmond Law and Tax, 2003, pp. 29–49.

'Harmful Tax Measures and Greying of Taxation in the Netherlands: What Went Wrong?', in Ashiabor, H., Deketelaere, K., Kreiser, L., & Milne, J. (eds.), *Critical Issues in Environmental Taxation: International and Comparative Perspectives*, Vol. II, Richmond, Richmond Law and Tax, 2005, pp. 521–532.

Faure, M. & Van den Bergh, R., 'Negligence, Strict Liability and Regulation of Safety under Belgian Law: An Introductory Economic Analysis', in *The Geneva Papers on Risk and Insurance*, 1987, pp. 95–114.

'Compulsory Insurance for Professional Liability', in *The Geneva Papers on Risk and Insurance*, 1989a, pp. 308–330.

*Objectieve aansprakelijkheid, verplichte verzekering en veiligheidsregulering*, Antwerp, Maklu, 1989b.

'Liability for Nuclear Accidents in Belgium from an Interest Group Perspective', *International Review of Law and Economics*, 1990, Vol. 10, pp. 241–254.

'Restrictions of Competition on Insurance Markets and the Applicability of EC Antitrust Law', *Kyklos*, 1995, Vol. 48, pp. 65–85.

Faure, M. G. & Visser, M., 'Law and Economics of Environmental Crime', in Sjögren, H. & Skogh, G. (eds.), *New Perspectives on Economic Crime*, Cheltenham, UK/Northampton, MA, Edward Elgar, 2004, pp. 57–75.

Faure, M. G. & Wang, H., 'Economic Analysis of Compensation for Oil Pollution Damage', *Journal of Maritime Law and Commerce*, 2006, Vol. 37, pp. 179–217.

Faure, M. & Wang, H., 'Compensating Victims of a European Deepwater Horizon Accident: OPOL Revisited', *Marine Policy*, 2015, Vol. 62, pp. 25–36.

Faure, M. G. & Weishaar, S. E., 'The Role of Environmental Taxation: Economics and the Law', in Milne, J. E. & Andersen M. S. (eds.), *Handbook of Research of Environmental Taxation*, Cheltenham, Edward Elgar, 2012, pp. 399–421.

Faure, M., Goodwin, M., & Weber, F., 'Bucking the Kuznets Curve: Designing Effective Environmental Regulation in Developing Countries', *Virginia Journal of International Law*, 2010, Vol. 51, pp. 95–156.

Faure, M., Koopmans, I., & Oudijk, J., 'Imposing Criminal Liability on Government Officials under Environmental Law: A Legal and Economic Analysis', *Loyola of Los Angeles International and Comparative Law Journal*, 1996, Vol. 18, pp. 529–569.

Feinberg, K., *Who Gets What? Fair Compensation after Tragedy and Financial Upheaval*, New York, NY, Public Affairs, 2012.

Fenn, P. & Veljanovski, C., 'A Positive Economic Theory of Regulatory Enforcement', *Economic Journal*, 1988, Vol. 98, pp. 1055–1070.

Field, B. C., *Environmental Economics: An Introduction*, New York, McGraw-Hill, 1994.

Firestone, J., 'Enforcement of Pollution Laws and Regulations: An Analysis of Forum Choice', *Harvard Environmental Law Review*, 2003, Vol. 27(1), pp. 105–176.

Fischel, W. A., 'Externalities and Zoning', *Public Choice*, 1980, Vol. 35, pp. 37–43.

*The Economics of Zoning Laws: A Property Rights Approach to American Land Use Controls*, Baltimore, MD, The John Hopkins University Press, 1985.

Fischman, R. L. & Barbarsh-Riley, L., 'Empirical Environmental Scholarship', *Ecology Law Quarterly*, 2018, Vol. 44, pp. 767–807.

Frank, R. H., *Microeconomics and Behavior*, 8th ed., Boston, MA, McGraw-Hill Irwin, 2010.

Frankel, M., *The Alkali Inspectorate: The Control of Air Pollution. Social Audit, A Special Report*, London, Headly Brothers, 1974.

Freeman, A. M., 'Economics, Incentives, and Environmental Regulation', in Vig, N. J. & Kraft, M. E. (eds.), *Environmental Policy in the 1990s: Reform or Reaction?*, 3rd ed., Washington, DC, CQ Press, 1997, pp. 187–207.

Freeman, J. & Kolstad, Ch. D. (eds.), *Moving to Markets in Environmental Regulation: Lessons from 20 Years of Experience*, Oxford, Oxford University Press, 2007.

Freestone, D. & Frenkil, D., 'Emissions Trading in the US: A New Regime Approaching?', in Roggenkamp M. & Hammer, U. (eds.), *European Energy Law Report VII*, Antwerp, Intersentia, 2009, pp. 75–94.

Frey, B. S., *Umweltökonomie*, 3rd ed., Göttingen, Vandenhoeck und Ruprecht, 1992.

Frey, B., 'FOCJ: Competitive Governments for Europe', *International Review of Law and Economics*, 1996, Vol. 16, pp. 315–327.

*Not Just for the Money: An Economic Theory of Personal Motivation*, Cheltenham, Edward Elgar, 1997.

Frey, B., 'Morality and Rationality in Environmental Policy', *Journal of Consumer Policy*, 1999, Vol. 22, pp. 395–417.

Frey, B. & Eichenberger, R., 'To Harmonise or to Compete? That's Not the Question', *Journal of Public Economics*, 1996, Vol. 60, pp. 335–349.

Friedmann, L., *Micro Economic Policy Analysis*, New York, McGraw-Hill, 1984.

'In Defence of Corporate Criminal Liability', *Harvard Journal of Law and Public Policy*, 2000, Vol. 23, pp. 833–858.

Friesen, L., 'Targeting Enforcement to Improve Compliance with Environmental Regulations', *Journal of Environmental Economics and Management*, 2003, Vol. 46, pp. 72–85.

Fullerton, D., 'Six Distributional Effects of Environmental Policy', NBER Working Paper No. 16703, National Bureau of Economic Research (January 2011), pp. 1–13.

Fullerton, D., Leicester, A., & Smith, S., 'Environmental Taxes', in Institute for Fiscal Studies (ed.), *Dimensions of Tax Design*, Oxford, Oxford University Press, 2010, pp. 423–535.

Galle, B., 'Carrots, Sticks, and Salience', *Tax Law Review*, 2013, Vol. 67, pp. 108–109.

Garoupa, N. & Klerman, D., 'Corruption and the Optimal Use of Non-monetary Sanctions', *International Review of Law and Economics*, 2004, Vol. 24, pp. 219–225.

Garoupa, N. & Gomez-Pomar, F., 'Punish Once or Punish Twice: A Theory of the Use of Criminal Sanctions in Addition to Regulatory Penalties', *American Law and Economics Review*, 2004, Vol. 6, pp. 410–433.

Geers, A. J. C. M., *Recht en humanisering van de arbeid*, Deventer, Kluwer, 1988.

Geers, A. J. C. M. & Gevers, J. K. M., 'Schadeloosstelling van slachtoffers van bedrijfsongevallen en beroepsziekten', *Nederlands Juristenblad*, 1977, pp. 951–959.

Gerard, D. & Wilson, E., 'Environmental Bonds and the Challenge of Long-Term Carbon Sequestration', *Journal of Environmental Management*, 2009, Vol. 90(2), pp. 1097–1105.

Gibbard, A., 'Manipulation of Voting Schemes: A General Result', *Econometrica*, 1973, Vol. 41(4), pp. 587–601.

Gilead, I., 'Tort Law and Internalization: The Gap between Private Loss and Social Cost', *International Review of Law and Economics*, 1997, Vol. 17(4), pp. 589–608.
Gilhuis, P. & Verschuuren, J., *Een Milieuschadefonds in Nederland; een Onderzoek naar de Mogelijkheden*, Publicatiereeks Milieubeheer, 1994.
Gilles, M., 'Public-Private Approaches to Mass Tort Victim Compensation: Some Thoughts on the Gulf Coast Claims Facility', *DePaul Law Review*, 2012, Vol. 61(2), p. 427.
Gilles, S., 'Rule-Based Negligence and the Regulation of Activity Levels', *Journal of Legal Studies*, 1992, Vol. 22, pp. 319–363.
Glasbergen, P. (ed.), *Cooperative Environmental Governance: Public-Private Agreements as a Policy Strategy*, Dordrecht, Kluwer Academic Publishers, 1998.
Gold, S., 'Causation in Toxic Torts: Burdens of Proof, Standards of Persuasion and Statistical Evidence', *Yale Law Journal*, 1986, Vol. 96, pp. 376–402.
Goldsmith, B. J. & Bergkamp, L., 'Introduction', in Bergkamp, L. & Goldsmith, B. J. (eds.), *The EU Environmental Liability Directive: A Commentary*, Oxford, Oxford University Press, 2013, pp. 1–6.
Gravelle, H. S. E., 'Accidents, Taxes, Liability Rules and Insurances', in *The Geneva Papers on Risk and Insurance*, 1987, Vol. 12, pp. 115–131.
Greenspan, D. & Neuberger, M., 'Blowout: Legal Legacy of the Deepwater Horizon Catastrophe: Settle or Sue? The Use and Structure of Alternative Compensation Programs in the Mass Claims Context', *Roger Williams University Law Review*, Winter 2012, Vol. 17, p. 97.
Greenstone, M., 'The Impacts of Environmental Regulations on Industrial Activity: Evidence from the 1970 and 1977 Clean Air Act Amendments and the Census of Manufacturers', *Journal of Political Economy*, 2002, Vol. 110(6), pp. 1175–1219.
Grimeaud, D., 'The Integration of Environmental Concerns into EC Policies: A Genuine Policy Development?', *European Environmental Law Review*, 2000, Vol. 9(7), pp. 207–218.
Grober, U., *Sustainability: A Cultural History*, Devon, UK, Green Books, 2012.
Groosman, B., 'Pollution Tax', in Bouckaert, B. & De Geest, G. (eds.), *Encyclopedia of Law and Economics, II: Civil Law and Economics*, Cheltenham, Edward Elgar, 2000, pp. 538–568.
Grossman, G. M. & Krueger, A. B., 'Environmental Impacts of a North-American Free Trade Agreement', in Garber, P. M. (ed.), *The US, Mexico Free Trade Agreement*, Cambridge, MIT Press, 1993, pp. 13–56.
'Economic Growth and the Environment', *Quarterly Journal of Economics*, 1995, Vol. 110, pp. 353–377.
Grossman, P. Z., Clearley, R. W., & Cole, D. H., 'Uncertainty, Insurance and the Learned Hand Formula', *Law, Probability and Risk*, 2006, Vol. 5(1), pp. 1–18.
Gunningham, M. & Grabosky, P., *Smart Regulation: Designing Environmental Policy*, Oxford, UK, Clarendon Press, 1998.
Guiso, L. & Paiella, M., 'Risk Aversion, Wealth, and Background Risk', *Journal of European Economic Association*, 2008, Vol. 6(6), pp. 1109–1150.
Gupta, S. van Houtven, G., & Cropper, M., 'Do Benefits and Costs Matter in Environmental Regulation? An Analysis of EPA Decisions under Superfund', in Revesz, R. L. & Stewart, R. B. (eds.), *Analyzing Superfund Economics, Science, and Law*, Washington, DC, Resources for the Future, 1995, pp. 83–113.
Gupta, S., van Houtven, G., & Cropper, M., 'Paying for Permanence: An Economic Analysis of EPA's Cleanup Decisions at Superfund Sites', *Rand Journal of Economics*, 1996, Vol. 27(3), pp. 563–582.

Haazen, O. A. & Spier, J., 'Amerikaanse toestanden en de nieuwe aansprakelijkheidsverzekering voor bedrijven en beroepen', *Nederlands Juristenblad*, 1996, Vol. 71, pp. 45–50.
Hahn, R. W., 'A New Approach to the Design of Regulation in the Presence of Multiple Objectives', *Journal of Environmental Economics and Management*, 1989a, Vol. 17, pp. 195–211.
*A Primer on Environmental Policy Design*, New York, Harwood Academic, 1989b.
'Economic Prescriptions for Environmental Problems: How the Patient Followed the Doctor's Orders', *Journal of Economic Perspectives*, 1989c, Vol. 3(2), pp. 95–114.
'Regulatory Constraints on Environmental Markets', *Journal of Public Economics*, 1990a, Vol. 42, pp. 149–175.
'The Political Economy of Environmental Regulation: Towards a Unifying Framework', *Public Choice*, 1990b, Vol. 65, pp. 21–47.
Hahn, R. W. & Hester, G. L., 'Where Did All the Markets Go? An Analysis of EPA's Emissions Trading Programme', *Yale Journal on Regulation*, 1989, Vol. 6, pp. 109–153.
Hahn, R. W. & Noll, R., 'Barriers to Implementing Tradeable Air Pollution Permits: Problems of Regulatory Interaction', *Yale Journal on Regulation*, 1983, Vol. 1, pp. 63–91.
Hansmann, H. & Kraakman, R. H., 'Toward Unlimited Shareholder Liability for Corporate Torts', *Yale Law Journal*, 1991, Vol. 100, pp. 1978–1934.
Hansson, I. & Skogh, G., 'Moral Hazard and Safety Regulation', *The Geneva Papers on Risk and Insurance*, 1987, Vol. 12, pp. 132–144.
Hardin, G., 'The Tragedy of the Commons', *Science*, 1968, Vol. 162(3859), pp. 1243–1248.
Harford, J. D. & Harrington, W., 'A Reconsideration of Enforcement Leverage When Penalties Are Restricted', *Journal of Public Economics*, 1991, Vol. 45, pp. 391–395.
Haritz, M., *An Inconvenient Deliberation: The Precautionary Principles Contribution to the Uncertainties Surrounding Climate Change Liability*, Alphen aan den Rijn, Wolters Kluwer, 2011.
Harrington, W., 'Enforcement Leverage When Penalties Are Restricted', *Journal of Public Economics*, 1988, Vol. 37, pp. 29–53.
Harrington, W. & Heyes, A., 'The Theory of Penalties: "Leverage" and "Dealing"', in Heyes, A. (ed.), *The Law and Economics of the Environment*, Cheltenham, UK/Northampton, MA, USA, Edward Elgar, 2001, pp. 185–197.
Harrison D. & Rubinfeld, D. L., 'Hedonic House Prices and the Demand for Clean Air', *Journal of Environmental Economics and Management*, 1978, Vol. 5, pp. 81–102.
Harrington, W., Morgenstern, R. D., & Sterner, Th. (eds.), *Choosing Environmental Policy: Comparing Instruments and Outcomes in the United States and Europe*, Washington, DC, Resources for the Future, 2004.
Hartlief, T. & Spier, J., 'Verzekering en aansprakelijkheid met "terugwerkende kracht"', *Aansprakelijkheid en Verzekering*, 1994, pp. 27–33.
Hartlief, T. & Tjittes, R. P. J. L., *Invloed van verzekering op de civiele aansprakelijkheid: Preadvies voor de Vereniging voor Burgerlijk Recht*, Lelystad, Vermande, 1990a.
'De aansprakelijkheid voor bedrijfsongevallen en – ziekten – recente ontwikkelingen met betrekking tot tewerkstelling en bewijslast', *Sociaal Recht*, 1990b, pp. 282–288.
*Verzekering en Aansprakelijkheid*, Deventer, Kluwer, 1994.
Hausman, J. A., *Contingent Valuation: A Critical Assessment*, Amsterdam, North-Holland, 1993.
Havercroft, I. & Macrory, R., *Legal Liability and Carbon Capture and Storage: A Comparative Perspective*, Melbourne, Global CCS Institute, 2014.
Hawkins, K., *Environment and Enforcement: Regulation and the Social Definition of Pollution*, Oxford, Clarendon Press, 1984.

Hayek, F. A., 'The Use of Knowledge in Society', *American Economic Review*, 1945, Vol. 35(4), pp. 519–530.

Hazelwood, S. J. & Semark, D., *P&I Clubs: Law and Practice*, London, Lloyd's List, 2010.

Heimert, A. J., 'How the Elephant Lost His Tusks', *Yale Law Journal*, 1995, Vol. 104(6), pp. 1473–1506.

Heine, G., 'Die Verwältungsakzessorietät im deutschen Umweltstrafrecht unter Berücksichtigung des österreichischen Rechts. Aktuelle Probleme und Reformüberlegungen', *Österreichische Juristenzeitung*, 1991, pp. 370–378.

Heine, G. & Meinberg, V., *Empfehlen sich Änderungen im strafrechtlichen Umweltschutz, insbesondere in Verbindung mit dem Verwaltungsrecht? Gutachten für den 57. Deutschen Juristentag*, Munich, Beck, 1988.

Hendrickx, R., 'Maritime Oil Pollution: An Empirical Analysis', in Faure, M. & Verheij, A. (eds.), *Shifts in Compensation for Environmental Damage*, Vienna, Springer, 2007, pp. 243–260.

Heringa, A. W., 'Private Life and the Protection of the Environment', European Court of Human Rights, 9 December 1994, Lopez Ostra v. Spain', *Maastricht Journal of European and Comparative Law*, 1995, Vol. 2, pp. 196–204.

Heyes, A. G., 'Eight Things about Enforcement That Seem Obvious But May Not Be', in Swanson, T. (ed.), *An Introduction to the Law and Economics of Environmental Policy: Issues in Institutional Design*, Amsterdam, Elsevier, 2002, pp. 519–537.

Heyes, A. G. & Liston-Heyes, C., 'Subsidy to Nuclear Power through Price-Anderson Liability Limit: Comment', *Contemporary Economic Policy*, 1998, Vol. 16(1), pp. 122–124.

Heyes, A. & Rickman, N., 'Regulatory Dealing – Revisiting the Harrington Paradox', *Journal of Public Economics*, 1999, Vol. 72, pp. 361–378.

Hirschman, A. O., *Exit, Voice and Loyalty: Responses to Decline in Firms, Organisations and States*, Cambridge, Harvard University Press, 1990.

Hirshleifer, J., 'The Expanding Domain of Economics', *American Economic Review*, 1985, Vol. 75, pp. 53–68.

Hoch, I. & Drake, J., 'Wages, Climate and the Quality of Life', *Journal of Environmental Economics and Management*, 1974, Vol. 1, pp. 268–295.

Hodas, D. & De Armey, P., 'North-American Greenhouse Gas Emission Trading Systems', in Farber, D. A. & Peeters, M. (eds.), *Climate Change Law*, Cheltenham, Edward Elgar, 2016, pp. 388–399.

Holcombe, R. G., 'Creating a Public-Private Partnership for Florida's Conservation Land Management', *Backgrounder*, 2009, Vol. 59, pp. 3–10.

Holley, C. & Sinclair, D., 'Enforcement Strategies: Inspection, Targetting and Escalation', in Paddock, L. C., Markell, D. L., & Bryner, N. S. (eds.), *Compliance and Enforcement of Environmental Law*, Cheltenham, Edward Elgar, 2017, pp. 101–113.

Hotelling, H., 'Stability in Competition', *Economic Journal*, 1929, Vol. 39(153), pp. 41–57.

Howarth, R. B. & Norgaard, R. B., 'Environmental Valuation under Sustainable Development', *American Economic Association*, 1992, Vol. 82(2), pp. 473–477.

Hsu, S.-L., 'Fairness versus Efficiency in Environmental Law', *Ecology Law Quarterly*, 2004, Vol. 31, pp. 303–401.

'Some Quasi-Behavioral Arguments for Environmental Taxation', *Critical Issues in Environmental Taxation*, 2008, Vol. V, pp. 29–52.

'The Accidental Postmodernists: A New Era of Skepticism in Environmental Policy', *Vermont Law Review*, 2014, Vol. 39, pp. 27–88.

Huber, B. R., 'Temporal Spillovers', in Mathis, K. & Huber, B., *Environmental Law and Economics*, Cham, Springer, 2017, pp. 43–57.

Huber, P., 'The Old-New Division in Risk Regulation', *Virginia Law Review*, 1983, Vol. 63, pp. 1025–1107.

Hughes, D., *Environmental Law*, 2nd ed., Oxford, Butterworths, 1992.

Huisman, W., *Tussen winst en moral, achtergronden van regelnaleving en regelovertreding door ondernemingen*, The Hague, Boom, 2001.

Huisman, W. & Van de Bunt, H. G., 'Sancties, organisatiecriminaliteit en milieudelicten', *Ars Aequi*, 1997, pp. 695–697.

Hulst, E., *Grondslagen van Milieuaansprakelijkheid*, diss., Arnhem, Gouda Quint, 1993.

'De werkelijkheid rondom een algemeen milieuschadefonds, een commentaar', Tijdschrift voor Milieuaansprakelijkheid, 1995, pp. 167–173.

Huther, J. & Anwar, S., 'Anti-Corruption Policies and Programs: A Framework for Evaluation', World Bank Working Paper 2501, 2001.

Hylton, K. N., 'When Should We Prefer Tort Law to Environmental Regulation?', *Washburn Law Journal*, 2002, Vol. 41, pp. 515–543.

Inman, R. & Rubinfeld, D., 'The EMU and Fiscal Policy in the New European Community: An Issue for Economic Federalism', *International Review of Law and Economics*, 1994, Vol. 14(2), pp. 147–161.

Innes, R., 'Self-Enforcement of Environmental Law', in Heyes, A. (ed.), *The Law and Economics of the Environment*, Cheltenham, UK/Northampton, MA, USA, Edward Elgar, 2001, pp. 150–184.

Innes, R. & Sam, A. G., 'Voluntary Pollution Reductions and the Enforcement of Environmental Law: An Empirical Study of the 33/50 Programme', *Journal of Law and Economics*, 2008, Vol. 51(2), pp. 271–296.

Interuniversitaire Commissie tot Herziening van het Milieurecht in het Vlaamse Gewest, *Voorontwerp Decreet Milieubeleid*, Brugge, die Keure, 1995.

Jacob, H., 'Deterrent Effects of Formal and Informal Sanctions', *Law & Policy*, 1980, Vol. 2(1), pp. 61–80.

Jaffe, A., Peterson, D., Portney, P., & Stavins, R., 'Environmental Regulation and the Competitiveness of US Manufacturing: What Does the Evidence Tell us?', *Journal of Economic Literature*, 1995, Vol. 33, pp. 132–163.

Jaffer, S. & Kay, J., 'The Regulation of Shop Opening Hours in the United Kingdom', in Graf von den Schulenburg, J. M. & Skogh, G. (eds.), *Law and Economics and the Economics of Legal Regulation*, Dordrecht, Nijhoff, 1986, pp. 169–183.

Jans, J. H., *European Environmental Law*, The Hague/London/Boston, Kluwer Law International, 1995.

*European Environmental Law*, 2nd ed., Groningen, European Law Publishing, 2000.

Jans, J. H. & Vedder, H. H. B., *European Environmental Law: After Lisbon*, 4th ed., Groningen, Europa Law Publishing, 2012.

Jeppesen, T., List, J. A., & Folmer, H., 'Environmental Regulations and New Plant Location Decisions: Evidence from a Meta-analysis', *Journal of Regional Science*, 2002, Vol. 42, pp. 19–49.

Johnston, J. S., 'The Law and Economics of Environmental Contracts', in Orts, E. W. & Deketelaere, K. (eds.), *Environmental Contracts: Comparative Approaches to Regulatory Innovation in the United States and Europe*, The Hague, Kluwer, 2001, pp. 271–304.

Jones, B., 'The Identification and Remediation of Contaminated Sites: The United Kingdom's Environment Act 1995', Tijdschrift voor Milieuaansprakelijkheid, 1995, pp. 159–166.

Jordan, A., Wurzel, R. K. W., & Zito, A. R., 'New Instruments of Environmental Governance: Patterns and Pathways of Change', *Special Issue Environmental Politics*, 2003, Vol. 12(1), pp. 1–24.

Josen, J., 'Catastrophe Bonds – Fear of the Unknown?', Derivative Times, 5 June, 2015.

Jost, P. J., 'Limited Liability and the Requirement to Purchase Insurance', *International Review of Law and Economics*, 1996, Vol. 16(2), pp. 259–276.

Kahan, D. M., 'Social Meaning and the Economic Analysis of Crime', *Journal of Legal Studies*, 1998, Vol. 27, pp. 609–622.

Kahneman, D. & Tversky, A., 'Prospect Theory: An Analysis of Decision under Risk', *Econometrica*, 1979, Vol. 47, pp. 263–281.

Kane, P., 'Using Tort Law to Enforce Environmental Regulations?', *Washburn Law Journal*, 2002, Vol. 41, pp. 427–467.

Kaplow, L., 'An Economic Analysis of Legal Transition', *Harvard Law Review*, 1986, Vol. 99, pp. 509–617.

Kapp, W., 'Environmental Disruption and Social Costs: A Challenge to Economics', *Kyklos*, 1970, Vol. 23(4), pp. 833–848.

Karpoff, J. M. Lott, J. R., & Ranike, G., 'Environmental Violations, Legal Penalties, and Repudiation Costs', University of Chicago John M. Olin Law & Economics Working Paper No. 71 (2nd series), 1998.

Kathuria, V., 'Controlling Water Pollution in Developing and Transition Countries – Lessons from Three Successful Cases', *Journal of Environmental Management*, 2006, Vol. 78, pp. 405–426.

Katzman, M. T., 'Pollution Liabilitiy Insurance and Catastrophic Environmental Risks', *Journal of Risk and Insurance*, 1988, Vol. 55(1), pp. 75–100.

Kaye, D., 'The Limits of the Preponderance of the Evidence Standard: Justifiable Naked Statistical Evidence and Multiple Causation', *Law & Social Inquiry*, 1982, Vol. 7(2), pp. 487–516.

Keenan, D. & Rubin, P., 'Shadow Interest Groups and Safety Regulation', *International Review of Law and Economics*, 1988, Vol. 8, pp. 21–36.

Keohane, N. O., 'Cost Savings from Allowance Trading in the 1990 Clean Air Act: Estimates from a Choice-Based Model', in Freeman, J. & Kolstad, Ch. D. (eds.), *Moving to Markets in Environmental Regulation: Lessons from 20 Years of Experience*, Oxford, Oxford University Press, 2007, pp. 194–229.

Ketchum, L., 'Epidemiologic Tables Law Groundwork for Future Radiogenic Cancer Claims', *Journal of Nuclear Medicine*, 1985, Vol. 26, pp. 967–972.

Kilchling, M., 'Comparative Perspectives on Forfeiture Legislation in Europe and the United States', *European Journal of Crime, Criminal Law and Criminal Justice*, 1997, Vol. 5, pp. 342–361.

Kilchling, M. (ed.), *Die Praxis der Gewinnabschöpfung in Europa*, Freiburg im Breisgau, Max Planck Institute for Foreign and International Criminal Law, 2002.

Kirchgässner, G. & Pommerehne, W., 'Tax Harmonisation and Tax Competition in the European Community: Lessons from Switzerland' (paper presented at the Cost Meeting in Luzern November 1993).

Kitzmueller, M. & Shimshack, J., 'Economic Perspectives on Corporate Social Responsibility', *Journal of Economic Literature*, 2012, Vol. 50(1), pp. 51–84.

Kloepfer, M., 'On the Codification of German Environmental Law', in Bocken, H. & Ryckbost, D. (eds.), *Codification of Environmental Law, Proceedings of the International Conference*, The Hague, Kluwer Law International, 1996, pp. 87–100.

Klosse, S., 'Bedrijfsongevallen en beroepsziekten: individuele of collectieve verantwoordelijkheid', *Nederlands Juristenblad*, 1993, pp. 1608–1613.

Knottenbelt, J., *Produktaansprakelijkheid*, diss., Erasmus Universiteit Rotterdam, 1990.

Koch, B. A. & Koziol, H., 'Comparative Conclusions', in Koch, B. A. & Koziol, H. (eds.), *Unification of Tort Law: Strict Liability*, The Hague, Kluwer Law International, 2002, pp. 395–435.

Kolstad, C. D., 'Uniformity versus Differentiation in Regulating Externalities', *Journal of Environmental Economics and Management*, 1987, Vol. 1, pp. 386–399.

Kolstad, Ch. D., Ulen, Th. S., & Johnson, G. V., 'Ex Post Liability for Harm vs. Ex Ante Safety Regulation: Substitutes or Complements', *American Economic Review*, 1990, Vol. 80, pp. 888–901.

Konar, S. & Cohen, M. A., 'Information as Regulation: The Effect of Community Right to Know Laws on Toxic Emissions', *Journal of Environmental Economics and Management*, 1997, Vol. 32, pp. 109–124.

Körber, A., 'Standards and Taxes in Environmental Law from a Public Choice Perspective', in Bouckaert, B. & De Geest, G. (eds.), *Essays in Law and Economics II*, Antwerp, Maklu, 1995, pp. 161–191.

Kornhauser, L. A., 'An Economic Analysis of the Choice between Enterprise and Personal Liability for Accidents', *California Law Review*, 1982, Vol. 70, pp. 1345–1392.

Kornhauser, L. A. & Revesz, R. L., 'Sharing Damages among Multiple Tortfeasors', *Yale Law Journal*, 1989, Vol. 98(5), pp. 831–884.

'Apportioning Damages among Potentially Insolvent Actors', *Journal of Legal Studies*, 1990, Vol. 19(2), pp. 617–651.

Kosonen, K. & Nicodème, G., 'The Role of Fiscal Instruments in Environmental Policy', CESifo Working Paper No 2719, July 2009.

Kottenhagen-Edzes, P. A., *Onrechtmatige daad en milieu. Het gebruik van het privaatrecht bij het voorkomen van milieuaantasting en het verhaal van milieuschade*, Arnhem, Gouda Quint, 1992.

Kozeltsev, M. & Markandya, A., 'Pollution Charges in Russia: The Experience of 1990–1995', in Bluffstone, R. & Larson, B. A. (eds.), *Controlling Pollution in Transition Economies: Theories and Methods*, Cheltenham, Edward Elgar, 1997, pp. 128–143.

Krämer, L., 'Community Environmental Law under the Maastricht Treaty on European Union and the Fifth Action Programme', in Abraham, T., Deketelaere, K., & Stuyck, J. (eds.), *Recent Economic and Legal Developments in European Environmental Policy*, Leuven, Leuven University Press, 1995, pp. 75–106.

'The Principle of Fighting Environmental Harm and Source (Source Principle)', in Krämer, L. & Orlando, E. (eds.), *Principles of Environmental Law*, Cheltenham, Edward Elgar, 2018, pp. 186–194.

Krutilla, J. V., 'Conservation Reconsidered', *American Economic Review*, 1967, Vol. 57, pp. 777–786.

Krutilla, J. V. & Fisher, A., *The Economics of Natural Environments: Studies in the Valuation of Commodity and Amenity Recourses*, rev. ed., Washington, DC, Recourses for the future, 1985.

Kuik, O. & Oosterhuis, F., 'Economic Impacts of the EU ETS: Preliminary Evidence', in Faure, M. & Peeters, M. (eds.), *Climate Change and European Emissions Trading. Lessons for Theory and Practice*, Cheltenham, Edward Elgar, 2008, pp. 208–222.

Kunreuther, H. & Freeman, P., 'Insurability, Environmental Risks and the Law', in Heyes, A. (ed.), *The Law and Economics of the Environment*, Cheltenham, Edward Elgar, 2001, pp. 302–318.

Kunreuther, H., Hogarth, R., & Meszaros, J., 'Insurer Ambiguity and Market Failure', *Journal of Risk and Uncertainty*, 1993, Vol. 7, pp. 71–87.

Kuznets, S., 'Economic Growth and Income Inequality', *American Economic Review*, 1955, Vol. 45,(1), pp. 1–28.

Landes, W. M. & Posner, R. A., 'The Private Enforcement of Law', *Journal of Legal Studies*, 1975, Vol. 4, pp. 1–46.

Landes, W. & Posner, R., 'An Economic Theory of Intentional Torts', *International Review of Law and Economics*, 1981a, Vol. 1, pp. 127–154.

'The Positive Economic Theory of Tort Law', *Georgia Law Review*, 1981b, Vol. 15, pp. 851–924.

'Causation in Tort Law: An Economic Approach', *Journal of Legal Studies*, 1983, Vol. 12, pp. 109–134.

'Tort Law as a Regulatory Regime for Catastrophic Personal Injuries', *Journal of Legal Studies*, 1984, Vol. 13, pp. 417–434.

*The Economic Structure of Tort Law*, Cambridge MA, Harvard University Press, 1987.

Lando, O., 'Die Regeln des Europäischen Vertragsrecht', in Müller-Graff, P. C. (ed.), *Gemeinsames Privatrecht in der Europäischen Gemeinschaft*, Baden-Baden, Nomos, 1993, pp. 473–474.

Laskowska, A. & Scrimgeour, F., 'Environmental Taxation: The European Experience', University of Waikato, Working Paper, 2002, available at: http://wms.soros.mngt .vaikato.ac.nz/NR/exeres/E33CCD10-4841-47AE-8A1A-C66E1B01E9FD.htm.

Lazarus, R. J., *The Making of Environmental Law*, Chicago, University of Chicago Press, 2003.

Lee, D. R., 'Rent-Seeking and Its Implications for Pollution Taxation', *Southern Economic Journal*, 1985, Vol. 51, pp. 731–744.

Lee, M., 'The Intersection between Environmental Law and Tort Law', in Paddock, L. C., Glicksman, R. L., & Bryne, N. S. (eds.), *Decision-Making in Environmental Law*, Cheltenham, Edward Elgar, 2016, pp. 62–72.

Legrand, P., 'The Impossibility of "Legal Transplants"', *Maastricht Journal of European and Comparative Law*, 1997, Vol. 4, pp. 111–124.

'Antivonbar', *Journal of Comparative Law*, 2008, Vol. 1(1), pp. 13–39.

Levinson, A., 'The Missing Pollution Haven Effect', *Environmental and Resource Economics*, 2000, Vol. 15(4), pp. 343–364.

'Environmental Regulatory Competition: A Status Report and Some New Evidence', *National Tax Journal*, 2003, Vol. 56(1), pp. 91–106.

Libecap, G. D. & Wiggins, S. N., 'Contractual Responses to the Common Pool: Prorationing of Crude Oil Production', *American Economic Review*, 1994, Vol. 74(1), pp. 87–98.

Lierman, S. & Veuchelen, L., 'The Optimisation Approach of ALARA in Nuclear Practice: An Early Application of the Precautionary Principle: Scientific Uncertainty versus Legal Uncertainty', *Water Science & Technology*, 2005, Vol. 52(6), pp. 81–86.

List, J. A., McHone, W. W., & Millimet, D. L., 'Effects of Air Quality Regulation on the Destination Choice of Relocating Plants', Oxford Economic Papers, 2003, pp. 657–678.

Litz, F. T., 'Harnessing Market Forces in Natural Resources Management: Lessons from the Surf Clam Fishery', *Boston College Environmental Affairs Law Review*, 1994, Vol. 21(2), pp. 335–361.

Liu, J., *Compensation for Ecological Damage: Comparative and Economic Observations*, Antwerp, Intersentia, 2013.

Livermore, M. A., 'The Perils of Experimentation', *Yale Law Journal*, 2017, Vol. 126(3), pp. 636–708.

Lofton, J. A., 'Environmental Enforcement: The Impact of Cultural Values and Attitudes on Social Regulation', *Environmental Liability*, 2001, Vol. 4, pp. 167–181.

Lokur, M. B., 'Environmental Law – Its Development and Jurisprudence', Green Law Lecture 2006, WWF-India, available at: www.wwfindia.org/news_facts/?1320.

Lomas, O., 'Current Survey: Environment', *Utilities Law Review*, Summer 1990, p. 62.

Lu, M., *Choose or Loose, Another Road to China's Sustainable Development: A Law and Economics Analysis of Corporate Sustainability Theories and Practices*, diss., Maastricht, Maastricht University, 2017.

Lu, M. & Faure, M. G., 'The Regulation of Corporate Environmental Responsibility', in Philipsen, N., Weishaar, S. E., & Xu, G. (eds.), *Market Integration: The EU Experience and Implications for Regulatory Reform in China*, Berlin/Heidelberg, Springer, 2016, pp. 239–265.

Lueck, D., 'The Economic Nature of Wildlife Law', *Journal of Legal Studies*, 1989, Vol. 18(2), pp. 291–324.

'Property Rights and the Economic Logic of Wildlife Institutions', *Natural Resources Journal*, 1995, Vol. 35, pp. 625–670.

'Property Institutions and the Limits of Coase', *Journal of Institutional Economics*, 2017, Vol. 13(4), pp. 793–800.

Lueck, D. & Micelli, T. J., 'Property Law', in Polinsky, A. M. & Shavell, S. (eds.), *Handbook of Law and Economics*, Vol. 1, Amsterdam, North-Holland, 2007, pp. 183–257.

Lutterer, W. & Hoch, H. K., *Rechtliche Steuerung im Umweltbereich. Funktionsstrukturen des Umweltstrafrechts und des Umweltordnungswidrigkeitenrechts: Empirische Untersuchungen zur Implementation strafbewehrter Vorschriften im Bereich des Umweltschutzes*, Freiburg im Breisgau, Max Planck Institute for Foreign and International Criminal Law, 1997.

MacDonell, C., 'The Gulf Coast Claims Facility and the Deepwater Horizon Litigation: Judicial Regulation of Private Compensation Schemes', *Stanford Law Review*, 2012, Vol. 64(3), p. 765.

Mackaay, E., *Economics of Information and the Law*, The Hague, Kluwer, 1982.

Majone, G., 'Unity in Diversity: European Integration and the Enlargement Process', *European Law Review*, 2008, Vol. 33, pp. 457–481.

Makdisi, J., 'Proportional Liability: A Comprehensive Rule to Apportion Tort Damages Based on Probability', *North Carolina Law Review*, 1989, Vol. 67, pp. 1063–1101.

Maler, K. G., 'A Note on the Use of Property Values in Estimating Marginal Willingness to Pay for Environmental Quality', *Journal of Environmental Economics and Management*, 1977, Vol. 4, pp. 355–369.

Maloney, M. & McCormick, R., 'A Positive Theory of Environmental Quality Regulation', *Journal of Law and Economics*, 1982, Vol. 25(1), pp. 99–123.

Markesinis, B. S., *The German Law of Torts: A Comparative Introduction*, Oxford, Hart Publishing, 2002.

Marshall, J., 'Moral Hazard', *American Economic Review*, 1976, Vol. 66, pp. 880–890.

Martinez Gandara, A., *The Law and Economics of Eco-labels*, diss., Rotterdam, Erasmus University Rotterdam, 2013.

Mashale, C., Moyo, T., & Mtapuri, O., 'An Evaluation of the Public-Private Partnership in the Lekgalameetse Nature Reserve in South Africa', *Mediterranean Journal of Social Sciences*, 2014, Vol. 5(20), pp. 855–862.

Massai, L., 'The Revision of the EU Emissions Trading System', in Roggenkamp M. & Hammer, U. (eds.), *European Energy Law Report VII*, Antwerp, Intersentia, 2009, pp. 3–25.

Mattei, U., *Comparative Law and Economics*, Ann Arbor, University of Michigan Press, 2000.

May, P. J. & Winter, S., 'Regulatory Enforcement and Compliance: Examining Danish Agro-Environmental Policy', *Journal of Policy Analysis and Management*, 1999, Vol. 18, pp. 625–651.

Mayers, D. & Smith Jr., C., 'On the Corporate Demand for Insurance', *Journal of Business*, 1982, Vol. 55(2), pp. 281–296.

Mburu, J. & Birner, R., 'Emergence, Adoption and Implementation of Collaborative Wildlife Management or Wildlife Partnerships in Kenya: A Look at Conditions for Success', *Society and Natural Resources*, 2007, Vol. 20(5), pp. 379–395.

McAllister, L. K., Van Rooij, B., & Kagan, R. A., 'Re-orienting Regulation: Pollution Enforcement in Industrialising Countries', *Law & Policy*, 2010, Vol. 32, pp. 1–13.

McCormick, R. & Tollison, R., *Politicians, Legislation and the Economy: An Inquiry into the Interest Group Theory of Governments*, Boston, MA, Martinus Nijhoff, 1982.

McPherson, M. A. & Nieswiadomy, M. L., 'African Elephants: The Effect of Property Rights and Political Stability', *Contemporary Economic Policy*, 2000, Vol. 18(1), pp. 14–26.

Medema, S. G., 'Juris Prudence: Calabresi's Uneasy Relationship with the Coase Theorem', *Law and Contemporary Problems*, 2014, Vol. 77(65), pp. 65–95.

Mehta, M. C., 'The Accountability Principle: Legal Solutions to Break Corruption's Impact on India's Environment', *Journal of Environmental Law & Litigation*, 2006, Vol. 21(1), pp. 141–156.

Meinberg, V., 'Empirische Erkenntnisse zum Vollzug des Umweltstrafrechts', *Zeitschrift für die Gesamte Strafrechtswissenschaften*, 1988, Vol. 100, pp. 112–157.

Merrill, T., 'Trespass, Nuisance and the Costs of Determining Property Rights', *Journal of Legal Studies*, 1985, Vol. 14(1), pp. 13–48.

Mettler, F. & Moseley, R., *Medical Effects of Ionizing Radiation*, Orlando, FL, Grune and Stratton, 1985.

Miceli, T., 'Optimal Prosecution of Defendants Whose Guilt Is Uncertain', *Journal of Law, Economics and Organisation*, 1990, Vol. 6, pp. 189–201.

Miceli, Th. J., 'Litigation Costs and the Statute of Limitations for Tort Suits', *International Review of Law and Economics*, 2000, Vol. 20(3), pp. 383–394.

Miller, J. G. & Justice, C., 'Organisational Liability for Environmental Crimes', in Paddock, L. C., Markell, D. L., & Bryner, N. S. (eds.), *Compliance and Enforcement of Environmental Law*, Cheltenham, Edward Elgar, 2017, pp. 200–214.

Millimet, D. L. & List, J. A., 'The Case of the Missing Pollution Haven Hypothesis', *Journal of Regulatory Economics*, 2004, Vol. 26, pp. 239–262.

Ministry of Housing, 'Spatial Planning and the Environment, the Netherlands' Energy Tax: Questions and Answers', The Hague, Ministry of Housing, 2004.

Mishan, E. J., 'Pangloss on Pollution', *Swedish Journal of Economics*, 1971a, Vol. 73(1), pp. 113–120.

'The Post War Literature on Externalities: An Interpretative Essay', *Journal of Economic Literature*, 1971b, Vol. 9(1), pp. 1–28.

*Cost-Benefit Analysis: An Informal Introduction*, London, Allen & Unwin, 2nd ed., 1974.

Moloney, M. T. & McCormick, R. E., 'A Positive Theory of Environmental Quality Regulation', *Journal of Law & Economics*, 1982, Vol. 25, pp. 99–123.

Monti, A., 'Environmental Risk: A Comparative Law and Economics Approach to Liability and Insurance', *European Review of Private Law*, 2001, Vol. 1, pp. 51–79.

Montini, M., 'The Principle of Integration', in Krämer, L. & Orlando, E. (eds.), *Principles of Environmental Law*, Cheltenham, Edward Elgar, 2018, pp. 139–149.

Moore, T. P., 'The Purpose of Licensing', *Journal of Law and Economics*, 1961, Vol. 4, pp. 93–117.

Morely, B., 'Empirical Evidence on the Effectiveness of Environmental Taxes', University of Bath, Working Paper No. 02/10, 2010, available at: http://opus.bath.ac.uk/18105/1/0210.pdf.

Mullenix, L., 'Prometheus Unbound: The Gulf Coast Claims Facility as a Means for Resolving Mass Tort Claims – A Fund Too Far', 2011, *Louisiana Law Review*, Vol. 71, p. 819.

Mullis, A. & Oliphant, K., *Torts*, London, Palgrave, 2011.

Myerson, R. B. & Satterthwaite, M. A., 'Efficient Mechanisms for Bilateral Trading', *Journal of Economic Theory*, 1983, Vol. 29(2), pp. 265–281.

Nash, J. R., 'Too Much Market? Conflict between Tradable Pollution Allowances and the "Polluter Pays Principle"', *Harvard Environmental Law Review*, 2000, Vol. 24, pp. 465–535.

Nash, J. R. & Revesz, R. L., 'The Design of Marketable Permit Schemes to Control Local and Regional Pollutants', *Ecology Law Quarterly*, 2001, Vol. 28, pp. 559–661.

'The Design of Marketable Permit Schemes to Control Local and Regional Pollutants', in Swanson, Th. (ed.), *An Introduction to the Law and Economics of Environmental Policy: Issues in Institutional Design*, Amsterdam, JAI Press, 2002, pp. 331–377.

Nelson, B., *Economic Analysis of Transportation Noise Abatement*, Cambridge, MA, Ballinger, 1978.

Nentjes, A. & Hommes, J., 'Handhaving van het milieurecht', *Tijdschrift voor Milieuaansprakelijkheid*, 1990, pp. 1–7.

Newman, P. (ed.), *New Palgrave Dictionary of Economics and the Law*, London, Macmillan, 1998.

Niessen, N., 'Decentralized Environmental Management', in Faure, M. & Niessen, N. (eds.), *Environmental Law in Development: Lessons from the Indonesian Experience*, Cheltenham, Edward Elgar, 2006, pp. 143–181.

Niezen, G. J., Raaijmaker, M. J. G. C., & Tervoort, A. J. S. M. (eds.), *Aansprakelijkheid voor milieuschade in de Europese Unie: Ongebonden Recht Bedrijven*, Deventer, Kluwer, 2000.

Nshimbi, M. & Vinya, R., 'Impacts of Public-Private Partnerships on Local Livelihoods and Natural Resource Dynamics: Perceptions from Eastern Zambia', *Resources*, 2014, Vol. 3(2), pp. 471–487.

Nyborg, K. & Telle, K., 'The Role of Warnings in Regulation: Keeping Control with Less Punishment', *Journal of Public Economics*, 2004, Vol. 88(12), pp. 2801–2816.

Oates, W., *Fiscal Federalism*, New York, Harcourt Brace Jovanovich, 1972.

'Book Review: The Uncertain Search for Environmental Quality', *University of Pennsylvania Law Review*, 1976, Vol. 124(3), pp. 864–891.

'The Regulation of Externalities: Efficient Behaviour by Sources and Victims', *Public Finance*, 1983, Vol. 38(3), pp. 362–375.

Oates, W. E., 'The Environment and the Economy: Environmental Policy at the Crossroads', in Quigley, J. & Rubinfeld, D. (eds.), *American Domestic Priorities: An Economic Appraisal*, Berkeley, CA, University of California Press, 1985, pp. 311–345.

'Market Incentives for Environmental Protection: A Survey of Some Recent Developments', in Peston, M. & Quandt, R. (eds.), *Prices, Competition and Equilibrium*, London, Philip Allen, 1986, pp. 251–267.

'Economics, Economists, and Environmental Policy', *Eastern Economic Journal*, 1990, Vol. 16(4), pp. 289–296.

Oates, W. & McGartland, A. M., 'Marketable Permits for the Prevention of Environmental Deterioration', *Journal of Environmental Economics and Management*, 1985, Vol. 12(3), pp. 207–228.

Oates, W. & Schwab, R., 'Economic Competition among Jurisdictions: Efficiency Enhancing or Distortion Inducing?', *Journal of Public Economics*, 1988, Vol. 35(3), pp. 333–354.

Oates, W. E., Portney, P. R., & McGartland, A. M., 'The Net Benefits of Incentive-Based Regulation: A Case Study of Environmental Standard Setting', *American Economic Review*, 1989, Vol. 79, pp. 1233–1244.

OCIMF, 'The U.S. Oil Pollution Act of 1990 ('OPA 90'): Why Has It Been so Successful at Reducing Spills', 2003.

O'Connor, D., 'Applying Economic Instruments in Developing Countries: From Theory to Implementation', *Environment and Development Economics*, 1998, Vol. 4(1), pp. 91–110.

OECD, *The Political Economy of Environmentally Related Taxes*, Paris, OECD, 2006.

*Ensuring Environmental Compliance: Trends and Good Practice*, Paris, OECD, 2009.

Ogus, A. I., 'Quantitative Rules and Judicial Decision-Making', in Burrows, P. & Veljanovski, C. (eds.), *The Economic Approach to Law*, London, Butterworth, 1981, pp. 210–225.

*Regulation: Legal Form and Economic Theory*, Oxford, Oxford University Press, 1994a.

'Standard-Setting for Environmental Protection: Principles and Processes', in Faure, M., Vervaele, J., & Weale, A. (eds.), *Environmental Standard in the European Union in an Interdisciplinary Framework*, Antwerp, Maklu, 1994b, pp. 23–37.

'Quality Control for European Regulation', *Maastricht Journal of European and Comparative Law*, 1995, Vol. 2, pp. 325–338.

Ogus, A., 'Competition between National Legal Systems: A Contribution to Economic Analysis to Comparative Law', *International and Comparative Law Quarterly*, 1999b, Vol. 48, pp. 405–418.

Ogus, A., 'Enforcing Regulation: Do We Need the Criminal Law?', in Sjögren, H. & Skogh, G. (eds.), *New Perspectives on Economic Crime*, Cheltenham, UK/Northampton, MA, USA, Edward Elgar, 2004a, pp. 42–56.

*Regulation: Legal Form and Economic Theory*, Oxford, Clarendon Press, 2004b.

'Corruption and Regulatory Structures', *Law & Policy*, 2004c, Vol. 26, pp. 229–246.

'Regulatory Arrangements and Incentives for Opportunistic Behaviour', in Eger, Th., Faure, M., & Zhang, N. (eds.), *Economic Analysis of Law in China*, Cheltenham, Edward Elgar, 2007, pp. 151–158.

'Regulation Revisited', *Public Law*, 2009, Vol. 2, pp. 332–346.

Ogus, A. & Abbot, C., 'Pollution and Penalties', in Swanson, T. (ed.), *An Introduction to the Law and Economics of Environmental Policy: Issues in Institutional Design*, Amsterdam, Elsevier, 2002a, pp. 493–516.

'Sanctions for Pollution: Do We Have the Right Regime?', *Journal of Environmental Law*, 2002b, Vol. 14, pp. 283–300.

Ogus, A. I. & Carbonara, E., 'Self-Regulation', in Parisi, F. (ed.), *Production of Legal Rules*, Cheltenham, Edward Elgar, 2011, pp. 228–252.

Olken, B. A., 'Corruption and the Costs of Redistribution: Micro Evidence from Indonesia', *Journal of Public Economics*, 2006, Vol. 90, pp. 853–870.

Olmstead, S. M. & Stavins, R. N., 'Comparing Price and Nonprice Approaches to Urban Water Conservation', *Water Resources Research*, 2009, Vol. 45, W04301, pp. 1–10.

Olson, M., *The Logic of Collective Action*, Cambridge, Harvard University Press, 1971.

*The Rise and Decline of Nations*, New Haven, Yale University Press, 1982.

Orts, E. W. & Deketelaere, K. (eds.), *Environmental Contracts: Comparative Approaches to Regulatory Innovation in the United States and Europe*, The Hague, Kluwer Law International, 2002.

Ostrom, E., 'Self-Governance and Forest Resources', 1999, available at: www.cifor.org/publications/pdf_files/OccPapers/OP-20.pdf.

Ostrom. E. et al., 'Revisiting the Commons: Local Lessons, Global Challenges', *Science*, 1999, Vol. 284(5412), pp. 278–282.

Ott, C. L. & Schäfer, H.-B., 'Die Vereinheitlichung des Europäischen Vertragsrechts: Ökonomische Notwendigkeit oder akademisches Interesse?', in Ott, C. L. & Schäfer, H.-B. (eds.), *Vereinheitlichung und Diversität des Zivilrechts in transnationalen Wirtschaftsraum*, Tübingen, Mohr Siebeck, 2003, pp. 203–236.

Otto, H. J., *General Prävention und externe Verhaltenskontrolle: Wandel von soziologischen zum ökonomischen Paradigma in der nord-amerikanischen Kriminologie?*, Freiburg im Breisgau, Max Planck Institute for Foreign and International Criminal Law, 1982.

Pagh, P., 'The New Danish Act on Strict Liability for Environmental Damage', *Environmental Liability*, 1995, Vol. 3, pp. 15–19.

'Experiences of and Plans for the Codification of Environmental Law in Denmark', in Bocken, H. & Ryckbost, D. (eds.), *Codification of Environmental Law, Proceedings of the International Conference*, The Hague, Kluwer Law International, 1996, pp. 143–153.

Palmer, T. & Riera, A., 'Tourism and Environmental Taxes: With Special Reference to the "Balearic Ecotax"', *Tourism Management*, 2003, Vol. 24, pp. 665–674.

Paloniitty, T. & Eliantonio, M., 'Scientific Knowledge in Environmental Judicial Review: Safeguarding Effective Judicial Protection in the EU Member States?', *European Energy and Environmental Law Review*, 2018, Vol. 27, pp. 108–114.

Panayotou, T., 'Economic Instruments for Environmental Management in Developing Countries', Prepared for the United Nations Environment Programme's Consultative Expert Group Meeting on the Use and Application of Economic Policy Instruments for Environmental Management and Sustainable Development, Nairobi, February 23–24, 1995; Environmental Economics Series Paper No. 16; 1–73.

Pallemaerts, M., 'De opkomst van het begrip duurzame ontwikkeling, het internationaal juridisch en politiek discours: een Conceptuele revolutie', *Recht en kritiek*, 1995, Vol. 21, pp. 60–77.

Parpworth, N., 'Enforcement in Environmental Regulation: The Defra Review', *Environmental Liability*, 2007, Vol. 15(1), pp. 15–26.

Partain, R. A., 'Moerman versus Pierson: The Nexus of Occupancy in Animals Ferae Naturae and Liability in Tort,' *Soongsil Law Review*, 2012, Vol. 28, pp. 241–290.

Partain, R., 'The Legally Pluralistic Tourist', in Sonnenburg, S. & Wee, D. (eds.), *Touring Consumption – Management – Culture – Interpretation*, Wiesbaden, Springer VS, 2015, pp. 261–284.

Pashigian, B. P., 'The Effect of Environmental Regulation on Optimal Plant Size and Factor Shares', *Journal of Law & Economics*, 1984, Vol. 27, pp. 1–28.

Pauly, M., 'The Economics of Moral Hazard: Comment', *American Economic Review*, 1968, Vol. 58, pp. 531–545.

Peeters, M., 'Emissions Trading as a New Dimension to European Environmental Law: The Political Agreement of the European Council on Greenhouse Gas Allowance Trading', *European Environmental Law Review*, 2003, Vol. 12, pp. 82–92.

'Enforcement of the EU Greenhouse Gas Emissions Trading Scheme', in Deketelaere, K. & Peeters, M. (eds.), *EU Climate Change Policy: The Challenge of New Regulatory Initiatives*, Cheltenham UK, Edward Elgar Publishing, 2006a, pp. 169–187.

'Inspection and Market-Based Regulation Through Emissions Trading: The Striking Reliance on Self-Monitoring, Self-Reporting and Verification', *Utrecht Law Review*, 2006b, Vol. 2(1), pp. 177–195.

'The Joint Governance of Transboundary River Basins: Some Observations on the Role of Law', in Faure, M. & Song, Y. (eds.), *China and International Environmental Liability: Legal Remedies for Transboundary Pollution*, Cheltenham, Edward Elgar, 2008, pp. 192–224.

'Greenhouse Gas Emissions Trading in the EU', in Farber, D. A. & Peeters, M. (eds.), *Climate Change Law*, Cheltenham, Edward Elgar, 2016, pp. 377–387.

Pelzman, S., 'Toward a More General Theory of Regulation', *Journal of Law and Economics*, 1976, Vol. 19, pp. 211–240.

Perez, O., 'Reflections on an Environmental Struggle: P&O, Dahanu and the Regulation of Multinational Enterprises', *Georgetown International Environmental Law Review*, 2002, Vol. 15(1), pp. 1–27.

Pernetta, A. P., 'A Disappearing Drylands Icon? White Rhinoceros Conservation and the Need for Public-Private Partnerships', *Biodiversity*, 2014, Vol. 15(2–3), pp. 231–233.

Perron, W., 'Vermögensstrafe und erweiterte Verfall', *Juristenzeitung*, 1993, pp. 919–920.

Pigou, A. C., *A Study in Public Finance*, London, Macmillan, 1951.

Polak, N. V., 'Algemene beginselen van rechterlijk overgangsrecht', *Themis*, 1984, Vol. 46, pp. 231–244.

Polborn, M. K., 'Mandatory Insurance and the Judgment Proof Problem', *International Review of Law and Economics*, 1998, Vol. 18(2), pp. 141–146.

Polinsky, A. M., 'Controlling Externalities and Protecting Entitlements: Property Rights, Liability Rule and the Tax-Subsidy Approaches', *Journal of Legal Studies*, 1979, Vol. 8, pp. 1–48.

Polinsky, M., *Introduction to Law and Economics*, Boston, MA, Little, Brown and Company, 1983.

Polinsky, A. M. & Shavell, S., 'The Optimal Trade-Off between the Probability and the Magnitude of Fines', *American Economic Review*, 1979, Vol. 69, pp. 880–891.

'A Note on Optimal Fines When Wealth Varies among Individuals', *American Economic Review*, 1991, Vol. 81, pp. 618–621.

'Should Employees be Subject to Fines and Imprisonment Given the Existence of Corporate Liability?', *International Review of Law and Economics*, 1993, Vol. 13, pp. 239–257.

Pommerehne, W. W., 'Measuring Environmental Benefits: A Comparison of Hedonic Technique and Contingent Valuation', in Bös, D., Rose, M., & Seidl, Chr. (eds.), *Welfare and Efficiency in Public Economics*, Berlin, Springer, 1988, pp. 363–400.

Porter, M., 'America's Green Strategy', *Scientific American*, 1991, Vol. 264(4), pp. 168–179.

Porter, M. E. & Van der Linde, C., 'Towards a New Conception of the Environment-Competitiveness Relationship', *Journal of Economic Perspectives*, 1995, Vol. 9, pp. 97–118.

Posner, R., *Economic Analysis of Law*, Boston, MA, Little, Brown and Company, 1973.

'Theories of Economic Regulation', *Bell Journal of Economics*, 1974, Vol. 5(2), pp. 335–358.

'Optimal Sentences for White-Collar Criminals', *American Criminal Law Review*, 1980, Vol. 17, pp. 400–418.

'An Economic Theory of the Criminal Law', *Columbia Law Review*, 1985, Vol. 85, pp. 1193–1209.

*Economic Analysis of Law*, 3rd ed., Boston, MA, Little, Brown and Company, 1986.

*Economic Analysis of Law*, 5th ed., New York, Aspen Law & Business, 1998.

*Economic Analysis of Law*, 6th ed., New York, Aspen Publishers, 2003.

*Economic Analysis of Law*, 9th ed., New York, Aspen Publishers, 2014.

Pozzo, B., 'The Liability Problem in Modern Environmental Statutes', *European Review of Private Law*, 1996, Vol. 4(2), pp. 111–144.

Priest, G. L., 'The Current Insurance Crisis and Modern Tort Law', *Yale Law Journal*, 1987, Vol. 96, pp. 1521–1590.

Prieur, M., 'Le parlement contre l'environnement', *Revue Juridique de l'Environnement*, 1977, Vol. 2(2), pp. 131–135.

*Droit de l'Environnement*, 6th ed., Paris, Dalloz, 2011.

Princen, S. B. M., 'The California Effect in the Transatlantic Relationship', diss., University of Utrecht, 2002, unpublished.

Raja, A. V. & Rathinam, F. X., 'Economic Efficiency and Public Interest Litigations (PIL): Lessons from India', paper presented at the first annual conference of the Asian Law and Economics Association 20 (June 25, 2005a) (Asian Law and Econ. Ass'n Conference, Kyung Hee Univ. [S. Korea]).

'Efficiency and Strategic Behaviour: The Case of Mass Torts' (unpublished working paper, on file with the University of Hyderabad, Dep't Econ.), 2005b.

'Regulatory Failure and the Economic Efficiency of Public Interest Litigation 22' (Dec. 8, 2006) (unpublished manuscript, University of Hyderabad) (on file with the Virginia Journal of International Law Association).

Rajamani, L., 'Public Interest Environmental Litigation in India: Exploring Issues of Access, Participation, Equity, Effectiveness and Sustainability', *Journal of Environmental Law*, 2007, Vol. 19(3), pp. 293–323.

Ranchordás, S., 'Innovation-Friendly Regulation: The Sunset of Regulation, the Sunrise of Innovation', *Jurimetrics*, 2015, Vol. 55(2), pp. 201–224.

Rea, S., 'The Economics of Insurance Law', *International Review of Law and Economics*, 1993, Vol. 13, pp. 145–162.

'Insurance Law', in Newman, P. (ed.), *The New Palgrave Dictionary of Economics and the Law*, London, Macmillan, 1998, pp. 342–348.

Reese, M., 'The Proximity Principle', in Krämer, L. & Orlando, E. (eds.), *Principles of Environmental Law*, Cheltenham, Edward Elgar, 2018, pp. 219–233.

Reny, Ph. J., 'Arrow's Theorem and the Gibbard-Satterthwaite Theorem: A Unified Approach', *Economics Letters*, 2001, Vol. 70(1), pp. 99–105.

Revesz, R., 'Rehabilitating Interstate Competition: Rethinking the Race-for-the-Bottom Rationale for Federal Environmental Regulation', *New York University Law Review*, 1992, Vol. 67, pp. 1210–1254.

'Federalism and Environmental Regulation: Lessons for the European Union and the International Community', *Virginia Law Review*, 1997a, Vol. 83, pp. 1331–1346.

Revesz, R. L., 'The Race-to-the-Bottom and Federal Environmental Regulation: A Response to Critics', *Minnesota Law Review*, 1997b, Vol. 82, pp. 535–564.

'Environmental Regulation, Cost-Benefit Analysis and the Discounting of Human Lives', *Columbia Law Review*, 1999, Vol. 99, pp. 941–1017.

'Federalism and Environmental Regulation: An Overview', in Revesz, R., Sands, Ph., & Stewart, R. (eds.), *Environmental Law: The Economy and Sustainable Development*, Cambridge, Cambridge University Press, 2000, pp. 37–79.

Revesz, R. L. & Livermore, M. A., *Retaking Rationality: How Cost Benefit Analysis Can Better Protect the Environment and Our Health*, Oxford, Oxford University Press, 2008.

Revesz, R. & Stewart, R. (eds.), *Analysing Superfund, Economics, Science and Law*, Washington, DC, Resources for the Future, 1995.

Richardson, B. J., *Environmental Regulation through Financial Organisations: Comparative Perspectives on the Industrialised Nation*, The Hague, Kluwer Law International, 2002.

Richardson, B. & Chanwai, K., 'The UK's Climate Change Levy: Is It Working?', *Journal of Environmental Law*, 2003, Vol. 15(1), pp. 39–58.

Richardson, G., Ogus, A., & Burrows, P., *Policy Pollution: A Study of Regulation and Enforcement*, Oxford, Clarendon Press, 1982.

Rizzo, M. & Arnold, F., 'Causal Apportionment in the Law of Torts: An Economic Theory', *Columbia Law Review*, 1980, Vol. 80, pp. 1399–1429.

'Causal Apportionment: Reply to the Critics', *Journal of Legal Studies*, 1986, Vol. 15, pp. 219–226.

Robinson, G., 'Probabilistic Causation and Compensation for Tortuous Risk', *Journal of Legal Studies*, 1985, Vol. 14, pp. 779–798.

Rody, M., 'Public Environmental Law in Germany', in Seerden, R. & Heldeweg, M., *Comparative Environmental Law in Europe, An Introduction to Public Environmental Law in the EU Member States*, Antwerp, Maklu, 1996, pp. 151–191.

Romano, C. P. R., *The Peaceful Settlement of International Environmental Disputes: A Pragmatic Approach*, London, Kluwer Law International, 2000.

Ronneberg, N. J., 'An Introduction to the Protection and Indemnity Clubs and the Marine Insurance They Provide', *University of San Francisco Maritime Law Journal*, 1990, Vol. 3, pp. 1–36.

Rose, C. M., 'Surprising Commons', *Brigham Young University Law Review*, 2014, Vol. 2014 (4), pp. 1257–1282.

Rose-Ackerman, S., 'Regulation and the Law of Torts', *American Economic Review/Papers & Proceedings*, 1991, Vol. 81, pp. 54–58.

'Environmental Liability Law', in Tietenberg, T. H. (ed.), *Innovation in Environmental Policy: Economic and Legal Aspects in Recent Developments in Environmental Enforcement and Liability*, Brookfield VT, Edward Elgar, 1992a, pp. 223–243.

*Re-thinking the Progressive Agenda, the Reform of the American Regulatory State*, New York, The Free Press, 1992b.

'Law versus Private Law in Environmental Regulation: European Union Proposals in the Light of United States Experience', *Review of European Community and International Environmental Law*, 1995a, Vol. 4, pp. 312–332.

*Controlling Environmental Policy: The Limits of Public Law in Germany and the United States*, New Haven, CT, Yale University Press, 1995b.

'Public Law versus Private Law in Environmental Regulation: European Union Proposals in the Light of United States and German Experiences', in Eide, E. & Van den Bergh, R. (eds.), *Law and Economics of the Environment*, Oslo, Juridisk Forlag, 1996, pp. 13–39.

Rosen, H. S., *Public Finance*, Chicago, Irwin, 1999.

Rosenberg, D., 'The Causal Connection in Mass Exposure Cases: A "Public Law" Vision of the Tort System', *Harvard Law Review*, 1984, Vol. 97(4), pp. 851–929.

Rousseau, S., 'Economic Empirical Analysis of Sanctions for Environmental Violations: A Literature Overview', Energy, Transport & Environmental Working Papers Series, Katholieke Universiteit Leuven, Centre for Economic Studies, Working Paper No. 2007a-03.

'The Impact of Sanctions and Inspections on Firms' Environmental Compliance Decisions', Katholieke Universiteit Leuven, Centre for Economic Studies, Working Paper No. 2007b-04.

'Timing of Environmental Inspections: Survival of the Compliant', *Journal of Regulatory Economics*, 2007c, Vol. 32, pp. 17–36.

'Evidence of a Filtered Approach to Environmental Monitoring', *European Journal of Law & Economics*, 2010, Vol. 29(2), pp. 195–209.

Rowell, A., 'Time in Cost-Benefit Analysis', *UC Irvine Law Review*, 2014, Vol. 4, pp. 1215–1239.

Rutagarama, E. & Martin, A., 'Partnerships for Protected Area Conservation in Rwanda', *Geographic Journal*, 2006, Vol. 172(4), pp. 291–305.

Salzman, J., 'Teaching Policy Instrument Choice in Environmental Law: The Five P's', *Duke Environmental Law & Policy Forum*, 2013, Vol. 23, pp. 363–376.

Salzman, J., Bennett, G., Carroll, N., Goldstein, A., & Jenkins, M., 'The Global Status and Trends of Payments for Ecosystem Services', *Nature Sustainability*, 2018, Vol. 1(3), pp. 136–144.

Salzman, J., Ruhl, J. B., & Nash, J. R., 'Environmental Law in Austerity', *Pace Environmental Law Review*, 2015, Vol. 32, pp. 481–491.

Sandmo, A., 'Environmental Taxation and Revenue for Development', WIDER Discussion Paper, No. 2003/86, The United Nations University World Institute for Development Economics Research (UNU-WIDER), Helsinki, 2003, pp. 1–28.

Sands, Ph., *Principles of International Environmental Law I: Frameworks, Standards and Implementation*, Manchester, Manchester University Press, 1994.

*Principles of International Environmental Law*, 2nd ed., Cambridge, Cambridge University Press, 2003.

Sands, Ph. & Peel, J., *Principles of International Environmental Law*, 3rd ed., Cambridge, Cambridge University Press, 2012.

Sathe, S. P., 'Judicial Activism: The Indian Experience', *Washington University Journal of Law & Policy*, 2001, Vol. 6, pp. 29–107.

Satterthwaite, M. A., 'Strategy-Proofness and Arrow's Conditions: Existence and Correspondence Theorems for Voting Procedures and Social Welfare Functions', *Journal of Economic Theory*, 1975, Vol. 10(2), pp. 187–217.

Schäfer, H.-B., 'Efficient Third Party Liability of Auditors in Tort Law and in Contract Law', *Supreme Court Economic Review*, 2004, Vol. 12, pp. 181–208.

'Rules versus Standards in Rich and Poor Countries: Precise Legal Norms as Substitutes for Human Capital in Low-Income Countries', *Supreme Court Economic Review*, 2006, Vol. 14, p. 113.

'Can Member State Liability for the Infringment of European Law Deter National Legislators?', in Eger, Th. & Schäfer, H.-B. (eds.), *Research Handbook on the Economics of European Union Law*, Cheltenham, Edward Elgar, 2012, pp. 82–94.

Schmitz, P. W., 'On the Joint Use of Liability and Safety Regulation', *International Review of Law and Economics*, 2000, Vol. 20, pp. 371–382.

Schoep, G. K. & Schuyt, P. M., *Feiten en percepties van de sanctionering van milieudelicten en delicten betreffende de volksgezondheid*, Leiden, Universiteit Leiden, 2008.

Schultze, Ch., *The Public Use of Private Interest*, Washington, DC, The Brookings Institution, 1977.

Schulze, W. & D'Arge, R., 'The Coase Proposition, Information Constraints, and Long Run Equilibrium', *American Economic Review*, 1974, Vol. 64(4), pp. 763–772.

Schwartz, A., 'Statutory Interpretation, Capture, and Tort Law: The Regulatory Compliance Defence', *American Law and Economics Review*, 2000, Vol. 2, pp. 1–57.

Schwartz, G., 'Mixed Theories of Tort Law: Affirming both Deterrence and Corrective Justice', *Texas Law Review*, 1997, Vol. 75, pp. 1801–1834.

Schwartz, P., 'The Polluter-Pays-Principle', in Krämer, L. & Orlando, E. (eds.), *Principles of Environmental Law*, Cheltenham, Edward Elgar, 2018, pp. 260–271.

Schwartz, A. & Wilde, L., 'Intervening in Markets on the Basis of Imperfect Information: A Legal and Economic Analysis', *University of Pittsburgh Law Review*, 1979, Vol. 127, pp. 630–682.

Seerden, R. & Heldeweg, M., 'Public Environmental Law in the Netherlands', in Seerden, R. & Heldeweg, M. (eds.), *Comparative Environmental Law in Europe: An Introduction* to *Public Environmental Law in the EU Member States*, Antwerp, Maklu, 1996, pp. 269–311.

Segerson, K., 'An Assessment of Legal Liability as a Market-Based Instrument', in Freeman, J. & Kolstad, C. D. (eds.), *Moving to Markets in Environmental Regulation: Lessons from Twenty Years of Experience*, Oxford, Oxford University Press, 2007, pp. 250–270.

Segerson, K. & Tietenberg, T., 'Defining Efficient Sanctions', in Tietenberg, T. H. (ed.), *Innovation in Environmental Policy*, Aldershot, UK/Brockfield, VT, Edward Elgar, 1992, pp. 63–65.

Sellenthin, M. O. & Skogh, G., 'Property Rights in Endangered Species: The Wolverine Case', *European Journal of Law and Economics*, 2004, Vol. 18(2), pp. 239–247.

Shapo, M. S., 'Tort Law and Environmental Risk', 1997, *Pace Environmental Law Review*, Vol. 14(2), pp. 531–544.

Sharon, O., Fishman, S. N., Ruhl, J. B., Olander, L., & Roady, S. E., 'Ecosystem Services and Judge-Made Law: A Review of Legal Cases in Common Law Countries', *Ecosystem Services*, 2018, Vol. 32, pp. 9–21.

Shavell, S., 'On Moral Hazard and Insurance', *Quarterly Journal of Economics*, 1979, Vol. 14, pp. 541–562.

'Strict Liability versus Negligence', *Journal of Legal Studies*, 1980a, Vol. 9(1), pp. 1–25.

'An Analysis of Causation and the Scope of Liability in the Law of Torts', *Journal of Legal Studies*, 1980b, Vol. 9, pp. 463–516.

'Liability for Harm versus Regulation of Safety', *Journal of Legal Studies*, 1984a, Vol. 13, pp. 357–374.

'A Model of the Optimal Use of Liability and Safety Regulation', *Rand Journal of Economics*, 1984b, Vol. 15, pp. 271–280.

'Uncertainty over Causation and the Determination of Civil Liability', *Journal of Law and Economics*, 1985a, Vol. 28, pp. 587–609.

'Criminal Law and the Optimal Use of Non-monetary Sanctions as a Deterrent', *Columbia Law Review*, 1985b, Vol. 85, pp. 1232–1262.

'The Judgment Proof Problem', *International Review of Law and Economics*, 1986, Vol. 6, pp. 45–58.

*Economic Analysis of Accident Law*, Cambridge, Harvard University Press, 1987.

*Foundations of Economic Analysis of Law*, Cambridge, Harvard University Press, 2004.

'The Corrective Tax versus Liability as Solutions to the Problem of Harmful Externalities', *Journal of Law and Economics*, 2011, Vol. 54, pp. 250–265.

Shimshack, J. P., 'Quantitatively Measuring Deterrence: Empirical Tools for Assessing the Impact of Environmental Monitoring and Enforcement Actions', in Paddock, L. C., Markell, D. L. & Bryner, N. S. (eds.), *Compliance and Enforcement of Environmental Law*, Cheltenham, Edward Elgar, 2017, pp. 221–241.

Siems, M., *Comparative Law*, Cambridge, Cambridge University Press, 2014.

Sigman, H., 'Environmental Liability in Practice: Liability for Clean-Up of Contaminated Sites under Superfund', in Heyes, A. (ed.), *The Law and Economics of the Environment*, Cheltenham, Edward Elgar, 2001, pp. 116–149.

Silberman, J. & Hindin, D., 'Effective Environmental Monitoring and Reporting', in Paddock, L. C., Markell, D. L. & Bryner, N. S. (eds.), *Compliance and Enforcement of Environmental Law*, Cheltenham, Edward Elgar, 2017, pp. 128–140.

Simon, J., 'Das Umwelthaftungsgesetz', in Ahrens, M. & Simon, J. (eds.), *Umwelthaftung, Risikosteuerung und Versicherung*, Berlin, Erich Schmidt Verlag, 1996, pp. 15–26.

Sinclair-Desgagné, B., 'The Environmental Goods and Services Industry', *International Review of Environmental and Resource Economics*, 2008, Vol. 2(1), pp. 69–99.

Sinden, A., 'Cost-Benefit Analysis', in Paddock, L. C., Glicksman, R. L. & Bryner, N. S. (eds.), *Decision-Making in Environmental Law*, Cheltenham, Edward Elgar, 2016, pp. 295–309.

Sioutis, G., 'Public Environmental Law in Greece', in Seerden, R. & Heldeweg, M., (eds.), *Comparative Environmental Law in Europe: An Introduction to Public Environmental Law in the EU Member States*, Antwerp, Maklu, 1996, pp. 193–211.

Skogh, G., 'A Note on Gary Becker's Crime and Punishment: An Economic Approach', *Swedish Journal of Economics*, 1973, Vol. 75, pp. 305–311.

'Public Insurance and Accident Prevention', *International Review of Law and Economics*, 1982, Vol. 2, pp. 67–80.

'The Combination of Private and Public Regulation of Safety', in Faure, M. & Van den Bergh, R. (eds.), *Essays in Law and Economics: Corporations, Accident Prevention and Compensation for Losses*, Antwerp, Maklu, 1989a, pp. 87–101.

'The Transactions Cost Theory of Insurance: Contracting Impediments and Costs', *Journal of Risk and Insurance*, 1989b, Vol. 56, pp. 726–732.

'Mandatory Insurance: Transaction Costs Analysis of Insurance', in Bouckaert, G. & De Geest, G. (eds.), *Encyclopedia of Law and Economics, II: Civil Law and Economics*, Cheltenham, Edward Elgar, 2000, pp. 521–537.

Skogh, G. & Stuart, C., 'An Economic Analysis of Crime Rates, Punishment and the Social Consequences of Crime', *Public Choice*, 1982, Vol. 38, pp. 171–179.

Smets, H., 'Pour une indemnisation garantie des victimes de pollution accidentelle', in Bocken, H. & Ryckbost, D. (eds.), *Insurance of Environmental Damage*, Brussels, Story-Scientia, 1991, pp. 397–423.

'COSCA: A Complementary System for Compensation of Accidental Pollution Damage', in Wettenstein, P, (ed.), *Harm to the Environment: The Right to Compensation and the Assessment of Damage*, Oxford, Clarendon Press, 1997, pp. 223–248.

Smettan, J. R., *Kriminelle Bereicherung in Abhängigkeit von Gewinnen, Risiken, Strafen und Moral*, Freiburg im Breisgau, Max Planck Institute for Foreign and International Criminal Law, 1992.

Smith, G. P. & Steenburg, D. M., 'Environmental Hedonism or, Securing the Environment Through the Common Law', *William & Mary Environmental Law & Policy Review*, 2015, Vol. 40, pp. 65–114.

Smith, H. E., 'Governing Water: The Semicommons of Fluid Property Rights', *Arizona Law Review*, 2008, Vol. 50, pp. 445–478.

Söderholm, P., 'Environmental Policy in Transition Economies: The Effectiveness of Pollution Charges', Center of Energy and Environmental Policy Research, Massachusetts Institute of Technbology, Working Paper No. 99-006, 1999.

Spence, M. & Zeckhauser, R., 'Insurance, Information, and Individual Action', *American Economic Review*, 1971, Vol. 61, pp. 380–391.

Spier, J., 'Verdere verscherping van de aansprakelijkheid van de werkgever voor arbeidsongevallen', *Aansprakelijkheid en Verzekering*, 1993, pp. 33–38.

'De Novelle inzake art. 47 lid 5 ontwerp inbouwwet bodemsanering', *Aansprakelijkheid en Verzekering*, 1994, pp. 43–44.

'Asbest en aansprakelijkheid', in Van Dunné, J. M. (ed.), *Asbest en aansprakelijkheid*, Arnhem, Gouda Quint, 1995, pp. 35–48.

Spier, J. & Haazen, O., 'The European Group on Tort Law ("Tilburg Group") and the European Principles of Tort Law', *Zeitschrift für Europäisches Privatrecht*, 1999, pp. 469–493.

Spier, J. & Sterk, C .H. W. M., 'The Draft Convention on Civil Liability for Damage Resulting from Activities Dangerous to the Environment', *Tijdschrift voor Milieu en Recht*, 1992, Vol. 591, p. 591.

Stavang, E., 'Tolerance Limits and Temporal Priority in Environmental civil liability', paper presented at the 13th annual conference of the European Association of Law and Economics, Haifa, Israel. [A version of this paper was published in the *International Review of Law and Economics*, 1997, Vol. 17, pp. 553–574.]

'Property in Emissions? Analysis of the Norwegian GHG ETS with References also to the UK and the EU', *Environmental Law and Management*, 2005, Vol 17, pp. 209–217.

Steinzor, R. I., 'Reinventing Environmental Regulation: The Dangerous Journey from Command to Self-Control', *Harvard Environmental Law Review*, 1998, Vol. 22, pp. 103–202.

Steinzor, R., 'How Criminal Law Can Help Save the Environment', *Environmental Law*, 2016, Vol. 46, pp. 209–239.

Stephan, G., 'Economic Impact of Emissions Standards: A Computational Approach to Waste Water Treatment in Western Europe', in Bös, D., Rose, M., & Seidl, Chr. (eds.), *Welfare and Efficiency in Public Economics*, Berlin, Springer, 1988, pp. 401–422.

Sterk, C. H. W. M., *Verhoogd gevaar in het aansprakelijkheidsrecht*, diss., KUB, Kluwer, 1994.

Sterner, Th. (ed.), *The Market and the Environment: The Effectiveness of Market-Based Policy Instruments for Environmental Reform*, Cheltenham, Edward Elgar, 1999.

Sterner, Th. & Hammar, H., 'Designing Instruments for Climate Policy', in Hansjürgens, B. (ed.), *Emissions Trading for Climate Policy: US and European Perspectives*, Cambridge, Cambridge University Press, 2005, pp. 17–36.

Stewart, R. B., 'Controlling Environmental Risks through Economic Incentives', *Columbia Journal of Environmental Law*, 1988, Vol. 13, pp. 153–169.

'Economic Incentives for Environmental Protection: Opportunities and Obstacles', in Revesz, R. L., Sands, Ph., & Stewart, R. B. (eds.), *Environmental Law, the Economy and Sustainable Development*, Cambridge, Cambridge University Press, 2000, pp. 171–244.

'Instrument Choice', in Bodanksy, D., Brunnée, J. & Hey, E. (eds.), *The Oxford Handbook of International Environmental Law*, Oxford, Oxford University Press, 2007, pp. 147–181.

Stigler, G., 'The Economics of Information', *Journal of Political Economics*, 1961, Vol. 69, pp. 213–225.

'The Optimum Enforcement of Laws', *Journal of Political Economy*, 1970, Vol. 78, pp. 526–536.

Stokey, E. & Zeckhauser, R., A *Primer for Policy Analysis*, New York, Norton, 1978.

Stone, Chr. D., *Should Trees Have Standing? Law, Morality, and the Environment*, 3rd ed., Oxford, Oxford University Press, 2010.

Strand, J., 'Environmental Kuznets Curves: Empirical Relationships between Environmental Quality and Economic Development', March 2002, Memorandum No. 04/2002, Department of Economics, University of Oslo, available at: www.oekonomi.uio.no/memo.

Sunstein, C. R., 'Behavioural Analysis of Law', *University of Chicago Law Review*, 1997, Vol. 64, pp. 1175–1195.

'Behavioural Law and Economics: A Progress Report', *American Law and Economics Review*, 1999, Vol. 1(1), pp. 115–157.

Sunstein, C. R. (ed.), *Behavioural Law and Economics*, Cambridge, Cambridge University Press, 2000.

Sunstein, C. R. & Pildes, R. H., 'Reinventing the Regulatory State', *The University of Chicago Law Review*, 1995, Vol. 62(1), pp. 3–129.

Svatikova, K., *Economic Criteria for Criminalisation: Optimizing Enforcement in Case of Environmental Violations*, diss. Rotterdam, Erasmus School of Law, 2011.

Svendsen, G. T., *Public Choice and Environmental Regulation: Tradable Permit Systems in the United States and $CO_2$ Taxation in Europe*, Cheltenham UK, Edward Elgar Publishing, 1998.

Thomas, T., 'Introduction, Symposium: Remedies for Big Disasters: The BP Gulf Oil Spill and the Quest for Complete Justice', *Akron Law Review*, 2012, Vol. 45, pp. 567, 570.

Thommes, K., Faure, M. G., & Heine, K., 'The Internal Market and the Consumer: What Consumers Actually Choose', *The Columbia Journal of European Law*, 2014, Vol. 21(1), pp. 47–70.

Tiebout, C., 'A Pure Theory of Local Expenditures', *Journal of Political Economy*, 1956, Vol. 64(5), pp. 416–424.

Tietenberg, H., 'Indivisible Toxic Torts: The Economics of Joint and Several Liability', *Land Economics*, 1989, Vol. 65(4), pp. 305–319.

Tietenberg, T., *Environmental and National Resource Economics*, Reading, Addison-Wesley, 2000.

Tietenberg, Th. & Johnston, M., 'Ex Post Evaluation of Marketable Permits: Methodological Issues and Literature Review', in *Tradable Permits: Policy Evaluation, Design and Reform*, Paris, OECD, 2004, pp. 9–44.

Tolley, G. S., Graves, P. H. F., & Blonquist, G. C., *Environmental Policy: Elements of Environmental Analysis*, Vol. I, Cambridge, Ballinger Publishing Company, 1981.

Totenberg, N., 'Supreme Court Weighs Exxon Valdez Damages', *NPR*, 27 February 2008.

Toy, Ch. R. & Leffler, A. M., 'Criminal Enforcement of Environmental Law', *Michigan Bar Journal*, 2001, Vol. 80(12), pp. 21–23.

Trabucchi, C. & Patton, L., 'Storing Carbon: Options for Liability Risk Management, Financial Responsibility', World Climate Change Report, Bureau of National Affairs 5, 2008.

Trebilcock, M. J., 'The Social Insurance-Deterrence Dilemma of Modern North American Tort Law: A Canadian Perspective on the Liability Insurance Crisis', *San Diego Law Review*, 1987, Vol. 24, pp. 929–1002.

Trebilcock, M. & Howse, R., 'Trade Liberalization and Regulatory Diversity: Reconciling Competitive Markets with Competitive Politics', *European Journal of Law and Economics*, 1998, Vol. 6, pp. 5–37.

Trebilcock, M. & Winter, R.A., 'The Economics of Nuclear Accident Law', *International Review of Law and Economics*, 1997, Vol. 17(2), pp. 215–243.

Turner, R. K., Pearce, D., & Bateman, I., *Environmental Economics: An Elementary Introduction*, New York, Harvester Wheatsheaf, 1994.

Tyran, J.-R. & Zweifel, P., 'Environmental Risk Internalization through Capital Markets (ERICAM): The Case of Nuclear Power', *International Review of Law and Economics*, 1993, Vol. 13, pp. 431–444.

Van, A. J., *Onzekerheid over daderschap en causaliteit: drie visies op civielrechtelijke aansprakelijkheid*, diss., Arnhem, Gouda Quint, 1995.

Van Acht, R. J. J., 'Onrechtmatige hinder', *Milieu en Recht*, 1993, pp. 220–228.

Van Boom, W. H., Lukas, M., & Kissling, Chr. (eds.), *Tort Law and Regulatory Law*, Vienna, Springer, 2007.

Van Dam, C., 'European Tort Law and the Many Cultures of Europe', in Wilhelmsson, Th. (ed.), *Private Law and the Cultures of Europe*, The Hague, Kluwer Law International, 2007, pp. 53–76.

Van den Bergh, R., 'Belgian Public Policy towards the Retailing Trade', in Graf von den Schulenburg, J. M. & Skogh, G. (eds.), *Law and Economics and the Economics of Legal Regulation*, Dordrecht, Nijhoff, 1986, pp. 185–205.

'Le droit civil face à l'analyse économique du droit', *Revue Internationale de Droit Economique*, 1988, pp. 229–254.

'Subsidiariteit rechtseconomisch bekeken. Adieu Bruxelles?' (1994): An English summary of this inauguration address has been published at Van den Bergh. R., 'The Subsidiarity Principle in European Community Law', *Maastricht Journal of European and Comparative Law*, 1994, Vol. 1(4), pp. 337–366.

'Subsidiarity as an Economic Demarcation Principle and the Emergence of European Private Law', *Maastricht Journal of European and Comparative Law*, 1998, Vol. 5(2), pp. 129–152.

'Economics in a Legal Strait-Jacket: The Difficult Reception of Economic Analysis in European Law' (paper presented at the workshop Empirical Research and Legal Realism. Setting the Agenda, Haifa, Israel, 6–9 June 1999).

'Towards an Institutional Legal Framework for Regulatory Competition in Europe', *Kyklos*, 2000, Vol. 53, pp. 435–466.

'Farewell Utopia? Why the European Union Should Take the Economics of Federalism Seriously', *Maastricht Journal of European and Comparative Law*, 2016, Vol. 23(6), pp. 937–964.

Van den Bergh, R., Faure, M. G. & Lefevere, J., 'The Subsidiarity Principle in European Environmental Law: An Economic Analysis', in Eide, E. & Van den Bergh, R. (eds.), *Law and Economics of the Environment*, Oslo, Juridisk Forlag, 1996, pp. 121–166.

Vanden Borre, T., 'Transplantatie van "kanalisatie van aansprakelijkheid" van het kernenergierecht naar het milieu(aansprakelijkheids)recht: een goede of een gebrekkige zaak?', in Faure, M. & Deketelaere, K. (eds.), *Ius Commune en Milieurecht. Actualia in het Milieurecht in België en Nederland*, Antwerp, Intersentia, 1997, pp. 329–382.

'Channelling of Liability: A Few Juridical and Economic Views on an Inadequate Legal Construction', in Horbach, N. (ed.), *Contemporary Developments in Nuclear Energy Law, Harmonising Legislation in CEEC/NIS*, Alphen a/d Rijn, Kluwer Law International, 1999, pp. 13–28.

*Efficiënte preventie en compensatie van catastroferisico's: het voorbeeld van schade door kernongevallen*, Antwerp, Intersentia, 2001.

'Shifts in Governance in Compensation for Nuclear Damage, 20 Years after Tchernobyl', in Faure, M. & Verheij, A. (eds.), *Shifts in Compensation for Environmental Damage*, Vienna, Springer, 2007, pp. 261–308.

Van den Heuvel, G., 'Corporate Crimes in East and West: In Search of Collusion', in Strang, H. & Vernon, J. (eds.), *International Trends in Crime: East Meets West*, Canberra, AIC, 1982, pp. 121–136.

Van Dunné, J. M. (ed.), *Transboundary Pollution and Liability: The Case of the River Rhine*, Lelystad, Vermande, 1991.

Van Dunné, J. M., 'Het Schelde-arrest en aansprakelijkheid voor asbest', in Van Dunné, J. M. (ed.), *Asbest en aansprakelijkheid*, Arnhem, Gouda Quint, 1995, pp. 19–34.

(ed.), *Non-point Source River Pollution: The Case of the River Meuse*, London, Kluwer Law International, 1996.

Van Dunné, J. M. & Snijder, E. E. I., 'Asbest en aansprakelijkheid', Tijdschrift voor Milieuaansprakelijkheid, 1991, pp. 60–71.

Van Rooy, B., *Regulating Land and Pollution in China: Law Making, Compliance, and Enforcement; Theory and Cases*, Leiden, Leiden University Press, 2006.

Van Zeben, J. A. W., 'The Untapped Potential of Horizontal Private Enforcement Within European Environmental Law', *The Georgetown International Environmental Law Review*, 2010, Vol. 22, pp. 241–269.

Van Zeben, J., 'Regulatory Competence Allocation: The Missing Link in Theories of Federalism', *Law, Institutions and Economics in Nanterre Workshop, Paris, France*, 2012, Vol. 11, pp. 1–37.

'Subsidiarity in European Environmental Law: A Competence Allocation Approach', *Harvard Environmental Law Review*, 2014, Vol. 38, pp. 415–464.

Veljanovski, C. G., 'The Economic Theory of Tort Liability – Toward a Corrective Justice Approach', in Burrows, P. & Veljanovski, C. G. (eds.), *The Economic Approach to Law*, London, Butterworths, 1981, pp. 125–150.

*The New Law and Economics: A Research Review*, Oxford, Centre for Social Legal Studies, 1982.

Verheij, A., 'Shifts in Governance: Oil Pollution', in Faure, M. & Verheij, A. (eds.), *Shifts in Compensation for Environmental Damage*, Vienna, Springer, 2007, pp. 133–196.

Verschuuren, J., *Het grondrecht op bescherming van het leefmilieu*, Zwolle, Tjeenk Willink, 1993.

'Naar een codificatie van beginselen van het milieurecht', *Recht en kritiek*, 1995, Vol. 21, pp. 421–445.

Victor, D. G., *The Collapse of the Kyoto Protocol and the Struggle to Slow Global Warming*, Princeton, NJ, Princeton University Press, 2001.

Viscusi, W. K., 'Frameworks for Analyzing the Effects of a Risk and Environmental Regulations on Productivity', *American Economic Review*, 1983, Vol. 73, pp. 793–801.

'Towards a Diminished Role for Tort Liability: Social Insurance, Government Regulation and Contemporary Risks to Health and Safety', *Yale Journal on Regulation*, 1989, Vol. 6, pp. 65–107.

'The Dimensions of the Product Liability Crisis', *Journal of Legal Studies*, 1991, Vol. 20, pp. 147–177.

Vogel, D., *Trading Up: Consumer and Environmental Regulation in the Global Economy*, Cambridge, MA, Harvard University Press, 1995.

'Environmental Regulation and Economic Integration', in Esty, D. C. & Geradin, D. (eds.), *Regulatory Competition and Economic Integration. Comparative Perspectives*, Oxford, Oxford University Press, 2001, pp. 330–347.

'Trade and the Environment in the Global Economy', in Vig, N. J. & Faure, M. G. (eds.), *Green Giants? Environmental Policies of the United States and the European Union*, Cambridge, MIT Press, 2004, pp. 231–252.

Vogenauer, S. & Weatherill, S., 'The European Community's Competence to Pursue the Harmonisation of Contract Law – An Empirical Contribution to the Debate', in Vogenauer, S. & Weatherill, S. (eds.), *The Harmonisation of European Contract Law*, Oxford, Hart, 2006, pp. 105–148.

Voinov-Kohler, J., 'The Basel Convention on the Control of Transboundary Movements of Hazardous Wastes and their Disposal', in Fitzmaurice, M., Tanzy, A. & Papantoniou, A. (eds.), *Multilateral Environmental Treaties*, Cheltenham, Edward Elgar, 2017, pp. 331–342.

Wagner, G., 'Die Aufgaben des Haftungsrechts – eine Untersuchung am Beispiel des Umwelthaftungsrechts – Reform', *Juristen Zeitung*, 1991a, Vol. 46(4), pp. 175–183.

'Umwelthaftung und Versicherung', *Versicherungsrecht*, 1991b, pp. 249–260.

'Die Zukunft der Umwelthaftpflichtversicherung', *Versicherungsrecht*, 1992, pp. 261–272.

'Umwelthaftung und Versicherung', in Ahrens, M. & Simon, J. (eds.), *Umwelthaftung, Risikosteuerung und Versicherung*, Berlin, Erich Schmidt, 1996, pp. 97–146.

'Tort Law and Liability Insurance', in Faure, M. (ed.), *Tort Law and Economics*, Cheltenham, Edward Elgar, 2009, pp. 377–405.

Wang, H., *Civil Liability for Marine Oil Pollution Damage: A Comparative and Economic Study of the International, U.S. & Chinese Compensation Regime*, The Hague, Kluwer Law International, 2011.

Wansink, J. H., 'Het DES-arrest in het perspectief van verzekerbare slachtofferbescherming', *Aansprakelijkheid & Verzekering*, 1993, pp. 7–12.

Weishaar, S., '$CO_2$ Emission Allowance Allocation Mechanisms, Allocative Efficiency and the Environment: A Static and Dynamic Perspective', *European Journal of Law and Economics*, 2007a, Vol. 24(1), pp. 29–70.

'The European $CO_2$ Emission Trading System and State Aid: An Assessment of the Grandfathering Allocation Method and the Performance Standard Rate System', *European Competition Law Review*, 2007b, Vol. 28(6), pp. 371–381.

Wessels, B., 'Zorgen om morgen: beheersing van beroepsaansprakelijkheid in discussie', *Nederlands Juristenblad*, 1995a, p. 235.

*Risicobeheer bij preadvisering, Preadvies Ne Voa*, Deventer, Law & Practice Publishers, 1995b.

Wheeler, N., 'The Use of Criminal Statutes to Regulate Product Safety', *Journal of Legal Studies*, 1984, Vol. 13, pp. 593–622.

Widmer, P., 'Switzerland', in Koch, B. A. & Koziol, H. (eds.), *Unification of Tort Law: Strict Liability*, The Hague, Kluwer Law International, 2002, pp. 323–350.

Wiener, J., 'Global Environmental Regulation: Instrument Choice in Legal Context', *Yale Law Journal*, 1999, Vol. 108, pp. 677–800.

Wiener, J. B., 'Precautionary Principle', in Krämer, L. & Orlando, E. (eds.), *Principles of Environmental Law*, Cheltenham, Edward Elgar, 2018, pp. 174–185.

Wilde, M., *Civil Liability for Environmental Damage: A Comparative Analysis of Law and Policy in Europe and the United States*, The Hague/London, Kluwer Law International, 2002.

Wils, W. P. J., 'Insurance Risk Classifications in the EC: Regulatory Outlook', *Oxford Journal of Legal Studies*, 1994, Vol. 14, pp. 449–467.

Wilson, E. J., Klass, A. B.; & Bergan, S., 'Assessing a Liability Regime for Carbon Capture and Storage', *Energy Procedia*, 2009, Vol. 1(1), pp. 4575–4582.

Winter, G. (ed.), *Multilevel Governance of Global Environmental Change: Perspectives from Science, Sociology and the Law*, Cambridge, Cambridge University Press, 2006.

Winter, G., 'The Climate Is No Commodity: Taking Stock of the Emissions Trading Community Scheme', *Journal of Environmental Law*, 2009, Vol. 22(1), pp. 1–25.

Wittman, D., 'First Come, First Served: An Economic Analysis of "Coming to Nuisance"', *Journal of Legal Studies*, 1980, Vol. 9(3), pp. 557–568.

Woerdman, E., *The Institutional Economics of Market-Based Climate Policy*, Amsterdam, Elsevier, 2004.

Woerdman, E., Clo, S., & Arcuri, A., 'European Emissions Trading and the Polluter Pays Principle: Assessing Grandfathering and Over-Allocation', in Faure, M. & Peeters, M. (eds.), *Climate Change and European Emissions Trading: Lessons for Theory and Practice*, Cheltenham, Edward Elgar, 2008a, pp. 128–150.

Woerdman, E., Arcuri, A., & Clò, S., 'Emissions Trading and the Polluter-Pays Principle: Do Polluters Pay under Grandfathering?', *Review of Law & Economics*, 2008b, Vol. 4(2), pp. 565–590.

Wong, H. & Wheeler, D., 'Financial Incentives and Endogenous Enforcement in China's Pollution Levy System', *Journal of Environmental Economics and Management*, 2005, Vol. 49(1), pp. 174–196.

Wood, C., *Planning Pollution Prevention: A Comparison of Siting Controls over Air Pollution in Great Britain and the United States*, Oxford, Heinemann Newnes, 1989.

Wurzel, R. K. W., Zito, A. R., & Jordan, A. J., *Environmental Governance in Europe: A Comparative Analysis of New Environmental Policy Instruments*, Cheltenham, Edward Elgar, 2013.

Xing, Y. & Kolstad, Ch. D., 'Do Lax Environmental Regulations Attract Foreign Investment?', *Environmental and Resource Economics*, 1995, Vol. 21, pp. 1–22.

Xu, G. & Faure, M. G., 'Explaining the Failure of Environmental Law in China', *Columbia Journal of Asian Law*, 2016, Vol. 29(2), 1–95.

Yang, T., 'The Emergence of the Environmental Impact Assessment Duty as a Global Legal Norm and General Principle of Law', *Hastings Law Journal*, 2019, Vol. 70(2), 525–572.

Yohe, G., 'Pollutors' Profits and Political Response: Direct Control versus Taxes: Comment', *American Economic Review*, 1976, Vol. 66, pp. 981–982.

Yoshida, R., 'GE Plan Followed with Inflexibility', *Japan Times*, 14 July 2011, available at: www.japantimes.co.jp/news/2011/07/14/news/ge-plan-followed-with-inflexibility/#.VowMH5MrLVo.

Zhu, L., 'International Convention on Civil Liability for Bunker Oil Pollution Damage, 2001: Liability and Insurance Aspects', in Basedow, J. & Magnus, U. (eds.), *Pollution of the Sea: Prevention and Compensation*, Berlin, Springer Verlag, 2007, pp. 171–180.

Zweigert, K. & Kötz, H., *Introduction to Comparative Law*, Oxford, Oxford University Press, 1998.

# Index

For EU product safety concerns, contact us at Calle de José Abascal, 56–1°, 28003 Madrid, Spain or eugpsr@cambridge.org.

www.ingramcontent.com/pod-product-compliance
Lightning Source LLC
LaVergne TN
LVHW011701200926
848484LV00004B/1027

* 9 7 8 1 1 0 8 4 2 9 4 8 1 *